KU-110-397

EVALUATING EDUCATION:
ISSUES AND METHODS

An Open University Reader

edited by

ROGER MURPHY and HARRY TORRANCE
Assessment and Examinations Unit
(Department of Education, Southampton University)

Published in association with
The Open University

UNIVERSITY OF WOLVERHAMPTON
LEARNING RESOURCES

Acc No.	CLASS
2157180	371.
CONTROL	27
0063183978	
DATE	SITE	EVA
23. NOV. 1998	WL	

GIFT

Harper & Row, Publishers
London

Cambridge
Mexico City
New York
Philadelphia

San Francisco
São Paulo
Singapore
Sydney

Copyright © 1987. Editorial and selection material © The Open
University. Individual chapters © as credited.

First published 1987

Harper & Row Ltd
28 Tavistock Street
London WC2E 7PN

All rights reserved. No part of this publication may be reproduced,
stored in a retrieval system, or transmitted in any form or by any
means, electronic, mechanical, photocopying, recording, or
otherwise, without the written permission of the publisher.

British Library Cataloguing in Publication Data

Evaluating education: issues and methods:
    an Open University reader.
    1. Students——Great Britain——Rating of
    I. Murphy, Roger   II. Torrance, Harry
    371.2'7'0941   LB1117

ISBN 0–06–318397–8

Typeset by Inforum Ltd, Portsmouth
Printed and bound by Butler & Tanner Ltd, Frome and London

CONTENTS

Section 4   REPORTING EVALUATION

ACKNOWLEDGEMENTS

The editors would like to thank Phil Clift, Mike Golby, Bob Moon, Martine Moon, Bill Prescott, members of the Educational Evaluation team, and Maurice Galton and Marten Shipman, the external assessors for the module, for their help in the preparation of this Reader. They would also like to thank Dot Purdon for her help with the references.

INTRODUCTION – TOWARDS BETTER SCHOOLS?

This reader is being published at a time of intense political and educational debate over both the need for and the most appropriate methods of evaluating the intentions and practices of the education service. A flurry of publications and policy statements from Her Majesty's Inspectorate (HMI) and the Department of Education and Science (DES) on the one hand (e.g. DES 1985a, 1985b and 1986), coupled with the specific requirements for evaluation from such agencies as the Manpower Services Commission (MSC) on the other, have led to the discussion and practice of evaluation on a far wider scale than hitherto, and in a much more politicized context. Many individuals have found themselves required to commission, or even conduct, evaluations with little time for reflection on either the purposes or methods of this activity. In this volume we aim to assist those who now wish to reflect on such issues. We have attempted to do this by gathering together some of the 'classic' papers extracted from some of the major debates that have occurred during the last twenty years or so. These are set amongst a number of more recent contributions relating to evaluations conducted on current initiatives in British education. We hope that the volume will be accessible to a wide audience, including teachers and advisers, regardless of whether or not it is read alongside the Open University Master's Degree module for which it has a specific function.

Such evaluation tradition as we have in the UK (as distinct from 'educational research' of one sort or another) has tended to be located in institutions of higher education, having grown out of the curriculum development projects of the 1960s and early 1970s. No single methodology has predominated; however, there has been a substantial reaction against a tradition of purely quantitative evaluation designs (much used in America), and some groups have worked hard at developing alternative approaches. This has often been a matter of balance rather than exclusivity, however. Parlett and Hamilton (Chapter 1.4) in a paper invariably quoted in support of solely qualitative methods argue for a range of methods to be used. Nevertheless in broad terms the tradition has indeed been one of asserting the importance of qualitative understandings of educative processes over the quantitative measurement of the outcomes of such processes, though exactly how such qualitative understandings are arrived at has been the subject of some debate between 'evaluators' and more social theory-oriented 'researchers' (cf. Stenhouse – Chapter 3.2 – and Hargreaves – Chapter 2.2). A number of individual evaluation studies have been grounded more in the traditional social sciences – particularly sociology – than in the emergent field of curriculum innovation and evaluation (cf. Atkinson and Delamont, 1985). However, the general thrust of this work has been towards collecting qualitative rather than quantitative data in order to understand better the process of curriculum change (and the factors which inhibit it).

This focus on understanding and the related activity of critique has often been at the expense of intervening in and contributing to the process of change, or of coming to judgements about the worth of such change. Both these issues are now firmly back on the evaluation agenda, as is a further issue related to the analysis of outcomes – value for money. This is not to say that such issues have never before been considered – the papers in Section 1 demonstrate that they have – but rather that changing circumstances make their consideration inevitable rather than optional and more often than not at the level of the school and the local education authority (LEA) rather than the university department.

What contribution, then, can our in many respects still emergent evaluation tradition make to current practice and policy-making in education? Our choice of papers for this reader – influenced of course by our discussion with other members of the Open University module team – contains our answer to the question: that the debates of the 1970s over broadening the range of methods used in evaluation and democratizing access to information are still relevant, indeed perhaps more so than ever, but only so long as the operational difficulties are acknowledged. These debates, exemplified in particular by the papers in Section 1, should be treated as sources of experienced comment rather than sources of prescriptive design which can all too easily just operate at the level of rhetoric – 'we're illuminating the issues' – while allowing hard decisions and the process by which they are made to escape scrutiny. This is a central argument which is addressed in many of the papers contained in the four sections of the reader. As an introduction to these wide-ranging contributions to a dynamic debate we will briefly review the development of evaluation as a field of intellectual and practical endeavour, over recent years, before turning to look at the changing context of evaluation in a little more detail.

Within the UK 'programme evaluation' – the summative evaluation of large-scale centralized initiatives which gave rise to papers such as those of MacDonald, and Parlett and Hamilton (Chapters 1.2 and 1.4) – very soon took on board issues of intervention and the promotion of curriculum and professional development. However, this was usually only at the level of the 'project team' and often led to the discovery that what the evaluation had to offer to curriculum development teams was too little and came too late, or was couched in the language of critique which, intentionally or not, could only add to the developing 'blame the teacher' syndrome of the accountability movement. Further developments were essentially twofold; some exponents and even opponents of evaluation took up the problem of the level at which intervention in curriculum development could be effective and argued for a much more school-based and formative approach, sometimes called 'action research'; others took up the issue of information-provision in a climate of accountability and began discussing the merits and possible practices of school 'self-evaluation'.

Such developments were in no sense discrete or linear of course; large-scale national evaluations still continue, while many of the advocates and practitioners of action-research have also contributed to the development of school self-evaluation (cf. McCormick and James, 1983, for a fuller account and analysis). Likewise many researchers, teachers and administrators, who have had little if any direct contact with programme evaluation and its offspring, have been attracted by the possibilities of a more school-based or school-focused approach to in-service training and curriculum development (cf. the papers by Wilcox, Harland, Hargreaves and Shostak in Section 2). The general point to be made, however, is that the educational community has by and large continued to talk about curriculum and professional development in terms defined by notions of professionalism, voluntarism and autonomy, with the focus of attention more often than not on the individual teacher in the individual classroom. Meanwhile the social and political context in which that talk is situated, and to which it must respond or be usurped, has been one of increasing attention to national standards and whole-school improvement – to the quality of education certainly, but the quality of management and outcome as well as teaching and learning processes. Curriculum and professional development on their own terms and for their own sake – which is how it might sometimes have appeared to the wider community – are no longer enough.

However, definitions of 'improvement' and of 'quality' and how they might be achieved are by no means unproblematic. Despite a generally perceived need for some sort of response to genuine concerns over variation in provision as well as standards, a major problem with recent government interventions has been the assumption that 'quality' must of necessity relate directly to the contribution of the education service to economic growth. Moreover, such assumptions and the way in which they have been articulated have led to considerable suspicion that what is meant by 'better schools' is more tightly controlled schools – approved, rather than improved. Thus we have had a whole series of initiatives which, taken together, have substantially altered the balance of power in curriculum decision-making: the General and National Criteria in GCSE, central funding through Educational Support Grants for specific developments, the reorganization of INSET funding, and most recently the proposals for a National Curriculum. The policy statements which have paralleled these developments have likewise raised issues concerning the control as against the improvement of education. Comments on mechanisms for school improvement, when linked with evaluation and appraisal in the context of already extant developments, suggest that it is the effectiveness of policy implementation which is at stake, rather than the effectiveness of schools.

Irrespective of particular policies however, and indeed particular governments, the fact remains that accountability and the improvement of schools are, quite rightly, on the public agenda. Similarly, while the framework in which teachers (and advisers and administrators) act is changing they remain fundamental to the educative process and its outcomes. Indeed, if schools and local authorities can manage and manipulate the various new funding arrangements that they are having to work with their power might yet increase. Well-conducted and well-utilized evaluation of policy as well as practice, and of products (perhaps we should say consequences) as well as processes, will be crucial to such an enterprise. It is a lot to ask, but it is a challenge that has to be met if the evaluation which the education service is being increasingly mandated to conduct is to be other than a *post hoc* legitimatory charade and if the service which is provided to the community is going to be seen to be responding to its concerns.

Roger Murphy and Harry Torrance

REFERENCES

Atkinson, P. and Delamont, S. (1985) Bread and dreams or bread and circuses: a critique of 'case study' research in education, in M. Hammersley (1987) *Controversies in Classroom Research*, Open University Press, Milton Keynes.
DES (1985a) *Better Schools*, HMSO, London.

DES (1985b) *Quality in Schools: Evaluation and Appraisal*, HMSO, London.
DES (1986) *Better Schools, Evaluation and Appraisal. Conference Proceedings*, HMSO, London.
McCormick, R. and James, M. (1983) *Curriculum Evaluation in Schools*, Croom Helm, London.

METHODOLOGICAL DEBATES: THE POLITICS AND PROCESS OF EDUCATIONAL EVALUATION

INTRODUCTION

As we have already suggested, educational evaluation has been the subject of some fairly involved debates during the past twenty or thirty years. In selecting the papers for this first section of the reader we have attempted to illustrate some of the major issues that have been at the heart of these debates.

There has been a good deal of reflection on the methods used by evaluators in collecting the evidence upon which they base their evaluations. Virtually all of the papers make at least some reference to the changes that have taken place in this respect. It has now become accepted for evaluations to employ a wider range of approaches than the traditional research designs that attempted to employ the essential features of scientific experiments. Cronbach (Chapter 1.1) sets out in considerable detail many of the reasons why evaluators were forced to shake off the shackles of the very narrow experimental research tradition. Evaluations take place in a dynamic, political, social context and there is rarely a single question that the evaluation is attempting to address. Because of this evaluations often need to be designed so that they are useful to a range of audiences who will make different assumptions and who will be interested in widely differing issues. Cronbach, along with Parlett and Hamilton (Chapter 1.4), thus puts the case for the collection of a broad range of evidence, including both qualitative and quantitative data. They also address the need for a wide range of questions to be considered throughout most evaluations, including the likelihood that the evaluation may itself raise questions that had not previously been considered.

Several of the papers address the need for rigour in the more loosely defined qualitative approaches. Cronbach, who came directly from the test-oriented tradition of psychometric research, gives the lead in this, but the theme is also picked up by Parlett and Hamilton and again by Stenhouse (Chapter 1.5).

Another major theme that has been at the heart of the debate about evaluation is the role of evaluators in relation to policy-making and policy-makers. MacDonald (Chapter 1.2) constructs ideal types of the different roles that can, perhaps unwittingly, be adopted by evaluators in this respect, and discusses their potential involvement or lack of it in the process of making policy decisions. Nisbet (Chapter 1.3) also picks up this theme in considering further the role and position of individuals who conduct evaluations, and the place of their own values in relation to the values of others involved in whatever is being evaluated.

There are many common themes that emerge from this section. There is a strong critique of narrowly conceived and poorly conducted evaluation studies – illustrated, for example, by Bennett's (Chapter 1.6) comments on the methods used by HMI in one of its surveys. There is a general striving towards evaluation studies that can be practically useful in the pursuit of educational change and improvement. For many of the writers this implies a need for those involved in evaluation to engage themselves fully within the complex arena of educational change, adapting their evaluation designs to improve their chances of capturing valuable evidence about the process of change that is occurring. There is also a general recognition that change needs to be understood within the context in which it occurs, and part of the move towards collecting a broader range of evidence involves creating a better understanding of that context.

Finally, the authors of the papers in this section are also aware of the reality that those conducting evaluations will often be subject to the authority of other agencies. Thus the need to negotiate with those commissioning or involved with evaluations is given much attention. Evaluators can just as easily become pawns in a larger political debate as they can make a worthwhile and substantial contribution to the understanding and proper consideration of education change and development.

1.1
ISSUES IN PLANNING EVALUATIONS*
Lee Cronbach

Designing an evaluative investigation is an art. The design must be chosen afresh in each new undertaking, and the choices to be made are almost innumerable. Each feature of a design offers particular advantages and entails particular sacrifices. Further merits and limitations come from the way various features combine. A broad theory of validity and utility is thus required to provide a base both for judging research plans and for generating more satisfactory ones.

A design is a plan for allocating investigative resources (Finney, 1956). In evaluation – as in basic science – the designer's task is to produce maximally useful evidence within a specified budget of dollars, a specified number of person-years from the evaluation staff and of person-hours from informants, and other such constraints. 'Maximally useful' is a key phrase. Most writings on design suggest that an investigation is to be judged by its form, and certain forms are held up as universal ideals. In contrast, I would argue that investigations have functions and that a form highly suitable for one investigation would not be appropriate for the next. This is to be, then, *a functional theory of design*.

The central purpose of evaluation differs from that of basic social research, and evaluations fit into a different institutional and political context. The strategy of evaluative research therefore requires special consideration. Logic is necessarily the same in all disciplined inquiry, but the translation of logic into procedure should depend on context, purpose, and expected payoff. Many recommendations appropriate for long-term programmes of scientific research are ill-suited to evaluation. Hence, general writings on design and scientific method are inadequate to guide the evaluator. General

* Cronbach, L.J. (1982) Issues in planning evaluations, in L.J. Cronbach *Designing Evaluations of Educational and Social Programs*, Jossey-Bass. San Francisco.

recommendations on evaluation can also mislead; evaluations should not be cast in a single mould. For any evaluation many good designs can be proposed, but no perfect ones . . .

Evaluations of programmes are the concern here. A programme – a treatment method – is an operational plan or directive (not necessarily detailed) for rendering some service. Such a plan is evaluated empirically after it has been realized in one or more sites. The fact that the plan could be realized elsewhere – that it, or at least its central hypothesis, could be propagated – motivates more formal evaluations than an everyday manager requires.

Programmes go through stages of development. *Toward Reform* (Cronbach, L.J. *et al.*, 1980, p. 107ff.; see also Berryman and Glennan, 1980) speaks of a breadboard (developmental) stage, a stage at which one or more pilot tests are made under ideal conditions, and a prototype stage (preferably a realistic field test). Out of this process there finally emerges an established operating programme. This chapter is chiefly concerned with prototype trials. At the breadboard stage, a programme is in such flux that the evaluation must be reoriented frequently and can scarcely be 'designed'. I shall not ignore ideal conditions ('superrealizations'), but they are too rare to be the main concern here. Established programmes are comparatively immune to serious evaluation, save as proposed modifications lead to a new study of prototypes . . .

The fact that my experience is mostly with evaluations of education and training influences the argument presented here. Responsibility for educational decisions is widely diffused, and those who participate in making them have discordant interests. The same directive or curriculum or administrative policy will turn into a different activity in different planes (McLaughlin, 1980). These characteristics call for a kind of inquiry that would be less appropriate in evaluating a standardized arrangement for traffic control, vaccination, or disbursement of welfare funds. Even so, the orientation toward education is not highly restrictive. Educational programmes range from a nationwide plan for providing daycare, to a system for instructing adults by means of telecasts, to a course of study being pilot-tested in one university, to an effort to improve the economic judgements made by prospective retirees. An analysis of evaluation that stretches over this range will apply to evaluations of many non-educational programmes.

I shall discuss planning as if a lone evaluator has already been given a broad commission and an allotment of funds and has accepted a target date for completing the evaluation. This is a rhetorical device. In the first place, no one individual is qualified to make all the judgements that go into design and interpretation; almost always, responsibility is shared within a team.

Moreover, it is often advisable to ask several groups to inquire into the same programme. Splitting up the work has logistical advantages. It brings in multiple perspectives and promotes healthy professional debate. In the second place, the commission given the evaluator ought to be tentative. Then the study can be extended, restricted, or redirected as fieldwork identifies critical uncertainties. Although my rhetorical device bypasses the decision to evaluate, all that will be said has implications for the timing, scale, and appropriateness of any proposed evaluation. Even the possibility of abandoning the evaluation remains open.

WHAT EVALUATIONS ARE OF MOST WORTH?

. . . . Nearly all the literature on evaluation speaks of it as an attempt to serve a decision maker. That language may be appropriate for technical studies commissioned by an official in a mature, stable organization. In such an agency, a consensus about goals and basic policies has been achieved, and responsibility for the programme operation has been delegated. The officers know what information is needed to adjust the operation. They specify what the evaluator is to look into and are attuned to use what he reports. (To avoid the clumsy gesture of 'he or she' and to reduce ambiguity of pronouns, I speak of the investigator as 'he' and of a significant other person (such as a decision-maker or a client) as 'she'.) When a firm considering whether to add a new product to its line commissions market research, the study does directly serve a defined decision-maker. So does measurement for quality control in a factory.

In a politically lively situation, however, a programme becomes the province of a policy-shaping community, not of a lone decision-maker or tight-knit group. Persons who play roles in approving the programme or in advocating alternatives, as well as most of those who carry out programme operations, are part of this community. Perhaps, nominally, the decision sits on one person's desk, but that person will need concurrence from other administrators, from legislators, and from interested publics. She becomes more an arbitrator, more an architect of compromise, than an independent weigher of evidence.

Evaluation design

Decisions about whether a programme will be evaluated and on what scale are often made before any thought is given to design. Large evaluations are typically undertaken at the request of an administrator or a central agency. The commissioning agent may reduce the evaluator to a technician by setting forth the questions to be answered and asking him simply to apply his skills of sampling, measurement and statistical analysis. But no one can judge whether an evaluation will be profitable without an impression of the kind and credibility of information likely to result from it. Administrators should ask evaluators to think through the design possibilities before agreeing to support a study (Wholey, 1979). The evaluator should not substitute his judgement for that of the sponsoring agency, but suggesting what and what not to investigate is a proper professional task.

Traditional writings on design tell an investigator who has already picked an aiming-point how to bring his weapons to bear. They tell him how to answer a fixed and limited question. Another question is for another day, that study to be designed when the time comes. Fixed and limited questions are suitable for basic research, since the available theory specifies a particularly timely question for any one study. The evaluator, in contrast, is not allowed to ask questions in endless series, mounting the thousand-and-first study of the problem after digesting the first thousand. He is not allowed the pure scientist's luxury of setting sub-questions aside for investigation in a future year. Therefore, he ought to spread his shots.

The evaluator's ultimate product is more than a summary of what occurred in certain sites where a certain programme was in operation. The community will want to know what can be expected in new sites and what can be expected of a modified programme. The evaluator, then, is called on to illuminate the whole problem area in a comparatively short period of time. In doing so, he may come to recognize a large number of politically relevant questions about the programme. But he cannot hope to answer them all and should not investigate each of them with equal intensity. To put extra effort into answering one question is to limit what will be learned about another. Identifying relevant questions and determining the emphasis each should have are central tasks in design. The selection among questions is guided by practical and political considerations, as well as by substantative ones.

Designing an evaluation is a continuing process. What variables deserve close attention will be discovered as the fieldwork proceeds. A decision to look intensively at one variable implies scanting investigation of some other variable. It may be reasonable to 'hold constant' some aspect of delivery, to draw a representative sample, or to administer a pre-test. But the designer cannot make those kinds of judgements purely in terms of logic of the proposed control. He must recognize the opportunities that will be forgone if a particular design feature is adopted, and he must determine whether, on balance, the credibility of the study will be increased or decreased by the choice. The cost of answering one question well must be weighed against the cost of leaving other questions unanswered.

The evaluator as teacher

It is not the evaluator's task to determine on his own whether a programme is worthwhile or what action should be taken. The evaluator cannot judge for others, any more than a counsellor can decide what career a student should prepare for. Still, the evaluator–teacher should feel free to take a stance. If he concludes that a policy has predominantly good consequences, attempting to persuade others to adopt it is entirely proper – as long as he does not suppress evidence inconsistent with his conclusion. Social institutions learn from experience; so do programme clients and political constituencies. The proper function of evaluation is to speed up the learning process by communicating what might otherwise be overlooked or wrongly perceived. The evaluator, then, is an educator. His success is to be judged by his success in communication; that is, by what he leads others to understand and believe. Payoff comes from the insight that the evaluator's work generates in others.

A study that is technically admirable falls short if what the evaluator learns does not enter the thinking of the relevant political community. That community may include clients, programme staffs, taxpayer leagues, environmentalist lobbies, legislators, bureaucrats, and interested citizens. An evaluation fulfils its function to the extent that it assists participants in the political process to resolve conflicts intelligently.

The evaluation can rarely play its proper role by letting a single decision-maker or a single centre of power set the questions for its attention. This statement runs counter to the recommendation of several astute commentators, notably Boruch and Cordray (1980) and a committee of the National Research Council (Raizen and Rossi, 1981). The committee would have the legislature or some other sponsor specify just what questions are relevant:

> Responding to the myriad, often conflicting expectations of all the audiences is likely to diminish the integrity of an evaluation and limit its usefulness to any one audience . . . The design of the evaluation should anticipate the primary audience(s), and the procedures, methods, analysis, and language of its reports should correspond to the needs and expectations of the primary audiences . . . Defining the audience and targeting the message will reduce the frustration that often accompanies the more eclectic attempts to speak simultaneously with many tongues in many groups.
>
> (Raizen and Rossi, 1981, p. 39)

The thinking of the Stanford Evaluation Consortium is reflected in the working title that *Toward Reform* once bore: 'Evaluation for a Free Society'. I quote Coleman and associates (1979, p. 6) to show that our view is not idiosyncratic:

The policy researcher is not the servant of the government official. He, like the official, is the agent of the people – the people not as a mass, but through their various roles, activities, and interests. In this conception, policy is the outcome of a clash of interests, not the product of a governmental policy-maker. The proper function of social policy research is to inform those interests – not a particular subset of those interests, not government, but the interests themselves – so that they may be better informed about their interests and thus press more rationally for them.

Evaluation ordinarily speaks to diverse audiences through various channels, supplying each with political ammunition, and with food for thought. Participants in political action use messages for many purposes. Some challenges to the report will be politically motivated; catch-as-catch-can counter-arguments are to be expected. It should surprise no one that the process by which evaluation contributes to community opinion is less disciplined than is the generation of scientific consensus.

A decade ago technical excellence was the accepted criterion for evaluation. In those terms the summative evaluation for Harvard Project Physics was exceptionally good, and it undoubtedly advanced the craft of evaluation. But if – as seems to be the case – the study had little influence on decisions and on thought about the teaching of science, it did not make the hoped-for contribution.

Teaching begins when the evaluator first sits down with members of the policy-shaping community to elicit their questions. It continues during every contact the evaluator has with programme participants or with others in his audience. The end report is only one means for enabling audiences to understand the programme and how it impinges on their interests. Teaching does more than transmit *answers*. The teacher's responsibility is not merely to know his subject-matter and convey relevant facts, conclusions, and techniques. Educating is as much a matter of raising questions as of providing answers. Especially where the topic is value-laden, the educator's responsibility is to help others ask better questions and determine what actions are appropriate to their aims. Ideally, the client comes to see the nature of the world more clearly and arrives at a better understanding of what she wants and of the political moves suitable for her purposes. Intellectual analysis is no substitute for that kind of negotiation.

Citizens do not serve their political interests if they operate on false assumptions. Instances abound of actions taken without sufficient understanding. Thus, unfortunate side effects sometimes appear after a programme has been accepted and put into use. Statements such as 'We never thought to check on that possibility' or 'We were misled by the developer's assurances' strongly suggest that the process of decision-making was inadequate. Other commonly heard remarks point to the same problem: 'If those facts had come to my attention, I'd have voted the other way.' 'I see now that we gave too much weight to the initial costs of the alternative programmes and not enough to the problems of maintaining each one.' 'We failed to realise how much our community differs from the tryout communities where the programme worked well.'

An evaluation ought to reduce uncertainties, but it should also challenge simplistic views (Cohen and Weiss, 1977). In so far as the evaluation activity and its reports enable everyone to appreciate the range of consequences that may follow a social action, the evaluation enables each participant to throw weight behind a truly preferred course of action. The foresight and open-mindedness of publics are limited, as are the resources for evaluation, and consequences are to some degree unforeseeable. The evaluator cannot hope to extinguish all doubts, nor can he hope to persuade all segments of the political community to make full use of his findings. Still, his target lies in that direction.

Since communication is a vital part of policy-oriented research, it ought to be considered at the planning stage. As Wilensky (1967, p. ix) has said, excellent policy research is

> *clear* because it is understandable to those who must use it; *timely* because it gets to them when they need it; *reliable* because diverse observers using the same procedure see it in the same way; *valid* because it is cast in the form of concepts and measures that capture reality (the tests include logical consistency, successful prediction, congruence with established knowledge from other sources); *adequate* because the account is full (the context of the act, event, or life of the person or group is described); and *wide ranging* because the major policy alternatives promising a high probability of attaining organizational goals are posed or new goals are suggested.

If the communications from the evaluation are the products that count, these questions should be asked of the completed evaluation:

- Did each fraction of the audience attend to the message?
- Did each understand it?
- Did each find it credible?
- Were the significant questions answered as well as possible?
- Did the answers alter the preconceptions of the audience?
- Was the dialogue leading to decisions enriched and elevated as a consequence of the evaluation?

The same questions phrased prospectively ('Will each fraction . . . attend to the message?') are to be raised when an evaluation plan is sketched out.

All the persons whose voices may be raised during the political discussion and all those who will shape the programme as it operates are part of the evaluator's target audience. Ideally, he will reach even further, to normally silent citizens whose voices *should* be raised. Even when a single manager or board appears to be in full control, an evaluator can alert a wider audience to its stake in the decisions. The influence of Ralph Nader and his team on decisions made by General Motors is a case in point. When an evaluator is commissioned by an official, his contract may restrict him from addressing outsiders directly, but he can still serve all parties by bringing the concerns of outsiders into the inquiry and its interpretation. The sponsor may not be cordial to an inquiry that recognizes the perspectives of clients and political adversaries. But as Coleman (1972) pointed out, a narrow evaluation serves the sponsor badly. If an evaluation does not collect data capable of dispelling (or validating) an objection voiced by critics of the programme, the evaluation may do nothing to change attitudes.

Formative use of findings

A single definite question is often the starting point of an evaluation. The question is usually cast in one of three forms:

1. 'Is the programme achieving its goals?'
2. 'Does the programme have an effect?'
3. 'How much larger, on the average, is the outcome under Plan A than under Plan B?'

These questions assume that the form of the programme has been fixed and that the aim of evaluation is to assess its merit. Scriven (1967) christened such evaluations *summative*, to contrast them with the *formative* study that regards the programme as fluid and seeks ways to better it. Scriven's terms are convenient, but they suggest a false division of studies into two classes.

Evaluation that focuses on outcomes can and should be used formatively. When a trial fails, the social planner wants to know why it failed and how to do better next time. When the trial succeeds and the proposal is considered for use under changed conditions, the intelligent planner does not conclude that its effectiveness has been proved. She now asks about the reasons and essential conditions for the success. Even when the trial of a plan has satisfactory outcomes, the policy-maker should be prepared to consider any alternative that has a chance of working appreciably better.

In principle, evidence of disappointing outcomes could lead administrators to cut off funds for a programme. But this almost never happens to established social programmes (Kaufman, 1976); once installed, such programmes generate their own political support. Moreover, to cut off a programme without substituting an alternative is to abandon the commitment to alleviate the social problem in question. To develop an alternative is a formative activity. [. . .]

Purely summative studies have been useful in the testing of drugs and vaccines. These can fairly be regarded as fixed treatments. A successful trial leads to acceptance of the substance as a treatment. If delivery during the trial was adequate and the treatment nevertheless fails, the investigator goes back to the test tube and the animal lab; no data from the field are likely to suggest what change in molecules would produce better results. The average summative result is convincing because the effect of the substance is almost surely independent of social circumstances and institutional arrangements. The substance may affect some types of individuals more than others, but soundly designed research will detect those interactions and will qualify accordingly the statement about average results. While educational and welfare systems do not have the fixed character and the independence of circumstances of the drug or vaccine, Gene Glass (personal communication, 1977) has pressed upon me the view that pure summaries of outcome can be profitable in social research. I shall comment on two examples that represent his thinking. Both have to do with treatments that were ill-conceived and on which the evaluation properly had a destructive effect.

First, consider a system for helping retarded readers that was promoted as a proprietary service by its inventors. The system had no roots in psychology, and the rationale offered for it seemed arbitrary. Research on the programme indicates that children treated in this manner were not demonstrably benefited, and a professional who knows of this finding will not refer children to the service. But evaluation makes only a limited contribution here, since it cannot guide improvement of the system. No plausible rationale links the prescribed exercises to performance in reading, so it is pointless to ask where the chain of intervening effects broke down. Yet that would be the first step toward worthwhile modifications.

The second example is the common practice of placing retarded pupils in separate classes; in principle, these special classes could adopt procedures suited to the children. Large-scale studies have reported, however, that children in special classes did no better on average than comparable children whose schools kept them in regular classes. Possibly some localities had effective special classes, but it became evident that the policy – as applied in schools generally – was not working. This average finding provided potent ammunition for reformers who favoured 'mainstreaming' of the retarded; partly as a response to these summative evaluations, policy has shifted toward mainstreaming. Still, I think formative research would have been a better investment. There is a chance that it might have shown how to benefit the slow learner.

Most educational programmes are loosely defined, allowing room for adaptation at the state, community, and classroom levels. An estimate of average or global benefit is only moderately helpful to national planners (Light and Smith, 1970), and it is much less helpful to local decision-makers. No group concerned with a particular site wants to know how a programme has operated in some mythical 'average' site. 'How will it work for us?' is the question. A national planner must consider whether changes in the social context in the course of a decade – a higher unemployment rate or more unionization of teachers, for example – are likely to affect outcomes. Similar variation over levels of government, over localities, and over time is found in many non-educational services.

When the programme is new, the image of a fixed programme is especially unrealisic. The pilot study of a new programme, installed in Year 1, may be scheduled to end in Year 5. The planners often speak as if in Year 5 a 'go/no-go' decision is to be made about the programme set up in Year 1. In actuality the decision is likely to be spread out in time and to be multiply branched. The programme will necessarily be modified by operational decisions during Years 2, 3 and 4. Even if assessment in Year 5 is encouraging, variants of the treatment or its delivery will be suggested. As insight into the limitations of the original plan emerges, fundamentally different programmes will be invented. Indeed, political developments or a changed perception of the social problem may have altered the whole direction of social action (Rivlin, 1974). The decision process profits little from a report that simply compares the end results of a now obsolete Plan A and a now obsolete Plan B.

Breadth and flexibility

Evaluation studies should be thoughtful, not mechanically objective. Modest studies buy more thought per person-year of effort than million-dollar ones, or so it has been in the past. To be sure, some questions can be addressed only on a large scale, and I am not defending penny pinching, whatever the size of the study . . .

Experienced and judicious members of the evaluation staff should be free to think deeply about events and data, and the senior investigators ought to dirty their hands by direct contact with events in the field. In large studies, however, the senior investigators are almost inevitably chairbound, free only to send the signals that guide a swarm of data collectors and data processers. For logistical and bureaucratic reasons, the design tends to become rigid; questions that emerge as the study progresses receive too little attention. As staff roles within the large team become differentiated, members become less able to see the programme whole and in living colour. The data reach the chief investigators as colourless aggregates. Hence, the final conclusions are likely to rest more on near-mindless data processing than on appreciation of the events themselves.

Consider a large evaluation of bilingual education that *was* thoughtfully interpreted (American Institutes for Research, 1977). The contractor was to assess outcomes of a federally supported programme of bilingual instruction intended primarily for children of Hispanic origin who had limited command of English. The programme was based on the idea that children who speak Spanish better than English would profit more if they were taught first to read in Spanish and were then shifted over to English. The investigators discovered, however, that the programme was not being applied to the intended population. Many schools were shunting into the bilingual programme all the Hispanic children who made a poor start in reading, even though, according to the teachers, a large fraction of them spoke English better than Spanish. Moreover, the planned transition to instruction entirely in English was not made; once the child could read in Spanish, the typical school did not return her to the mainstream of instruction. The summative evaluation had to be discounted. It would have been sensible to call off the effort, but Congress had ordered an evaluation and the wheels could not be stopped. Elaborate testing was not needed to establish that it is counterproductive to teach in Spanish when a child understands Spanish poorly or not at all. The merits of transitional bilingual education for the Spanish-dominant child could not be observed if instruction was directed wholly toward maintenance of Spanish. The point of the example is that this evaluative study was exceptionally perceptive. Many a large-scale study, failing to check how a programme was actually carried out, has 'appraised' an innovation that was never tried.

In diverse and changing circumstances, an evaluation is a better guide to action when the outcome information is supplemented by information on situational variables and intermediate processes that condition the results. Resources should therefore be allocated to describing the sites where the intervention was implanted, as well as the events that interacted with and modified treatment events and the client's response. These kinds of narratives tell what went on and so give some basis for inferring what is likely to occur under changed conditions. The evaluation is then as much a historical inquiry as a scientific one . . .

Beyond the stand-alone study

Enthusiasts for 'hard' evaluation have offered the dubious suggestion that a single firmly designed study, standing alone, can provide the signal to continue a programme or abandon it. But Baker (1967, p. 211), writing when large evaluations were just beginning to appear, saw that the requirements of complex fieldwork cannot be captured within the Fisherian model of narrowly targeted stand-alone studies: 'The current situation presents an opportunity for a new conceptualization of experimental design which is as great as that which existed during the 1920s' (when Fisher did his seminal work). Planning an evaluative inquiry is more like planning a campaign of investigation than like planning a single experiment, as was noted by Berryman and Glennan (1980). The designer has to prevision the work as a whole, but he should not harden the plans. The *Viking* investigations of Mars (Lee, 1976) provide an analogy to the evaluator's work. Each day the automated lander gathered data on a dozen kinds of questions and sent them to earth, where scientists examined them. A few hours later the command team transmitted back to Mars the lander's instructions for the next day's work. The messages reflected priorities emerging from the interpretation of the latest printouts. Evaluation at its best has the same fluid responsiveness to incoming observations and to the changing concerns of the political community.

Sophisticated writers are aware that conclusions about programmes are based on the cumulation of findings and not on one study, and they favour an evolving pattern of diversified studies rather than a single focused trial (Raizen and Rossi, 1981). The literature on design, however, does not adequately reflect this view . . .

Understanding comes out of accumulated knowledge, not from the stand-alone trial. Finney (1956, p. 15), a successor of Fisher, has written:

> In agricultural research today, advance rarely comes from a single dramatic experiment. More commonly, improvements in agricultural practice can be based only on the critical appreciation of evidence from a large number of experiments which are not necessarily all of the same type or even all from the same organized program.

Finney called for the synthesis of information from all past research on the subject, including studies with weak designs. Although he finds value in experimental control, Finney sees no one comparative trial as pivotal. Cook and Campbell (1976, p. 227) think similarly: 'We would delude ourselves if we believed that a single experiment, or even a research program of several years' duration, would definitely answer the major questions associated with confidently inferring a causal relationship, naming its parts, and specifying its generalizability.'

Rivlin (1974), who, like Cook and Campbell, is a strong advocate of tightly designed social research, goes further in circumscribing the use of formal experiments. To develop proper programme designs and measures for studying complex instructional treatments takes several years, she says; and by the time the plans are set, policy-makers may no longer be interested in such programmes. As for programmes such as tuition vouchers and performance contracting, which would alter whole institutions, 'it may never be possible to do "experiments" on which firm statistical inferences can be based' (p. 353). Why? Because the policy leads to different local responses. It becomes far more important to trace the effects of the unplanned variations than to average the outcomes over the heterogeneous trials (Berryman and Glennan, 1980; Cook, 1981).

Experiments are most clearly worth their cost, Rivlin (1974) argues, when the treatment is easily specified and controlled and can be delivered to individuals or households. Prime examples would be cash payment plans, as in the well-known New Jersey income maintenance experiment (Rossi, 1978, p. 588). The controlled study can give information on significant variables affecting individual response even if the conditions of delivery during the trial are quite unlike those of an operational programme. An educational counterpart would be the laboratory studies with very small groups of children that were used in developing lessons for 'Sesame Street' and 'Electric Company' (Boruch, 1975, p. 39).

Some who find merit in large, strongly controlled tests of government programmes would reserve such tests for exceptional political decisions. Some of the social scientists at the helm of the New Jersey income maintenance experiment came to believe that the government should support such experiments only when they provided information relevant to *major* policy questions and when such information could not be attained without a controlled experiment (Timpane, 1970).

Conceptual uses of results

Evaluations have typically been seen as ways of reaching better decisions about the programme being evaluated. In truth, evaluative findings frequently have no direct effect on the programme studied, whereas large consequences follow from indirect, 'conceptual' uses of the information (Rein, 1976; Weiss, 1977; Lindblom and Cohen, 1979). Beliefs about the central problem – about the causes of poverty and unemployment, for example – are altered. So are social goals and priorities, and beliefs about the probity and efficacy of schools or other institutions and of public servants generally. The direction that new programme proposals take is influenced by perceptions that grew out of experience with earlier programmes; evaluation is only one means of capturing and dramatizing that experience . . .

A programme manager may have highly specific questions; but inquiries of many kinds, not all of them evaluations and not all of them on the same specific topic, feed into conversations of the policy-shaping community. The studies of Piaget, as transmitted by Hunt (1961) and others, had as much influence on thinking about compensatory education in the late 1960s as did the Westinghouse evaluation of Head Start. Intensive tryouts of particular forms of training (along Piagetian lines, for example) affected thinking as much as did the large-scale assessments. The evaluator does not have the responsibility to deliver – indeed, should not deliver – a firm answer to a specified policy question. The evaluator's responsibility is that of any other social agent who seeks to help in selecting action alternatives: to illuminate the corner of the world where the problem resides. In this, evaluation research does not differ from basic research on child development or income or delinquency.

CONFLICTING IDEALS FOR EVALUATION

The typical essay on how to conduct or judge evaluations rests on a preconception of proper form. Sometimes the essay makes the preconception explicit and argues for it; sometimes not. Radically though some of these preconceptions differ, direct confrontation of one with another has been rare. Typically, a writer ignores ideals other than his own, dismisses them as 'not really evaluation', or acknowledges that they are appropriate in studies he regards as comparatively unimportant. I hope instead to offer a synthesis of views.

I overdramatize only slightly when I contrast a scientistic school of evaluators with a humanistic one (as Campbell, 1975a, has done before me). Writers at one pole prize experiments; those at the opposite extreme find evaluative experiments misinformative.

I shall not treat the scientistic and humanistic positions symmetrically. I shall comment particularly on literature advocating or criticizing strong designs, since quantitative studies have been reviewed with a sharp eye and balanced assessment of them seems to be possible. Qualitative evaluation has become more prominent recently, and much has been said in favour of the approach. Enthusiasts vary widely in their practice and concept of qualitative evaluation, but they have felt it necessary to present a united front to gain a hearing for unorthodox practices. When their spokespersons feel secure enough to critize naturalistic evaluations that illustrate one or another of the particular heresies, issues will be defined and clarified as they have been during debates over experiments and quasi-experiments. Advice on integrating qualitative methods into plans for programme evaluation can then become more pointed than the advice that I can offer here.

My predilections colour what I say. In forty years of evaluative work and methodological studies, I have specialized in quantitative and statistical methods and have been a technical consultant for large surveys, experiments, and near-experiments. I have supervised a number of pure-experiment dissertations, but a design with controlled assignment has never seemed appropriate for a study of my own. I have switched back and forth between measurements and less formal methods. In evaluating a Stanford programme of courses in Values, Technology, and Society during the 1970s (with a report restricted to internal use of the programme staff), I relied almost entirely on interview, observation, questionnaire, and judgement. But during the same time period, my students and I piled up mountains of computer printout in an effort to devise a statistical framework for certain parts of a nationwide study of school violence.

The scientistic ideal

A true experiment, as described in the literature on evaluation, concentrates on outcome or impact and embodies three procedures:

1. Two or more conditions are in place, at least one of them being the consequence of deliberate intervention.
2. Persons or institutions are assigned to conditions in a way that creates equivalent groups.
3. All participants are assessed on the same outcome measure(s).

Fairweather (1980) insists that an adequate effort toward social change must be scientific, and he equates the term *scientific* with *experimental*. Although surveys, correlational studies, and quasi-experiments have a place, he says, 'finally, for an accurate evaluation . . . it is *absolutely essential* that an experiment be carried out with random assignments of participants' (p. 248). Writers whose language is less absolute quite commonly equate high quality in evaluation with this particular design, seeing all other qualities as secondary. According to Gilbert, Mosteller, and Tukey (1976, p. 296), 'Ethical justification for failing to make a randomized trial [comparison of new and old, or new and null, treatment] is never easy and often impossible. Inadequately evaluated programs can usually be regarded as "fooling around" with the people involved.'

Significantly, a new report commissioned to advise Congress regarding evaluation policy (Boruch and Cordray, 1980) identifies evaluation with estimating the comparative effects of programmes having similar aims, calls emphatically for quality of design, and equates quality with the randomized experiment. Similar language appears in the companion volume of recommendations to Congress from a committee of the National Research Council (Raizen and Rossi, 1981).

Although Boruch and Cordray admit that the randomized trial is not always to the point, the alternatives they mention are limited inquiries into strictly political questions: Is the programme politically feasible? How much service does a programme deliver to whom? Hence, Congress is being given the message that, if the aim is to study the consequences of installing a programme, only the randomized experiment rises above the level of 'ambiguous', 'misleading', 'inadequate', and 'inept' (section 5, p. 20). Non-experimental approaches to the study of consequences are considered reluctantly, and only because of the political infeasibility, costs, and practical difficulties of random assignment.

The humanistic ideal

Writers at the humanistic extreme find experiments unacceptable. For them, naturalistic case studies are the panacea. A humanist would study a programme already in place, not one imposed by the evaluator. If persons are asssigned to a treatment, that is because the policy under study calls for assignment; assignments are not made for the sake of research. The programme is to be seen through the eyes of its developers and clients. Naturalistic investigators would ask different questions of different programmes. Benefits are to be described, not reduced to a quantity. Observations are to be opportunistic and responsive to the local scene, not prestructured. Some of the humanists abjure objectivity; their ideal is the sensitive, appreciative observer. Several members of this school are conveniently represented in a work provocatively titled *Beyond the Numbers Game* (Hamilton *et al.*, 1978) . . .

THE EMERGING RECONCILIATION

Extreme statements imply greater conflict between the two schools than exists. The strong recommendations on either side are intended to apply in limited circumstances (though it is the rare writer who tells us what circumstance he has in mind). Most advocates of strong designs in evaluation see them as serving central decision-makers who are looking for a standard policy to be applied over a large region. Naturalistic evaluators are usually interested either in improving services in the site(s) studied or in leading those on the front line elsewhere (principals and teachers, for example) to perceive their own circumstances and activities differently.

It is good to see a recent article with the title 'Beyond Qualitative Versus

Quantitative Methods' (Reichardt and Cook, 1979) and to come across a work on 'multiple-method approaches' (Saxe and Fine, 1979), in which it is argued that the more an evaluative effort is spread over multiple studies, the greater the place for a mixture of styles. Saxe and Fine, seeing the worth of large, less controlled studies and small rigorous experiments that give strong answers to pointed questions, urge that the approaches be made deliberately *complementary*:

> The data developed from the macro and micro studies should not be viewed as orthogonal. They interact to identify those aspects of the program worthy of investigation by the alternative form of analysis . . . Data from the two levels feed into each other in a cyclical fashion in order to identify those program elements requiring revision or special attention.
>
> (Saxe and Fine, 1979, p. 64)

While these tolerant writings are welcome, eclectic tolerance is not enough to guide the designer. The evaluator has to decide how to distribute investigative effort month by month. Broadly speaking, the scientific method consists in imposing controls on what would otherwise be casual and perhaps untrustworthy observations. This is true of naturalistic as well as quantitative inquiries. Both kinds of science must be concerned with, for example, the sampling of sites and informants and with the framing of questions; and each has developed devices to improve the quality of observations. Each control has a particular purpose, and a control that strengthens a study in one respect is almost certain to restrict it in another or to increase its cost. These trade-offs should be brought to the forefront of consciousness.

On several matters members of both schools seem to agree. To begin, they agree that society should innovate. Social institutions and services are by no means as good as they could be, and arrangements that once worked well may collapse when social conditions change. They also agree that a well-intentioned change – even one supported by a strong rationale – may do little good and may do harm. Whenever the character of an innovation and the political tempo permit, the change should be tentative and reversible (Campbell, 1969).

Evaluation should be empirical, examining events in sites where the programme is tried and scrutinizing the reactions and subsequent performance of the persons served. The 'objective' scientist gives a stronger meaning to empiricism than the humanist does. The humanist would judge a human creation in its own terms; if the audience at a play fails to respond, for example, the fault may lie in the audience and not in the work of art. The study of *Hamlet* in school is defended by Stenhouse (1978) simply on the grounds that *Hamlet* is worth studying; and, in his opinion, no one can say what effect on particular students the instructor should want Shakespeare's play to have, and very little of the effect is measurable.

Although Stenhouse and other writers contributing to *Beyond the Numbers Game* (Hamilton *et al.*, 1978) trust sensitive observers much more than they trust measurements, the hard-nosed test of a hypothesis can be worth its cost when the hypothesis is properly mature and important to verify. Cook and Campbell (1979, p. 345) put it this way: 'It is rarely desirable to conduct an experiment until [one is sure] that the manipulations are exactly the ones of interest.' This is true for both the experimental and the control or contrast conditions. But while a programme is evolving, Cook and Campbell add, less formal methods of study are appropriate. Indeed, all evaluators favour pilot work, and few would call for a high degree of 'control' at that stage. If there is a difference of opinion, it is about the duration of the exploratory phase. Advocates of experimentation usually speak of less controlled trials as 'pre-experimental', implying that in time a hard test will follow.

The statisticians Gilbert, Mosteller, and Tukey (1976, p. 297) speak of the rigorous confirmatory test as the capstone of a development effort that starts with 'insights' derived in part from 'anecdotal evidence – that is, careful case studies'. What language could be more congenial to the humanists? In principle, exploratory work can lead ultimately to a well-defined scientific proposition. To confirm that proposition for the record, the scientist designs a formal experiment with experimental and control treatments. It can be run off with little likelihood of surprise; the comparison is expected to document what has already been learned. Textbooks on 'design of experiments' discuss the study-for-the-record, not the pilot work. In contrast, humanistic evaluators tend to oppose freezing a policy in a form that can be tested and made permanent if it passes the test. They prefer to keep plans and operations in flux. They presumably would never get around to a hard-nosed appraisal.

Writers of all persuasions accept the importance of the 'threats to validity' that Campbell and Stanley (1963) made the litany of a generation of graduate students. However the investigator proceeds, awareness of these threats brings a caution to his interpretation that was frequently lacking in quantitative fieldwork prior to 1963. The critical logic of Campbell and Stanley (restated in Cool and Campbell, 1976, 1979) plays a large part in commentary on evaluations (though caution in the planning and interpretation of evaluations is less than universal).

The quantitative-minded are now inclined to agree with the humanists that compressing evaluative data into a single index of benefit or into a significance test cannot do justice to the reality being evaluated. Some evaluators try to sum up costs and benefits, but translations of multiple outcomes into simple indexes are in truth no more than heuristic devices. Utility analysis cannot displace political negotiation, according to the experts (Keeney and Raiffa, 1976). Even the goals set for the programme are subject to reconsideration. What compression gains in succinct communication is offset by loss of information and by the concealing of value judgements. Some time back, many professional evaluators were content to try to answer a yes-or-no question: Did the programme achieve its goals? Today everyone would want to be informed about side effects and would want to see a fuller description of the levels of the several outcomes.

Randomized experiments were once regarded as quite distinct from trials where comparison groups are not strictly equivalent. Now the quantitative options are all seen as approximations to experiments (Boruch, 1975). The term *quasi-experiment* was introduced by Campbell and Stanley (1963) to encompass studies that examine data collected under contrasting conditions, without random assignment of subjects. Those who press for rigour have always been ambivalent about quasi-experiments because the category includes both close and distant approximations. In fact, Campbell and Stanley overshot their mark. Aiming to show that careful interpretation could make *good* use of quasi-experiments, they inadvertently led some less sophisticated readers to believe that quasi-experiments are suspect. Some readers were even persuaded that a design that classifies subjects into types before assigning them to treatment at random is inferior to a fully random assignment. Readers were also led to think of experiments as impeccable, but the ideal experiment can rarely be achieved. A randomized design in a field study is likely to produce no more than an approximation to a true experiment, because of attrition and other departures from the plan.

In emphasizing degrees of approximation to the true experiment, I shall refer to 'strong' and 'weak' designs, the former including controlled-assignment and repeated-measures designs. The strong designs (ideally executed) are unbiased. That is to say, if the design is used to compare two treatments whose effects on a certain population and in a certain setting are identical, the difference found in comparisons of samples, averaged over many samples, will be zero.

Whether a design is strong or weak, all conclusions from it are inferences. They reach beyond the data with the aid of assumptions or presuppositions, and each one has a degree of credibility. Some advocates of strong designs suggest that conclusions from them can be 'certain', but that is not the case. An interpretation rests not on data alone but also on a large body of understandings, many of them potentially open to challenge (Lakatos and Musgrave, 1970, especially pp. 76–79, 99–103, 131). Even a determined operationist will fail to make explicit the presuppositions that separate him from other theorists in his field; that is, his operational definitions will ignore those aspects of the experimental setting that, in his mind, make little difference anyway (MacKenzie, 1977, pp. 132–133). Campbell has written much about the inevitable need to rely on plausible inference and common-sense knowing in interpreting even true experiments (see especially Campbell, 1974). Gilbert, Mosteller, and Tukey (1976, pp. 369–370) have this to say on the same point:

> Even if we are able to follow the best guidance we now have – when we must evaluate either a natural experiment or an unrandomized trial – namely, to seek out alternative methods of error-prone inference, to use a few or even several that appear likely to be prone to separate sources of error, and then to discuss their results together, recognizing their fallibility – even if we do all this, we cannot be sure of our results, only somewhat less uncertain. But we have an obligation to do as well as we may with the data we have.

BASIC QUESTIONS

Four main questions run through many of the discussions and disagreements between and within schools of evaluation:

1. Are causal conclusions required in evaluation?
2. Should evaluation have a conservative influence?
3. Should inquiry be targeted?
4. Should treatment conditions be standardized?

Although these questions are interconnected, I shall try to consider each in turn.

Are causal conclusions required in evaluation?

The following statement is representative of the scientistic point of view: 'Evaluation research . . . attempts to show causal relationships – for example, that A, the program Head Start, causes B, the desired outcome, equalization of cognitive skills among all pre-school children. To be useful, the investigator must be able to rule out alternative explanations for changes noted' (Bernstein and Freeman, 1975, p. 88). Approximations to experiments are accepted by Boruch and other writers of this school only in reluctant acknowledgement that controlled assignment may be practically or politically unfeasible. Investigations with weak designs are likely to be dismissed as inadequate. Outright rejection of certain designs is a tradition going back to the Campbell–Stanley monograph of 1963. In the 1970s, however, Campbell (1974, 1975c) came to see case studies as playing a legitimate role and retracted as a 'caricature' his earlier remarks that they were 'of almost no scientific value' and 'unethical' as dissertation research.

Those who see a causal statement as the intended fruit of an evaluation envision a conservative, hard-to-convince decision-maker who will accept an innovation only when its worth has been proved. The Rossi–Freeman–Wright text (1979) illustrates how stern was the scientistic ideal of just a few years back:

> Impact evaluation needs to be undertaken as systematically and rigorously as possible in order to document the causal linkages between intervention inputs and program outcomes. Such a task requires, to the best of our abilities, ruling out other explanations for the results (or lack of results) of social interventions [p. 161] . . . The problem of discerning the effectiveness of a program is identical with the problem of establishing causality [p. 162] . . . The basic aim of impact evaluation is to estimate the *net effects* or *net outcomes* of an intervention . . . free and clear of the effects of other elements present in the situation under evaluation [p. 163].

. . . There is also reason to doubt that decision-makers are crucially interested in causal inference; they need 'a rough, but constantly refined, set of understandings as to what is associated with what', says Moynihan (1969, p. 194). Simon (1960) describes most decision-making as 'satisficing'. The executive, like the person in the street, notes the state of affairs subsequent to an action. If that is within a satisfactory range, she continues with the same course of action – unless an alternative that might yield even better outcomes attracts her attention. She needs information on consequences, but a satisfactory state of affairs is a gift horse that she is unlikely to anatomize.

Should evaluation have a conservative influence?

The stress on causal testing in evaluation seems to arise from a sceptical, if not a conservative, political position. Riecken (1976, p. 43) criticizes those who act without providing for assessment of results:

> The history of social reform and amelioration is littered with examples of large-scale and costly catastrophes . . . as well as more modest mistakes . . . and simply ineffective treatments that appear to have done neither good nor harm, but only expended public funds. None of these programs was undertaken in the spirit of playing with people's lives, yet they affected the lives of a larger number of people at a considerably greater cost than experimental programs would have done.

Experimentation is prescribed as an antidote of overselling by those who cater to putative beneficiaries of a programme. Moreover, it puts a check on administrators who cover up the defects of weak programmes. Thus, Stanley (1972, p. 69) advocates strong designs because 'powerful methods can yield results from which the administrator may have no place to hide'.

Although some support for evaluations comes from conservatives who oppose public spending and new services, those who favour strong designs generally advocate vigorous attack on social problems. The conservatism of these evaluators is best articulated by Campbell (1975b): Existing institutional arrangements have emerged from centuries of societal evolution and have passed pragmatic tests in the process. Further evolution requires ceaseless innovation, but mutants are many whereas improvements are few. Constant culling is required, and early evaluation increases the likelihood that only genuine improvements will come into regular use. Berk and Rossi (1976), however, fear that evaluation is undermining the impulse to seek improvements. The accumulation of evidence that weak interventions have weak effects or no detectable effects contributes to 'a growing sense of social problem intractability' (p. 338).

The methodological conservatism of the experimentalists has a political slant, as is seen in the formulation of impact assessments as tests of null hypotheses. Size of effect is to be considered only *after* the data show a dependable 'treatment effect' (Cook and Campbell, 1979, p. 41; Rossi, Freeman, and Wright, 1979, p. 161). When 'no significant difference' is interpreted as a programme failure, the burden of proof is placed on the innovation . . .

As Robert Stake points out (personal communication, 1978), the arguments about method are to a significant degree an outcropping of divergent opinions about the complexity of the world. Some social scientists and social planners believe or hope that straightforward general conclusions can describe the main features of social processes. They believe that some treatments or policies are better than others and that these should become standard practice. For them, standardization is a feature of rational management, not just of investigation. Other social observers believe that probabilistic generalizations are almost worthless, since much of what happens is determined by the specifics of a situation and the perceptions of participants. Those who perceive this complexity fear that authorities who trust a generalization are likely to take Procrustean action.

The evaluator serves one or more political forces. As was pointed out in *Toward Reform*, evaluators help political figures remain in power if they supply them with information that other participants in the political process do not possess, and this may contribute to centralization of power. It should be possible, however, for the evaluator to cast himself as adviser to the entire polity if his information is disseminated and speaks to the concerns of the many constituencies with interests at stake. MacDonald (1976, p. 133) suggests that an evaluator places himself in one of three groups – 'autocratic', 'democratic' or 'bureaucratic' – by the commissions he accepts. (The third category matches a context of command, where a manager has been charged with executing defined plans and needs the evaluator purely as a technician. As *Toward Reform* argues, programmes rarely operate in that context, and I neglect it here.)

Those pressing for strong designs want the evaluator's role in governance to be large. In MacDonald's phrase, the role they seek is one of 'policy validation' or, one might say, policy legitimation. The evaluator offers to certify that a policy, if adopted, will live up to its advertising (or will not). For his report to be strongly persuasive, he must have adopted strong techniques. Also, he must be perceived as impartial, free from political interference and censorship. If a policy question can be defined as empirical, rationalists say hopefully, answers can be certain and decisions can be removed from politics (from the people?). This aspiration, for MacDonald, is 'autocratic' (but it seems fairer to say that the intent is to be 'authoritative'). If the question the design addresses directly is *the* pivotal question, if the design is powerful enough, and if there is no prospect that the relationship will change from year to year, evaluation might resolve the question. But even if the evaluation achieved that end, to remove a topic from politics by narrowing the issue has a disenfrachising effect because the concerns of some parties are left out of the account.

MacDonald, in discouraging the evaluator from taking an autocratic stance, is typical of the humanistic school. Studying the political function of evaluation, my colleagues and I in the Stanford Evaluation Consortium reached a similar judgement. In a pluralistic system, different participants will weigh facts differently, and too many questions arise for definitive evidence to be collected. Facts affect the participants' negotiations, but the fate of the programme is never removed from politics. The democratic evaluator therefore should help each participant to judge the legitimacy of the policy; focusing on a predefined question may push into the background what would be most pertinent to some of the parties.

Humanistic evaluators see a large payoff in what the community learns first-hand during the evaluation; some see this as more important than the learning that comes from the evaluator's reports. Robert Stake (personal communication, 1978) suggests this contrast: The scientist sees the rank and file as suppliers of data and as an audience awaiting what he distils from the data; the humanist is a teacher who turns the rank and file into investigators. They are to refine their perceptions without the aid of an intermediary or authority. Evaluation and use of evaluation thus become a communal process. This approach minimizes the role of power and expertise.

Should inquiry be targeted?

On the one hand, a communication system can send out many bits of information in a fixed time, accepting the risk that a comparatively large fraction of the message will be lost in transmission or garbled. To communicate with minimum loss and distortion, on the other hand, the communicator has to make his message simple and the transmission redundant. Neither represents the ideal; a balance between bandwidth and fidelity is wanted (Shannon and Weaver, 1949). In research the term *fidelity* refers to the dependability of an answer to a particular question. The term *bandwidth* refers to the number of questions for which an answer is offered, whether dependable or not. Focusing all resources on one limited message improves fidelity. That is the reason for making the SOS message highly redundant: nothing but the cry for help and the all-important map co-ordinates of the ship, over and over.

Distributing resources over possible questions, an evaluator strikes a balance between focus and diffusion. A narrow investigation provides a peak amount of information on one question. On other questions it provides tangential information that reduces uncertainty slightly. About the remaining matters, it does not reduce uncertainty at all. The report therefore has high fidelity on some point. A wide-band inquiry spreads attention more uniformly, yielding information of medium fidelity on most matters. As bandwidth increases, fidelity drops. At some threshold the evaluation planner becomes unwilling to reduce further the fidelity of evidence on major questions for the sake of learning a small amount about some minor ones . . .

When the design is so structured and the sample so large that two persons carrying out the same study would reach the same conclusion, the conclusion on the operationally specified question can be taken as definitive. When a study speaks to several questions, each answer has its own degree of reproducibility. A premium on reproducibility is warranted when certain well-defined questions are of overriding importance, but ordinarily it makes sense to reduce uncertainty about a larger number of issues, many of which are loosely defined. Strong tests of hypotheses are intended to ensure reproducibility. By standardizing treatment and by reporting only 'significant' relations, the designs limit bandwidth. Few resources go into the recording of variables and events that do not enter into the hypothesis. Moreover, some descriptions of the ideal experiment suggest specifying plans so exhaustively that the study could be executed by aides who scrupulously followed the detailed guidelines; no place is left for exploring what is not anticipated.

Naturalistic investigators spread resources widely over treatment, process, and outcome variables, and they sift subsets of data for patterns. They report and interpret relations that are not statistically significant. That is, they opt for bandwidth and sometimes accept dubious reproducibility. Though a scientistic evaluator prefers to narrow an inquiry for the sake of reproducibility, a formal experiment can be broad. Testing multiple hypotheses, as in a factorial design, increases bandwidth. A person concerned with many outcomes of several treatment variants on many demographic subgroups or types of community could in principle build each comparison into a randomized design.

The choice between bandwidth and fidelity arises in reporting as well as in data collection. At one extreme, what the study learned can be compressed to fit into a headline. At the opposite extreme, a narrative report (or a film) tries to give the reader a vicarious experience that will allow her to arrive at a personal interpretation of the observations. In so far as the evaluation plan has reduced the bandwidth of the data, the report is sure to be focused. The converse does not hold. A wide-band inquiry can be brought to as pointed a conclusion as a narrow inquiry.

In traditional writings on psychological research methods, the investigator is advised to design a study with high fidelity to settle a sharp question. These ideas have strongly influenced writings on evaluation. I came to a contrary view thirty years ago, as I considered the multiscore tests then coming into use for measuring aptitude profiles and for appraising personality. When a test devotes an hour to checking on a dozen aspects of an individual, no one of its findings can have the precision of a test that concentrates an equal effort on measuring one aspect. In applied measurement it is often appropriate to sacrifice some fidelity to increase bandwidth; the balance depends on the specifics of the problem. I take the same position here (for earlier statements see Cronbach, 1954, or Cronbach and Gleser, 1957) . . .

The usual emphasis on strict and precise inferences found in advice to social scientists is tempered in a statement for evaluators by the statistician Walter Deming. Writing on 'the logic of evaluation', Deming (1975) emphasizes causal interpretation and finds virtue in strong designs – and then turns to their pitfalls:

> The most important lesson we can learn about statistical methods in evaluation is that circumstances where one may depend wholly on statistical inference are rare [p. 55] . . . Statistical inference in an analytic [causally oriented] problem is most effective when it is presented as conclusions valid for the frame studied and for the

range of environmental conditions specified for the tests . . . Other conditions may well be encountered [p. 62] . . . Extreme accuracy in an analytic study is wasted effort [p. 65].

Deming goes on to say that an overwhelming outcome difference in an experiment may justify a decision in favour of the winner but that a modest difference cannot provide a firm basis for decision because an experiment almost invariably leaves important variables out of account. Similarly, Gilbert and Mosteller (1972, p. 376), even as they campaign for strong designs, recognize that interactions can undercut conclusions about the main effect of a treatment contrast: 'When the same treatment under controlled conditions produces good results in many places and circumstances, then we become confident that we have found a general rule. When the payoff is finicky – gains in one place, losses in another – we are wary because we can't count on the effect.'

Social action, Deming says, always relates to situations, treatments, measures, and/or populations other than those of the direct investigation. Two questions lead one away from direct reliance on the experimental result. Is the treatment truly fixed? If not, it can possibly be adapted on the basis of an understanding of its effects. Second, is it possible that the treatment interacts with characteristics of clients, the institutional setting, or other conditions? As Deming says, only an expert in the subject-matter can deny that a change in one of these respects will make little difference in the outcome. Once these questions are raised, the evaluator finds it important to look within the treatment and within the population to identify differentiated effects. When contentious rhetoric is put aside, it appears that everyone wants to make predictions that reach beyond the fixed experimental situation and wants both bandwidth and fidelity to some degree.

Should treatment conditions be standardized?

In field research one uses whatever sites and participants come conveniently to hand, draws a representative or deliberately diverse sample, or selects a near-uniform set. The researcher lets treatments take their natural course or specifies exactly what service is to be delivered. Standardization appeals to the experimentalist, outcome-oriented investigator. For him, tampering with a treatment in mid-trial – even to make it work – spoils the experiment. Natural variation in events from unit to unit makes interpretation equivocal; the treatment should be fixed. Freeman (1964, p. 194) would have the evaluator 'remain within the environment, like a snarling watchdog ready to oppose alterations in program and procedures that would render his evaluation efforts useless'. The humanist is sceptical of standardization of social interventions and services, and doubly sceptical of attempts to make them standard for the sake of investigation. To do so is to lose the variety of human response he finds most instructive.

The Fisherian model of experimentation identifies a limited number of factors believed to be causally significant and crosses them to define cells (for example, seed 3 and fertilizer level b). All plots of land assigned to that cell are treated the same way with respect to the control variables. Factors not specified for control, such as slope and orientation of terrain, are allowed to vary. Fisherian designs are not much seen in evaluation, but Fisherian control is often held up as an ideal. Thus, in *Social Experimentation* (Riecken and Boruch, 1974) we read that 'the most important variables will be treated factorially if possible, and . . . *they must be* if causal inferences about their effects are sought' (p. 68; emphasis added). Cook and Campbell (1979, p. 43) value strict control for another reason: 'Lack of standardization both within and between persons [delivering services] will inflate error variance and decrease the chance of obtaining true differences. The threat . . . can be most obviously controlled by [making] the treatment . . . as standard as possible across occasions of implementation.'

But doubts about standardization arise even among the experimentally minded. I shall later quote Fisher himself in favour of *not* standardizing any variable save the main ones. Cook and Campbell (1979, p. 65) favour controlled diversity: 'There is really no substitute for deliberately varying two or three exemplars of a treatment, *where possible.*' Their example is a study of the effect of a communication delivered by prestigious communicators. Only the use of several prestigious figures, each with a different sub-group, gives confidence that a result is attributable to the general variable of prestige and not to the unique characteristics of a lone communicator. Although the tradition is to standardize measuring operations, they too may be chosen with an eye to representativeness and diversity. Cook and Campbell (1979, pp. 66–80, 366) call for observing diverse treatment realizations, subjects, and indicators of outcome for the same reason that Gilbert and Mosteller (1972) wanted to check out a programme in many localities.

To get diversity one may reach out for maximally dissimilar instances or draw a representative and, hence, mixed, sample. Brunswik (1956) introduced 'representative design' as an alternative to laboratory controls. Research on perception, Brunswik thought, could well ask the subject to judge targets sampled from her everyday environment – instead of asking her to judge squares of standard size and uniform colour, presented at a standard distance under standard illumination. In the natural environment, some variables tend to be associated. The Fisherian design 'unties' the variables to form unnatural situations. This can be good science, but it can also lead to false interpretations.

An unsophisticated evaluator assessing grouping of grade school students by ability would standardize by requiring fast, slow, and mixed class sections to study the same arithmetic lessons, thus holding constant all variables but one. The evaluator who accepts the Fisherian ideal would create at least two standard treatments, one easy and one difficult. If naïve, he would form unnatural cells – for example, he would require some of the slow sections to struggle with difficult lessons. The Brunswikian would avoid such constraints and would instead look at naturally occurring events (Snow, 1974). He would like to know what happens when teachers' decisions about content and pace of lessons produce a correlation between the treatment and student ability – 'confounding them', a Fisherian would say. Accepting a rationale similar to that of Brunswikians, sociologists such as Kish (1975) value the realism and representativeness of survey research. The sociologist would find it reasonable to correlate the school-by-school averages of fourth graders on a state-wide achievement test with principals' descriptions of the grouping practices in their respective schools.

Even experimenters concerned with a fixed national policy (with guidelines regulating bilingual instruction, for example) may consider it useful to observe what happens when the fixed directive is implemented by staff members in typical sites. The experimenter could not hope to ensure that every site will follow the directive in every particular; and if he could cause that to happen, the situation would be unnatural. Does it really make sense for the applied scientist to investigate a standard treatment that is unlikely to operate once the investigator's pressure for compliance is removed? Or should he permit, and collect data on, the heterogeneous interpretations that schools place on the directive under normal operating conditions? . . .

Standardization of data collection fosters objectivity, but humanists prize subjective information. Typically, they want the observer to pick out events he considers significant and to filter what he observes through his conceptual system. Great value is placed on the observations and interpretations of participants. The approach that ethnographers take to distant cultures has recently commanded the enthusiasm of humanistic evaluators. The ethnographer sets out to comprehend how the native observer apprehends events; he tries to set aside his preconceptions and categories in order to register the mental world of the informant. This approach to evaluation reflects several themes of the humanists. First, no outsider can specify in advance what is important to observe. Second, only the person affected by the programme knows what is important to her, and each person's values should be treated respectfully. Finally, even though the intervention may have a fixed plan, it is interpretations by programme staff and clients than determine the outcomes. What is important, then, cannot be manipulated, standardized, objectified, or quantified.

TOWARD A SOPHISTICATED DIFFERENTIATION

The contrast with which this discussion began is now seen to refer to views on a number of aspects of research planning and reporting. A person with a scientistic viewpoint will prefer re-planning, focusing, standardization, quantification, and controls; a humanistically oriented evaluator will lean toward greater openness. But few individuals would adopt either style for every aspect of an investigation, and none would insist on applying a uniform style to all studies.

Speaking of experiments and naturalistic case studies as polar opposites is a rhetorical device; evaluation planning is not a matter of choosing between irreconcilables. It almost always makes sense to impose control on some aspects of data collection when treatments are naturalistic and to do some naturalistic observation when the treatment plan is elaborately controlled. The balance between the styles will vary from one sub-question to the next and may well shift (in either direction) after early evaluation activities change the evaluator's sense of the job to be done. Experimental control is not incompatible with attention to qualitative information or subjective interpretation, nor is open-minded exploration incompatible with objectification of evidence.

Campbell (1975a, p. 10) makes a positive recommendation: Evaluations with strong designs should also

> attempt to systematically tap all the qualitative commonsense program critiques and evaluations that have been generated among the program staff, program clients and their families, and community observers . . . Where such evaluations are contrary to the quantitative results, the quantitative results should be regarded as suspect until the reasons for the discrepancy are well understood. Neither is infallible, of course. But for many of us, what needs to be emphasized is that the quantitative results may be as mistaken as the qualitative.

Campbell goes on to lament the polarization he sees in American evaluation practice, where sponsors have sometimes opted for an anthropological study of an innovation and sometimes for a formal quantitative assessment, but not for the evaluation in which the two kinds of activities support each other.

Evaluators need not – in fact, they should not – decide which school of thought they 'belong to'. Something is gained when an evaluation becomes more objective, more reproducible, more concentrate. Something else is gained when the evaluation becomes more phenomenological, more flexible, broader in its coverage. The choices should differ from evaluation to evaluation . . .

REFERENCES

American Institutes for Research (1977) *Evaluation of the Impact of ESEA Title VII Spanish/English Bilingual Education Program*, American Institutes for Research, Palo Alto, California.

Baker, F.B. (1967) Experimental design considerations associated with large-scale research projects, in J.C. Stanley (ed.) *Improving Experimental Design and Statistical Analysis*, Rand McNally, Chicago.

Berk, R. and Rossi, P. (1976) Doing good or worse: evaluation research politically re-examined, *Social Problems*, Vol. 23, pp. 337–49.

Bernstein, I.N. and Freeman, H.E. (1975) *Academic and Entrepreneurial Research*, Russell Sage Foundation, New York.

Berryman, S.E. and Glennan, T.K. Jr (1980) An improved strategy for evaluating federal programs in education, in J. Pincus (ed.) *Educational Evaluation in the Public Policy Setting*, Report R 2505 RC, Rand Corporation, Santa Monica, California.

Boruch, R.F. (1975) Coupling randomized experiments and approximations to experiments in social program evaluation, *Sociological Methods and Research*, No. 4, pp. 31–53.

Boruch, R.F. and Cordray, D.S. (1980) *An Appraisal of Educational Program Evaluations: Federal, State and Local Agencies*. Unpublished report (ED 192466), Northwestern University, Evanston, Illinois.

Brunswik, E. (1956) *Perception and the Representative Design of Experiments*, University of California Press, Berkeley.

Campbell, D.T. (1969) Reforms as experiments. *American Psychologist*, No. 24, pp. 409–29.

Campbell, D.T. (1974) *Qualitative Knowing in Action Research*. Occasional Paper, Stanford Evaluation Consortium, Stanford University.

Campbell, D.T. (1975a) Assessing the impact of planned social change, in G.M. Lyons (ed.) *Social Research and Public Policies*, Hanover, N.H., Public Affairs Center, Dartmouth College.

Campbell, D.T. (1975b) Conflicts between biological and social evolution and between psychology and moral tradition, *American Psychologist*, No. 30, pp. 1103–26.

Campbell, D.T. (1975c) Degrees of freedom and the case study, *Comparative Political Studies*, No. 2, pp. 178–93.

Campbell, D.T. and Stanley, J.C. (1963) Experimental and quasi-experimental designs for research on teaching, in N.L. Gage (ed.) *Handbook of Research on Teaching*, Rand McNally, Chicago.

Cohen, D.K. and Weiss, J.A. (1977) Social science and social policy: schools and race, *Educational Forum*, No. 41, pp. 393–413.

Coleman, J. S. (1972) *Policy Research in the Social Sciences*, General Learning Press, Morristown, New Jersey.

Coleman, J.S. et al., (1979) *Policy Issues and Research Design*, National Opinion Research Center, Chicago.

Cook, T.D. (1981) An evolutionary perspective on a dilemma in the evaluation of ongoing social programs, in M.B. Brewer and B.E. Collins (eds.) *Scientific Inquiry and the Social Sciences: A Volume in Honor of Donald T. Campbell*, Jossey-Bass, San Francisco.

Cook, T.D. and Campbell, D.T. (1976) The design and conduct of quasi-experiments and true experiments in field settings, in M.D. Dunnette (ed.) *Handbook of Industrial and Organizational Psychology*, Rand McNally, Chicago.

Cook, T.D. and Campbell, D.T. (1979) *Quasi-Experimentation: Design and Analysis Issues for Field Settings*, Rand McNally, Chicago.

Cronbach, L.J. (1954) Report on a psychometric mission to clinicia, *Psychometrika*, No. 19, pp. 263–70.

Cronbach, L.J. and Gleser, G.C. (1957) *Psychological Tests and Personnel Decisions*, University of Illinois Press, Urbana.

Cronbach, L.J. et al. (1980) *Toward Reform of Program Evaluation: Aims, Methods and Institutional Arrangements*, Jossey-Bass, San Franciso.

Deming, W.E. (1975) The logic of evaluation, in E.L. Struening and M. Guttentag (eds.) *Handbook of Evaluation Research*, Vol. I, Sage, Beverly Hills, California.

Fairweather, G.W. (1980) Community psychology for the 1980s and beyond, *Evaluation and Program Planning*, No. 3, pp. 245–50.

Finney, D.J. (1956) The statistician and the planning of field experiments, *Journal of the Royal Statistical Society*, No. 119, pp. 1–27.

Freeman, H.E. (1964) Conceptual approaches to assessing impacts of large-scale intervention programs, *Proceedings, American Statistical Association* (Social Statistics Section), pp. 192–8.

Gilbert, J.P. and Mosteller, F. (1972) The urgent need for experimentation, in F. Mosteller and D.P. Moynihan (eds.) *On Equality of Educational Opportunity*, Random House, New York.

Gilbert, J.P., Mosteller, F. and Tukey, J. (1976) Steady social progress requires quantitative evaluation to be searching, in C.C. Abt (ed.) *The Evaluation of Social Programs*, Sage, Beverly Hills, California.

Hamilton, D., Jenkins, D., King, C., MacDonald, B. and Parlett, M. (eds.) (1978) *Beyond the Numbers Game*, McCutchan, Berkeley, California.

Hunt, J. McV. (1961) *Intelligence and Experience*, Ronald Press, New York.

Kaufman, H. (1976) *Are Government Organizations Immortal?*, Brookings Institution, Washington, DC.

Keeney, R.L. and Raiffa, H. (1976) *Decisions with Multiple Objectives: Preferences and Value Trade-Offs*, Wiley, New York.

Kish, L. (1975) Representation, randomization and control, in H.M. Blalock et al. (eds.) *Quantitative Methodology*, Academic Press, New York.

Lakatos, I. and Musgrave, A. (eds.) (1970) *Criticism and the Growth of Knowledge*, Cambridge University Press.

Lee, B.G. (1976) Mission operations strategy for Viking, *Science*, No. 194, pp. 52–62.

Light, R.J. and Smith, P.V. (1970) Choosing a future: strategies for designing and evaluating new programs, *Harvard Educational Review*, No. 40, pp. 1–28.

Lindblom, C.E. and Cohen, D.K. (1979) *Usable Knowledge*, Yale University Press, New Haven, Connecticut.

MacDonald, B. (1976) Evaluation and the control of education, in D. Tawney (ed.) *Curriculum Evaluation Today: Trends and Implications*, Macmillan, London.

MacKenzie, B.D. (1977) *Behaviourism and the Limits of Scientific Method*, Humanities Press, Atlantic Highlands, New Jersey.

McLaughlin, M.W. (1980) Evaluation and alchemy, in J. Pincus (ed.) *Educational Evaluation in the Public Policy Setting*. Report R 2502 RC, Rand Corporation, Santa Monica, California.

Moynihan, D.P. (1969) *Maximum Feasible Misunderstanding*, Free Press, New York.

Raizen, S. and Rossi, P.H. (1981) *Program Evaluation in Education: When? How? To What Ends?*, National Academy Press, Washington, DC.

Reichardt, C.S. and Cook, T.D. (1979) Beyond qualitative versus quantitative methods, in T.D. Cook and C.S. Reichardt (eds.), *Qualitative and Quatitative Methods in Evaluation Research*, Sage, Beverly Hills, California.

Rein, M. (1976) *Social Science and Public Policy*, Penguin Books, New York.

Riecken, H.W. (1976) Social experimentation, in C.C. Abt (ed.) *The Evaluation of Social Programs*, Sage, Beverly Hills, California.

Riecken, H.W. and Boruch, R.F. (eds.) (1974) *Social Experimentation*, Academic Press, New York.

Rivlin, A.M. (1974) Allocating resources for policy research: how can experiments be more useful?, *American Economic Review*, No. 64, pp. 346–54.

Rossi, P.H. (1978) Issues in the evaluation of human services delivery, *Evaluation Quarterly*, No. 2, pp. 573–99.

Rossi, P.H., Freeman, H.E. and Wright, S.R. (1979) *Evaluation: A Systematic Approach*, Sage, Beverly Hills, California.

Saxe, L. and Fine, M. (1979) Expanding our view of control groups in evaluations, in L.E. Datta and R. Perloff (eds.) *Improving Evaluations*, Sage, Beverly Hills, California.

Scriven, M. (1967) The methodology of evaluation, in R.E. Stake *et al.* (eds.) *Perspectives on Curriculum Evaluation*. AERA Monograph Series on curriculum Evaluation, No. 1, Rand McNally, Chicago.

Shannon, C.E. and Weaver, W. (1949) *The Mathematical Theory of Communication*, University of Illinois Press, Urbana.

Simon, H.A. (1960) *The New Science of Management Decision*, Harper & Row, New York.

Snow, R.E. (1974) Representative and quasi-representative designs for research on teaching, *Review of Educational Research*, No. 44, pp. 625–6.

Stanley, J.C. (1972) Controlled field experiments as a model for evaluation, in P.H. Rossi and W.Williams (eds.) *Evaluating Social Programs*, Seminar Press, New York.

Stenhouse, L. (1978) Some limitations of the use of objectives, in D. Hamilton *et al.* (eds.) *Beyond the Numbers Game*, McCutchan, Berkeley, California.

Timpane, P.M. (1970) Educational experimentation in national social policy, *Harvard Educational Review*, No. 40, pp. 547–66.

Weiss, C.H. (ed.) (1977) *Using Social Research in Public Policy Making*, Lexington Books, Lexington, Mass.

Wholey, J.S. (1979) *Evaluation: Promise and Performance*, Urban Institute, Washington, DC.

Wilensky, H. (1967) *Organizational Intelligence: Knowledge and Policy in Government and Industry*, Basic Books, New York.

1.2
EVALUATION AND THE CONTROL OF EDUCATION*
Barry MacDonald

Evaluators seldom if ever talk about themselves as political figures, persons involved in the distribution of power. To do so would verge on bad taste. Do we not share, with those who teach and those who do research and those who administer, a common commitment to the betterment of the educational system we serve? Let the journalists monitor the tilting balance of control, or talk of 'secret gardens'.[1] We have a job to do, a technology to perfect, a service to render. Political language is rhetorical or divisive, when it is not both. It is a dangerous discourse for evaluators to engage in.

It is therefore with some trepidation that I address myself to the political dimension of evaluation studies. That I should do so at all is not, as some readers may surmise, because all the legitimate facets of evaluation have been fully explored in other chapters, thus driving me to speculative invention. Rather, it is because I have increasingly come to view evaluation itself as a political activity, and to understand its variety of styles and approaches as expressions of differing stances towards the prevailing distribution of education power. I intend to propose a simple classification system for evaluation studies. My trepidation will be readily appreciated when I say that the terms I propose to employ are three words which are familiar enough in political discussion, but generally excluded from the vocabulary of dispassionate description. I refer to the words 'bureaucratic', 'autocratic' and 'democratic'. Although it may not be immediately apparent that these are useful words to employ in an interpretative description of evaluation studies, I suggest that we attempt to analyse it and see to what

* MacDonald, B. (1974) Evaluation and the control of education, in B. MacDonald and R. Walker (eds.) *Innovation, Evaluation, Research and the Problem of Control* (SAFARI), Centre for Applied Research in Education, Norwich.

extent we feel comfortable with the perspective it generates. Our task is to relate the style of an evaluation study to the political stance it implicitly adopts. The analysis is not intended to be divisive, but to encourage wider reflection on the alternative roles available.

I am aware that only the academic theorist uses these political terms referentially; most of us employ them when we wish to combine a definition of an action or structure with the expression of an attitude towards it. 'Bureaucracy' and 'autocracy' carry overtones of disapproval, while 'democracy' at least in Western societies can still be relied upon to evoke general approval. Nor am I free from such affective responses myself, and it will not escape the reader that my own stance falls conveniently under the 'democratic' label. Nevertheless, my major argument is not directed against what I will call bureaucratic and autocratic evaluation stances, but towards the need to make explicit the political orientation of the evaluation so that we can define the kind of evaluation studies that we want and need. And it may be worth while reminding the reader that we belong to a society which aspires to a form of democracy in which a highly developed bureaucracy is reconciled with individual freedom of action.

I want to begin, however, by giving a historical account of some of the considerations which led me to formulate such a typology. Four occasions stand out in mind. The first was a few years ago, during a visit to the United States of America. I met a research worker who had recently completed an evaluation of the effects of a particular state school 'bussing' programme. She was in a mood of deep gloom. 'What's the point of educational research?' she said. It turned out that the evaluation report, commissioned by the state authority for a review of its bussing policy, was then ignored when the review took place. The evaluation strongly endorsed the educational value of the prevailing policy but the decision was to discontinue bussing. The evaluation report was confidential to its sponsors.

I cannot recall how I responded at the time, but now I would say that it was a good piece of educational research but a bad piece of evaluation. Bad for two reasons. Firstly, because it paid insufficient attention to the context of the policy decision it sought to serve, and secondly, because it allowed the conditions of contract to pre-empt the right of those affected to be informed.

A couple of weeks afterwards I had a brief conversation with one of the most respected exponents of educational evaluation in America, whose views I sought on this issue. He was extremely scathing about the service role adopted by evaluators. A 'cop-out' was what he called it, implying that my new-found profession was little more than the hired help of the bureaucracy. As a Schools Council project evaluator, I found this at the time rather difficult to relate to my own situation. No one, except my mother-in-law and a few well-meaning friends, had told me how to do my job or placed other than financial restrictions on me. I asked this man to tell me how he envisaged the responsibility of evaluation, indeed, how he exercised it, since he was, and still is, a very powerful practitioner. 'It is the duty of the evaluator,' he told me, 'to reach a conclusion about the comparative merits of alternative courses of educational action. It is also his duty,' he added, 'to ensure that his judgement is implemented by those who control the allocation of resources.'

Taken aback by this remarkably interventionist conception of evaluation, I asked my informant how he could justify such a stance. The answer was twofold. An evaluator's judgement is based on objective evidence of accomplishment, evidence gathered by means of a technology of public procedures and skills. The whole process of conclusion-reaching is guaranteed by the evaluator's peer group, the research community. Muscling in on policy decisions, on the other hand, can be justified by an appeal to democratic principle enshrined in the constitution, principles which the bureaucracy cannot be trusted always to uphold.

I did not find this argument attractive. The 'evaluator king' role appealed to me even less than the role of the hired hack. It seemed to me that the act of evaluation is not value-free. Also, the technology is alarmingly defective, and the whole process of conclusion-reaching far from transparent. What is more, although the research community might be notionally construed as custodian of the scientific detachment of its members and guarantor of the validity of their conclusions, in fact such a function is only systematically carried out in relation to academic awards. Indeed, the community has shown few signs of any desire to extend that jurisdiction. Perhaps it's just as well. When research is closely related to ideology, as is the case with educational research, history suggests that we lock up the silver.

My third conversation took place more than two years ago, at a gathering of evaluators at Cambridge. This time I can name the other party, something I could not do in the first two instances because I am unsure about the detailed accuracy of my recall, and because it would be wrong to turn casual remarks into enduring statements. We were discussing the role of the evaluator in relation to education decision-making, when Myron Atkin, of the University of Illinois, spelled out what he saw to be a dangerous trend in America, a growing attempt on the part of the research community to use its authority and prestige to intefere in the political process. It was no part of the researcher's right, *qua* researcher, to usurp the functions of elected office–holders in a democratic society.

Now I realize that anyone reading this who had a part-time job of evaluating, say, the effect of certain reading materials on children's oral vocabulary in a primary school in Wytown, may think this anecdote extremely peripheral to his concerns. I want to argue that the underlying issue is one which no evaluator can dismiss, and furthermore, that the resolution of the issue is a major factor in determining his choice of evaluation techniques.

But first, my fourth anecdote, involving yet another American. No apology will be called for on that account, I hope, although I anticipate having to resist charges of incipient élitism. We are fledgelings in a specialism that is well established across the Atlantic. Robert Stake was addressing a recent meeting of the Schools Council Evaluators Group at a time of high electoral fever. The then Prime Minister, Edward Heath, had declared the key election issue to be 'Who rules Britain?', and Stake began his presentation by suggesting that an important issue for evaluators was 'Who rules education?'. Relating this question to the accountability movement in America, Stake argued a strong case for recognizing the informational needs of different groups affected by curriculum decisions (Stake, 1974).

The phrase 'Who rules education?' stuck in my mind, and began to interact with other questions and concerns, including those already mentioned. At that particular time I had written a couple of things myself that were relevant, and I hope the reader will forgive me for quoting from them. In the first, a proposal to the Department of Education and Science advocating the funding of an evaluation of computer-assisted learning, the following passage occurred:

> The everyday meaning of the word 'evaluate' is unambiguous. It means quite simply to judge the worth of something. This is a long-established usage, and it is hardly surprising that many people assume that the task of the educational evaluator is to judge the worth of educational programmes. Some evaluators do, in fact, share this assumption, and a few would even argue that the evaluator has a right to expect that his judgements would be suitably reflected in subsequent policy. But there are others, including the present writer, who believe that the proper *locus* of judgements of worth and the responsibility for taking them into account in the determination of educational policy, lie elsewhere. In a society such as ours, educational power and accountability are widely dispersed, and situational diversity is a significant factor in educational action. It is also quite clear that our society contains groups and individuals who entertain different, even conflicting, notions of what constitutes educational excellence. The evaluator has therefore many audiences who will bring a variety of perspectives, concerns and values to bear upon his presentations. In a pluralist society, he has no right to use his position to promote his personal values, or to choose which paticular educational ideologies he shall regard as legitimate. His job is to identify those who will have to make judgements and decisions about the programme, and to lay before them those facts of the case that are recognized by them as relevant to their concerns.
>
> (MacDonald, 1973)

It did not occur to me when I wrote it that this is an essentially political statement, involving an acknowledgement of the distribution of power and values, an affirmation of a decision-making process, and an assertion of the evaluator's obligation to democratize his knowledge. The second piece I had written was an introduction to a section of a book on readings in curriculum evaluation (Hamilton *et al.*, 1977). The section was concerned to illustrate the objectives model of evaluation and its development from the early papers of Ralph Tyler to current applications in America and Britain. Getting the section ready, I was puzzled still by the difficulty in explaining why this approach to curriculum planning, so popular for so long in America, had really failed to take root in our own country, despite the elegance of its logic and the absence of alternative models. Then it suddenly struck me that the model could be viewed as a cultural artefact, as American as popcorn. It was an ideological model harnessed to a political vision. I wrote:

> The inclination of so many American curriculum developers and evaluators to perceive educational change as a technological problem of product specification and manufacture, is by itself unremarkable. Mechanistic analogies have a peculiar appeal for a people who see themselves as the raw materials of a vision which can be socially engineered. Their culture is characteristically forward-looking, constructionist, optimistic and rational. Both the vision and the optimism are reflected in the assumption that goal consensus, a prerequisite of engineering, is a matter of clarification rather than reconciliation. In contrast British culture is nostalgic, conservationist, complacent and distrustful of rationality. Our schools are the agents of continuity, providing discriminating transmission of a culture that has stood the test of time and will continue to do so, given due attention to points of adaptive growth. Goal consensus is neither ardently desired nor determinedly pursued. Such pursuit would entail a confrontation of value-systems which have so far been contained within an all-embracing rhetoric of generalized education aims.
>
> (Hamilton *et al.*, 1977)

The piece concluded: 'The theory and practice of the objectives model of evaluation is thus wedded to an American view of society, and an American faith in technology. Pluralist societies will find it difficult to use. Unified societies will use it, and discover they are pluralist.'

Having now aired a number of questions related to the uses and abuses of evaluation from a politico/ideological perspective, I want, before drawing them together, to remind the reader of some crucial distinctions between evaluation and research.

EVALUATION AND RESEARCH

It is possible to emphasize, as John Nisbet did most lucidly at the inaugural meeting of the British Educational Research Association in April 1974 (Nisbet, 1980), that curriculum evaluation is an extension of educational research, sharing its roots, using its methods and skills. It was salutory too, as Nisbet understood, to remind us of the dangers of engaging in our own internecine territorial power games. While I have no wish to quarrel with the assertion of many commonalities shared by evaluation and research, it is important for my present purpose to emphasize one major distinction, and a particular danger in subscribing too readily to the continuity thesis.

The distinction is one to which Hemphill (1970) has drawn attention in a paper on this theme. After stating that the basic and utilitarian purpose of evaluation studies is to provide information for choice among alternatives, and that the choice is a subsequent activity not engaged in by the evaluators, Hemphill says:

> This fact might lead to the conclusion that an evaluation study could avoid questions of value and utility leaving them to the decision-maker, and thus not need to be distinguished from research, either basic or applied. The crux of the issue, however, is not *who* makes a decision about what alternatives or *what information* serves as the basis for a decision; rather, it is the *degree to which concern with value questions is part and parcel of the study*.
>
> (Hemphill, 1970)

A matter of 'degree' may not suggest a worthwhile distinction. It is necessary to be more explicit. Of course, values enter into research, in a number of ways. There are many people in this country who have resisted the conclusions of a great deal of educational research since the war, on the grounds of value bias inherent in problem selection and definition. This was notable in the response to research into educational opportunity, and seems likely to characterize the reception of current research in the field of multi-ethnic education. Other value judgements of the researcher are less perceptible and lie buried in his technology. The more esoteric the technology, the less likely are these values to be detected. Test and survey instruments are wrongly assumed to be value-free because of the depersonalized procedures of administration and analysis that govern their application. There is more value bias in research than is commonly recognized. Nevertheless, it remains the responsibility of the researcher to select the problem and devise the means, a responsibility safeguarded by the totem of 'academic freedom'. He construes his task in these terms: 'Which of the questions I judge to be important can I answer with my technology?'

The position of the evaluator is quite distinct, and much more complex. The enterprise he is called upon to study is neither of his choosing nor under his control. He soon discovers, if he failed to assume it, that his script of educational issues, actions and consequences, is being acted out in a socio/political street theatre which affects not just the performance, but the play itself. He finds he can make few assumptions about what has happened, what is happening, or what is going to happen. He is faced with competing interest groups, with divergent definitions of the situation and conflicting informational needs. If he has accepted narrowly stipulative terms of reference, he may find that his options have been pre-empted by contractual restraints that are subsequently difficult to justify. If, on the other hand, he has freedom of action, he faces acute problems. He has to decide which decision-makers he will serve, what information will be of most use, when it is needed and how it can be obtained. I am suggesting that the resolution of these issues commits the evaluator to a political stance, an attitude to the government of education. No such commitment is required of the researcher. He stands outside the political process, and values his detachment from it. For him the production of new knowledge and its social use are separated. The evaluator is embroiled in the action, built into a political process which concerns the distribution of power, i.e. the allocation of resources and the determination of goals, roles and tasks. And it is naïve to think of educational change as a game in which everybody wins, seductive though that implication of the rhetoric is. One man's bandwagon is another man's hearse.

When evaluation data influences power relationships, the evaluator is compelled to weigh carefully the consequences of his task specification. The much-used term 'independent evaluator' obscures rather than clarifies the problem. Independent of whom? The people who fund the evaluation? The curriculum development team? The pupils, parents, teachers, local education authorities, publishers, critics? His own values and needs? The independent evaluator is free only to choose his allegiance, to decide who he shall listen to, whose questions will be pursued, whose priorities shall have primacy, who has the right to know what. In this sense, the degree of his involvement with values is so much greater than that of the researcher that it amounts to a difference in kind. It also makes explicit the political dimension of evaluation studies.

I said earlier that there was a danger in subscribing too readily to the continuity thesis. It is this. The researcher is free to select his questions, and to seek answers to them. He will naturally select questions which are susceptible to the problem-solving techniques of his craft.

In a sense, as Tom Hastings (1969) has pointed out, he uses his instruments to define his problems. The evaluator, on the other hand, must never fall into the error of answering questions which no one but he is asking. He must first identify the significant questions, and only then address the technological problems which they raise. To limit his inquiries to those which satisfy the critical canons of conventional research is to run a serious risk of failing to match the 'vocabulary of action'[2] of the decision-maker. The danger therefore of conceptualizing evaluation as a branch of research is that evaluators become trapped in the restrictive tentacles of research respectability. Purity may be substituted for utility, trivial proofs for clumsy attempts to grasp complex significance. How much more productive it would be to define research as a branch of evaluation, a branch whose task it is to solve the technological problems encountered by the evaluator.

The relevance of this issue to my present thesis is easy to demonstrate. The political stance of the evaluator has consequences for his choice of techniques of information-gathering and analysis. Recently, I bumped into a researcher whose completed report was being considered for publication for the Schools Council. He was somewhat impatient over a criticism that had been made. 'Some of these people at the Council,' he observed caustically, 'seem to think that everything one writes should be understandable to teachers.' This raises the issue nicely I think. A great deal of new knowledge is produced by researchers and evaluators by means of techniques and procedures which are difficult to understand. Conclusions are reached and judgements made by the few who are qualified to make them. Others accept or reject these conclusions according to the degree of respect they feel towards those who make them, or the degree to which the conclusions coincide with their beliefs and self-interests.

For many years now those concerned with the failure of the educational system to make full use of the results of educational research have pleaded the case for all teachers to be trained in the techniques of research. Perhaps some of that effort should have been expended in exploring techniques that more closely resemble the ways in which teachers normally make judgements, techniques that are more accessible to non-specialist decision-makers. The evaluator who sees his task as feeding the judgement of a range of non-specialist audiences faces the problem of devising such techniques, the problem of trying to respond to the ways of knowing that his audiences use. Such an effort is presently hampered by the subjection of evaluators to a research critique which is divorced from considerations of socio-political consequences.

A POLITICAL CLASSIFICATION OF EVALUATION STUDIES

Evaluators do not only live in the real world of educational politics; they actually influence its changing power relationships. Their work produces information which functions as a resource for the promotion of particular interests and values. Evaluators are committed to a political stance because they must choose between competing claims for this resource. The selection of roles, goals, audiences, issues and techniques by evaluators, provides clues to their political allegiances.

I think it would be useful at this point to describe the three distinct types of evaluation study – bureaucratic, autocratic and democratic. In doing so I am using the familiar device of ideal-typology, that is, I am describing each type in pure form. When one compares real examples with the 'ideal', there is rarely a perfect fit, although frequently an approximation. My analysis of ideal types is an attempt to present them equally, to characterize accurately their central features. It would be ironic, however, if I failed to acknowledge that I am hampered in this effort by a personal preference for the 'democratic' stance, and to recognize that an analysis which precedes an argument is always suspect. The field of evaluation has been characterized by studies which fall into one or other of the first two types. The democratic evaluation study is an emerging model, not yet substantially realized, but one which embodies some recent theoretical and practical trends. It is, in part, a reaction to the dominance of the bureaucratic and autocratic types of study currently associated with American programmes.

Bureaucratic evaluation

Bureaucratic evaluation is an unconditional service to those government agencies which have major control over the allocation of educational resources. The evaluator accepts the values of those who hold office, and offers information which will help them to accomplish their policy objectives. He acts as a management consultant, and his criterion of success is client satisfaction. His techniques of study must be credible to the policy-makers and not lay them open to public criticism. He has no independence, no control over the use that is made of his information, and no court of appeal. The report is owned by the bureaucracy and lodged in its files. The key concepts of bureaucratic evaluation are 'service', 'utility' and 'efficiency'. Its key justificatory concept is 'the reality of power'.

Autocractic evaluation

Autocratic evaluation is a conditional service to those government agencies which have major control over the allocation of educational resources. It offers external validation of policy in exchange for compliance with its recommendations. Its values are derived from the evaluator's perception of the constitutional and moral obligations of the bureaucracy. He focuses upon issues of educational merit, and acts as expert adviser. His technique of study must yield scientific proofs, because his power base is the academic research community. His contractual arrangements guarantee non-interference by the client, and he retains ownership of the study. His report is lodged in the files of the bureaucracy, but is also published in academic journals. If his recommendations are rejected, policy is not validated. His court of appeal is the research community, and higher levels in the bureaucracy. The key concepts of the autocratic evaluator are 'principle' and 'objectivity'. Its key justificatory concept is 'the responsibility of office'.

Democratic evaluation[3]

Democratic evaluation is an information service to the whole community about the characteristics of an educational programme. Sponsorship of the evaluation study does not in itself confer a special claim upon this service. The democratic evaluator recognizes value pluralism and seeks to represent a range of interests in his issue formulation. The basic value is an informed citizenry, and the evaluator acts as broker in exchanges of information between groups who want knowledge of each other. His techniques of data gathering and presentation must be accessible to non-specialist audiences. His main activity is the collection of definitions of, and reactions to, the programme. He offers confidentiality to informants and gives them control over his use of the information they provide. The report is non-recommendatory, and the evaluator has no concept of information misuse. The evaluator engages in periodic negotiation of his relationships with sponsors and programme participants. The criterion of success is the range of audiences served. The report aspires to 'best-seller' status. The key concepts of democratic evaluation are 'confidentiality', 'negotiation', and 'accessibility'. The key justificatory concept is 'the right to know'.

THE CONTEMPORARY CONTEXT OF EVALUATION STUDIES

What progress can be made towards the task of comparing these ideal types with manifestations in the real world? It is important to avoid the dangers of labelling and stick to the notion of comparison. To judge by the sudden rash of accountability legislation in the United States, bureaucratic evaluation has American education by the throat, and is tightening its grip. Although it would be an exaggeration to suggest that the long tradition of local control of schools has been seriously undermined, we cannot lightly dismiss the fact that in 1973 thirteen states enacted legislation tying teacher tenure and dismissal to the achievement of performance-based objectives, predetermined by administrators and assessed by evaluators. Strenuous opposition from teacher unions to this mechanistic oversimplification of complex problems is falling to the argument that soaring educational costs demand proof of 'pay off'. Some observers suspect ulterior motives. House (1973) writes: 'I believe such schemes are simplistic, unworkable, contrary to empirical findings, and ultimately immoral. They are likely to lead to suspicion, acrimony, inflexibility, cheating, and finally control – which I believe is their real purpose.' If he is correct in this interpretation, and it is at least plausible, then the lack of professional ethic for evaluators is exposed. This is 'hired help' with a vengeance, and it gives a wry twist to the Stufflebeam definition of the purpose of evaluation – 'aiding and abetting the decision makers' (Stufflebeam and Guba, 1968).

The logic of the accountability movement bears a family resemblance to the engineering paradigm of evaluation pioneered by Tyler and accorded powerful legitimation by the federal bureaucracy in monitoring its massive investment in curriculum development over the past decade, even though the potential of evaluation studies as instruments of control was noted. Cohen (1970) writes: 'the Congress is typically of two minds on the matter of program evaluation in education – it subscribes to efficiency, but it does not believe in Federal control of the schools. National evaluations are regarded as a major step toward Federal control by many people, including some members of Congress.'

It is also possible to see evidence of autocratic trends in the American evaluation scene. Federal allocation of educational expenditure has always tended to be more sensitive to the need for external validation than policy at the state level, and the expensive national programmes of recent years have seen the rise to powerful advisory positions of evaluators such as Michael Scriven. 'Blue ribbon' panels of evaluation experts are called upon by federal bureaux to decide which of two or more existing programmes should continue to receive support. In this way the bureaucracy controls expenditure and deflects criticism on to the academic 'autocrat'.

What of the democratic model? Some of its central ideas can be detected in the views currently advanced by Robert Stake (1976). Evaluation studies which operationalize his recognition of value pluralism and multiple audiences will meet some of the criteria of democratic evaluation which I characterized earlier.

Turning to this country, the contemporary scene is in one sense at least much simpler. If we agree to regard evaluation as distinct from research, then relatively few evaluation studies have been carried out, and only a handful of people would categorize their profession as 'educational evaluation'. Most evaluations have been one-off jobs done by people without prior or subsequent experience, usually teachers on secondment to curriculum projects. We have no evaluation experts. Investment in evaluation studies is marginal at the national level, and almost non-existent at the local level.

But that situation could change rapidly. There is concern here too with the rising cost of educational expenditure, together with recognition of the need for schools to respond effectively to changing social and economic conditions. These are the conditions of growth for evaluation, which could have a significant role to play in the next decade. What influence will evaluators exert on the changing pattern of control? . . .

One of the most striking contemporary educational events in Western industrialized societies is the forceful intervention of national government in the affairs of the school. Effective curriculum development has become an internationally recognized need, and evaluation will be a sought-after service in this effort. Evaluation costs money, and those who commission evaluation studies will be those who command resources. Who will serve the powerless if the evaluator flies the 'gold standard' (Stake, 1976)?

The independent foundations like Nuffield, Gulbenkian and Leverhulme, may have an even more important role to play in the future than they have had in the past. Although their American equivalents have come under attack recently, accused variously of conservative conceptualizations, political meddling and ineptness, the independent sponsors may fulfil the need for checks and balances in changing power relationships.

One final point. The boundaries between educational and social programmes are becoming increasingly blurred; nursery provision, ethnic education and compensatory programmes are prime examples. Values seem likely to enter increasingly into the considerations of evaluators. There will be a place in the future for the three types of evaluation study outlined here, but there may be a special case for exploring in practice some of the principles which characterize the democratic model. Democratic evaluation is essentially a process model. For those who believe that means are the most important category of ends, it deserves refutation or support.

NOTES

1. The phrase 'the secret garden of the curriculum' was coined in 1960 by the then Minister of Education, Sir David Eccles, in the Parliamentary debate on the Crowther Report. It was a sardonic acknowledgement of the extent to which control of educational policy lay outside national government. The phrase has since become popular with educational journalists.
2. The phrase was coined by Ernest R. House. See (1972) The conscience of

educational evaluation, *Teachers' College Record*, Vol. 73, No. 3, pp. 405–414. 3. This approach to evaluation is currently guiding fieldwork in the Ford SAFARI Project, which is developing a case-study method of educational inquiry. I am indebted to my colleague, Rob Walker, who shares with me responsibility for this conceptualization.

REFERENCES

Cohen, D.K. (1970) Politics and research: evaluation of social action programs in education, *Review of Education Research*, Vol. 40, No. 2.

Hamilton, D., Jenkins, D., King, C., MacDonald, B. and Parlett, M. (eds.) (1977) *Beyond the Numbers Game*, Macmillan, London.

Hastings, J.T. (1969) The kith and kin of educational measures, *Journal of Educational Measurements*, Vol. 6, No. 3.

Hemphill, J.K. (1970) The relationship between research and evaluation studies, in Ralph W. Tyler (ed.) *Educational Evaluation: New Roles, New Means*, University of Chicago Press.

House, E.R. (1973) *The Price of Productivity: Who Pays?*, Centre for Instructional Research and Curriculum Evaluation, University of Illinois, Urbana-Champaign, mimeograph.

MacDonald, B. (1973) *Educational Evaluation of the National Development Programme in Computer Assisted Learning*, Centre for Applied Research in Education, Norwich.

Nisbet, J. (1980) Educational research – the state of the art. In W.B. Dockrell and D. Hamilton, (eds.) *Rethinking Educational Research*, Hodder and Staughton, London.

Stake, R.E. (1974) Responsive Evaluation, *New Trends in Evaluation*, Institute of Education, No. 35, January.

Stake, R.E. (1976) *The Measuring of Education*, McCutchan, California, in press.

Stufflebeam, D.L. and Guba, E. (1968) Evaluation: the process of stimulating, aiding and abetting insightful action, address delivered at the second national symposium for professors of educational research, Evaluation Centre, College of Education, Ohio State University, November.

1.3
THE ROLE OF EVALUATORS IN ACCOUNTABILITY SYSTEMS*
John Nisbet

ACCOUNTABILITY AND POWER

When accountability is superimposed on educational evaluation, it brings in a new dimension – the political dimension of power. Since evaluation implies judgement, there is always an undercurrent of power in evaluation procedures; but accountability makes this explicit, bringing evaluation into the power structure in education. Accountability is itself an aspect of power: Kogan (1979) describes accountability as 'one mode only of the wider set of authority and power relationships'. For the evaluator, an accountability system is evaluation 'with teeth', armed with sanctions and charged with responsibility. Consequently, when evaluators are involved in accountability procedures, they must declare their stance. Is their function to support the status quo in the distribution of power (among institutions as well as among persons); or are they to challenge the status quo, or – if that sounds extreme – to question it or open up the possibility of changing it? The usual answer to this is that it depends on how the results work out; but the answer is more complex than this, and has implications for policy in the design of evaluation procedures for accountability.

Evaluators as gatekeepers

Accountability structures put the evaluator into a powerful position. They give him the role of 'gatekeeper', in that the evaluator controls access to information. Information is the 'currency' of accountability and, like money in a market situation, information is the token form of the power element in

* Nisbet, J. (1979) The role of evaluators in accountability systems, CIRCE seminar paper.

the accountability situation. The evaluator decides which information will be gathered, how it will be processed, which parts will be reported and the survival of institutions and individuals may be affected by the evaluator's decisions. In so far as this is a new role for evaluators, it is important that they should understand it, and be aware of how other people perceive what evaluators are doing.

A perceived threat

The evaluator operating within an accountability structure is likely to be seen by teachers as a threat to their freedom of action. Even the decision to set up an accountability procedure implies that teachers have some explaining to do, that there is some slack in the system which needs tightening up. The threat may be a veiled one, but it is unmistakable. 'What are they going to do to us?' or 'How are they going to get at me?' are the questions which arise first in the teacher's mind, not 'Will this help me, or protect me from unfair criticism?' Two factors have contributed to produce this reaction: the teachers' feeling of vulnerability, and the recent emergence of evaluation as a distinctive specialism.

Teachers, says Wolcott (1977) in *Teachers versus Technocrats*, feel bitter at being treated as 'passive recipients of resources . . . from local and central government', for then they are at the mercy of administrators or politicians who (in the teachers' view) do not understand their position. 'Teachers are nagged by feelings of vulnerability: they are fond of referring to their plight as defenceless, powerless and unappreciated individuals . . . Teachers become increasingly antagonistic toward providing information that seems not to improve their own position, but threatens to increase others' control over them.'

Accountability makes us all feel vulnerable, for it makes explicit the power structure which conventionally is covered over. Even a superintendent may feel this: Wolcott quotes one as saying, 'Changes are coming so fast . . . we feel powerless and defenceless.'

Evaluation as a new specialism

Teachers' feelings of hostility are accentuated by a feature which is pecular to the American context, in contrast with Britain, France, Australia, New Zealand and other countries – the emergence of *evaluation* as a new specialist profession and the absence of *inspectors* who perform a related function in other national systems of education.

It may be too much to claim evaluation as a new profession, but the activity now has many of the features of a profession: its own training courses, its own literature and even its own code of ethics (Stufflebeam, 1979). The role did not exist fifteen years ago, and it is still relatively unusual outside the USA to find people who call themselves 'evaluators'. There is evaluation, but it is not seen as a specialism, but rather as a function performed by someone with a general knowledge of the educational situation, and by short-term contract. In Europe and Australia and elsewhere, the evaluator's function is commonly performed by inspectors. In the USA, the autonomy of school boards, and of states, rendered unacceptable the appointment of national inspectors. The absence of a service like the inspectorate has left a gap – some means of checking on standards and maintaining coherence and comparability across the nation – and this is the gap which evaluators have moved in to fill. In Britain, inspectors are appointed by the Queen, thus separating them from identification with either the political government or the administrative bureaucracy. They are recruited from the ranks of teachers, all inspectors being expected to have a record of successful teaching experience and to be able to demonstrate their teaching competence on occasion. Consequently, teachers and inspectors share a common professional base. Inspectors tend to be seen as ex-teachers, their style is subjective and non-technical; they do not use highly specialized techniques; their credibility depends on their status. Admittedly, teachers are often suspicious of or hostile to inspectors (especially in Australia, where they tend to be identified with the administration); but generally the shared professional base improves the quality and ease of communication between teachers and inspectors. (Pinar, 1978, makes a similar point about the relation of researchers and practitioners in the field of medicine, where the shared professional outlooks are in contrast to the field of education where researchers often have no school experience.)

Evaluators are liable to have difficulty in performing this inspectional function. They lack the assigned status of inspectors and must rely instead on the authority of the specialism which they have established. This specialism weakens the common professional base of evaluators and teachers, and may therefore accentuate divisiveness in the educational system. Certainly during the peak period of the accountability movement in Britain, from 1861 to 1890, the era of payment by results, inspectors incurred much hostility from teachers, and possibly may be said to have generated it by the distinctive testing function which inspectors were obliged to perform. In recent years in the USA, the unprecedented flow of federal funds into evaluation has increased the risk of resentment, envy and hostility from teachers.

Risk of backlash

A situation like this has all the ingredients which result in a rebound or backlash, a violent public reaction in which a practice or set of values previously widely accepted is now repudiated. If this happens, evaluators are the obvious target for blame for the defects and consequences of accountability procedures. There is at present a strong public pressure for accountability, and there are many ways in which an appropriate system can be beneficial; but there are also many ways in which the system can go wrong. Then the evaluators may reap a whirlwind from the accountability procedures which they are sowing; and because they are a new separate specialist group, they will be exposed and defenceless.

A parallel is the position of psychologists in the eleven-plus controversy in Britain. Until the mid-1950s, the eleven-plus testing procedures were widely accepted as a contribution to equality of opportunity (giving a fair chance by valid tests to children who had not the advantage of coaching for conventional examinations). Critics of the system had been vocal since the 1920s, but it was not until the late 1950s that public attitudes changed sharply. Psychologists were subsequently identified as responsible for the élitist concept of IQ (now 'redefined' as a device to maintain class privilege). Other examples of such changes of public opinion may suggest themselves: anti-pollution, equal rights. Vietnam, the student revolt of 1986. The specialist evaluator should study the legend of Faust, who was given access to unlimited power but had to pay the price in the end. However, the predicted backlash may never happen. Or perhaps it may have happened already – prematurely, so that it went off at half-cock – in the deschooling, alternative education movement, which failed to gain sufficient support.

NEUTRALITY AND COMMITMENT

Evaluators in an accountability system cannot adopt a neutral pose. They must either work with the authority structure, or challenge it, either supporting the status quo or seeking to change it.

No neutral pose?

The usual answer by evaluators to an assertion such as this is to compare their role to that of the referee, or judge, impartial and fair, or to that of the scientist, detached and uncommitted to any cause except truth. The evaluator may be the agent of authority but he is not the authority itself. He is the technician who gathers information for someone else to base a decision on. 'We provide the data base: others add the value judgements. Thus we are not responsible.'

This neutral pose may be tenable in some circumstances (see 'Neutrality when consensus' below); but in an accountability procedure the evaluator is brought into the power structure and this gives him an influence, direct and indirect, which he cannot avoid.

Direct and indirect influence

The influence of the evaluator may be likened to that of the secretary of a committee, who prepares the agenda, writes the minutes, controls the mode of working, has a say in membership, decides the form of public reports, and yet claims to be a neutral servant of the group. The direct influence of evaluators is on the curriculum of schools, because what is tested often determines what is taught. Their indirect influence operates through an organizational effect which tightens bureaucratic divisions and limits participation.

According to Weber's analysis of bureaucratic systems, 'formal organizations' have a hierarchy of office, each official has a specified sphere of action, and his authority derives from the authority of those above him in the hierarchy. Most schools are formal organizations. Accountability 'tightens' this bureaucratic structure. The use of tests strengthens the hand of the expert, excluding the uninitiated from participation. Once a list of objectives is agreed, it cuts out the possibility of further debate. Each level in the hierarchy tends to be 'loyal' in not undermining the higher authority, since his own authority depends on that of the level above him.

Neutrality when consensus

Evaluators cannot pose as neutral in a situation like this. However, there may be circumstances which permit a neutral course of action, namely where there is a wide consensus about aims and values. Within areas where there is such a consensus, the task of the evaluator is then limited to decisions on techniques, within an accepted and unquestioned framework. But if there is no consensus, the evaluator has to make judgements (or to go along with others' judgements) on what to include or omit, what criteria to use, what methods to adopt, and so on.

Examples of areas where there is consensus are: business where there is wide agreement on the aim of profit; medicine, an agreed aim of health; sport, an agreed aim of winning. But even in sport, evaluation becomes problematic immediately the consensus is questioned: when judges have to assess 'artistic merit' (in gymnastics, diving, skating), certain values are explicitly or implicitly declared preferable by the judging procedure, and the judges impose these values on the competitors.

It was once easy to be a judge in a beauty competition, for it was quite obvious what qualities were prized. More recently, as beauty competitions are seen as an exploitation of sex and the woman's position in society and are challenged, the judge must now consider carefully the values which are to be the basis of his assessment.

Forcing the evaluator into commitment

The procedures which are adopted for an accountability system express some philosophy or set of values. If these values are not in accordance with the evaluator's own philosophy, they must express someone else's prior judgement; and since the evaluator is caught up in the power structure, he has to accept the philosophy of those above him in the structure. The danger of this is that the evaluator also imposes these values on others, becoming an agent of hidden coercion.

Accountability is sometimes regarded as 'democratic', because it opens up schools to public inspection, and breaks the jealously guarded control of teaching by the teaching profession. By enrolling the evaluator as an agent of coercion, accountability can work against democratic principles, limiting freedom of decision and giving power to central authorities and to technical 'experts.'

If the evaluator does not accent the philosophy of the established authority, he is unlikely to be employed, or to continue in employment. He has no natural right to impose his own values, nor has he much chance of getting away with this. In the choice between maintaining the status quo and challenging it, he usually must give support if he is to have any leverage in the system.

A PLURALIST SOLUTION

The evaluator cannot impose his own values in the choices he makes, and it has been argued that he cannot fall back on 'neutral scientific values'. But he is not therefore obliged to follow the lines prescribed for him by others. The solution lies in adopting a complex procedure to match the complexity of the situation he faces. The evaluator's choices should reflect the values of *a range of participants* in the process he is evaluating. Thus, in an accountability system in education, evaluation should aim to spread the responsibility and to spread the coverage.

Spread the responsibility

Spreading the responsibility involves a diffusion of decision-making, involving others, especially teachers, in as extensive a participation as is possible. This pluralist solution is justifiable not only in offering the evaluator protection from blame, but also in being more likely to produce a complete and fair report, more likely to be accepted as valid. It imposes checks on excess or misuse of power. However, spreading the responsibility has weaknesses, in that it requires time (and therefore resources) and it can offer no guarantee to those in authority that they will be able to retain control. More seriously, it means using forms of evaluation which tend to lack credibility. Accountability procedures may be categorized as:

(a) external evaluation, such as tests or examinations set by an outside agency;
(b) peer evaluation, as in accreditation or inspection by colleagues;
(c) self evaluation, as in self-report systems.

Spreading the responsibility necessarily means making more use of peer evaluation and self evaluation, both of which do not stand up well to public challenge. The inspectorate system is a form of peer evaluation, but it has a status element which gives it credibility. This has enabled the English system to avoid the worst excesses of accountability (the Assessment of Performance Unit, set up to prepare suitable tests, has an inspector in charge), while the Scottish system has rejected use of tests in any accountability procedure. At the secondary education or high school stage, the existence in Britain of a long-standing national system of traditional examinations in which teachers' panels have a part to play, goes some way towards satisfying pressures for accountability.

Spread the coverage

Spreading the coverage recognizes that what is tested often determines what is taught, and therefore it is necessary to generate *a wide range of aspects for assessment* in any accountability procedure. This implies more than including a range of studies beyond the 'basics'. It means taking account of moral education and the development of personality as well as academic studies. It also means looking at methods, organizations and relationships within schools, as well as standards of achievement – that is, it should be concerned with process as well as product. All this is easier said than done. There is no consensus on what should be covered, and wide coverage adds to time and cost. It is extremely difficult to devise measurement instruments for many areas of the curriculum in a form which is valid across schools and across the country. The 1973 survey of programmes (Educational Testing Service, 1973) states:

Twenty-seven out of the fifty-three states [or state-level agencies] have stated a goal concerned with human relations. However, only three states report that they have been able to conduct an assessment of progress toward such a goal. Several are in the process of developing the necessary instrumentation, but have not yet achieved results which are a satisfactory solution to the measurement problems.

Some of the tests which have been developed since that survey are merely factual or checklist items of dubious and untested validity. The Assessment of Performance Unit in England has fared no better: having set out to cover six areas – language, number, science, aesthetic subjects, physical education and moral education – it is already in difficulties at number three on the list. Even if tests were developed, it is doubtful if they would carry credibility. Self-report and peer evaluation are necessary to deal with this aspect.

The pluralist solution has limitations. Certainly, it is easier to win agreement when there is something for everyone in the recipe; but limits imposed by time and costs force some element of choice. Spreading the responsibility and coverage, resisting the pressure to limit, are nevertheless useful guiding principles to aspire to.

REFERENCES

Educational Testing Service (1973) *State Educational Assessment Programs: 1973 Revision,* Educational Testing Service, Princeton, New Jersey.

Kogan, M. (1979) *Private Communication.*

Pinar, W.F. (1978) Notes on the curriculum field, *Educational Researcher,* Vol. 7, No. 8, pp. 5–12.

Stufflebeam, D.L. (1979) *Standards for Evaluations of Educational Programs, Projects and Materials* (draft), Joint Committee on Standards for Educational Evaluation, University of Western Michigan, Kalamazoo.

Wolcott, H.F. (1977) *Teachers versus Technocrats: An Educational Innovation in Anthropological Perspective,* Center for Educational Policy and Management, Eugene, Oregon.

1.4
EVALUATION AS ILLUMINATION: A NEW APPROACH TO THE STUDY OF INNOVATORY PROGRAMMES*
Malcolm Parlett and David Hamilton

INTRODUCTION

This paper advocates a total reappraisal of the rationale and techniques of programme evaluation. Characteristically, conventional approaches have followed the experimental and psychometric traditions dominant in educational research. Their aim (unfulfilled) of achieving fully 'objective methods' has led to studies that are artificial and restricted in scope. We argue that such evaluations are inadequate for elucidating the complex problem areas they confront, and as a result provide little effective input to the decision-making process.

Illuminative evaluation is introduced as belonging to a contrasting 'anthropological' research paradigm. Attempted measurement of 'educational products' is abandoned for intensive study of the programme as a whole: its rationale and evaluation, its operations, achievements, and difficulties. The innovation is not examined in isolation, but in the school context or 'learning milieu'. The paper then describes the methodological strategies of illuminative evaluation. Observation, interviews with participants (students, instructors, administrators and others), questionnaires, and analysis of documents and background information are all combined to help 'illuminate' problems, issues, and significant programme features.

The paper concludes with a discussion of the problems and potentialities of the new approach: its range of applicability; the validity and generalizability of evidence; the professional skills and obligations of the research worker; how explorations of the learning milieu can meet the need for

---

* Parlett, M. and Hamilton, D. (1972) Evaluation as Illumination: A New Approach to the Study of Innovatory Programmes, Occasional Paper No. 9, Centre for Research in the Educational Sciences, Edinburgh.

theoretical advance; and how the illuminative approach can clarify and interpret the programme for the various groups of decision-makers who look to the evaluation study for assistance in their task.

Innovation is now a major educational priority. For nearly two decades it has expanded and proliferated. It absorbs increasing sums of public and private money. Its impact is felt throughout the world. Curricula are restructured, new devices introduced, forms of teaching permutated. But decisions to change are more than educational: questions of politics, ideology, fashion and finance also intervene.

More recently – to aid decision-making – innovation has been joined by evaluation. Increasingly, committees and foundations fund evaluation studies as an integral part of innovation programmes. Like innovation itself, evaluation has rapidly developed a legitimacy and importance of its own: professional journals have been launched and research centres established. The 'evaluator' has emerged as a new and influential figure.

In short, both innovation and evaluation have become 'big science' (Price, 1963).

As a new field, programme evaluation has encountered a wide range of problems, both theoretical and methodological. Current concerns include the 'roles' of evaluation; the neutrality of the evaluator; the value of classroom observation; the function of 'formative' evaluation; the use of 'objectives'; and the value of long-term studies. Confusion is engendered as rival proposals, models and terminologies are voiced and then rapidly countered.

As a developing field of study, evaluation proceeds in the absence of coherent or agreed frames of reference.

More generally within educational research two distinct paradigms can be discerned. Each has its own strategies, focuses and assumptions. Dominant is the 'classical' or 'agricultural-botany' paradigm (Parlett, 1972), which utilizes a hypothetico-deductive methodology derived from the experimental and mental-testing traditions in psychology. Almost all evaluation studies have resided within this traditional paradigm.

More recently, a small number of empirical studies have been conceived outside the agricultural-botany framework, and relate instead to social anthropology, psychiatry, and participant observation research in sociology (cf. Henry, 1971; Jackson, 1968; Young, 1971).

Such research can be thought of as representing a second and contrasting paradigm, with a fundamentally different research style and methodology from that of mainstream educational research. We outline here an approach to evaluation that belongs to this alternative, or 'social anthropology' paradigm.

TRADITIONAL EVALUATION AND THE AGRICULTURAL-BOTANY PARADIGM

The most common form of agricultural-botany type evaluation is presented as an assessment of the effectiveness of an innovation by examining whether or not it has reached required standards on pre-specified criteria. Students – rather like plant crops – are given pre-tests (the seedlings are weighed or measured) and then submitted to different experiences (treatment conditions). Subsequently, after a period of time, their attainment (growth or yield) is measured to indicate the relative efficiency of the methods (fertilizers) used. Studies of this kind are designed to yield data of one particular type, i.e. 'objective' numerical data that permit statistical analyses (cf. Light and Smith, 1970). Isolated variables like IQ, social class, test scores, personality profiles and attitude ratings are codified and processed to indicate the efficiency of new curricula, media or methods.

Recently, however, there has been increasing resistance to evaluations of this type. The more notable shortcomings may be briefly summarized as follows.

First, educational situations are characterized by numerous relevant parameters. Within the terms of the agricultural-botany paradigm these must be randomized using very large samples; or otherwise strictly controlled. The former approach entails a major data collection exercise and is expensive in time and resources. It also runs counter to the need, widely acknowledged, for evaluation before large-scale application rather than after it. The latter procedure – of strict control – is rarely followed. To attempt to simulate laboratory conditions by 'manipulating educational personnel' is not only dubious ethically, but also leads to gross administrative and personal inconvenience. Even if a situation could be so unnervingly controlled, its artificiality would render the exercise irrelevant; rarely can 'tidy' results be generalized to an 'untidy' reality. Whichever approach is used, there is a tendency for the investigator to think in terms of 'parameters' and 'factors' rather than 'individuals' and 'institutions'. Again, this divorces the study from the real world.

Second, before-and-after research designs assume that innovatory programmes undergo little or no change during the period of study. This built-in premise is rarely upheld in practice. Yet it remains fundamental to the design, constraining the researchers from adapting to the changed circumstances that so frequently arise. It may even have a deleterious effect on the programme itself, by discouraging new developments and redefinitions midstream. Longitudinal studies, for these reasons, rarely can serve an effective 'formative' or 'cybernetic' function.

Third, the methods used in traditional evaluations impose artificial and arbitrary restrictions on the scope of the study. For instance, the concentration on seeking quantitative information by objective means can lead to neglect of other data, perhaps more salient to the innovation, but which are disregarded as being 'subjective', 'anecdotal', or 'impressionistic'. However, the evaluator is likely to be forced to utilize information of this sort if he is satisfactorily to explain his findings, weight their importance and place them in context.

Fourth, research of this type, by employing large samples and seeking statistical generalizations, tends to be insensitive to local perturbations and unusual effects. Atypical results are seldom studied in detail. Despite their significance for the innovation, or possible importance to the individuals and institutions concerned, they are ironed out and lost to discussion.

Finally, this type of evaluation often fails to articulate with the varied concerns and questions of participants, sponsors, and other interested parties. Since classical evaluators believe in an 'objective truth' equally relevant to all parties, their studies rarely acknowledge the diversity of questions posed by different interest-groups.

These points suggest that applying the agricultural-botany paradigm to the study of innovation is often a cumbersome and inadequate procedure. The evaluation falls short of its own tacit claims to be controlled, exact and unambiguous. Rarely, if ever, can educational programmes be subject to strict enough control to meet the design's requirements. Innovations, in particular, are vulnerable to manifold extraneous influences. Yet the traditional evaluator ignores these. He is restrained by the dictates of his paradigm to seek generalized findings along preordained lines. His definition of empirical reality is narrow. One effect of this is that it diverts attention away from questions of educational practice towards more centralized bureaucratic concerns.

ILLUMINATIVE EVALUATION AND THE SOCIAL-ANTHROPOLOGY PARADIGM

Although traditional forms of evaluation have been criticized in this way, little attempt has been made to develop alternative models. The model described here, *illuminative evaluation* (cf. Trow, 1970, and Parlett, 1969), takes account of the wider contexts in which educational programmes function. Its primary concern is with description and interpretation rather than measurement and prediction (cf. Smith and Pohland, 1971). It stands unambiguously within the alternative anthropological paradigm. The aims of illuminative evaluation are to study the innovatory programme: how it operates; how it is influenced by the various school situations in which it is applied; what those directly concerned regard as its advantages and disadvantages; and how students' intellectual tasks and academic experiences are most affected. It aims to discover and document what it is like to be participating in the scheme, whether as teacher or pupil; and, in addition, to discern and discuss the innovation's most significant features, recurring concomitants and critical processes. In short, it seeks to address and to illuminate a complex array of questions: 'Research on innovation can be enlightening to the innovator and to the whole academic community by clarifying the processes of education and by helping the innovator and other interested parties to identify those procedures, those elements in the educational effort, which seem to have had desirable results' (Trow, 1970, p.302).

The paradigm shift entailed in adopting illuminative evaluation requires more than an exchange of methodologies: it also involves new suppositions, concepts, and terminology. Central to an understanding of illuminative evaluation are two concepts: the 'instructional system' and the 'learning milieu'.

The instructional system

Educational catalogues, prospectuses, and reports characteristically contain a variety of formalized plans and statements which relate to particular teaching arrangements. Each of these summaries can be said to constitute or define an instructional system; and includes, say, a set of pedagogic assumptions, a new syllabus, and details of techniques and equipment. This 'catalogue description' is an idealized specification of the scheme: a set of elements arranged to a coherent plan. Despite their immense variation, the Dalton Plan, performance contracting, programmed learning, the integrated day, team teaching, 'Sesame Street' and 'Man: A Course of Study' can all be considered as instructional systems in these terms.

The traditional evaluator builds his study around innovations defined in this way. He examines the blueprint or formalized plan and extracts the programme's goals, objectives, or desired outcomes. From these, in turn, he derives the tests and attitude inventories he will administer. His aim is to evaluate the instructional system by examining whether, for example, it has 'attained its objectives' or met its 'performance criteria'.

This technological approach fails to recognize the catalogue description for what it is. It ignores the fact that an instructional system, when adopted, undergoes modifications that are rarely trivial. The instructional system may remain as a shared idea, abstract model, slogan or shorthand, but it assumes a different form in every situation. Its constituent elements are emphasized or de-emphasized, expanded or truncated, as teachers, administrators, technicians and students interpret and reinterpret the instructional system for their particular setting. In practice, objectives are commonly reordered, redefined, abandoned or forgotten. The original 'ideal' formulation ceases to be accurate, or indeed, of much relevance. Few in practice take catalogue descriptions and lists of objectives very seriously, save – it seems – for the traditional evaluator.

To switch from discussing the instructional system in abstract form to describing the details of its implementation is to cross into another realm. Here the second new concept is required.

The learning milieu

This is the social-psychological and material environment in which students and teachers work together. The learning milieu represents a network or nexus of cultural, social, institutional, and psychological variables. These interact in complicated ways to produce, in each class or course, a unique pattern of circumstances, pressures, customs, opinions, and work styles which suffuse the teaching and learning that occur there. The configuration of the learning milieu, in any particular classroom, depends on the interplay of numerous different factors. For instance, there are numerous constraints (legal, administrative, occupational, architectural and financial) on the organization of teaching in schools; there are pervasive operating assumptions (about the arrangement of subjects, curricula, teaching methods, and student evaluation) held by faculty; there are the individual teacher's characteristics (teaching style, experience, professional orientation, and private goals); and there are student perspectives and preoccupations.

Acknowledging the diversity and complexity of learning milieux is an essential prerequisite for the serious study of educational programmes. The argument advanced here is that innovatory programmes, even for research purposes, cannot sensibly be separated from the learning milieux of which they become part. If an evaluation study hinges on the supposed perpetuation of the instructional system in more or less its original form, it makes an arbitrary and artificial distinction: it treats the innovations as a self-contained and independent system, which in practice it is manifestly not.

The introduction of an innovation sets off a chain of repercussions throughout the learning milieu. In turn these unintended consequences are likely to affect the innovation itself, changing its form and moderating its impact. For example, at the Massachusetts Institute of Technology, it was found that switching from 'distributed' to 'concentrated' study (a change from students taking several subjects concurrently to intensive full-time study of a single subject) was, in the event, far more than a rescheduling arrangement (Parlett and King, 1971). It demanded new pedagogic forms (continuous lecturing would have led to 'overload'); it resulted in new role relationships between faculty and students (daily contact encouraged a degree of informality impossible with two meetings a week of one hour each); and it changed peer relations between students (their working alongside the same students continuously led to much greater interaction than is usual in MIT sophomore classes). Such profound shifts in the learning milieu produced a further range of important secondary effects, apparently far removed from the innovation as such, but ultimately deriving from it.

To attempt to gauge the impact of the innovation (in this instance 'concentrated study') without paying attention to factors such as these, would clearly be absurd. In the above study it was possible to trace how each of these milieu effects had its corollary in the intellectual sphere: e.g. the informality encouraged normally silent students to ask questions; and though the range of different learning activities was regarded as excellent for achieving basic comprehension of the subject-matter, it might have put the students at a disadvantage in a conventional exam.

Connecting changes in the learning milieu with intellectual experiences of students is one of the chief concerns for illuminative evaluation. Students do not confront 'knowledge' in naked form; it comes to them clothed in texts, lectures, tape-loops, etc. These form part of a wider set of arrangements for instructing, assessing, and counselling which embody core assumptions about how knowledge and pedagogy should be organized. This 'management' framework, in turn, is embedded within wider departmental and institutional structures, each with its own set of procedures, and professional and societal allegiances. Though apparently far removed from the assimilation and schematization of knowledge at the classroom level, these 'higher-order' aspects of the school or college environment cannot be ignored. To take an example: teaching and learning in a particular setting are profoundly influenced by the type of assessment procedures in use; by constraints of scheduling; by the size and diversity of classes; by the availability of teaching assistants, library, computing, and copying facilities. These, in turn, are dependent on departmental priorities; on policies of faculty promotion; on institutional myths and traditions; and on local and national pressures.

The learning milieu concept is necessary for analysing the interdependence of learning and teaching, and for relating the organization and practices of instruction with the immediate and long-term responses of students. For instance, students' intellectual development cannot be understood in isolation but only within a particular school or college milieu. Equally, there are phenomena of crucial educational significance (such as boredom, interest, concentration, 'floundering' and intellectual dependency) that make non-sense of the traditional psychological distinction between 'cognitive' and 'affective' and which customarily arise as responses to the total learning milieu, not to single components of it. Students do not respond merely to presented content and to tasks assigned. Rather, they adapt to and work within the learning milieu taken as an interrelated whole. They pay close attention to 'hidden' as well as 'visible' curricula (Snyder, 1971). Besides acquiring particular habits of studying, reading and responding, they also assimilate the conventions, beliefs, and models of reality that are constantly and inevitably transmitted through the total teaching process.

ORGANIZATION AND METHODS OF ILLUMINATIVE EVALUATION

Illuminative evaluations – like the innovations and learning milieux that they study – come in diverse forms. The size, aims and techniques of the evaluation depend on many factors: the sponsor's preoccupations; the exact nature and stage of the innovation; the number of institutions, teachers, and students involved; the level of co-operation and the degree of access to relevant information; the extent of the investigator's previous experience; the time available for data collection; the format of the required report; and, not least, the size of the evaluation budget.

Illuminative evaluation is not a standard methodological package but a general research strategy. It aims to be both adaptable and eclectic. The choice of research tactics follows not from research doctrine, but from decisions in each case as to the best available techniques: the problem defines the methods used, not vice versa. Equally, no method (with its own built-in limitations) is used exclusively or in isolation; different techniques are combined to throw light on a common problem. Besides viewing the problem from a number of angles, this 'triangulation' (Webb *et al.*, 1966) approach also facilitates the cross-checking of otherwise tentative findings.

At the outset, the researcher is concerned to familiarize himself thorough-ly with the day-to-day reality of the setting or settings he is studying. In this he is similar to social anthropologists or to natural historians. Like them he makes no attempt to manipulate, control or eliminate situational variables, but takes as given the complex scene he encounters. His chief task is to unravel it; isolate its significant features; delineate cycles of cause and effect; and comprehend relationships between beliefs and practices, and between organizational patterns and the responses of individuals. Since illuminative evaluation concentrates on examining the innovation as an integral part of the learning milieu, there is a definite emphasis both on observation at the classroom level and on interviewing participating instructors and students. Characteristically in illuminative evaluation there are three stages: investigators observe, inquire further and then seek to explain. Thus, in our study of a pilot project in independent learning in British secondary schools, early visits to participating schools yielded a number of common incidents, recurring trends, and issues frequently raised in discussion. These we either observed ourselves, or heard about from teachers and pupils. (For example, we noticed that teachers spoke in different ways about the independent learning materials provided for use with their classes. While some regarded the sets of materials as constituting, collectively, a course of study, others saw the same materials as having a supplementary or ancillary function; to be used simply as a collection of resources to draw upon as, when or if necessary.)

The second stage began with the selection of a number of such phenomena, occurrences or groups of opinions as topics for more sustained and intensive inquiry. A change of emphasis accompanied this development. During the first, exploratory stage, we had become 'knowledgeable' about the scheme. At the second stage this enabled our questioning to be more focused; communication to be more coherent and relaxed; and, in general, observation and inquiry to be more directed, systematic and selective. (Thus – in our contacts with the teachers – we sought to find out more about the status they assigned to the independent learning materials and the extent to which they integrated them with others.)

The third stage consisted in seeking general principles underlying the organization of the programme; spotting patterns of cause and effect within its operation; and placing individual findings within a broader explanatory context. It began with our weighing alternative interpretations in the light of information obtained. Thus, why did teachers differ in their attitudes towards the materials? It seemed in general that teachers' views depended on the availability of related materials in the school; on their previous experience with similar methods; and – most critically – on whether or not they saw the material as 'displacing' or as 'supporting' the teacher. A number of other lines of investigation led to the same central issue: that of the changed role of the teacher in an independent learning setting.

Obviously the three stages overlap and functionally interrelate. The transition from stage to stage, as the investigation unfolds, occurs as problem areas become progressively clarified and redefined. The course of the study cannot be charted in advance. Beginning with an extensive data base, the researchers systematically reduce the breadth of their inquiry to give more concentrated attention to the emerging issues. This 'progressive focusing' permits unique and unpredicted phenomena to be given due weight. It reduces the problem of data overload; and prevents the accumulation of a mass of unanalysed material.

Within this three-stage framework, an information profile is assembled using data collected from four areas: observation; interviews; questionnaires and tests; documentary and background sources.

Observation

As noted above, the observation phase occupies a central place in illuminative evaluation. The investigator builds up a continuous record of ongoing events, transactions and informal remarks. At the same time he seeks to organize this data at source, adding interpretative comments on both manifest and latent features of the situation. In addition to observing and documenting day-to-day activities of the programme, the investigator may also be present at a wide variety of other events (e.g. faculty and student meetings, open days, examiners' meetings, etc.) (cf. Smith and Keith, 1971).

Much of the on-site observation involves recording discussions with and between participants. These provide additional information which might not otherwise be apparent or forthcoming from more formal interviews. The language conventions, slang, jargon and metaphors that characterize conversation within each learning milieu can reveal tacit assumptions, interpersonal relationships and status differentials.

Finally, there is a place for codified observation, using schedules for recording patterns of attendance, seating, utilization of time and facilities, teacher–pupil interaction, etc. The illuminative evaluator is cautious in the deployment of such techniques. In that they record only surface behaviour they do not facilitate the uncovering of underlying, more meaningful features.

Interviews

Discovering the views of participants is crucial to assessing the impact of an innovation. Instructors and students are asked about their work, what they think of it, how it compares with previous experience; and also to comment on the use and value of the innovation. Interviews vary as to the type of information or comment that is sought. While brief, structured interviews are convenient for obtaining biographical, historical or factual information, more open-ended and discursive forms are suitable for less straightforward topics (e.g. career ambitions and anxieties).

Though desirable, it is rarely possible to interview every participant, except in small innovatory programmes or with large research teams. Interviewees, therefore, must usually be selected randomly or by 'theoretical' sampling (Glaser and Strauss, 1967). This latter mode requires seeking out informants or particular groups who may have special insight or whose position makes their viewpoints noteworthy (e.g. students who have won prizes or failed altogether; marginal faculty members, who may have close knowledge of the innovation but have stayed outside it; young assistants teaching in their first semesters, etc.). Those interviewed can also include more distant but equally relevant figures: e.g. at the college level, deans, administrators and student counsellors; and, beyond the college, curriculum developers and foundation officials from whom the innovation stemmed.

Questionnaire and test data

While concentrating on observation and interviews, the illuminative evaluator does not eschew paper and pencil techniques. Their advantage in larger-scale illuminative studies is especially evident. Also survey-type questionnaires used late in a study can sustain or qualify earlier tentative findings. Free- and fixed-response formats can be included to obtain both quantitative summary data and also open-ended (and perhaps new and unexpected) comment.

There are, of course, several valid objections to questionnaires, particularly if they are used in isolation. Unless most carefully prepared, questionnaires can lead to mindless accumulations of uninterpretable data. Expensive in time and resources, such careful preparation must be weighed against the benefits likely to accrue. A second drawback is that many recipients regard questionnaires as impersonal and intrusive. Others, keen to express their complicated views, find the questionnaire a frustrating, indeed trivializing medium. From these dissatisfied groups, some do not reply; yet these non-respondents may be the most important in certain respects.

Besides completing questionnaires, participants can also be asked to prepare written comments on the programme; to go through checklists; or compile work diaries that record their activities over a specific period of time.

Finally there are published or custom-built tests of attitude, personality and achievement. Such tests enjoy no privileged status within the study. Test scores cannot be considered in isolation; they form merely one section of the data profile. Interest lies not so much in relating different test scores, but in accounting for them using the study's findings as a whole.

Documentary and background information

Innovations do not arise unheralded. They are preceded by committee minutes, funding proposals, architectural plans, and consultants' reports. Also other primary sources are obtainable: e.g. non-confidential data from registrars' offices; autobiographical and eye-witness accounts of the innovation; tape recordings of meetings; and examples of students' assignments.

The assembly of such information can serve a useful function. It can provide a historical perspective of how the innovation was regarded by different people before the evaluation began. The data may also indicate areas for inquiry (e.g. how representative were the students taking part?); may point to topics for intensive discussion (e.g. why were certain major features of the original proposal later abandoned?); or may expose aspects of the innovation that would otherwise be missed (e.g. why were subject requirements not fulfilled?).

PROBLEMS AND POSSIBILITIES OF ILLUMINATIVE EVALUATION

First encounters with the radically different perspective of illuminative evaluation prompt a number of important questions.

Foremost is usually concern over the 'subjective' nature of the approach. Can 'personal interpretation' be scientific? Is not collection, analysis and reporting of data, sceptics ask, entirely at the discretion of the researchers themselves?

Behind such questions lies a basic but erroneous assumption: that forms of research exist which are immune to prejudice, experimenter bias and human error. This is not so. Any research study requires skilled human judgements and is thus vulnerable. Even in evaluation studies that handle automatically processed numerical data, judgement is necessary at every stage: in the choice of samples; in the construction or selection of tests; in deciding conditions of administration; in selecting the mode of statistical treatment (e.g. whether or not to use factor analysis); in the relative weight given to different results; and, particularly, in the selection and presentation of findings in reports.

Nevertheless, the extensive use of open-ended techniques, progressive focusing, and qualitative data in illuminative evaluation still raises the possibility of gross partiality on the part of the investigator. A number of precautionary tactics are possible. During the investigation different techniques can be used to cross-check the most important findings; open-ended material can be coded and checked by outside researchers; consultants to the evaluation can be charged with challenging preliminary interpretations and playing devil's advocate; and members of the research team can be commissioned to develop their own interpretations. At the report stage, in addition to the findings, critical research processes can also be documented: theoretical principles and methodological ground rules can be discussed and made explicit; criteria for selecting of rejecting areas of investigation can be spelled out; and evidence can be presented in such a way that others can judge its quality.

Even with such precautions, the subjective element remains. It is inevitable. When the investigator abandons the agricultural-botany paradigm his role is necessarily redefined. The use of interpretative human insight and skills is, indeed, encouraged rather than discouraged. The illuminative evaluator thus joins a diverse group of specialists (e.g. psychiatrists, social anthropologists and historians) where this is taken for granted. In each of these fields the research worker has to weigh and sift a complex array of human evidence and draw conclusions from it.

A further issue also focuses on the position of the investigator. Does not his presence have an effect on the conduct and progress of the innovatory scheme he is studying? Certainly it does; indeed, any form of data collection creates disturbance. Illuminative evaluators recognize this and attempt to be unobtrusive without being secretive; to be supportive without being collusive; and to be non-doctrinaire without appearing unsympathetic.

This leads to an important point: that research workers in this area need not only technical and intellectual capability, but also interpersonal skills. They seek co-operation but cannot demand it. There may be times when they encounter nervousness and even hostility. They are likely to be observing certain individuals at critical times in their lives (e.g. students about to leave, or instructors with a high personal investment in the innovation). The researchers need tact and a sense of responsibility similar to that pertaining in the medical profession. They seek and are given private opinions, often in confidence. They are likely to hear, in the course of their study, a great deal about personalities and institutional politics that others might be inquisitive to know. There are especially difficult decisions to make at the report stage: though full reporting is necessary it is essential to safeguard individuals' privacy.

Such problems, confronting many research workers in the human sciences, are exacerbated in the case of close-up, intensive studies of the type outlined here. The price of achieving the richer, more informative data of illuminative evaluation is the greatly increased attention that must be paid to the evaluator's professional standards and behaviour. Though there can be no fixed rules, there are certain guidelines for the illuminative evaluator.

For instance, to retain the viability and integrity of his research position and the trust of the participants in the programme, the investigator needs, from the outset, to clarify his role; to be open about the aims of his study; and to ensure that there is no misunderstanding or ambiguity about who, for example, will receive the report.

Besides concern with the investigator's special position, illuminative evaluation also prompts questions concerning the scope of the investigation. Is illuminative evaluation confined to small-scale innovations? Can it be applied to innovations that are being widely implemented? Detailed studies of specific learning milieux may be insightful and valid, but are the results and analyses generalizable to other situations? Is it possible to move from the particular to the universal?

Despite its basis in the close-up study of individual learning milieux illuminative evaluation can also be applied on a wider scale. Suppose an innovatory programme had been adopted by many different schools. At the beginning of the evaluation a small sample of schools could be selected for intensive study. As the study progressed, and as it focused on selected salient issues arising in the different learning milieux, the number of schools studied could be expanded. The new investigations, now more selective, could be pursued more speedily, with concentration more on noting similarities and differences between situations, than on full documentation of each learning milieu. Finally, with this further information assimilated, short visits, or even – in the last resort – mailed questionnaires could be used for the remainder of the institutions.

The full progression – from small sample studies to larger-scale inquiries – is often only necessary in widely applied programmes. But there is another way in which perceptive and rigorous study of specific situations can yield more generally applicable insights with either large- or small-scale investigations. Learning milieux, despite their diversity, share many characteristics. Instruction is constrained by similar conventions, subject divisions, and degrees of student involvement. Teachers encounter parallel sets of problems. Students' learning, participation, study habits and examination techniques are found to follow common lines; and innovations, as such, face habitual difficulties and provoke familiar reactions. There is a wide range of overlapping social and behavioural phenomena that accompany teaching, learning and innovating. This is widely acknowledged. However, few of these phenomena have been pinpointed, adequately described or defined accurately. Illuminative evaluation aims to contribute to this process. There is a need for abstracted summaries, for shared terminology and for insightful concepts. These can serve as aids to communication and facilitate theory-building. They have been conspicuously absent from most research in education. Yet, without this conceptual equipment, the universals of teaching will be cyclically discovered, described, forgotten, rediscovered and described again.

DECISION-MAKING, EVALUATION AND ILLUMINATION

The principal purpose of evaluation studies is to contribute to decision-making. There are at least three separate but related groups of decision-makers to whom the evaluator addresses his report: the programme's participants; the programme's sponsors, supervisory committee or educational board; interested outsiders (such as other researchers, curriculum planners, etc.).

Each group or constituency will look to the report for help in making different decisions. The participants, for example, will be anxious to correct deficiencies, make improvements and establish future priorities. The sponsors and board members will be concerned with pedagogic issues but will also want to know about the innovation's cost, use of resources and outside reputation. The outsiders will read the report to decide whether or not the scheme has 'worked', or to see whether it could be applied or adapted to their own situations.

Clearly, if the evaluator is to acknowledge the interests of all these groups, he cannot – even if requested – provide a simple 'yes' or 'no' on the innovation's future. A decision based on one group's evaluative criteria would, almost certainly, be disputed by other groups with different priorities. A 'mastery of fundamentals' for one group is for another a 'stifling of creativity'. The investigator does not make decisions. Indeed, in these terms he cannot – except as a representative or agent of one of the interest-groups.

Illuminative evaluation thus concentrates on the information-gathering rather than the decision-making component of evaluation. The task is to provide a comprehensive understanding of the complex reality (or realities) surrounding the programme: in short to 'illuminate'. In his report, therefore, the evaluator aims to sharpen discussion, disentangle complexities, isolate the significant from the trivial and to raise the level of sophistication of debate.

SUMMARY

When an innovation ceases to be an abstract concept or plan, and becomes part of the teaching and learning in a school or college, it assumes a different form altogether. The theatre provides an analogy: to know whether a play 'works' one has to look not only at the manuscript but also at the perform-ance, that is, at the interpretation of the play by the director and actors. It is this that is registered by the audience and appraised by the critics. Similarly, it is not an instructional system as such but its translation and enactment by teachers and students that is of concern to the evaluator and other interested parties. There is no play that is 'director-proof'. Equally, there is no innova-tion that is 'teacher-proof', or 'student-proof'.

If this is acknowledged, it becomes imperative to study an innovation through the medium of its performance and to adopt a research style and methodology that is appropriate.

This involves the investigator leaving his office and computer printout to spend substantial periods in the field. The crucial figures in the working of an innovation – learners and teachers – become his chief preoccupation. The evaluator concentrates on 'process' within the learning milieu, rather than on 'outcomes' derived from a specification of the instructional system. Observation linked with discussion and background inquiry enables him to develop an informed account of the innovation in operation.

Ideally, the output of his research will be regarded as useful, intelligible and revealing by those involved in the enterprise itself. Further, by address-ing key educational issues it can also be seen as a recognizable reality by others outside the innovation. If the report is seen merely as an arcane or irrelevant addition to a research literature already ignored by practising educators, clearly the evaluator will have failed.

In attempting to document the teacher–student interactions, intellectual habits, institutional constraints, etc., that characterize classroom life, the investigator contributes to a field that has received only minimal attention from social scientists. Until recently, perceptive accounts of learning milieux have, more often than not, been found in 'travellers' tales' or 'non-fiction' novels rather than in educational research reports (e.g. Holt, 1964, or Herndon, 1965). The investigator has, therefore, not only short-term goals, but also the long-term goal of contributing to a developing and urgently required new field of study.

This approach does not cure all ills, nor can any one approach. Certainly, no simplified instant solutions to perennial educational questions will be delivered by such studies. Indeed, by discarding a spurious 'technological' simplification of reality, and by acknowledging the complexity of education-al process, the illuminative evaluator is likely to increase rather than lessen the sense of uncertainty in education. On the other hand, unless studies such as these are vigorously pursued there is little hope of ever moving beyond helpless indecision or doctrinal assertion in the conduct of instructional affairs.[2]

NOTES

1. The original version of this paper contains almost fifty footnotes, which amplify some of the points and give supporting references. Only essential citations have been retained here [Eds.].

2. The authors are grateful to the following for their comments on a previous draft: Clem Adelman, Tony Becher, Sara Delamont, Oliver Fulton, Liam Hudson, Carolyn Miller, Peter Sheldrake, Deirdre Snyder, Kim Taylor, Brian Torode, Martin Trow, Rob Walker and members of M. Parlett's seminar at the 1972 Danforth Foundation Workshop on Liberal Arts Education at Colorado Springs.

The preparation of this paper has been supported by a grant from the Nuffield Foundation, London.

REFERENCES

Glaser, B. and Strauss, A. (1967) *The Discovery of Grounded Theory,* Aldine, New York.

Henry, J. (1971) *Essays on Education,* Penguin, Harmondsworth.

Herndon, J. (1965) *The Way It Spozed to Be,* Simon & Schuster, New York.

Holt, J. (1964) *How Children Fail,* Dell, New York.

Jackson, P. (1968) *Life in Classrooms,* Holt, Rinehart & Winston, New York.

Light, R. and Smith, P. (1970) Choosing a future: strategies for designing and evaluating new programs, *Harvard Educational Review,* No. 40, pp. 1–18.

Parlett, M. (1969) Undergraduate teaching observed, *Nature,* No. 223, pp. 1102–4.

Parlett, M. (1972) Evaluating innovations in teaching, in H. Butcher and E. Rudd (eds.) *Contemporary Problems in Higher Education,* McGraw-Hill, London.

Parlett, M. and King, J. (1971) *Concentrated Study,* Society for Research in Higher Education, London.

Price, D. (1963) *Little Science, Big Science,* Columbia University Press.

Smith, L. and Keith, P. (1971) *Anatomy of Educational Innovation,* Wiley, New York.

Smith, L. and Pohland, P. (1971) *Technology and the Rural Highlands,* AERA Monograph, No. 8.

Snyder, B. (1971) *The Hidden Curriculum,* Knopf, New York.

Trow, M. (1970) Methodological problems in the evaluation of innovation, in M. Wittrock and D. Wiley (eds.) *The Evaluation of Instruction,* Holt, Rinehart & Winston, New York.

Webb, E. *et al.* (1966) *Unobtrusive Measures: Non Reactive Research in the Social Sciences,* Rand McNally, Chicago.

Young, M. (ed.) (1971) *Knowledge and Control,* Collier-Macmillan, London.

1.5
THE STUDY OF SAMPLES AND
THE STUDY OF CASES*
Lawrence Stenhouse

Let me begin by recalling that last year I offered this conference a definition of research as 'systematic inquiry made public'. Such inquiry is a response – alternative, for example, to prayer or contemplation – to a problem, and it aims to solve the problem by the achievement of understanding. Two kinds of problems of understanding to which systematic inquiry is a possible response are: problems of understanding the world in which we are called upon to act and problems of understanding what we ought to try to do.

In basic research – as opposed to applied research in such a field as education – these two problems are integrated by theory which is created by and addressed to researchers. Theory is such an understanding of the world as enables us to decide how to act as *researchers*. It structures knowledge in such a way as to let us plan by what research act we shall attempt to advance knowledge. The function of academic or 'pure' theory is to support the planning of research acts.

Educational research has as its overriding aim the support of educational acts – it is not 'pure' but 'applied'. Yet it must also support the planning of research acts in educational settings. Our problem is to find approaches to research which produce theory which is of use both to practitioners of education and to practitioners of educational research and which enables both to act in the light of systematic intelligence.

Now, I could attempt to build on this foundation an analysis of the relation of theory and practice in educational research; but that is not my purpose today. I want to hunt a dichotomy, which I perceive not merely as a logical distinction, but also as embodied in the social transactions of the educational

*Stenhouse, L. (1980) The study of samples and the study of cases, *British Educational Research Journal*, Vol. 6, No. 1, pp. 1–6.

research community, which as a consequence, may allegorically be thought of as a two-headed animal. The two heads are constantly disagreeing but the terms of the dispute change. As the chameleon changes its colours and Proteus his shape, so this dichotomy changes its verbiage. The tête-à-tête distinction is now between 'quantitative' and 'qualitative', now between 'psychostatistical' and 'ethnographic' and now again between 'positivist' and 'humanist'.

The product model is opposed to the process model, the conceptually abstracted to the naturalistic approach. Each of these categorizations reflects differences of value or taste: the formal garden on the one hand, the cunning simulation of nature on the other. Each too reflects individual abilities and disables one of the dichotomy's heads; for words fail the psychostatistician and the ethnographer does not count. These underlying differences of temperament and training are by no means irrelevant. They reflect real determinants of style.

But my purpose is to conjure the dichotomy to chop logic; to seek a formulation that will establish some logical – rather than stylistic or psychological – relationships across the cloven heads as a basis for reflective discourse rather than competitive banter. The problem is to get our dichotomy's heads equipped to speak to each other.

In this spirit I will try asserting that the most important distinction in educational research at this moment is that between the study of samples and the study of cases.

Scientific experimenters in such a field as chemistry use samples – of such substances as zinc or hydrochloric acid or ammonium – and generalize the results from a laboratory experiment to a defined 'target population'. The basis of their procedure is control: the control of the purity of the substances. Pure samples represent accurately the behaviour of all possible samples of the pure substances subjected to the same processes.

In the life sciences control of purity cannot often be established. Instead it seems one must represent in the sample the range of variation in the population to which one must generalize. It would seem that the sample needs to be judged because it cannot be tested or controlled for purity.

It was the striking virtue of Ronald Fisher's *The Design of Experiments* (1935) that he recognized and presented so clearly the idea that in experimental situations where we aspire to predictive generalization random sampling is to be preferred to judgemental sampling, the reason for this being that the error in judgemental sampling is inaccessible to estimate whereas the error in random sampling can be calculated by an application of the mathematics of probability. The so-called 'psychostatistical paradigm' in educational research was founded upon this insight.

Now, although Einstein rebelled against the use of probabilistic results to support theory in physics, nevertheless we might well concede that at any particular time in the progress of a pure science, the discrimination between competing theories might be a matter of probability and such a situation could well guide research acts. Fisher, however, was working not in a pure science, but in the applied science of agriculture, where the purpose of experiment was to choose among alternative cultures of crops or animals. A decision as how best to act agriculturally was at stake.

The criterion for this decision was gross crop yield, and the assumption was that of consistent treatment within the field. That is, treatment could not be differentiated from plant to plant on an individual or sub-group basis.

This experimental procedure was adapted to education, sometimes with good results. But there were always limitations. While in agriculture it is normally accepted that the fate of individual seeds of corn or individual battery hens does not matter unless it makes the relation of investment to gross yield unfavourable, in education the fate of individual students is generally held to be an appropriate concern. Furthermore, while in agriculture it was assumed that the expense of differentiating treatments between individuals could only be justified in clinical cases on expensive animals, in education it was widely believed that the treatment of students should be a differential response to diagnostic assessments of their needs.

Experiments concerned to guide the choice of curricula or teaching methods threw into relief the limitations of an approach dependent on sampling and the application of the statistics of probability.

At first the reactions to the exposure of these limitations treated the problem as technical. This is true of the classic papers by Campbell and Stanley (1963), Bracht and Glass (1968) and Snow (1974). To an extent it is residually true of Walker and Schaffarzick's (1974) consideration of the criteria of yield.

However, it became clear that the problem went deeper than this. Statistically significant preferences for one treatment as opposed to another generally meant that in a substantial minority of cases – as many as 40 per cent it could be – the treatment which showed better overall was in fact worse. What was sauce for the goose proved not to be sauce for the gander!

From this observation came the pursuit – through mathematical analysis – of trait-treatment, or, as Cronbach called them, 'aptitude-treatment' interactions. The hope was that it might be possible so to define the properties of individuals and institutions which interacted with the treatment to differentiate the outcomes that the application of a schedule or test to an institution or individual could tell us immediately what to do in that case.

Thus an anxious child of nine in a formal authoritarian school in Lancashire and a relaxed child of seven in an informal free-disciplined school in the West Riding might require different treatment and yet by feeding in data about all the interacting variables we should be able to prescribe at least the outlines of the two differentiated treatments. And note that it is the researcher who offers that prescription without depending on the judgement of the teachers involved in the context and with the children in question.

Of course, something *can* be said by way of such guidance, but the hope that this might come close to a recommendatory prescription has not been justified, as was signalled by an important paper from Cronbach (1975).

To make refined judgements about what educational action to take in particular cases lodged in particular contexts, we need much more information than can at present be reduced to indices and we need to present our conclusions in a way that feeds the judgement of the actors in the situation, a way that educates them rather than briefs them.

To gather about the subjects of our study evidence sufficiently rich to support the kind of discussion from which judgements can be made as conjectures and then subjected to refutation or confirmation in the light of evidence, is a far more laborious and extensive task than gathering data on samples by schedules or tests. We are closer to the historian or to the clinician in style. It is as if we were committing ourselves to studying a sample of 1,500 children in 100 schools by means of individual tests and clinical histories of each child and detailed historical and sociological studies of each school. We should need, let us say, 100 researchers working in parallel, and even then we should have difficulty in reducing the evidence they gathered to data which were comparable and quantifiable. And the problems of working in such intimate detail with schools and children make any approach to random sampling virtually impossible.

A natural strategy in this situation is to set about the patient cumulation of studies of cases. We need to go back to careful direct observation of educational institutions and processes. This is a laborious business and we must work cumulatively. It is the fate, too, of the archaeologist. Digging takes time. His equivalent of the sampling problem is the decision which site to dig next. This decision can be made wisely only in the light of the cumulated work of other archaeologists.

I believe that the description of cases and the analytic categorization of samples are complementary and necessary approaches in educational research, and it is high time that the superficial stylistic differences between their proponents were recognised as impediments to good sense in the research community. There may of course be gulfs of value and commitment within that community, but I believe that the important party divisions exist on both sides of the sample study/case study fence.

I do not want on this occasion to give detailed consideration to the methodology of the study of cases – it is an area in which colleagues and I are at present working with the support of an SSRC grant and as we do so it becomes clear that others here and elsewhere abroad are engaged in parallel activity. But there are one or two selected points I want to make.

The first is that there is an acute need for attention to be paid to quantitative aspects of case study. It seems to me quite clear that descriptive case studies should not confine themselves to words. What indices might best be gathered to describe a school and to locate it within the population of schools? Some – number of pupils, teachers, library books – are obvious. But what of site value, average travelling distance for sports fixtures, geographical distribution of former pupils, age of textbooks and other possibilities? And what testing and measurement might we do in a case study; what, for example, is the potential of time series analysis? What would Bennett's data on teacher styles and pupil progress look like if they were organized as thirty-seven classroom case studies rather than as a sample? I very much hope that we shall find attention being given to such problems in the next years.

A second problem is the achievement of an understanding of the relative status of observation and interview in case study, and of what is going on in each.

It seems to me that in talking of observation in educational case study the analogy with participant observation has too readily been drawn. Can one participate in a school, whose roles are functionally defined, in the same way that one can participate in a community which is a setting for living in a much broader sense?

The observer who relies on or gives priority to his own perceptions and the interviewer who gives priority to the perceptions of others both gather evidence. I use the term evidence to contrast with the alternative term data. Data are standardized – and attenuated – at the point at which they are gathered in order to make them comparable: evidence is not comparable except by virtue of a critical process. Such a process is comparable with the critical methods of the historian. The point is well made by comparing Wragg's (1978) Rediguide on Interviewing, which is concerned with structured interviews whose intention is to gather data (i.e. information made as comparable as it can be by the process through which it is gathered), with Ronald Blyth's (1969) oral history interviews behind Akenfield whose intention is to gather evidence (i.e. information whose comparability is later to be established by critical process).

The problem of field research in case study is to gather evidence in such a way as to make it accessible to subsequent critical assessment, to internal and external criticism and to triangulation. Here it seems to me that interview is at present better placed than observation in spite of the sociologist's prejudice in the other direction. This is because historians have over many years developed critical tools for dealing with evidence of the kind provided by the voices of participants. But we have as yet a long way to go in developing parallel critical techniques to discount the biases and distortions which may arise from an observer's attachment – not to self-esteem and self-interest in their common forms – but to a theoretical stance.

Such problems as these point to the need for us to establish conventions for the conduct and reporting of fieldwork in case studies, which attempt to secure a basis for verification and for cumulation. Such conventions should never be thought of as binding: they offer either guidance or a position against which to rebel. They are themselves hypothetical. But they must address the two closely related questions: how can a reader verify a case study? How can a reader who is a researcher use another's case study as a contribution to his own work? Think back to my analogy with archaeology.

These questions – which have yet to be resolved even in a hypothetical form – seem to me to show great promise as growing points of our thinking. They are also fundamental to the proper supervision of students at doctoral and master's levels. They are entitled to advice about them.

My own view has recently come to be that all fieldwork should yield a case record – of observational field-notes or of interview transcripts – which serves as an evidential base to underwrite a descriptive case study. Such case records might be made available either in print or possibly in microfiche, pouched in the cover of a dissertation, and these should be footnoted as a historian footnotes his sources. The reader will follow into the record his doubts or his interests.

It is an exciting possibility that current interest in the careful study of cases might produce a national archive of such case records. If we had such an archive now, we could understand in much greater intimacy and depth the recent history of our schools.

Of course one of the problems is that educational researchers have for the most part become impatient for results. Few relish the discipline of the historian who takes years in archives before he can move from the paper or monograph to the large canvas. In fact, however, the problems are – as any good historian knows – less daunting than they appear to social scientists. The fact is that you spend less time reading theory and more time reading primary sources!

But I fear my prejudices are showing!

Behind all descriptive case study of the kind we are discussing there lies another and extremely serious problem: access to data in terms of the rights of the subjects who are studied. I believe that this should be an easier problem in a professional field like education than in a personal and private field, but a great deal of work needs to be done to make good that belief. In particular perhaps theory and discussion which emerges from such work needs to be fully accessible to teachers. It is absurd that educational research should make itself less accessible to teachers than political history is to politicians, or than, say, the Webbs' studies of trade unionism are to trade unionists.

It would be useful to our field if the attempt to assess critically the process of case study in respect of its collection of evidence or data, its problems of verification and cumulation and its responsibility to address educators led to a similar review of the processes of sample study. Recent revelations about Cyril Burt might suggest the need for a check-up.

Such monitoring of standards is necessarily in all fields of educational research a responsibility of the research community. It is not one for the enterprise of individuals. At present a group of colleagues and I are seeking a framework within which such a communal enterprise can be undertaken by those who feel some responsibility for the conduct of case study. It is an activity of the research community in which I hope BERA will play an important part; for an educational research association exists to support precisely the kind of discussion in the research community that is needed.

NOTES

1. Presidential Address to the Annual Conference of the British Educational Research Association, September 1979.

REFERENCES

Blyth, R. (1969) Akenfield, Penguin, Harmondsworth.
Bracht, G.H. and Glass, G.V. (1968) The external validity of comparative experiments in education and the social sciences, American Educational Research Journal, No. 5, pp. 437–74.
Campbell, D.T. and Stanley, J.C. (1963) Experimental and quasi-experimental designs for research on teaching, in N.L. Gage (ed.) Handbook of Research on Teaching, Rand McNally, Chicago.
Cronbach, L.H. (1975) Beyond the two disciplines of scientific psychology, The American Psychologist, No. 30, pp. 116–27.
Fisher, R.A. (1935) The Design of Experiments, Oliver & Boyd, Edinburgh.
Snow, R.E. (1974) Representative and quasi-representative designs for research on teaching, Review of Educational Research, No. 44, pp. 265–91.
Walker, D.F. and Schaffarzick, J. (1974) Comparing curricula, Review of Educational Research, No. 44, pp. 83–111.
Wragg, E.C. (1978) Conducting and Analysing Interviews, Rediguide No. 11, School of Education, University of Nottingham.

1.6
SURVEYED FROM A SHAKY BASE*
Neville Bennett

The report *Primary Education in England* represents the first concrete outcome of Plowden's suggestion that surveys of the quality of primary schools should be undertaken by HMI at regular intervals.

The scope of the survey was impressive, comprising randomly selected classes of seven-, nine- and eleven-year-old children in a random selection of 542 schools. Information about the schools, their organization and teaching, was acquired by questionnaire, and the range and quality of pupil work assessed by observational techniques. In addition about one half of the nine and eleven-year-old children observed completed tests of reading and mathematics to provide an indication of standards.

The results and recommendations have already received wide media coverage even though the report itself is still strike-bound. The concern here therefore is not with the findings but with the quality and status of the data on which these findings are based. This is a necessary and legitimate concern given that investigations of classroom life present many methodological difficulties, that the report is addressed to those 'who carry responsibility at any level for decisions about education' and as such is likely to be used as the basis for consultation and change. This assessment of the quality of the evidence and its interpretation is limited to the observational aspects of the inquiry since these data provide the major findings on which the recommendations are based.

No investigator of classroom processes observes without a focus. This focus is derived from theory, informal or formal, explicit or implicit, which delineates those aspects deemed worthy of attention given the purpose(s) of the study. This rationale is normally made clear, but in this report there is little hint, other than the statement that the rating schedules used were

*Bennett, N. (1978) Surveyed from a Shaky Base (HMI Survey), *Times Educational Supplement*, 3 November.

constructed 'on the basis of their knowledge of primary schools and teaching and on their collective experience of assessing the work of children in primary schools'.

One of the central but implicit theoretical strands of the study is the 'match' defined as 'the relationship between the standard of work children in the groups were doing and that which they were considered by HMI to be capable of doing'. The match has of course a respectable theoretical, if little empirical, underpinning but there is no discussion as to why this particular theoretical orientation was adopted to the exclusion of other demonstrably important constructs or theories.

Lack of clarity in rationale is matched by lack of methodological detail making it difficult to assess the reliability of the data gathered. Two HMIs inspected each class together, a process which took two or three days if the school was large enough to provide a group of seven-, nine- and eleven-year-olds. This allows approximately one day per class. In that day they had to make approximately 150 ratings, presumably on each child, by assessing work in progress, previously completed exercise books, paintings and models, and concluding with a discussion with pupils and teacher. This sounds impossible, but if some kind of within-class sampling of pupils was adopted there is no mention of it in the report.

Rating scales of the type used are notoriously unreliable due to rate subjectivity. This is particularly so when the behaviours to be rated are not specifically defined. Items in the schedules used required judgements on, for example, the quality of songs, pupils' emotional development, exercise of leadership and whether engaged in developing sympathy with the predicament of others.

For such studies the raters are normally required to undergo training in an attempt to achieve consistency and for an index of rater agreement to be computed. However, there is no indication of this process in this study. Details might also have been expected of the agreement between the two HMIs observing the same class or pupils but again none is provided. All we are told is that they filed agreed returns.

HMI ratings of the quality of the match also raise questions of reliability. Teachers grouped their class into high, average and low ability prior to HMIs making their subjective judgement. But HMI had no notion of level of pupil ability in an absolute sense – high ability in one class could equate with low ability in another. How this problem was coped with is not recorded.

One of the major problems in observing is the possibility that the presence of the observer significantly alters normal patterns of behaviour, particularly if the observed is aware of the purpose of the study. This could lead to a grossly distorted picture.

In this study the teachers knew beforehand the purpose of the observation and the date of the visit. These visits took place between late 1975 and 1977. Given this information it is worth posing a question. If you were a primary teacher operating in the educational climate of 1976–77 when the air was full of talk of declining standards and William Tyndale (not to mention teaching styles) and you were informed that you were to be observed by two HMIs, how would you have reacted? Could this be one of the reasons why a mere 5 per cent of teachers were observed to be using exploratory methods?

There may also be one or two problems of interpretation. Of particular importance are those relating to the question of the match since these are embedded in a number of the recommendations. The relevant findings are that the match is better when a teacher teaches his or her specialism and when didactic and mixed teaching approaches are adopted. Pupil achievement is also higher in such circumstances.

On the other hand match is poor in inner city classes, in vertically grouped classes and when exploratory teaching approaches are used. In these cases pupil achievement is lower.

It is tempting on the basis of such evidence, albeit correlational, to imply a causal link between a good match and high achievement, and such thinking does underlie a number of the recommendations. Unfortunately this interpretation cannot be supported by more controlled classroom-based research. The most recent studies clearly argue that average and low-ability pupils perform better with a reasonable or poor match since this allows adequate practice, indeed overlearning, of material. The latest study found overestimation to be a consistent negative predictor of achievement and underestimation, i.e. poor match, to be a consistent positive indicator of achievement.

No doubt these studies also had methodological inadequacies but this example does highlight the fact that to base recommendations for change on the basis of the interpretations of one study is a dangerous practice.

These criticisms are not designed to be destructive; there is much in the report to be admired. They are made to highlight the fact that investigations into classroom behaviours and their relation to pupil outcomes is one of the most difficult, yet important, areas of educational research. And that reports of this kind, backed by the authority and expertise of HM Inspectorate, are just as prone to methodological shortcomings as any other piece of research.

Read carefully the report will be of great value in sensitizing teachers and decision-makers to the complex issues involved in teaching primary children. However, the value of studies of this kind do not in my view lie in the provision of pedagogic prescriptions, but in raising levels of awareness, and that, I am sure, is what this report will achieve.

A CHANGING CONTEXT FOR EVALUATION IN BRITAIN

INTRODUCTION

The debates over the politics and the process of educational evaluation highlighted in Section 1 had their origins in the expansionary projects and programmes of the 1960s and 1970s. Essentially the debates took place within the educational community itself: between researchers with regard to the appropriate research methods to be brought to bear on the task of evaluation and, occasionally, between researchers and teachers (or perhaps one should say researchers and action-researchers) with regard to where the balance ought to lie in the twin evaluation tasks of improving practice and increasing knowledge. Latterly however, debates over the role, purpose and conduct of evaluation have begun to take place in an explicitly political, and indeed politicized, context, with central government intervening to attempt to define the parameters of the debate. Debates over methodology are still relevant of course, and, many would argue, all the more so in an era of potentially blinkered utilitarianism and empiricism. Likewise politics has always mattered, as MacDonald (Chapter 1.2) pointed out almost fifteen years ago. However, the nature of the political realities which educators, including evaluators, now face have become much more manifest of late, and the selection of papers in Section 2 attempts to reflect this, particularly with regard to the changing funding arrangements for curriculum development, evaluation and in-service training.

Wilcox (Chapter 2.1) argues that the nature of the research community itself has changed over recent years with teachers doing much more research, particularly of an evaluative nature, and with local education authorities becoming much more interested in it. Hargreaves (Chapter 2.2.), however, questions the value of much of this work and raises essential issues with regard to how fragmented, localized studies can produce generalizable findings. In a somewhat similar vein Harland (Chapter 2.3) suggests that a certain amount of 'divide and rule' is apparent in the local operation and evaluation of centrally prescribed initiatives, with local authorities and teachers being reduced to the role of agents and technicians in curriculum change, rather than analysts and active developers. Shostak (Chapter 2.4) reflecting on the sorts of developments which Wilcox and Harland describe argues that local education authorities must take control of evaluation 'to support the development of practice'. Taken together these four papers raise major questions about whether local education authorities can develop coherent policies for their schools – both within authorities and across them – and then make 'principled' bids for short-term 'categorical' funds, building a balanced programme of school development out of the myriad of often contradictory initiatives which are being launched.

A broader and more pessimistic overview of similar issues is provided by Kushner and MacDonald (Chapter 2.5). Their review is written from the perspective of external evaluators trying to disseminate information about educational initiatives to the public at large, i.e. still trying to operationalize democratic evaluation in what they characterize as an increasingly anti-democratic political context. They argue that evaluation is being increasingly marshalled to justify policy rather than to interrogate it and document its effects. Tempted to withdraw altogether rather than be implicated in such potential fraud, they nevertheless conclude that the effort to render policy-making public is still worth while.

The last two chapters in this section (2.6 and 2.7) focus on a much more long-standing concern of teachers and parents, that of examination results. They draw attention to three essential features of any debate about the use and abuse of examination results in evaluation: first, despite the current proliferation of initiatives in education the publication of examination results reasserts the primacy of a fairly traditional, academic view of what counts as 'good education' and indeed appropriate evaluation; second, that the interpretation of examination results is by no means straightforward and if they are to be used in evaluative studies then much more than a comparison of raw results is required; third, that even a sophisticated use of examination data does not necessarily lead to school *improvement* – that must also draw on qualitative understandings of classroom activities and processes. The issues addressed here anticipate much of the forthcoming debate about current steps to institute formal tests and exams for 7, 11 and 14 year-olds. The results from this national programme of testing will provide further opportunities for inappropriate judgements about the performance of pupils, teachers and schools.

2.1
RESEARCH COMMUNITIES, THE WHITE PAPER CHASE AND A NEW RESEARCH ECUMENISM*

Brian Wilcox

THE RESEARCH COMMUNITY

Of late there have been some interesting changes in the range of people involved in educational research. Up until fairly recently most educational researchers would have been located in the education and social science faculties of universities and polytechnics and in the small number of national research institutes such as the NFER. Although this is still the case at least three other groups have emerged which could reasonably be regarded as part of a larger research community.

Perhaps it may surprise you to know that I would include Her Majesty's Inspectorate (HMI) as one of those groups. Of course it could be said that HMI, because of its inspection activities, has always been an exponent of that branch of research known as evaluation. I think that the case for regarding inspectors as a rather special kind of educational researcher, at least for part of their job, is supported by some significant changes in their method of working since the mid-1970s. First there is the way they have carried out the series of major surveys on various sectors of the education service starting with the primary survey (HMI, 1978), followed by the secondary one (HMI, 1979), and concluding most recently with the middle schools 8–12 survey (HMI, 1985). These surveys have involved teams of inspectors using structured checklists, observational schedules, and the back-up of sophisticated statistical analyses – in fact a range of methodological paraphernalia comparable to that of the conventional researcher – in

*Wilcox, B. (1986) Research communities, the white paper chase and a new research ecumenism, *British Educational Research Journal*, Vol. 12, No. 1, pp. 3–13.

addition to the traditional HMI approach based on informed professional judgement. The reports of these surveys must be regarded as substantial and authoritative contributions to our understanding of schools and I think to the research literature generally.

A second major development has been the introduction in the last couple of years of inspections of whole local education authorities (LEAs). These are attempts to evaluate the full range of an LEA's education provision and represent in conventional research terms multi-site evaluations of complex proportions. They require the resolution of many difficult methodological issues including the sampling of institutions and the programmes and activities within them, the standardization of judgements amongst the dozens of inspectors involved, and the analysis of the resultant data base obtained. These activities and those associated with the more familiar inspections of individual institutions represent in my view a distinctive and largely unrecognized approach to case study methods.

A second group of emergent researchers are teachers. In the past teachers' involvement in research was limited very often to being the *objects* of research rather than the *doers* of it. There are at least two major developments which have changed that situation. One is the Teacher as Researcher movement which owes much to the personal influence and writings of the late Lawrence Stenhouse and the talented team that he assembled at the University of East Anglia in the late 1960s and early 1970s (Stenhouse, 1975). The use of the term 'movement' here is not to be taken to imply the existence of a single coherent organization. Basically the movement unites teachers who are committed to the disciplined analysis of their own classroom activities with the aim of increasing their professional expertise. The practice is methodologically eclectic and may be regarded as a form of classroom action research (Nixon, 1981). The second development relevant here is the growth of post-graduate opportunities for the study of education, particularly represented by master's degree courses in universities and polytechnics. The number of teachers who have completed such courses, either through full-time secondment or on a part-time basis, is now many times greater than was the case only ten years ago. Most of these courses have a dissertation requirement that can include the carrying out of a piece of empirical research. The result is that we now have a significant minority of teachers in our schools who have had the experience of doing research and, for a period of time at least, of being part of the research community.

My third group are those employed within the education department of LEAs. In the past relatively few LEAs have employed staff primarily as researchers. The ILEA is still the only education authority which, through its research and statistics branch, has a substantial number of full-time researchers. In other LEAs a range of staff may have a partial commitment to research within some wider developmental, planning or advisory role. Typically then, and perhaps somewhat surprisingly, LEAs have in the past had a somewhat undeveloped role in relation to research. That situation is changing – one manifestation of this is the emergence over the last two years of a Local Education Authorities Research Group (LEARG).

To speak of these three groups (HMI, teachers, LEA staff) and the other two (academic staff and professional researchers) as a community is to exaggerate the links which exist between them. Rather they constitute a set of relatively independent communities each of which are themselves loose constellations of individuals. In my view the conduct, quality and impact of educational research would very likely be improved if closer links leading to more active collaboration were established between the groups.

Events are I think moving in that direction and in a way which suggests that the natural location of such collaboration is that of the LEA. Much of educational research at the present time inevitably takes place anyway within the bailiwick of the LEA. This is because educational research is pre-eminently the study of the maintained sector. Such workers as Geoffrey Walford who research the independent school sector are very much in the minority (Walford, 1985). In most LEAs then there will generally be a good deal of individual research under way in their schools, colleges and other educational institutions. This will be carried out by a whole variety of people from individual teachers to researchers associated with major national projects. The degree of involvement of the LEA in much of this research may be very slight and limited simply to agreeing that researchers may approach institutions with a view to seeking their participation. The extent to which this collective body of research activity relates to LEA concerns may be largely fortuitous.

LEAs need to have a research policy. It is probably the case that very few do. A provisional policy might indicate the specific areas of special interest to the LEA on which research would be welcomed and encouraged. Such a policy could be circulated to local and other researchers. This would not necessarily imply that the LEA would provide funds for research – although that might be feasible for some topics. The purpose of circulating the policy would be to see whether the LEA's research interests coincided with those of researchers already involved in particular investigations or about to be so. Clearly where there was a correspondence of interest the LEA would be able to offer appropriate facilities to the researchers, e.g. access to schools. The existence of a policy would also help an authority in responding, one way or another, to the many unsolicited requests that it receives from individuals and agencies to conduct research within its institutions.

The extent to which an LEA is able to articulate a research policy is dependent on how clearly its general policies are expressed concerning the development of its institutions, services and programmes. Thus an LEA which has a policy on the co-ordination of provision for the 'under-fives' and is considering its possible implementation in a particular area, might well decide that research on parental views would be useful. An approach could therefore be made perhaps to the local university or polytechnic to see whether a member of staff or a student might undertake an appropriate survey.

THE WHITE PAPER *BETTER SCHOOLS:* SOME IMPLICATIONS FOR RESEARCH

Although LEAs have a wide range of organizational, administrative, and financial policies governing their many activities, those concerned with more specifically educational matters, e.g. the school curriculum, have often at best been implicit in general procedures and ways of working rather than explicitly stated. That position is likely to change – and it is the present government's intention that it should so do. The recent White Paper *Better Schools* (White Paper, 1985) sets out clearly the government's concern to raise educational standards. This is to be effected *inter alia* by requiring LEAs (and schools) to identify priorities and formulate specific policies in a range of areas including the curriculum, in-service education, and deployment of the teacher force.

Assuming that the government's polices, as outlined in the White Paper, are implemented successfully as intended, they are likely to have two consequences relevant to research. First by making LEAs define more precisely the nature of their activities they will be more able, as already indicated, to specify areas where research would be helpful. Secondly some of the enabling strategies referred to in the White Paper would help to define possible areas of collaborative research within the LEA context.

The establishment and implementation of curricular policies is an example of one of the intended strategies. The government believes that the present curricula of many schools are inadequate for preparing pupils for their future adult life and also exhibit an unacceptable level of variation from school to school and from area to area. The White Paper stresses the need to secure a broad agreement about the objectives and content of the school curriculum. The government intends therefore, after consultation, to issue statements of policy supported by more general discussion papers from Her Majesty's Inspectorate. This concern to achieve greater curricular clarity and agreement is consistent with the movement within the DES, discernible from the mid-1970s and increasingly apparent following the change of government in 1979, towards a more dirigiste and centralist role (Lawton, 1980, 1984). It is envisaged that the objectives will have practical effect by becoming the basis of curricular policies of the Secretaries of State, the LEAs and the schools. It is intended that the objectives will be applied with differences of emphasis and balance to reflect local circumstances and local judgement.

The school system then is to conform to a rational planning model in which curricular goals are to be set nationally and transmitted down through the LEAs to schools and thence to individual teachers in policy statements of increasing specificity. Whether or not the school system should operate in this manner is a moot point, but the indications are that it does not at the moment (Wise, 1977). There is need for research here on the effectiveness of this kind of rational model. Do teachers in fact conceptualize their teaching in terms of the kind of hierarchy of influences which the model proposes? If they do, are such teachers more effective with their pupils than those who operate under different conceptual frameworks? Although studies of teaching behaviour have been a significant field of educational research during the last decade (e.g. Galton, Simon and Croll, 1980), they have generally been carried out with little or no reference to the external influences of one kind or another operating on the teacher. Research studies are needed then of how curricular consensus can be achieved within schools and LEAs, how that process can be formally represented in useful policy statements, and how such statements can affect the actual behaviour of teachers and other educationists.

A second enabling strategy is one in which large-scale curriculum development is supported by what Harland (1985) calls categorical funding. In essence this consists of encouraging LEAs to bid for allocations from central funds by submitting proposals, within defined guidelines and criteria, to mount local development programmes reflecting specific government priorities. The Technical and Vocational Educational Initiative (TVEI) and the Lower Attaining Pupils' Programme (LAPP), administered by the MSC and DES respectively, are examples of this strategy. Both of these are seen as major vehicles for exploring the possibilities of establishing a more practical and relevant curriculum. This strategy of competitive funding has been developed further through the Education Support Grant (ESG) scheme to support work under priority headings which include the teaching of mathematics in school, science teaching as part of primary education and the improvement of the quality of education in urban primary schools (DES, 1984).

All of these schemes (TVEI, LAPP, ESG) are examples of a common strategy to ensure a greater degree of correspondence between curricular priorities at national and LEA levels. From a research perspective the strategy is of special interest since it offers a somewhat different approach to curriculum development. In the past, curriculum development has been mainly concerned with national projects of the Schools Council kind (Stenhouse, 1980) and individual school-based initiatives (Eggleston, 1980). Schemes like TVEI may be said to offer potentially the advantages of both types of development. Thus, although the schemes represent national initiatives, the curriculum development associated with them does not take place centrally but at the level of the individual LEA and its institutions. They offer to an LEA, through the provision of external funds, the possibility of adopting a concentrated attack on a major aspect of the curriculum which it would not otherwise find easy to do. Strings are attached of course, i.e. commitment to implementing certain general principles, and it will be interesting to know whether or not these cramp unduly the style of local curriculum developers.

The schemes provide opportunities for evaluating local programmes and testing specific curricular hypotheses. Both TVEI and LAPP are the subject of major externally funded evaluations by the NFER. In addition, activities have been established involving institutions of higher education in the evaluation of individual LEA programmes. Similar opportunities exist for the ESG scheme since one of the requirements is that proposals should indicate how projects will be evaluated. If we consider then the evaluation and research activity either already under way, or capable of being developed as more LEAs become involved in schemes of this kind, it represents a very substantial effort and one of the best opportunities ever of investigating systematically the process of curriculum change.

Complementary to the initiatives for transforming the curriculum outlined in the White Paper are others concerned with examinations and assessment, in-service education, and the management of the teacher force. Each of these will provide, and indeed already is providing, opportunities for research. Although the introduction of GCSE will generate a major research programme for the new examination boards, other researchers are likely to be attracted to such matters as the effect on teaching and learning of the new methods of assessment and the 'national criteria' on which individual syllabuses will be based. The government's parallel development of records of achievement is already being supported by nine pilot schemes in individual LEAs or in LEA consortia. Each scheme will have its own internal evaluation and the project as a whole will also be the subject of a national evaluation.

The new approach to the funding of in-service education expected for 1987/88 is likely to require LEAs to develop more sophisticated methods of identifying teacher needs and to devote rather more attention to the evaluation of their programmes than is generally the case at the moment. The most contentious aspect of the section in the White Paper on the management of the teacher force is that of teacher appraisal. It is to be hoped that existing projects concerned with this issue and others which will certainly emerge in the near future not only draw on the considerable body of relevant research already at hand but are also associated with their own research and evaluation programmes.

Although the White Paper is replete with research possibilities for individual aspects of policy, it should also be said that the rational planning model which underpins the White Paper as a *whole* is also eminently researchable. Rarely has that model been made so explicit in a major government document on education. Never before perhaps has there been such apparent agreement, not only amongst politicians but also amongst educationists, that the model is appropriate. Although the school system is essentially 'bureaucratic' in the Weberian sense and therefore 'rational' there may nevertheless be limits on how far rationalization can proceed without the process becoming dysfunctional. Indeed, Wise (1977) looking at the American scene argues that the trend is so pronounced that it should be characterized as the hyperrationalization of education and that paradigms other than the dominant rational one are needed to explain the process of schooling. Whether the policy implications of the White Paper merit the pathological description of hyperrationalization remains to be seen. What is important is that researchers somewhere should be looking critically at the implementation of that policy over the next few years.

Particularly important to my argument here is that the programmes of evaluation and research associated with the various initiatives outlined in the White Paper will be conducted within a local context and will inevitably involve close collaboration between LEA and academic researchers. Teachers will be involved not only as participants within the programmes but also potentially as researchers and evaluators. Collaboration may in certain circumstances involve other agencies like the NFER as external evaluators. Since HMI is also watching these developments keenly, collaboration could, therefore, potentially embrace all groups of the research community.

COLLABORATIVE RESEARCH IN LEAs

I anticipate then that LEAs, as a result of their involvement in implementing the White Paper initiatives and their consequent and growing sense of being at the sharp end of a policy- and priority-driven education service, will be seeking to develop a closer working relationship with researchers, particularly those based in nearby institutions of higher education and with whom they already have well-established links through perhaps the provision of in-service education. That relationship may involve officers and advisers in commissioning research using perhaps LEA funds or those made available through various government initiatives. It is worth stressing however that good research may also be done with little or no direct funding. Perhaps one of the unfortunate effects of the present system of organizing research is the tendency for it to be dominated by the pursuit of prestigious research grants from external funding bodies such as the ESRC. Much useful research can be done by academics in fulfilling their 'contractual' commitment to re-search not only as individuals but also, and this appears to be rare, as a team on a common unfunded project. Given the increasing difficulties of securing research grants from the conventional funding agencies the kind of col-laboration with LEAs which I have suggested would also seem to be good sense for academic researchers.

Collaboration can also be achieved in a very cost-effective manner through the potential represented by teachers on secondment. I suspect that my own LEA is not exceptional in being more concerned than perhaps formerly with using the secondment programme, at least in part, to research issues of special local interest. Such an opportunity is also provided by the Teacher Fellowship scheme (DES, 1983) which allows experienced teachers to work in a university or polytechnic on a study or inquiry – research in the broadest sense – of significance not only to the individuals concerned but to their schools and LEAs. At its best the Fellowship scheme focuses the different expertise and perspective of teacher, academic supervisor, head-teacher perhaps, and LEA officer or adviser, on to a real practical issue or problem. Although the 'teacher as researcher' notion is increasingly recog-nized as providing a distinctive contribution to educational research, it has been concerned in the main with improving the individual teacher's own classroom practice. Up until fairly recently perhaps there has been slower re-cognition of the complementary notion of teacher as researcher *for* the LEA.

The greater involvement of LEAs in research of the kind I have advocated may also do much in tackling the enduring and vexed issues of dissemination and impact. Only a small proportion of practitioners have regular access to the traditional mechanisms for the dissemination of research findings, i.e. academic journals, books, specialist conferences. Making the LEA the locale and target for at least a substantial part of research activity has several advantages in this respect. The LEA provides a tangible and coherent entity within which 'policy-makers', 'practitioners', 'teachers' and the other groups to which researchers usually implicitly offer their results are not anonymous generalized creations vaguely 'out there' but identifiable real human beings who are accessible. Depending on the nature of the research the appropriate audience may be a relatively small number of individuals who can be easily assembled to consider the findings. For example a study done on pastoral care in secondary schools may only need to be disseminated to a small specialist audience of several dozen people (assistant heads perhaps) for the results to be considered by those able to act on them. In some cases the prime dissemination audience may consist of one person. To engage a chief education officer in considering a piece of research may on occasions be enough!

LEAs also have well-established internal communication networks which can provide effective routes for the dissemination and discussion of research. These might include meetings of professional groups, the local INSET organization, LEA committees and working parties and many others which offer, according to the topic, opportunities to bring researchers and their results face to face with relevant audiences. The use of these is likely to be more potent in their effects on practitioners than standard journal articles important though these are in the wider dissemination process and as contributions to scholarship. The LEA therefore might provide a missing link in that long-desired chain uniting the activities of researchers to those of teachers and other practitioners.

Ed Stones, referring specifically to teacher education, has argued that training institutions should become more self-consciously research institutions (Stones, 1985). I would suggest that notion could be developed further in two ways. First training institutions should fulfil their research function in collaboration with neighbouring LEAs and secondly as well as including research on teaching it should also encompass other aspects of educational research. The planning of educational research jointly by appropriate LEA staff and those in faculties of education, and utilizing the talents of teachers – particularly those on secondment – might yield research which in Stones's words is systemic in education rather than parasitic on it. This kind of collaboration would also provide a research counterpart to the partnership arrangements envisaged for initial teacher training by the White Paper *Teaching Quality* (White Paper, 1983).

To make collaborative research possible requires someone in an LEA with a special remit for research. He or she would need to hold a senior position so as to be familiar with current policy issues and interests and have access to a wide range of LEA personnel. A broad knowledge of research methodology, the range of research being undertaken nationally and 'who's who' in the research community would also be essential requirements. In the past LEAs, in terms of research, have often provided little more than free markets for research entrepreneurs. A research co-ordinator, or perhaps the term 'broker' might be more appropriate, is needed to know who is in the market, to bring those in the market with particular interests together, to encourage others to come in whose research wares look interesting, and most importantly to bring researchers together with those concerned with educational practice and policy. Who might hold such a role? In my own authority it is filled by an adviser with the special designation of 'research and evaluation'. It does make good sense to vest this responsibility within the advisory service of an LEA. Advisers are an LEA's main agents for innovation (Bolam, 1979; Wilcox, 1985). They have the specific responsibility of co-ordinating local in-service and curriculum development programmes. The co-ordination of an LEA's research programme represents then a natural complement to these functions (Wilcox, 1982). Advisers also have a wide network of contacts within and beyond their own LEAs and these include links with higher education and the research community generally.

In developing the notion of research collaboration at the LEA level it may seem that there is little opportunity for involving the first of the research groups which I identified – Her Majesty's Inspectorate. But it should be noted that inspectors are often involved as assessors to research projects and members of project steering committees. They also give advice on research proposals submitted to the DES for funding. In addition, HMI, I believe, has much to offer in terms of its research experience – the kind I attributed to it at the beginning of this paper. One current research concern which is common to HMI and other researchers can be expressed simply as 'how do you judge a school?' This issue is expressed in different terms by the various groups with a stake in it. For HMI and perhaps LEAs, it is 'inspection', for particular researchers it is 'school effectiveness' and for those in schools 'self-evaluation'.

Some inspectors might demur at the suggestion that they are researchers for some of their time. I think, however, that in doing so they would either be expressing an unnecessary modesty or reflecting an inappropriate conception of what counts as research. They are, as I indicated earlier, the possessors of a range of techniques and ways of working which are essentially concerned with evaluation. They have an established tradition of working in this field from which perhaps conventional researchers could learn much. To take one example – they have considerable experience of working in teams and have developed procedures for combining their individual judgements into an agreed collective view. Knowledge of their methods would have considerable interest and value for researchers. I am aware that the question of whether or not HMI and LEA advisers might collaborate together on appropriate activities has been raised within the DES. If that were to occur its extension further to include academic researchers would present a very interesting prospect. How far, however, it would be feasible and allowable for HMI, given its special position within the education system, to share more openly its methods of working remains to be seen.

SUMMARY AND IMPLICATIONS

The purpose of this paper has been to argue the advantages of bringing together the various groups that constitute the research community into a closer working relationship. This perhaps might be the beginning of what could be called an ecumenical research movement. I have suggested that this would be achieved most naturally at the LEA level in terms of potentially effective types of collaborative research associated with some of the policy initiatives summarized in the White Paper *Better Schools*. In drawing the attention of researchers to the White Paper I am not necessarily recommending its educational virtues. I personally have some reservations – particularly about its underlying educational philosophy. This basically reflects the perceived primacy of scientific, technological and economic imperatives. Despite references to a balanced curriculum and the importance of developing individual talents there is an implicit relegation of the arts and the aesthetic side of education generally to a subordinate position. References to the existential purposes of education – the pursuit of meaning and discovery of the self – are not to be found in current official documents on education. They are clearly démodé in the hard-nosed world of the 1980s.

However, whatever view we have of the individual merits of the White Paper it does have the advantage of being, in its own terms, a logically coherent package which is unequivocal about its intentions and how they are to be realized.

Generally speaking the more clearly the policies of education are expressed the easier it is to define a large part of the research agenda. Paradoxically perhaps one can have an inadequate – or even downright bad educational policy and still have good research flow from it. As they say, 'It is an ill wind . . .' I would, however, stress that collaborative research should not be defined solely by the framework of the White Paper. One development which I discern in schools at the present time is that some headteachers have moved on from the stage of conducting reviews of the organization and surface structures of the curriculum to wanting to tackle seriously the nature of classroom process. This focuses on a concern about teaching methods which often conform to an etiolated version of the old didactic style. Although TVEI and LAPP will hopefully contribute to the development and evaluation of new approaches to teaching and learning, there is a need for more sustained research in this field representing as it does a common concern of those in schools, LEAs and in academic research.

The organization of collaborative research of the kind I have outlined puts the LEA into a much more prominent position with respect to the initiation, planning and dissemination of research than has usually been the case in the past. I find it surprising that we have bemoaned for years the marginal role of educational research without apparently recognizing, given the way our educational system is organized, that the LEA is a necessary key factor in the processes of dissemination and impact. If we really do take seriously the view that research should influence educational events more discernibly and predictably than it appears to at the moment, then the LEA must be a major partner in the research enterprise. What I have suggested is entirely feasible and many of the features I have described are already apparent here in Sheffield where the university, the polytechnic, the LEA and its schools have, I believe, the firm sense of being members of a collaborative community in which research is both carried out and applied and where theory and practice influence each other.

I would not, however, wish to risk the possibility of my views being taken to imply an unjustifiable appropriation of the total research enterprise. There needs obviously to be a national perspective on educational research and research activities that transcend the immediate needs of individual LEAs. I would certainly not wish research to be trammelled by the perceived urgencies and priorities of policy-makers of whatever kind. I think there needs to be, as in other disciplines, a balance between those two aspects of research which, for want of better brief titles, we can call the 'pure' and the 'applied'. What I have essentially drawn attention to is the neglect of the LEA in current conceptions of educational research both as a context for research and as a potentially important influence on its organization and planning. I believe this neglect to be harmful to the cause of educational research and the ideas I have put forward should if implemented help to redress the situation.

There is widespread recognition of the importance of teachers' contributions to research. Their increasing involvement has done much to both demystify and humanize the notion of research. BERA has itself underscored the value of teachers as collaborators in research by extending membership to them. We need now to recognize more fully the contribution of the LEAs and seek to encourage the research traditions and activities within them. In particular there is a need to involve three key groups in LEAs more closely in the Association's activities – education officers, education advisers and educational psychologists. Perhaps we should be talking about 'advisers as researchers', 'education officers as researchers' and 'school psychologists as researchers'. As the first member of an LEA education department to hold the office of President of BERA I intend to discuss with the Executive Council ways in which the Association might give practical support to the realization of effective collaborative research and the greater involvement of LEAs in the process.

NOTES

1. This paper was the presidential address delivered at the Conference of the British Educational Research Association, BERA, Halifax Hall, University of Sheffield, 29 August–1 September 1985.

REFERENCES

Bolam, R. (1984) Local education authority advisers: their role and future, in P. Harling (ed.) *New Directions in Educational Leadership,* Falmer Press, Brighton.

DES (1983) *School Teacher Fellowships,* Teaching Training Circular 4/83, DES, London.

DES (1984) *Education Support Grants,* Circular 6/84, DES, London.

Eggleston, J.S. (ed.) (1980) *School-Based Curriculum Development in Britain,* Routledge & Kegan Paul, London.

Galton, M., Simon, B., and Croll, P. (1980) *Inside the Primary Classroom,* Routledge & Kegan Paul, London.

Harland, J. (1985) *TVEI: A Model for Curriculum Change.* Paper presented at the BERA Annual Conference, University of Sheffield, 29 August.

HMI (1978) *Primary Education in England.* A survey by HMI Inspectors of Schools, HMSO, London.

HMI (1979) *Aspects of Secondary Education in England.* A survey by HMI Inspectors of Schools, HMSO, London.

HMI (1985) *Education 8 to 12 in Combined and Middle Schools.* An HMI survey, HMSO, London.

Lawton, D. (1980) *The Politics of the School Curriculum,* Routledge & Kegan Paul, London.

Lawton, D. (1984) *The Tightening Grip,* Bedford Way Papers 21, London University, Institute of Education.

Nixon, J. (1981) *A Teachers' Guide to Action Research,* Grant McIntyre, London.

Stenhouse, L. (1975) *An Introduction to Curriculum Research and Development,* Heinemann, London.

Stenhouse, L. (1980) *Curriculum Research and Development in Action,* Heinemann, London.

Stones, E. (1985) *Towards a Systematic Approach to Research on Teaching: The Place of Investigative Pedagogy.* Paper presented at the BERA Annual Conference, University of Sheffield, 29 August.

Walford, R. (1985) *Change in Public Schools: A Revolution in Chains.* Paper presented at the BERA Annual Conference, University of Sheffield, 29 August.

White Paper (1983) *Teaching Quality,* Cmnd 8836, HMSO, London.

White Paper (1985) *Better Schools,* Cmnd 9469, HMSO, London.

Wilcox, B. (1982) What an LEA can do about research in the schools, *Education,* Vol. 160, no. 12, p. 216.

Wilcox, B. (1985) Clarifying the role of the adviser, *Education,* Vol. 165, No. 15, p.331.

Wise, A.E. (1977) Why educational policies often fail: the hyperrationalisation hypothesis, *Journal of Curriculum Studies,* Vol. 9, No. 1, pp. 43–57.

2.2
THE RHETORIC OF
SCHOOL-CENTRED INNOVATION*
Andy Hargreaves

INTRODUCTION

Two very different movements can be detected in contemporary patterns of curriculum development and change in England. On the face of it, they are worlds apart, diametrically opposed even. The first concerns the growing involvement of 'the Centre', of national government and the Department of Education and Science (DES) in the direct control, administration and monitoring of the school curriculum. Because of wide media coverage of the host of official educational documents which have marked the state's long and sustained endeavour to exercise greater control over what is learned and by whom in schools – its attempt to bind schools more firmly in the service of society – this movement has become the best-known one to the public at large and the most contentious among professional educators. With the publication of each Green Paper, Yellow Book and curriculum document, the teaching profession – raised on a tradition of school and classroom autonomy – has been voluble in its protests; and academics of different persuasions have registered their own dissatisfactions about the secret activities of the 'mandarins' of the DES (Lawton, 1980); about their attempt, with parliamentary government, to control the educational system by much closer regulation of the school curriculum and teacher practice than the broader and looser *licensed* autonomy that had been granted to teachers during the era of educational and economic expansion (Dale, 1979). And they have shown themselves to be wary of the ideologically loaded language in which HMI and DES documents have been couched (Donald, 1977;

*Hargreaves, A. (1982) The rhetoric of school-centred innovation, *Journal of Curriculum Studies*, Vol. 14, No. 3, pp. 251–66.

Halpin, 1981). Publicly, the centralizing tendency of curriculum change is the most visible and best-known one, and professionally it is certainly the most contentious, occasioning the greatest amount of controversy and dissent.

Not so well known to those outside schooling, but making itself felt more pervasively in the everyday experience of teachers, is the decentralizing or localizing tendency towards innovation in curriculum provision and in-service training (these things tend to be linked) at the level of the school. This pattern is variously referred to as school-based curriculum development, school-focused curriculum development, school-based in-service education and training (INSET) and school-focused INSET. I shall refer to them all as school-centred innovation (SCI) for short, since it is their common localizing tendency rather than the fine distinctions which separate them that concerns me here. The proponents of SCI have claimed that it has had a staggering impact on the educational system over the last decade, far in excess of the amount of public recognition accorded it (Eggleston, 1979, 1980). In part, the suggested strength and novelty of SCI has possibly been overrated by its advocates since the processes to which it refers had been going on unnoticed many years before the advent of the 'school-based' 'school-focused' label. However, the movement is not, as some have implied (for example Skilbeck, 1976), simply a modest extension of a long-established trend, but has been shaped through definite, concerted and co-ordinated initiatives, that together far outweigh the previously disparate activities of thoughtful and enlightened teachers and heads in separate schools. That concerted effort can be seen in the very sizeable body of literature on SCI – in primers and readers for those new to the field (for example Warwick, 1975; Henderson and Perry, 1981; Eggleston, 1980), as well as in well-known educational journals,[1] especially those which have published special issues on the subject.[2] In addition, conferences on different aspects of SCI are held year by year;[3] and various initiatives of some magnitude have been taken to generate, co-ordinate and evaluate large-scale programmes of school-centred work across the country.[4] To some, all this frenetic activity might seem an elaborate smoke-screen to disguise the more overtly and politically contentious efforts of the state to exercise central direction over the curriculum. While there is some truth in this, SCI has not been just talk and rhetoric. A good deal of real and consequential work has been going on within the schools themselves. This appears, in fact, to be one of those proverbial cases where there is no smoke without fire.

However, when one peers into the flames of SCI, what is most discomforting about it is the absence of that scepticism and watchfulness among academics and practitioners which so strongly characterizes the debate surrounding the centralizing tendency of curriculum change. In effect, SCI has been optimistically and zealously advanced as both guardian, if not modern patron, of teacher automony and professionalism and as a likely cure for much of the current educational malaise. This is not to deride the *principles* of SCI; principles which, in large part, accounted for its emergence. Against the backdrop of the failure of nationally based programmes of curriculum change, and the difficulties that teachers commonly experience when trying to apply the insights of university, college and local education authority (LEA) provided courses to the everyday demands of school life, SCI undoubtedly offers the very real hope that curriculum development and in-service training can be successfully related to the particular needs of each school for which it caters. And into the bargain, it almost certainly achieves these ends at considerably less expense than non-school-centred programmes (see, for example, Simmons, 1980). More recently, in an educational system beleaguered by falling rolls and economic cuts, SCI has also been viewed as a way of compensating for the erosion of career opportunities by involving teachers in school decision-making processes. Thus, SCI has come to be regarded as a way of allowing innovation to 'take' at low cost while maintaining motivation and morale among teachers.[5] It is not in the least bit surprising, then, that so much hope, faith, time and energy should have been invested in it.

However, what gives cause for concern is the fact that hope, faith and optimism do not so much permeate the discussions and evaluations of SCI as consume them. In these discussions and commentaries, the virtues and successes of SCI appear to be legion; its drawbacks and failures few. In this article my argument is that such a heavy skewing of discussion away from sharp and constructively critical analysis of SCI has created quite serious and widespread misunderstandings of the actuality of decision-making processes and their consequences at the level of the school. Given that strong wave of optimism, sometimes amounting to only mildly restrained self-congratulation on the part of those involved as leading participants in SCI, those misunderstandings may well be politically apposite ones, confirming an optimistic, democratic and 'sensibly' pragmatic ideology of SCI which serves to direct professional attention away from those things which other educational researchers have long held to be at the heart of the schooling process and which give it life – processes of conflict and struggle, power and constraint, domination and persuasion, the creation of consent and the suppression of opposition, and so forth. If a proper appraisal is to be made of SCI and the likelihood of its long-term success, then these other, less obviously appealing and benign aspects of formally democratic and collaborative decision-making processes must be subjected to the most rigorous scrutiny. So far, in the discussions of SCI, that task has hardly been begun.

TELLING IT LIKE IT OUGHT TO BE: ACCOUNTS OF SCI

When one surveys the SCI literature, what is most striking is the dearth of rigorous, critical and empirically grounded accounts of particular schemes and projects. It is hard to find dispassionate studies of the actuality of decision-making processes, the particular forms that participation in decision-making takes and the effects that such participation has in the moment-by-moment process of deliberation. As Reid (1978, 1979) reminds us, curriculum decision-making is a process of eminently *practical* deliberation made in an institutional context and within a formal distribution of power and experience between teachers and heads that places constraints on the sorts of decisions that are and can be made and on the kinds of accounts that teachers and heads tend to put forward to justify those decisions.[6] It is disappointing, then, that so little of the SCI literature gives any sense of the dynamics of the decision-making process and its effects on the perceptions, indeed on the motivation and morale, of those involved. Instead, what most writers in this field are concerned to do is either to persuade people of the importance of SCI, to outline the many possible forms it might take, or, somewhat anecdotally, to assert its success in particular cases. These kinds of accounts I shall call exhortatory, taxonomic and reflective.

Exhortatory accounts

Exhortatory accounts seek to persuade people that SCI *should* take place.[7] Like most statements published during the early stages of educational movements, these accounts are at once intensely programmatic, issuing spirited moral and professional injunctions about the importance of school-centred work, and also rather vague, providing little guidance about the forms SCI might take, and the problems that might be encountered along the way. After identifying the failure of centralized and non-school-based forms of curriculum development and in-service training in the past, and outlining the challenge that a contracting school system presents to the educational imagination in the present, the authors of exhortatory accounts fervently recommend the participation and collaboration of teachers in SCI. But the way in which 'participation' is advocated does little to further people's understandings or expectations of the particular forms that participation might take. Thus, in answer to the question 'what kind of a context is best for promoting teacher development?', Eraut (1977, p. 11) includes 'participative decision-making and flexible policies' as one of the five defining characteristics of such a context, but never explains what these things mean. Similarly, Sayer proclaims that

> a strategy of INSET which has the school as its starting point, is likely to encourage groups of teachers to do things themselves; the initiative is theirs, the exercise becomes one of self-development and active participation rather than 'being sent' on a course.
>
> (Sayer, 1979, p. 95)

Once again, though, what such participation would look like in practice and whether it would then be endorsed by all concerned is never specified. In this sense, terms like 'participation' and 'self-development' have barely any explanatory value at all. Their role in the SCI discourse is largely symbolic, their purpose being to arouse sympathy and support by locating SCI within the cherished tenets of social democratic thought and practice. Few could demur from the principle of participation advocated in this way, since all it seems to be doing is extolling virtue and pronouncing against sin.

Like primary school teachers who speak to each other as if they all know and agree what 'progressive education' means, then go away to operate widely different teaching styles in their own classrooms (Sharp and Green, 1975), the enthusiastic proponents of 'participation' are almost certainly hiding more than they reveal. Although, temporarily, this might help to secure professional commitment to the cause of SCI, it is also probable that those about to embark on such schemes will as a result be ill-prepared for the difficulties they are likely to encounter in the process of deliberation.

In a period of contraction, with all the problems that this presents for the internal management of schools, the need to be cautious about advancing overly simplistic internal solutions to large-scale problems that affect the educational system as a whole is especially great, since the collapse of these proposals may not only fail to *raise* staff motivation and morale, but might actually *depress* it still further. The recommendations of those who see SCI as a useful strategy for dealing with the effects of contraction should therefore be treated very warily. For instance, one solution proposed by Hunter and Heighway (1980) to the morale and motivation crisis takes the form of the highly dynamic-sounding principle of *creative turbulence*. Though never clearly defined, this appears to refer to an increase of staff participation in school decision-making, a fundamental reassessment of the goals of the school and a blurring of the roles of teacher, senior teacher and headteacher in determining educational outcomes. The brunt of Hunter and Heighway's policy recommendations is expressed as follows:

Such aspects as school-based or school-focused in-service training and development of staff could become an integral part of the ongoing structure of the school. Greater participation in curriculum planning, assessment procedures and organizational decision-making could be elements which generate wider accountability and responsibility-sharing in a more open organistic school structure, rather than in the closed mechanistic management structures which still exist. Such changes give cause to review fundamentally the roles of teacher, head, head of year/ department, etc. in the light of the potentially changing career structure in the teaching profession due to decreasing mobility within and between schools.

(Hunter and Heighway, 1980, p. 485)

The proposers of this programme do mention, as an aside, that the extent to which participation in curriculum planning and decision-making is realized in practice is 'open to empirical study', but apart from this brief qualification the optimism of their recommendations is unyielding. In this sense it is not unlike the picture of enlightened yet cautious advance towards democracy in school decision-making outlined elsewhere by Razzell (1979). He states:

I feel that we are moving steadily towards the position where primary schools will see it to be highly desirable, if not essential, to function as a team of professionals sharing fully in the decision-making. The day of the autocratic head setting his personal thumb-print clearly on his school is almost over.

(Razzell, 1979, p. 5)

Now, it would be as churlish to dismiss out of hand such optimism about the growth of enlightened forms of school management, as it would be naïve to accept it on trust. However, there does appear to be a danger that a bland advocacy of increased participation in school decision-making or, even further, a claim that such a trend is already well under way, might lead specialists in INSET and curriculum innovation to embrace dangerously simplistic panaceas. What is really required is close examination of the forms that participation takes when it is implemented in particular programmes of staff development and curriculum change. What needs to be adduced in particular is whether teacher participation leads them at present to being *in control* of the curriculum, or to their remaining *in service* to ends formulated by others. 'In service' or 'in control'? Paternalistic consultation or radical staff democracy? These are just some of the alternative meanings of teacher participation that need to be identified and examined in actual cases of educational change, for the consequences are likely to be very different in each case. In this respect, it is illuminating to contrast Hunter and Heighway's (1980) faith in participation with an earlier paper of Hunter's (1980) on staff participation in a comprehensive school where it was noted that the concept of participation was 'being used as a legitimating strategy for forms of social control, by securing the commitment of teachers to decisions they do not in fact make'.

Taxonomic accounts

Taxonomic accounts are also programmatic, but more elaborately so. In meticulous detail, they outline the many different kinds of SCI that might, in theory, be developed. The language in which such schemes are described is a hypothetical and conditional language of the possible. The authors of taxonomic accounts take it for granted that SCI *should* take place: their more precise purpose is to specify the different conceivable ways in which it *could* be organized, and their repetitive use of 'could', 'might' and 'may' reflects this nicely. A good example of the genre is Henderson and Perry's (1981) work on school-focused in-service education. In it, they suggest that:

> Some needs *may* be met within the school, through staff conferences, curriculum development activities or personal study. Some *may* involve short-term visits to other schools, longer-term exchanges of staff between schools, or study groups involving two or more schools in a locality . . . Other types of need *may* be met by a consultancy approach; by the schooling inviting, say a local authority adviser, a training institution lecturer, or a teacher from elsewhere into the school to work with the whole staff, a small group of teachers, or an individual teacher . . . One mode of consultancy operation *might* be the school-based course. An extension of this, when the same needs are being felt by a number of neighbouring schools, is a locally-based course or study group on a more conventional pattern, based in one of the schools concerned, a teachers' centre, or a local training institution.
>
> (Henderson and Perry, 1981, emphasis added)

Though writers such as Henderson and Perry draw a number of important fine conceptual distinctions within SCI (for example between school-based and school-focused work), the most powerful theme that pervades their accounts is that of the immensely, almost infinitely diverse forms that SCI *might* take.

This celebration of an open horizon of possibilities for SCI has been taken one stage further by a small but influential group of writers who have constructed formidably complex taxonomies in an attempt to illustrate all the possible intersections between the many different dimensions along which varieties of SCI might be arranged. Bolam (1979), for instance, has devised an analytic framework for classifying different ways of evaluating INSET programmes. Here, the particular nature of an INSET evaluation activity is defined in a three-dimensional matrix at the intersection of the type of INSET evaluator (school, LEA, etc. – four types in all); the nature of the evaluation task (negotiating access, disseminating findings, etc. – six types in all); and the target of the evaluation (school, LEA, etc. – five types in all). This creates a total of 120 different possible varieties of evaluation activity. Alexander (1980) presents an even more complex framework than this, which extends into four dimensions. Perhaps because this would be rather difficult to represent diagrammatically, he opts to collapse two of the dimensions – the mode of the INSET programme (course-based, non-course-based, etc.), and the location of the programme (school, teachers' centre, etc.) – into one. But even with this simplified framework, the matrix still generates as many as 486 different permutations of possible kinds of school-focused INSET.

Undoubtedly these armchair exercises are very impressive undertakings. For all their taxonomic grandeur, though, their major effect is to draw attention away from the actual and patterned differences that can in practice be found between real, rather than hypothetical instances of SCI. Just as importantly, they lead to a neglect of those common difficulties and constraints that *all* SCI schemes are likely to face within the confines of the existing educational, economic and political situation. The conjuring up of potentially relevant indices and dimensions 'in the air', as it were, aside from the everyday situational demands that teachers and heads face in different kinds of schools, creates a pluralistic and individualistic image of SCI which makes it look *as though* there were as many kinds of SCI as there were intersections of variables, and *as though* these intersections were in every case almost random, determined by the particular nature and needs of each school in its own specific locality. Thus while the fascination for constructing elaborate taxonomies – the great strength of curriculum theory – has certainly given a sense of the diversity of SCI, it has, at the very same time precluded the careful description, explanation and evaluation of the nature and effects of teacher participation in different schemes. For the moment, what it has, in effect, done is to place the extremely important work of SCI outside the explanatory embrace of social science.

Reflective accounts

In contrast to the speculative and hypothetical character of exhortatory and taxonomic accounts, reflective accounts do at least present reports on actual instances of SCI. However, instead of being presented as carefully constructed research-based analyses, reflective accounts normally take the form of journalistic recollections authored by leading participants in or instigators of the programmes that are being described. Though the reports are not always unreservedly flattering about the schemes concerned, criticism is rarely more than mild or sporadic. Any reservations that are expressed are usually rather brief and placed in parentheses. For the most part, the dominant interest is in providing an account of 'how it was done' as a contribution to the overall pool of professional experience of those involved in SCI in order to develop and enhance a tradition of 'good practice' in the area.[8]

While I would not wish to impugn the honesty and integrity of these storytellers, the accuracy of their accounts is always bound to be open to a number of substantial doubts. Firstly, this is because of the mode of reporting: reflective accounts, rather like HMI reports, are presented as somewhat loose forms of description that do not allow the reader to check out the data on which that description is based, and therefore to assess its accuracy. The second problem concerns the status and interests of the reporter. Because of their commitment to particular projects, the authors of reflective accounts have a strong stake in witnessing them reach a satisfactory conclusion and may therefore be unreceptive to evidence to the contrary. Furthermore, given their relatively senior position within the school or the project team, that evidence may simply be withheld from them – they are unlikely, for instance, to be fully cognizant of the perspectives and reactions of all their staff, especially those of their more junior colleagues, or of any teachers who nurture hidden reservations and resentments about the change.

It is not unreasonable, then, to ask for accounts that are more open to checking and scrutiny. There are many ways in which greater openness could be secured, but some might include giving examples of the kinds of data on which accounts are based, identifying the people whose perspectives have been elicited, noting what kind of interaction processes have been observed, indicating how accurately these have been documented, and so forth. Certainly, a wider range of accounts than those offered by leading and committed participants needs to be sampled. Only when these kind of precautionary measures have been taken, might it then be possible to determine whether any raconteur is an astutely observant participant, or an imaginatively unobservant one.

AN IDEOLOGY OF SCI

The overall outcome of the speculative outlines and retrospective views contained in exhortatory, taxonomic and reflective accounts, is an ideology of SCI which gives a distorted picture of the practice that occurs in many schools and of the consequences of that practice. That ideology emphasizes and encourages increased teacher *participation* in SCI, but does not assess the different forms that participation actually takes, nor the uses to which it tends to be put. In particular, it fails to acknowledge the resistance of many teachers, especially probationers, to the very idea of participation (Bullock, 1980; Richardson, 1981) or to recognize the ways in which senior staff use a range of strategies in the decision-making process having the effect of frustrating the involvement and undercutting the contributions of other enthusiastic teachers within the school (Hunter, 1980; Weston, 1979; Hargreaves, 1980a). Secondly, the ideology of SCI stresses the value of *collaboration* between teachers, but neither examines the ways in which such collaboration is secured nor admits the presence and importance of conflict and struggle between different teachers, subject departments and so on, in the process of educational innovation (Ball, 1981). Thirdly, the ideology celebrates the evolution of SCI as an instance of *grass-roots democracy,* which presents an important alternative and counterbalance to the encroachment of centrally generated curriculum initiatives (Eggleston, 1980, p. x) but, in so opposing these movements, fails to examine the extent to which the educational rhetoric and curriculum categories of 'standards', 'accountability' and so forth, employed in local discussions are themselves central in origin (Halpin, 1981). Attention has been focused so heavily on the centre's unsubtle attempts to storm the front gates of the citadel of teacher autonomy, that its quiet entry through the back door of SCI has been virtually undetected. Fourthly, the ideology posits a virtually infinite range of different possible kinds of SCI, according to the needs and demands of particular schools, but does not match this elusive *diversity* against any substantive study of existing practice. In other words, SCI writing does not *demonstrate* the presence of value-pluralism, it is simply predicated on the assumption of its existence.

Overall, then, the SCI literature encapsulates the highest ideals of liberal democracy as worthy and readily attainable goals in the management of schools. In effect, it promises no less than the realization of liberty (individual diversity), equality (participation and grass-roots democracy), and fraternity (collaboration).[9] Cast in these terms, it is not surprising therefore, that the ideology of SCI should have been imbued throughout with a widespread *optimism* about the necessity and impending success of the venture. In the light of the above observations, though, this seems less than fully warranted. However, more disconcerting still than the distortions created by the 'hard sell' approach of much of the SCI literature, is the fact that the rather limited amount of empirical research that is to be found in this area is of a kind which tends, because of its methodological orientation, to reinforce rather than dispel the myths that programmatic and retrospective accounts have generated. This research will now be examined carefully in order to elucidate the exact ways in which it tends to confirm rather than challenge existing professional assumptions.

RESEARCH ON SCI

In the small amount of research that has been conducted on SCI, two strands are dominant. These are the traditions of survey research and 'tied' evaluation. Though the merits and demerits of each of these traditions are now reasonably well known, the appreciation of their limitations has not really penetrated into the SCI literature. For that reason, while the following points are hardly 'news' in the most general sense, they are worth reiterating in this particular context.

The survey tradition

A small number of studies of involvement in school decision-making have tried to discover staff perceptions of the decision-making process on the basis of questionnaires administered to a large sample of teachers. One of the largest surveys of this kind is Cohen and Harrison's (1979) study of decision-making in Australian schools. Amongst other things, they were interested in who participates in making curriculum decisions. As part of their research, they carried out a national survey of the principal, three heads of departments and ten teachers in each of ninety-eight secondary schools. One of their findings – for them a lamentable one – was that only 24 per cent of the sample considered that school objectives were written by the total staff. The researchers then claimed that this finding – an alleged indicator of low rates of teacher participation – was, as the others, 'generalizable to all Australian secondary schools because of the rigorous methods of sampling' (a stratified random sample). This led them to bemoan the widespread absence of systems of participatory decision-making in Australian secondary schools.

In advancing strong claims for the generalizability of their findings about school decision-making, Cohen and Harrison (1979) are drawing sensibly on the traditional strength of survey research – its capacity to generate findings which are broadly applicable to a large number of people and institutions. But the crucial question which is begged in research which tries to get at people's perspectives on social life, via the survey method, is not the generalizability of the findings but their validity. Simply put, what people write 'in the cold' as a response to a brief item on a questionnaire, is often a poor document of their everyday working perspectives. If researchers want to examine the complexity of decision-making processes and people's perceptions of those processes, the questionnaire is therefore likely to prove a rather clumsy, inaccurate and imprecise tool. For instance, Cohen and Harrison give no indication of what 'participation' means to the participants;

nor is their indicator of teacher participation – the staff's inclusion in writing curriculum objectives – a self-evidently valid one. The writing of curriculum objectives may be only one small part of the curriculum decision-making process and an unimportant one at that. Nowhere is it stated that teachers attribute any great importance to formally written objectives. For them, this may be only a nominal exercise, 'real' participation taking other forms. Furthermore, the statement that objectives were written by 'the whole staff' may mean a host of different things – written simultaneously? Written by a working party chairman then co-ordinated with the statements of other working party chairmen? Written by the headteacher, after canvassing the views of individual members of staff? With or without their knowledge? Or what?

The overall consequence of such survey studies of teacher participation in curriculum decision-making is that unwarranted claims are made about allegedly generalized features of the decision-making process on the basis of what, given the methodology, are unavoidable simplifications and mis-understandings of the nature, process and meaning of participation. Such misunderstandings usually lead to shoring up rather than questioning of existing political and professional values and assumptions about school decision-making. This is not because of what *is* asserted, but more because of what is left out – because of certain possible meanings of participation and collaboration that are kept off the agenda.

A good illustration of this is the influential research of Rutter *et al.* (1979) on secondary schools and their effects. In their survey of twelve secondary schools, Rutter and his colleagues found that one of the variables correlating with favourable pupil outcomes was the existence of a curriculum in the school that was group-planned rather than fragmented according to the interests and whims of individual teachers. 'Schools where most teachers planned jointly,' they argue 'tended to have better attendance and less delinquency' (Rutter *et al.*, 1979, p. 136). They acknowledge that 'group planning took many different forms', but emphasize that 'in the less success-ful schools, teachers were often left completely alone to plan what to teach with little guidance or supervision from their senior colleagues and little co-ordination with other teachers to ensure a coherent course from year to year'. The pattern of decision-making that was found to be most closely correlated with favourable outcomes was one where 'decisions were made at a senior level rather than in the staff room' but where teachers's own views were represented at the 'appropriate decision-making level' (Rutter *et al.*, 1979, p. 138). The conclusion the authors draw on the basis of these findings amounts to a vindication of democracy by consultation: 'The combination of decision-making by senior staff, after consideration of the views of the whole staff,' they suggest, 'may be a good one' (p. 138). In the light of 'findings' such as these, it is not difficult to see why many critics have discerned a 'tight ship' philosophy in Rutter's model of the good school. And yet the basis on which that model rests is exceedingly fragile. In effect, the most important distinctions – between different *kinds* of consultation – are not made in the study. It is a banal truism that most headteachers and departmental heads consult their staff about curriculum decisions, at some level, in one form or another. What it is more important to know is the particular forms that such consultation takes and which of those forms are more effective. All that Rutter and his team do, though, is to oppose a self-evidently virtuous model of order (group-planned curriculum, teachers' views taken into account) against an equally self-evidently unacceptable model of chaos (individually determined curriculum, teachers' views not represented). All the vital distinctions that separate 'ordered' schools from one another – and most British schools are of this kind – are glossed by unhelpfully vague phrases which refer to things like consultation at the 'appropriate decision-making level'. The most crucial and contentious questions concerning the *kinds* of consultation that are most effective – for instance whether a consistently pursued policy of 'left-radical' staff democracy of the kind seen at William Tyndale school or Countesthorpe College is better or worse than an occasional series of paternalistic (or maternalistic) chats between heads of departments and their junior staff – are never asked. The fact that these kinds of distinctions are not drawn and cannot be drawn because of the rather bland and indiscriminating kinds of questions that teachers are asked, and the fact that schools are not selected for study precisely so that those very distinctions might be highlighted, then enable the researchers to preach a homogeneous philosophy of consultation, and to give that philosophy one particular interpretation. That interpretation – which as the HMI (1979) document *Ten Good Schools* also makes clear, views consultation as taking place within a framework of firm but humane leadership – therefore serves to reinforce rather than question by close comparison what is claimed to be existing 'good practice'.

The tied-evaluation tradition

Much closer insights into the fine details of school decision-making have been provided by curriculum and INSET evaluators. The great merit of their work is that, in comparison to survey research, it certainly enriches our understanding of the dynamics of the curriculum decision-making process and of the perceptions of those who participate in that process. A strong sense is given of what actually happens during the long and tortuous process of deliberation, and in some of the very best accounts, as in much of the work produced by the Centre for Applied Research in Education (CARE) at the University of East Anglia, the authors have a commendable capacity to carry the reader along with the drama of innovation as it unfolds. Here, the power of human observation is sensitively put to work so as to bring alive the dynamics of decision-making among teachers. It is not without some justification that this tradition is often termed *illuminative* evaluation (Parlett and Hamilton, 1976).

However, the immense potential of first-hand observation, as a resource for explaining complex processes of social interaction in the schooling system, is never fully harnessed because of the use to which that observation is put – *evaluating* rather than *explaining* school-centred innovation. Of course, evaluation does not exist apart from explanation; indeed it is highly dependent on it. The problem, though, is that the quality of the explanation in terms of its *accuracy,* its *scope*, and its possible *generalizability* to institutions beyond the ones being studied is severely restricted by its being subordinated to the requirements of evaluation. This is especially true in those currently fashionable forms of 'democratic' evaluation (MacDonald, 1974), where the subjects of the evaluation are involved all along the line in the process of evaluation to the extent of exerting a large influence over the collation of data, the production of explanations, and the release of research reports. A flavour of this tradition is given in Henderson's (1979) work on school-focused INSET, though other examples would serve just as well.[10] Henderson's argument is that

> evaluation should be a co-operative activity undertaken as an integral part of the INSET activities by the participants themselves. Information thus collected might then be collated by the LEA or local training institution (and therefore, perhaps, at the regional and national levels) in order that experience can be distilled and fed back to the schools.
>
> (Henderson, 1979, p. 24)

As with other SCI literature this writing is redolent with the irresistibly appealing symbols of participation, collaboration and grassroots democracy. If Henderson's prescriptions were acted upon, though (and in many places they are), it is difficult to see just how any generalized and rigorous explanations of SCI could be produced when the evaluation is explicitly consumer-serving, internal, informal and judgemental (Henderson and Perry, 1981, p. 167). Why is this?

The most central and obvious point is that the very existence of evaluation and evaluators in a school has an immense impact on the process being evaluated. Often, this is precisely what is wanted since one clear purpose of evaluation is the improvement of existing practice. In one sense, there is nothing wrong with this: few people would wish to impede the process of bringing about change for the better in schools. But, it seems to me, it is not possible to have it both ways – to change the decision-making process under review even as it proceeds *and* to produce potentially generalizable explanations of the dynamics of that process as it would have unfolded had no evaluators been present. In this sense, the distillation of *experience* (in the manner suggested by Henderson, 1979) is a poor substitute for the generation and accumulation of rigorous *knowledge*. Of course, some evaluators might attempt to get round this problem by delaying the feedback of results to the school concerned, but, even here, their very presence in the school as evaluators who are known as such is still likely to have a restricting effect on the sorts of knowledge and practices that teachers are prepared to disclose.

The very nature of evaluation, therefore, makes it almost impossible for its proponents to tell either the truth (the problem of accuracy) or the whole truth (the problems of scope and generalizability). The latter difficulty is further exacerbated by the tendency of school-centred evaluation to be, in Henderson's words, both internal and consumer-serving; in short, school-centred evaluators tend to *tie* the analysis, findings and recommendations of the evaluation to a programme of change that can be practically carried out within the context of the school. This means that, while issues such as the time allowed for decision-making and the way in which working parties are composed receive full attention (Abbs, 1980), rather grander interpretations of the dynamics of school decision-making, the implications of which might extend beyond the problems of particular schools to things like the desirability of the very institution of headship (Weston, 1979, p. 226), or the level of financing of the educational system (Weston, 1979), tend to be ignored: these are just not 'practical' issues for any one school. The point is, though, that while such problems may be the least tractable ones, they could well be the most crucial. By keeping them off the agenda, the tradition of 'tied' evaluation may therefore be doing the cause of school-centred innovation a considerable disservice.

One particular strand of 'tied' evaluation, the 'theorizing practice' tradition, attempts to make a virtue out of this fundamental weakness, by pursuing a programme of action where 'the analysis of practice is followed by the application of relevant theory' (Carnie, 1980). This theory is not introduced from the outside, as it were, but is based on the already existing organizing categories of the practising teacher (Ashton and Merritt, 1979). The aim, then, is to theorize teachers' existing craft knowledge for them (or, rather, with them) in order to help them cope better with their professional work (Desforges and McNamara, 1979). The act of theorizing practice is therefore consciously related to the immediate practical needs of the classroom and, to that extent, is seen to be superior to the formal teaching of educational theory through the disciplines in a way that subsequently proves frustrating when teachers try to apply it to the classroom situation. The fundamental drawbacks (and political attractiveness) of this eminently practical approach are not hard to see. It isolates the classroom from its wider determinants, whether these are in the authority structure of the school or in the economics of education, and treats existing practice more or less as given, attempting only to identify and theorize its 'best' features. Alternative educational practices and the political and economic conditions that might be needed to establish them are therefore precluded from consideration. Furthermore, the use of teachers' present experience as the mainstay of the explanation of classroom practice, offers little hope of moving beyond the bounds of existing practice, of constructing collective and critical revisions of the nature of teaching. While teachers are left to innovate in this way by drawing on their experience alone, it is difficult to see how, in the absence of any dialogue with those who have undertaken rigorous observations of school life, that experience can be extended or transcended.

In the confines of the present schooling system, then, the truth of SCI is neither 'democratic' nor is it 'plain-tongued', as the theorizers of practice and advocates of CARE seem to imply (Kushner and Norris, 1981). It is not 'democratic' because, in the present system, teachers have particular interests to defend, especially those that attach to their subject identities. The prospect of establishing truth through free, open and undistorted dialogue between researcher and researched (Elliott, 1980), therefore seems a remote one at present. Nor is the teacher necessarily the most likely party to breach the terms of the democratic bargain between researcher and researched. The researcher, while advocating plain-speaking at one level, also retains unequal access to the world of formal theory and its concepts at another, introducing these concepts into discussion in a way that leaves their origins and contentious nature unclear to teachers (Barton and Lawn, 1981). Moreover, the researchers may also exercise indirect control over the release of findings by drawing on their own privileged knowledge about tight publishing schedules and so on (Jenkins, 1978).

When taken together, these various difficulties – the distorting effects of evaluation on the processes being observed, the limiting effects of teachers' experience as a main platform for the generation of theory, and the covert importation by researchers of additional assumptions and unspecified theoretical and practical knowledge into the process of 'democratic' evaluation – are not conducive to the production of a theoretically rigorous, methodologically cautious and potentially generalizable understanding of the nature and consequences of SCI. For these reasons, it is therefore somewhat regrettable that the very great capacity of first-hand observational research to get to the heart of the actuality of school decision-making has barely been exploited because of its containment within a widespread programme of 'applied' educational research and evaluation. This is not to deride the undeniable value of applied research in other respects, especially as a device for changing the particular schools under scrutiny; but it does cast doubt on its worth as a means of producing valid and potentially generalizable understandings of the everyday dynamics of SCI.

CONCLUSION

To sum up, it would appear that while great amounts of time, energy and resources, and not a little hope and optimism, have been invested in SCI, its success has by no means been demonstrated, nor is its future effectiveness in raising (or even maintaining) staff motivation and morale in any sense assured. In effect, although the heady rhetoric of SCI persists, promising everything from an effective method of managing innovation in schools, to the realization of staff democracy, fraternity and liberty, its practical success in actual instances of school change is, judging by the very limited amount of research available to date, precariously balanced on a knife-edge of uncertainty. For that reason, it is a matter of some urgency that SCI be subjected to a thorough, rigorous examination. Within that examination, it is of paramount importance that questions such as the following are not shuffled off the agenda. What, even in the terms which the SCI movement has itself set concerning the raising of staff motivation and morale, makes a successful or an unsuccessful scheme? What influence do head and deputy, for instance, exert in the moment-by-moment process of deliberation, and what implications do their interventions have for staff perceptions of the democratic process? More fundamentally, perhaps, is 'democracy' a realizable goal so long as heads retain final and long-standing responsibility for the decisions that are taken within schools? Can teachers reasonably be expected to participate in a democratic process of SCI when the majority are excluded from other important centres of decision-making – such as governors' meetings, contacts with HMIs and advisers and so on – that may run against the democratic grain? What effect does the relative exclusion of ordinary teachers from the wider governance of education, their restricted access to educational theory and other kinds of school practice, and the consequent overwhelming centrality of classroom practicalities to teachers, have on the kinds of *contributions* they make to staff discussion? What implications do the inequality of access between teachers and heads, to educational theory, experience of other schools, contact with educational politicians and administrators and familiarity with decision-making skills, for instance, have on the 'democratic' nature of SCI?[11]

These questions are perhaps uncomfortable ones to ask at a time when a number of heads and deputies are attempting to establish more open procedures of school management in a spirit of altruism and sincerity. But they are absolutely essential ones for academics and school practitioners to discuss, if the possible progeny of SCI – lower rather than higher staff motivation and morale – is not to be the next great irony of educational change.

The call for 'more research' then, is not just a matter of academic curiosity, but one of great educational importance. The everyday dynamics of the SCI process have as yet more or less eluded detailed academic study.[12] There are three groups of educational researchers who might, however, wish to turn their attention to such matters. The first, curriculum theorists, have to date, perhaps because of their generally greater preoccupation with taxonomy and evaluation, tended to shy away from this kind of endeavour. The second group – sociologists of the curriculum – have been equally remiss in carrying out empirical studies of curriculum decision-making. While they have produced a good deal of high-quality, imaginative and speculative theorizing about the curriculum, and how it is determined, few have chased up the implications of their work through empirical study. The third group, ethnographers of schooling – an assortment of sociological and psychological researchers of school processes – have certainly grasped the empirical nettle, but in doing so they have devoted most of their research attentions to teacher–pupil relations in the classroom at the expense of studying what Keddie (1952) calls the 'educationist context', the context of teacher decision-making outside the classroom. However, if some of these imbalances in the research community can begin to be rectified, and the whole nature of SCI can be placed on the agenda of academic research and professional discussion, there may then be a growing awareness not only of the different forms SCI might take along with their practical effects, but also of the context in which SCI takes place – a context of resource levels, authority structures and so on, that may be equally vital to the success or failure of the SCI enterprise. It is in the spirit of generating such kinds of inquiry that this paper is written.

NOTES

1. Foremost amongst these is the *British Journal of In-Service Education* but the *British Journal of Teacher Education* also has devoted many of its pages to the various aspects of SCI, and to school-based and school-focused INSET in particular.

2. See, for instance, (1980) *Curriculum,* No. 1, and (1979) *Cambridge Journal of Education,* Vol. 9, Nos. 2 and 3.

3. One of the best known of these was the 1976 Priorities in In-Service Education conference at La Sainte Union College of Higher Education, Southampton.

4. Most notably the SITE project organized and co-ordinated by Bolam and Baker (Bolam, 1979; Baker, 1979), The Open University IT/INSET project, organized by Ashton and Merritt (1979)

5. For discussion of the role of SCI in a period of educational and economic recession see Lightfoot (1978); Dennison (1979); Hewitt (1978); Harlen (1977); Bradley (1979); Sayer (1979); Hunter and Heighway (1980).

6. For an interesting development of this view in relation to empirical data about teacher decision-making, see Walker (1975).

7. For examples of exhortatory accounts see Watkins (1973); Warwick (1975); Partington (1976); Jones (1980) and Fish (1980).

8. Examples of 'reflective' literature can be found in collections edited by Eggleston (1980); Henderson and Perry (1981); and articles by Broome (1980); Carnie (1980); Simmons (1980); Keast and Carr (1978).

9. Ideological features of this kind are by no means confined to SCI, but are common in educational discourse. For examples of their influence on writing about middle school education, for instance, see Hargreaves (1980b); and Nias (1980).

10. As, for instance the work of the SITE team reported in Bolam (1979) and Baker (1979).

11. I have touched on some of these matters in another empirical paper on the dynamics of staff decision-making (Hargreaves, 1980a).

12. Most existing studies of curriculum innovation in practice tend to focus on the impact of national projects on school life (Shipman and Jenkins, 1974; Gleeson, 1979; or on the effects of innovation in the classroom (Smith and Keith, 1971; and Gross, Giacquinta and Bernstain, 1971), rather than on collective staff decision-making as such.

REFERENCES

Abbs, P. (1980) Continuing curriculum change at Codsall School, in J. Eggleston (ed.) *School-based Curriculum Development in Britain,* Routledge & Kegan Paul, London.

Alexander, R. (1980) Towards a conceptual framework for school-based INSET, *British Journal of In-Service Education,* Vol. 6, No. 2.

Ashton, P. and Merritt, J. (1979) INSET at a distance, *Cambridge Journal of Education,* Vol. 9, Nos. 2 and 3.

Baker, K. (1979) The SITE project: an experiment in approaches to INSET, *Cambridge Journal of Education,* Vol. 9, Nos. 2 and 3.

Ball, S. (1981) *Beachside Comprehensive,* Cambridge University Press, Chapter 6.

Barton, L. and Lawn, M. (1981) Back inside the whale: a curriculum case study, *Interchange,* Vo. 11, No. 4.

Bolam, R. (1979) Evaluating in-service education and training: a national perspective, *British Journal of Teacher Education,* No. 5.

Bradley, H. (1979) INSET now – taking stock, *Cambridge Journal of Education,* Vol. 9, Nos. 2 and 3.

Broome, M. (1980) Professional self development through participation in curriculum development, *Curriculum,* Vol. 1, No. 1.

Bullock, A. (1980) Teacher participation in school decision-making, *Cambridge Journal of Education,* Vol. 10, No. 1.

Carnie, J.M. (1980) IT–INSET: a school-focused programme of initial training and in-service education, *Curriculum,* Vol. 1, No. 1.

Cohen, D. and Harrison, M. (1979) Curriculum decision-making in Australian education: what decisions are made within schools?, *Journal of Curriculum Studies,* Vol. 11, No. 3.

Dale, R. (1979) The politicisation of school deviance: reactions to William Tyndale, in L. Barton and R. Meighan (eds.) *Schools, Pupils and Deviance,* Nafferton Books, Driffield.

Dennison, W.F. (1979) Falling rolls: teachers and shrinking schools, *Durham and Newcastle Research Review,* No. IX, p. 43.

Desforges, C. and McNamara, D. (1979) Theory and practice: methodological procedures for the objectification of craft knowledge, *British Journal of Teacher Education,* Vol. 5, No. 2.

Donald, J. (1977) Green Paper: noise of crisis, *Screen Education,* No. 30.

Eggleston, J. (1979) *School-Based Curriculum Development,* OCED, Paris.

Eggleston, J. (1980) *School-Based Curriculum Development in Britain,* Routledge & Kegan Paul, London.

Elliott, J. (1980) Methodology and ethics. Unpublished paper delivered to British Educational Research Association Conference, Cardiff.

Eraut, M. (1977) Strategies for promoting teacher development, *British Journal of In-Service Education,* Vol. 4, Nos. 1 and 2, p. 11.

Gleeson, D. (1979) Curriculum development and social change: towards a reappraisal of teacher action, in J. Eggleston (ed.) *Teacher Decision Making in the Classroom,* Routledge & Kegan Paul, London.

Golby, M. and Fish, M.A. (1980) School-focused INSET: clients and consultants, *British Journal of In-Service Education,* Vol. 6, No. 2.

Gross, N.E., Giacquinta, J.B. and Bernstain, M. (1971) *Implementing Organizational Innovation: A Sociological Analysis of Planned Educational Change,* Harper & Row, London.

Halpin, D. (1981) Exploring the secret garden, *Curriculum,* Vol. 1, No. 2.

Hargreaves, A. (1980a) Contrastive rhetoric and extremist talk: teachers, hegemony and the educationist context, in L. Barton and S. Walker (eds.) *Schools, Teachers and Teaching,* Falmer Press, Brighton.

Hargreaves, A. (1980b) The ideology of the middle school, in A. Hargreaves and L. Tickle (eds.) *Middle Schools: Origins, Ideology and Practice,* Harper & Row, London.

Harlen, W.A. (1977) Stronger teacher role in curriculum development?, *Journal of Curriculum Studies,* Vol. 9, No. 1.

Henderson, E. (1979) The concept of school focused in-service education and training, *British Journal of Teacher Education,* Vol. 5, No. 1, p. 24.

Henderson, E. and Perry, W. (1981) *Change and Development in Schools: Case Studies in the Management of School-Focused Education,* McGraw-Hill, London.

Her Majesty's Inspectorate (1979) *Ten Good Schools: A Secondary School Enquiry,* HMSO, London.

Hewitt, F.S. (1978) Teacher participation in planning and provision: the identification of pertinent factors, *British Journal of In-Service Education*, Vol. 5, No. 1.

Hunter, C. (1980) The politics of participation – with special reference to teacher–pupil relationships, in P. Woods (ed.) *Pupil Strategies*, Croom Helm, London.

Hunter, C. and Heighway, P. (1980) Morale, motivation and management in middle schools, in T. Bush, J. Goodey and C. Riches (eds.) *Approaches to School Management*, Harper & Row, London.

Jenkins, D. (1978) An adversary's account of SAFARI's ethics of case study, in C. Richards (ed.) *Power and the Curriculum*, Nafferton Books, Driffield.

Jones, J.A.G. (1980) An in-school approach to in-service training, *Curriculum*, Vol. 1, No. 1.

Keast, D.J. and Carr, V. (1978) School-based INSET – interim evaluation, *British Journal of In-Service Education*, Vol. 5, No. 3.

Keddie, N. (1971) Classroom knowledge, in M.F.D. Young (ed.) *Knowledge and Control*, Collier-Macmillan, London.

Kushner, S. and Norris, N. (1981). Interpretation, negotiation and validity in naturalistic research, *Interchange*, Vol. 11, No. 4, p. 30.

Lawton, D. (1980) *The Politics of the School Curriculum*, Routledge & Kegan Paul, London.

Lightfoot, M. (1978) The educational consequences of falling rolls, in C. Richards (ed.) *Power and the Curriculum*, Nafferton Books, Driffield.

MacDonald, B. (1974) Evaluation and the control of education, in B. MacDonald and R. Walker (eds.) *Innovation, Evaluation Research and the Problem of Control*, SAFARI, CARE, Norwich.

Nias, J. (1980) The ideal middle school: its public image, in A. Hargreaves and L. Tickle (eds.) *Middle Schools: Origins, Ideology and Practice*, Harper & Row, London.

Parlett, M. and Hamilton, D. (1976) Evaluation as illumination, in D. Tawney (ed.) *Curriculum Evaluation Today*, Macmillan, London.

Partington, G. (1976) School-focused INSET, *British Journal of In-Service Education*, Vol. 3, No. 1.

Razzell, A. (1979) Teacher participation in school decision-making, *Education*, Vols. 3–13, No. 7, p. 1.

Reid, W.A. (1978) *Thinking About the Curriculum*, Routledge & Kegan Paul, London.

Reid, W.A. (1979) Practical reasoning and curriculum theory: in search of a new paradigm, *Curriculum Inquiry*, Vol. 9, No. 3.

Richardson, D.A. (1981) Student–teacher attitudes towards decision-making in schools before and after taking up their first appointments, *Educational Studies*, Vol. 7, No. 1.

Rutter, M., Maughan, B., Mortimore, P. and Ouston, J. (1979) *Fifteen Thousand Hours: Secondary Schools and Their Effects on Children*, Open Books, London.

Sayer, J. (1979) INSET strategy of a large comprehensive school, *Cambridge Journal of Education* Vol. 9, Nos. 2 and 3, p. 95.

Sharp, R. and Green, A. (1975) *Education and Social Control*, Routledge & Kegan Paul, London.

Shipman, M., Bolam, D. and Jenkins, D. (1974) *Inside a Curriculum Project*, Methuen, London.

Simmons, L.M. (1980) Staff development in schools, *Curriculum*, Vol. 1, No. 1.

Skilbeck, M. (1976) School-based curriculum development and the task of in-service

education, in E. Adams (ed.) *In-Service Education and Teachers' Centres*, Pergamon Press, Oxford.
Smith, L.M. and Keith, P.M. (1971) *Anatomy of Educational Innovation*, Wiley, London.
Walker, D.F. (1975) Curriculum development in an art project, in W.A. Reid and D.F. Walker (eds.) *Case Studies in Curriculum Change*, Routledge & Kegan Paul, London.
Warwick, D. (1975) *School-Based In-Service Education*, Oliver & Boyd, Edinburgh.
Watkins, R. (ed.) (1973) *In-Service Training: Structure and Content*, Ward Lock Educational, London.
Weston, P. (1979) *Negotiating the Curriculum*, NFER, Windsor.

2.3
THE NEW INSET:
A TRANSFORMATION SCENE[1]*

Janet Harland

A great deal has already been said and written about the new arrangements for the planning, management and funding of INSET [In-Service Education and Training for Teachers], first as piloted in TRIST (TVEI [Technical and Vocational Education Initiative] Related In-Service Training) and then from 1987 continued via special grant from the DES [Department of Education and Science]. Rather than debate the issue at the level of detail, I propose to develop an argument that these changes imply a fundamental transformation in the role of teachers which goes beyond all or any of these elements. Firstly I intend to suggest that this transformation will happen as a result of the shift towards categorical funding (of which specific grant is a common form) and of the mechanisms which attach to such funding; and secondly, that it will be further strengthened as the DES imports ideas about in-service training from the sphere in which categorical funding strategies have been worked out and developed in relation to schools and colleges, i.e. in the Manpower Services Commission (MSC).

This shift towards categorical funding is one which is gathering pace as it is increasingly adopted by the DES (e.g. in the Lower Attaining Pupils Programme; the limited in-service grant schemes of 1983, 1984 and 1986; and the Education Support Grants established under the 1984 Education Act). It is widely interpreted as a conscious strategy chosen by the present administration to speed and increase the impact of government policies for education, and recent statements by the new Secretary of State seem to endorse this explanation. On the other hand, it may also be that a preference

*Harland, J. (1987) The new INSET: a transformation scene, *Journal of Educational Policy*, Vol. 2, No. 3, pp. 235–244.

for specific grant is a more or less inevitable aspect of the management style adopted by modern bureaucracies, including government departments, concerned to demonstrate closer links between inputs and outputs (Salter and Tapper, 1981). It certainly fits well with the kind of creeping centralism which has marked the past decade in most spheres of public life.

But the focus of this paper is a concern not with motivation but rather with impact. For it is certainly possible that the effects of this, or any other, new policy may go beyond that which is predicted or intended; and may indeed carry implications which are as damaging as the ills (and INSET has its share) which it is supposedly addressing.

The mid-1970s was a period of uncertainty about the nature and purpose of the in-service education and training of practising teachers. The James Report (DES, 1972) turned out to be yet one more impossible dream; in the utilitarian and pragmatic 1980s the rationale offered there for a 'professional' model sounds brave but foolish: 'to reflect and enhance the status and independence of the teaching profession and of the institutions in which many teachers are educated and trained'.

The 1978 report of the Advisory Committee on the Supply and Training of Teachers (ACSTT) sub-committee (DES, 1978) marked the beginning of a co-ordinated attempt to rationalize and plan for INSET in a manner which recognizes the needs of the system alongside those of the individual teacher (DES, 1978). But in the intervening years a new approach to curriculum change and development and the role of the teacher within it had emerged from the work of Lawrence Stenhouse and others associated with him, and had taken a firm grip on the practice of many of those providing INSET for teachers. This approach argues that teachers are central to the process not just of curriculum implementation but also of development; indeed that the problem of effecting genuine curriculum change had defied solution just because the task had so often been undertaken by project teams far away from the classroom and not directly involved in teaching children. The Stenhouse slogan of 'no curriculum development without teacher development' became the battle-cry of this approach and it has been identified with much of the most exciting INSET work over the past decade and a half. In this, the pace has undoubtedly been set by those who worked closely with Stenhouse himself.

This is not the place for an extended analysis of Stenhouse's thinking on the professional role of teachers but it is important to note that the slogan which acts as the shorthand for his views is essentially ambiguous. Does it mean that without sparky, innovative teachers no real curriculum development will take place? Or does it mean that if you want to change the curriculum, you had better ginger up the teachers (or else, by implication, they will undermine your efforts)? Put diagrammatically are we to read the statement as:

curriculum development → teacher development

or as

curriculum development ← teacher development

In the early and middle 1970s many saw the arrow moving firmly from right to left. Stenhouse (1975, 1980) himself continued to urge this interpretation; in his 1975 book he developed the concept of 'teacher as researcher (into her own practice)' and later, in 1980, he wrote that 'curriculum development is about teacher development'. The rationale, therefore, behind much INSET has been that by expanding the professional knowledge and understanding of teachers, we could ensure healthy curriculum development even if it proved difficult to predict what form that might take; indeed unpredictability is seen as a value in terms of both the curriculum itself and also of pupil-learning outcomes. The concept of teacher professionalism is here somewhat different from that of the James Report (DES, 1972) in that it is firmly focused on the classroom: the teacher is required to be the critic of his/her own practice, self-aware and therefore self-directing, and preferably acting in co-operation with colleagues.

Since the mid-1960s many factors had served as both a challenge and an opportunity for teacher-initiated change – the ending of selection, the raising of the school leaving age, the development of CSE, and the perennial expansion in numbers and types of pupil. The Schools Council's rhetoric encouraged (or perhaps did not choose to challenge) this situation though many commentators have remarked on the tension between the emphasis on teacher freedom and the parallel attempt to sponsor and to see adopted a range of often somewhat prescriptive projects developed by teams of experts. When the Council switched its policy in the late 1970s from projects to programmes it appeared, *inter alia*, to be looking for new ways to endorse the old principle of the centrality of teachers in the curriculum process. It has been pointed out that the Council in its projects (and to a degree in its programmes) was in the main taking up and systematizing innovation that was already established in some exceptional classroom practice. A somewhat parallel idea to this was the view that the central function of HMI should properly be the promotion of good practice on the Johnny Appleseed model of carrying news of innovation in one school to others on their circuit (see, for example, Lady Plowden's evidence given in the mid-1970s to the Expenditure Committee (1976) on Policy Making in the DES). Maurice

Kogan (1979) has summed up this faith in grass roots development: 'one of the glories of British school education is the way in which development has been practitioner-based'.

The importance of this conviction has been reflected in the practice of many of those institutions providing advanced courses for teachers. Though one can point to exceptions, there has persisted a notion that the primary rationale behind courses leading to an advanced qualification should be to produce a more informed, critical, reflective teacher who would then be better able to fill the 'professional' role; that this is a valuable INSET objective for very many teachers; and that INSET which is more specifically 'delivery orientated' is of obvious but more limited value. The whole character therefore of much INSET work – and indeed of much initial training – is based on a conception of teacher professionalism which stresses the primacy of the practitioner in the process of change and development.

Much of the development within the world of INSET since 1978 and particularly since 1983 has called this view into question. However, it is not enough to discuss these developments in isolation without first setting them in the context of the past decade. These ten years have seen the steady build-up of a deficit model of the education system in general, and teachers in particular; the story is well known to those who work in the field and is clearly strongly antipathetic to the notion that teachers are at first base in curriculum development. Less often remarked as part of the context for INSET change is the truly astounding growth of the 'training' industry across all aspects of national life, a movement responsible for creating a healthy amount of employment but which has sadly produced a veritable plague of spurious and ill-conceived workshops, seminars, courses and conferences. Thus there arises a view that when a school has a problem, rather than resolve the matter from within its own resources, someone should go on a course in order to bring back some expertise from elsewhere. And further, that someone outside the problem has a solution to offer.

To turn again to the particular, we must consider first the ACSET document of November 1984 (the name of ACSTT is now recast as the Advisory Committee on the Supply and *Education* of Teachers) and then the subtle transformation of its proposals in the DES response since the publication of *Better Schools* in March 1985 (DES, 1985). ACSET's document (DES, 1984) clearly built on the earlier report of their sub-committee (DES, 1978) in arguing for a much more coherent INSET policy. They wanted an emphasis on the *institution* in the assessment of need; in the identification of appropriate forms of delivery and of key people to receive the required training; and in the development of proper procedures for feeding the fruits of that training back into the institution so that its contribution to collective goals might be properly evaluated. The report envisages that each school should make an annual submission to the local education authority (LEA) which the authority would then reconcile with 'regional and national developments'. LEAs should receive a general grant for this purpose (possibly at the rate of 5 per cent of the teachers' salary bill) over which they should exercise discretion – though the committee accepts that the existing 'national priority scheme [see below] might be operated in parallel'. The present pooling arrangements should go, and short courses should be paid for 'at cost' so that LEAs would be in a position to gauge 'value for money' and therefore the relative costs of different types of provision.

When these ideas were reflected back in DES policy, there had been some significant transformations. It would seem, for a start, that the DES (1985, para. 174) judged that 'the in-service teacher training grants scheme introduced in 1983–84 has succeeded in stimulating training in selected national priority areas'. That scheme had offered limited funding for specified INSET activities and from this experience two lessons were clearly learned: firstly that it is highly efficacious to identify areas for training which support DES curriculum priorities and secondly, that a high level of control can be maintained through the mechanisms of categorical funding which oblige LEAs and INSET providers to march in step with DES policy. In *Better Schools* a new policy for all in-service training was accordingly set out. The DES accepted ACSET arguments for coherence, and the balancing of institutional need against LEA priorities; but from 1987 it was proposed to switch to specific rather than general grant in order that LEA INSET programmes should be subject to the oversight, guidance and approval of the DES. Within each programme the DES planned to look for a balance between 'national priority areas of training' and 'locally assessed priorities' (DES, 1985, para. 176) thus incorporating and expanding the limited grant schemes piloted in 1983 and 1984 while extending DES oversight to the whole of INSET.

The TRIST programme announced a month after the publication of *Better Schools* (MSC, 1985) was quite explicitly a dummy run for the new system. In implementing this trial, the MSC acted with its usual alacrity. Thus, in the summer of 1986 we saw the DES endeavouring to emulate that agility by asking LEAs to submit their plans for 1987–88 by October despite the fact that significant details about the global sum available, the basis of its distribution, the exact list of priority areas, and the looked-for balance between local and national needs were all not then known. Finally, in late August, the long-awaited circular was published and at last LEAs and others saw the precise figure for grant-aided expenditure (£200 million – rather less than hoped for), the list of priority areas (largely but not wholly predictable) and the balance between national and locally determined needs (35:65, a ratio more slanted to national needs than anticipated, and containing a further bias in that the national element is to be supported at the rate of 70 per cent of approved expenditure, whereas local needs will attract only 50 per cent). LEA advisers were thus able to devote the rest of their summer holiday to completing outline submissions.

But rather than go further into the details of the new scheme I want to attempt two distinct analytical exercises. In the first place I intend to look at the 'mechanisms' through which this new INSET strategy is to be implemented and to suggest that it will display certain significant characteristics that have already been explored through the MSC's TVEI and TRIST programmes, characteristics which are inherent in the nature of categorical funding. Secondly, I want to explore the relationship between curriculum development and teacher development implied by these strategies and show how this too has been shaped by MSC techniques which, in these matters, have been influenced by the interaction between the Commission and the Further Education Unit (FEU) a development unit sponsored by, and until recently a part of, the DES.

First then, the mechanisms. In implementing TVEI, I want to suggest that the MSC built on the experience of their previous ventures into low-level vocational training and special programmes of one kind and another for the young school leaver. To do this they used the inducement of resources in what I take to be a form of categorical funding, whereby a body which has neither the statutory right nor the means to implement its own policies, seeks to do so through agencies that have both and are prepared to deliver in exchange for the necessary moneys. In so far as the process relates to statutory rights, categorical funding acts as an effective, even if temporary, substitute for legislation: in so far as it relates to finding agencies to do something which the principal to the agreement either cannot or does not wish to do for itself, categorical funding comes very close to the kind of sub-contracting arrangements common in industry.

Within this strategy for policy implementation there appear to be certain key elements:

1. *Criteria* – by which it is made clear what is expected of those schemes to be submitted for approval.
2. *Bid* – the process by which the would-be provider indicates his proposals. This is invariably followed by a process of *negotiation* during which the original bid is brought as close as possible to the 'ideal' as set out by the criteria.

3. *Contract* – this represents the deal struck between the parties concerned. It forms the basis on which the licensee may proceed and the expectation is that any deviation not specifically allowed for (e.g. agreement about permitted scope for virement) should be *re-negotiated*.

4. *Monitoring* – normal patterns of accountability would indicate that the agency providing the funds should be able to satisfy itself that the terms of the contract are being met so a flow of information as to numbers, categories, outcomes and expenditure is demanded. This of course extends to the certification of expenditure and the auditing of accounts.

5. *Evaluation* – categorical funding requires of evaluation two somewhat contradictory characteristics: firstly a degree of independence so that special pleading and self-justification do not act as a smoke-screen to the provider's ineptitude; and yet secondly, a focus on the processes of implementation rather than any form of fundamental critique concerning the underlying goals or strategies of the programme.

6. *Replication* – a key task for the evaluator, and indeed for the agency receiving the funding, is to demonstrate the manner in which ripples are spreading through the system as a result of lobbing in the targeted money. In TVEI this is called *replication*; in INSET programmes it will presumably be called *impact*.

Those of us with a close acquaintance with TVEI have been aware of all these elements in the MSC's strategies and indeed have not found them universally negative. They do however have certain implications and these will in all probability have the same importance within the new arrangements for INSET for, without labouring the issue to the point of tedium, I want to suggest that here too it seems we can anticipate a process which includes elements of criteria, bid, negotiation, contract, monitoring, evaluation and replication. Those implications include the following:

● a notion that a successful bid equals a successful strategy, i.e. if the proposal is rewarded by funds it is by definition a good one;

● a devaluation of the concept of local autonomy: the apparent freedom *not* to bid, or not to bid at a particular level, is a sham;

● a conception of the LEA and its teachers as licensed agents of the DES, free to exercise initiative but within specified bounds (rather as the encyclopaedia salesman is encouraged to be enterprising but within the streets and using the credit arrangements authorized by the company);

● a key role for the prior identification of goals and needs (this in preference to an emergent and adaptive policy) which facilitates the monitoring and evaluation of performance and which fits so well with the planning models favoured by modern bureaucracy.

My argument is therefore that in the switch to new methods of funding, and therefore planning, in-service education LEAs will have to live with the characteristics of categorical funding, which are preoccupying in themselves for those who must operate within the rules and far-reaching in their implications for all those who are involved in schemes sponsored in this manner. The DES will control the criteria and may therefore rewrite them from time to time. It can also control the timing of the whole process. Crucially it will be able to use the negotiation phase to ensure that its conception of INSET is enshrined in LEA proposals and thereafter it can exploit its right to enforce a contract to keep a close watch on the process. Moreover, through requirements laid on the INSET programme, the DES will be able to reinforce the other demands it is, or might be, making on LEAs: for example to develop and enforce curriculum policies for their schools which accord with national guidelines; to make technical and vocational education available to all; to prioritize particular curriculum areas such as primary science, or computer studies for all; and many more. For their part schools and colleges will have to recognize that their LEA is operating under a system which has implications for them too.

I now turn to the relationship between curriculum development and teacher development implied by the new INSET, a relationship which I have already discussed in the early part of this paper. Here I want to argue that, if we accept that the DES has now developed a strategy which permits it to shape the style, delivery and even content of INSET to its own conception, we should now try to analyse what that conception might be and where it has come from. To do this I intend to begin by referring to the influence of the FEU.

Not only should the FEU receive the credit for systematizing pre-vocational education, turning an inchoate mass of local and regional responses to an emerging student need into a major element in curriculum provision for fourteen–eighteen-year-olds; but we should also recognize the efficiency with which the Unit has conceptualized and promoted a staff development strategy to go with it.

In considering this approach to staff development, I think we must at all times remember that it has emerged from a further education tradition of both curriculum design and pedagogy and therefore comes from the world of vocational training where it is quite normal and proper for those who practise a particular craft or trade to lay down what is required of the young people who are being prepared to join them. In that context it is easy to understand the FEU's slogan 'curriculum-led staff development'. It is also interesting to compare the phrase with that of Stenhouse: in terms of its key words we find that the FEU replaces one appearance of the word 'development' in the Stenhouse formulation with the word 'led' and there are clearly echoes between the two, perhaps even intentional ones. Indeed this apparently innocuous phrase has met with little criticism even in the school sector where it has appeared in connection with the development of pre-vocational courses. Moreover it is an apt description of the 'cascade' model use for GCSE staff training.

But let us consider further the elements within 'curriculum-led staff development'. It is suggested that teachers or lecturers preparing to cope with curriculum change should:

1. develop a checklist of skills and qualities derived from and demanded by the key components of the curriculum;
2. assess skills and experiences already possessed by teachers both collec-tively and individually;
3. identify staff needs as a basis for initiating staff development programmes (derived from FEU, 1982).

A later formulation of this process (Coombe Lodge, 1985) reduces it to a simple recipe:

Demands → Strengths → Needs

The FEU acknowledges that there are wide differences of opinion associ-ated with the concept of staff development (FEU, 1982). It identifies the 'professional' model favoured by the James Committee (DES, 1972) and it contrasts that with an 'organizational' model which is 'rooted in the needs of institutions and systems rather than those of individuals'. Its own model is one which is 'curriculum-led' thus, it claims, resolving the 'confusion' caused by other conflicting definitions 'by focusing on that which brings profession-als and organizations together, the demands of the curriculum'.

This formula and its justification is indeed neat and is undoubtedly effective in helping a group of teachers face the task of implementing a new course. Such an approach is clearly useful within the new orthodoxy of pre-vocational education where terms such as negotiation, experiential learning and problem-solving have become reifications rather than aspira-tions within curriculum discourse. As such this definition of staff develop-ment has, I suggest, penetrated first TVEI, then TRIST and now perhaps INSET as a whole.

But what is missing? Why does it seem so easy? Is it that we are now operating in a context where *the curriculum is a given*? In the FEU formula the curriculum is there, and it can and should lead staff development. But in the Stenhouse version it remains to be developed – or at least (as has already been proposed) that is the interpretation of his words which has largely shaped the work of teacher educators for a decade or more. Apple and Teitelbaum (1986) have written recently of the trend to divest teachers of any responsibility for conception in relation to the curriculum and to restrict them to matters relating to execution. They have pointed also to the de-skilling that results from this: loss of opportunity to use a skill results all too soon in the loss of the skill itself. What the FEU model offers us I suggest is a scenario in which the arrow inevitably moves from the predetermined curriculum towards teacher development, and never from the teacher's conception to the developing curriculum.

Of course such an interpretation can be hotly refuted. Much of the rhetoric coming from the DES, from the FEU and from the Joint Board for Pre-Vocational Education suggests that there is much for teachers to do in 'fleshing out the bones' of the courses they will teach. After all, so much curriculum formulation now comes to schools and colleges in the form of frameworks, guidelines, lists of core elements and skills, assessment procedures and so forth – surely these are mere skeletons leaving space for teacher input? Again I would refer to the analogy of the encyclopaedia salesman whose initiative is indeed welcomed by the company; but I suggest that freedom within tight rules is scarcely freedom in a sense which invites or permits genuine grass-roots innovation.

How does this reformulation of the relationship between curriculum development and teacher development align with the apparent intentions of the DES in engineering a very substantial change in in-service education and training? *Better Schools* provides a clue. There the theme is the

increasing demands which the government's policies for the schools will make on the teachers'
● practical teaching skills;
● breadth and depth of subject knowledge;
● knowledge of and skills in assessment.
Extensive in-service training will be needed to equip teachers to respond to these demands.
(DES, 1985, para. 172)

Essentially this paragraph maintains the deficit model of teachers. They are people who lack some or all of what is needed to meet the government's 'demands' and they must therefore be 'equipped' accordingly. Whether this is an organizational or a curriculum model of staff development seems to me to be immaterial, for whichever it is the clear implication is that staff development is going to be 'curriculum led'. It is clearly not a professional model and perhaps we would not want it to be in the status-orientated version of the James Report (DES, 1972). But neither is it a Stenhouse model and that does seem to undermine a conception of teacher professionalism which is heavily entrenched in the system and even appears fairly frequently in DES rhetoric. Yet it fits admirably in a scenario where teachers are not concerned or involved with curriculum development in anything but a trivial sense; in other words where, as in the FEU formulation, curriculum is a given in the staff development process. Such is the world of centrally controlled examinations with national criteria and core content, broadly agreed objectives across much of the curriculum, HMI-commended pedagogies based on experience gained from inspections and APU testing, and an increasingly 'managed' rhetoric about what should or should not be in the curriculum. If we are to move to a 'national curriculum' in the even tighter form proposed by the present Secretary of State, Kenneth Baker, no one will be pretending that teachers are much more than part of the delivery system. Yet the whole transformation has been and is being adroitly cloaked in phrases, words and slogans which have echoes and overtones of others that have captured the commitment of educators. Many LEAs have welcomed what they perceive as a chance to exercise more control over in-service education and training. They should perhaps consider these words of Apple's (1982): 'The strategic import of the logic of technical control in schools . . . lies in its ability to integrate into one discourse what are often seen as competing ideological movements and hence, to generate consent from each of them.' Perhaps some LEAs are proving too ready to read into the new arrangements the messages they prefer to hear rather than to think through the implications of curriculum led staff development.

The argument of this paper is then, that the funding of in-service education and training through specific grant involves mechanisms such as bid and contract (and others already described) which reinforce and rigidify a conception of curriculum control and development as something logically prior to teacher development; and therefore, intentionally or not, it undermines the professionalism of teachers in a form which has been the object and rationale of much of the best of both initial and in-service education.

NOTES

1. Lest the imagery of the transformation scene escape some readers who lack the benefit of my North country wartime childhood, I should say that such delights come at the end of Act I of the traditional pantomime. With all the technical gadgetry at his command, the producer transforms the stage into fairyland, or the magician's cave, or Neptune's ocean kingdom. The flying ballet swings out over the more expensive seats in the stalls, and a few already privileged children scramble for toffees from heaven. So we are all transported to the land of make-believe: eyes open wide and jaws drop. But it is over all too soon: the magic was just a trick. We are left in our utility (utilitarian?) world where there aren't even any choc-ices.

REFERENCES

Apple, M. (1982) *Cultural and Economic Reproduction in Education*, Routledge & Kegan Paul, London.

Apple, M. and Teitelbaum, K. (1986) Are teachers losing control of their skills and curriculum?, *Journal of Curriculum Studies*, Vol. 18, No. 2, pp. 177–84.

Coombe Lodge (1985) *Staff Development Analysis*, FESC Working Paper.

DES (1972) *Teacher Education and Training* (the James Report), HMSO, London.

DES (1978) Advisory Committee on the Supply and Training of Teachers (ACSTT), *Making INSET Work*, HMSO, London.

DES (1984) Advisory Committee on the Supply and Education of Teachers (ACSET), *Proposals on INSET*, HMSO, London.

DES (1985) *Better Schools*, HMSO, London.

DES (1986) *Local Education Authority Training Grants Scheme: Financial Year 1987–88*, Circular 6/86, DES, London.

Expenditure Committee of the House of Commons (1976) *Policy Making in the DES*, Cmnd 6678, HMSO, London.

FEU (1982) *Teaching Skills*, Further Education Unit, London.

Kogan, M. (1979) Educational policy making and analysis, *Educational Analysis*, Vol. 1, No. 2, pp. 5–14.

MSC (1985) Letter from Bryan Nicholson to LEAs.

Salter, B. and Tapper, T. (1981) *Education, Politics and the State*, Grant McIntyre, London.

Stenhouse, L. (1975) *An Introduction to Curriculum Research and Development*, Heinemann, London.

Stenhouse, L. (1980) *Curriculum Research and Development in Action*, Heinemann, London.

2.4
THE ROLE AND PRACTICE OF EVALUATION IN LOCAL EDUCATION AUTHORITIES OR EVALUATION . . . SO WHAT

Ray Shostak*

INTRODUCTION

This chapter explores some of the issues which surrounded the move towards a greater emphasis on evaluation in the UK education service. It suggests that to date local education authorities (LEAs) have developed approaches to evaluation by unsystematically exploring different ways of reviewing their work.

1. Historically there has been little call for LEAs and schools to account for what they were doing and only cursory attempts at evaluation. The service was characterized by an over-reliance on myth and tradition.
2. Early evaluation then responded to an increasingly questioning public and was, at this stage, characterized by the 'self-evaluation' movement.
3. Later, evaluation efforts responded to categorical funding and the battle for control over education. This stage was characterized by the use of external evaluators.

It is argued that this developing process and change of emphasis has led to the realization that the search for information and evidence to help decision-making has to replace the previous reliance on tradition and myth. In simple terms evidence had to replace hunch.

The chapter concludes by offering a set of principles and a strategy for LEAs to structure their educational evaluation for the 1990s.

* First publication.

There are those who pose the simple question 'What good is education?' and those who have to answer it. Clearly, the answers have not convinced the questioners for they continue to repeat the question. Perhaps, as educationalists, we have provided answers of insufficient clarity or detail. Perhaps this is because we have been 'haters of information' and too 'committed to mythology'. Indeed, it could be argued that evidence has often been presented to help us improve practice, but we have chosen to ignore it.

For an intriguing parallel we can look to the work of Ignac Semmelweis. He collected evidence about hospital practice and from his observations suggested that patients were dying for reasons other than those commonly believed in the medical profession. He presented evidence that doctors were often going directly from the morgue to maternity patients and inferred that this fact might be connected with the high death rate. He suggested that doctors should wash their hands before touching mothers in labour. There was outrage.

He continued to present his data and his analysis but he continued to be ignored. The simple truth was that his process of collecting data and analysing it to inform practice was less believable than the 'mythology' which allowed the medical profession to retain its traditional practices.

Education in the UK may similarly be described as teetering on a foundation of mythology and tradition. Evidence, as with Semmelweis, is not something which is heavily traded in educational circles. Personal and professional change is always difficult – the seduction of the security and the power of the past can result in the impotence of complacency – the challenge of evidence has to be faced.

For the purposes of this exploration the following definition of educational evaluation is used: The systematic collection and analysis of evidence with a view to improving the quality of the educational experience.

Two fundamental principles underpin what follows. The first is that the only thing of importance within the educational service is the quality of the educational experience for students. The second principle is that LEA decision-makers have a right to seek and provide evidence about the quality of the education their students experience.

What follows should be read as an attempt to put our evaluation work within a developmental context. Although the approaches to evaluation may have been right at the time, they may no longer be appropriate. We can perhaps learn from considering these developments. We too must not ignore the evidence. The challenge for LEAs is to define and develop evaluation programmes and strategies which contribute more powerfully to the development of their practice.

Ray Shostak 137

THE FIRST AGE OF EVALUATION: AN AGE OF SELF EVALUATION

The first age of evaluation began in the UK in the late 1960s and early 1970s. It was developed, as is much change in education, in response to the demands of the time and it represented a step towards the search for evidence about what was happening in schools. Although short lived, there remain within the service remnants of this early approach. These first attempts at formal educational review were problematic because:

(a) there was little tradition of educational review or accountability rooted in evidence within which to place the work;
(b) the people who had practised educational evaluation previously had confused roles and little or no credibility with their variety of audiences;
(c) there was not an adequate or common language with which to report educational practice to the audiences.

Until this point education had been under the jurisdiction of 'the individual professional' and evaluation was something done in the privacy of one's own classroom, except on odd occasions between two consenting adults. The system was relatively unaffected by control or interference from outside the school by HMI, LEA, governors and parents. The service had been hitherto run by 'gentlemen' in a 'civilized' way and remained rooted, if not ossified, in tradition. HMI reports were confidential documents, government reports on education were few and far between and in general there was an unquestioned confidence in the work of schools. There was an expansion of higher education and school leavers were finding employment; all in the secret garden was blooming.

The service, then, could truly be characterized as one based on hunch rather than evidence. Myths and folk traditions abound in the absence of evidence. There was the myth of the 'ideal teacher' who, whilst being a pillar of the community, had a vocation and worked for love. There was the myth of the 'school' as a natural place for children to learn. There were myths about 'child-centred education', 'open-plan schools', 'new mathematics', 'comprehensive schools' – without any hard evidence and certainly no established channels of communication the myths surrounding such aspects of the service turned into legends. It was as though the service was perpetuated and sustained at every level by a belief that all was well – all was assumed to be well because so few were questioning in depth.

In the early 1970s, however, questions began to be asked with increasing vehemence about what was being taught within schools, the way in which it was being taught and, more fundamentally, by whom. Questions came from parents, governors and government in both local and national forums. Quite simply, people wanted to know what was going on in their schools. This was interpreted as the stakeholders wanting to hold the system to account. The reasons for this are documented elsewhere but the response from the educational service was to produce evidence – of a kind.

Those within LEAs charged with the task began to search for ways to produce the evidence, which they believed was there, to assure those outside that all was indeed well. From a protected lack of information about what went on in schools these early moves signalled the beginning of the information revolution.

Evidence began to be produced and often it received the same response as that to Semmelweis. This was partly because of the perceived credibility of those who were producing it and partly because of the quality of the evidence itself. Reports began to emerge from HMI and LEA advisers, but mostly from teachers themselves.

HMI's contribution to LEA work, traditionally in the arena of the full school inspection, began to be replaced by a broader 'system-wide' approach to information. This change may be documented in a study of DES publications during and after the 'Great Debate'. Full inspections of individual schools by HMI would subsequently be only one contribution to the quest of raising standards in our schools. There was also a recognition, perhaps for the first time, that cycles of full inspections across the educational spectrum with a limited inspectorate was not a realistic proposition. More significantly it began to be questioned whether there were not more appropriate staff to do such work, such as the local authority inspectors and advisers. As the traditional role of HMI shifted from full inspection of schools the implications for the role of LEA inspectors and advisers was put on the educational agenda. As HMI reported to central government, the LEA inspectors and advisers in turn could serve local government – it was a logical step to suggest that appropriate responsibility should be undertaken by appropriate people in the appropriate arena.

The subsequent expectations about the contribution of LEA inspection and advisory services in this first age of evaluation led to a clearer understanding of the tension and duality within the role. Were they the evaluators for the LEA or were they the teachers' friend? This tension was not new, indeed it is exemplified by the contrasting use of the words 'inspector' and 'adviser' across and within LEAs. In the 'soft' educational world this tension could be avoided but the new 'hard' world of information began to challenge the status quo. LEA decision-makers began to make more 'inspectorial' demands upon advisers only to discover that many were inspecting work they had advised teachers to do – in a very real sense they were inspecting their own work. Issues relating to the generation of criteria for evaluation and the skill development of the LEA advisers and inspectors relating to their fitness to evaluate began to be raised – mostly to be avoided.

Perhaps the largest proportion of the evaluation work carried out at this time was that undertaken by teachers through a process of 'self-evaluation'. The response to the demand for more information about what was happening was instantaneous. In a short space of time schools and LEAs began paper-based approaches which were soon labelled as 'death by a thousand questions'. The purpose of these schemes and schedules was often unclear. Were they designed to improve teacher practice by suggesting a range of laudable activities? Were they to glean evidence for a political defence of the school? Were they to meet LEA requirements? Although some of these evaluation schemes led to serious questioning and development, many were exercises in creative writing. There was little preparation for teachers to do this work and the skills relating to the administration of such evaluations were rarely developed. It was another demand to be absorbed by the mythologically omnicompetent teachers.

Teachers, officers and advisers who had previously just got on with their job were now required formally to evaluate their work. All of a sudden public documents were being demanded in an arena where there was no tradition of asking, let along answering, searching questions. Apart from a consideration of the new skills required for such a process there were questions posed relating to the ethics of such work, the time taken and the processes needed to validate the nature of the evaluation. Such considerations left many schools and teachers perplexed. A common result was a lack of clear purpose for such evaluations leading to compromise and questionable evidence, often in an unusable state. Reports were regularly written in a quasi-academic language which became meaningless to many of the audiences who were to receive them.

Evaluations with a complexity of purpose tend to become broad-based inquiries, and if this is coupled with reports aiming to serve a variety of stakeholders the process seems destined for failure. At best such processes raise more questions than they answer. Indeed the 'self-evaluation movement' may be characterized by much wasted teacher time, a great deal of paper-based activity, no clear criteria for judgement and little ownership by many teachers, schools or LEAs: all this resulting in a poor defence of the system – one of the points of the exercise. This work often failed to fulfil either the service's need to account for itself, or the individual's need to develop professionally.

In this atmosphere, which extended into the early 1980s, parents and governors, the government and the public at large merely increased the volume of their demand to be informed about the work of schools and, more significantly, began to request clear judgement about the quality of teacher performance. After all, if you ask a question and receive an inadequate answer the least you do is ask the question again. There were additional demands for the DES to 'give a firmer lead' to the work in schools and although there was still respect for the legitimate use of professional judgement, the view that only teachers had a right to give direction to education was challenged. Teacher autonomy was now an outdated concept; the myth, as well as the legend, had been exposed.

So education, and the evaluation of it, became a populist issue in the UK in the late 1960s and the 1970s. The age of accountability had dawned but the belief that the profession could be accountable to itself was no longer sustainable.

THE SECOND AGE OF EVALUATION: THE EXTERNAL EVALUATOR

The political climate of the 1980s saw a continued disenchantment with the education service. The questions which were being raised about teachers and teaching continued and the increased intervention by central government in education brought a new demand for evaluation. The lack of clarity about the role of LEAs in evaluating the work of schools was to be compounded by the battle over control of the curriculum.

In 1982 the DES introduced the first of what was to become a new approach – categorical funding or specific grants, intended to improve a particular area of work in schools. Finance for such initiatives was allocated through a competitive bidding system, allegedly enabling LEAs to have access to additional funding for those purposes identified by the DES. This early funding was followed swiftly by Technical and Vocational Education Initiative (TVEI), Education Support Grants (ESGs), TVEI Related In-Service Training (TRIST) and recently by the funding of all in-service teacher training.

So came the second age of educational evaluation, on the coat-tails of the new educational imperatives. The Lower Attaining Pupils Programme TVEI, 'specific grants' for In-Service Education and Training for Teachers (INSET) and educational projects each demanded educational evaluation. What was notable was that although the audience shifted, the purposes continued to remain unclear, masked by the demand for 'value for money'.

The evaluation debate was focused sharply on specific initiatives but many of the questions from the first age remained unanswered. In an economy which left local authorities with restricted finances, with a falling school population and in a time of educational consumerism, LEAs had little choice but to play the game 'Hunt the new money'. This became an important task within education departments and one of the rules of the game was to give a clear commitment to evaluation.

In many of these schemes the DES or MSC commissioned 'outsiders' to provide judgements about the work being undertaken on their behalf. Not surprisingly, many LEAs began to mirror this approach by commissioning 'external evaluations' of the execution of the scheme at LEA level. Central government through either the DES or MSC advertised for evaluators and research agencies, and researchers began framing proposals for such external educational evaluation. Once again the precise purposes of these evaluations were often confused and LEAs were still uncertain about the use of the evidence and information gathered.

Projects and programmes started to have their evaluator, or team of evaluators. As there was little clarity regarding what criteria could be used for making judgements about practice, evaluations were often framed as 'formative'. Consequently, LEAs had a range of 'external evaluators' working to inform the development of often very complex projects involving a number of schools. The new evaluators marketed skills which, by implication, were not held in LEAs, but although providing external evaluations became big business they were regularly done on a part-time basis from an LEA perspective.

One difficulty of working part-time on an evaluation was that evaluators had difficulty keeping up with the work of large programmes. Indeed, given the range and complexity of project work, adopting the formative approach meant that feedback was often so incomplete or slow it had limited value to the individuals and LEAs involved. This time-lag in response created a distance, not dissimilar to that created with the 'central teams' of the old centre-periphery curriculum development projects. Consequently problems began to arise where the evaluators, who themselves were informing 'value for money decisions', were being questioned in relation to their own worth. The lack of clarity and clear contracting left many unfulfilled expectations and generated a loss of confidence in the role of the external evaluator. In reality, given the lack of clear purpose, the dimensions of most evaluation tasks, the limited time to do them and the climate in which they were working, the evaluators' contribution was always likely to be peripheral to the work of the project or programme.

Nevertheless, the trend continued and external evaluations continued to be a source of revenue for the research community. This led to the roles of researcher, evaluator and development worker becoming blurred and confused. Often those doing the evaluations were operating as researchers and developers simultaneously. The emerging troupe of evaluators began to suffer in practice from the same dilemma as the local authority advisers and inspectors. They often became marginal and unable to detach themselves from the actual programme they were evaluating because of their natural desire to influence its development. In other cases they discovered that they could not deliver what LEAs wanted them to. The evaluation scene continued to be characterized by confused purposes, expectations and audiences.

In the wider context, the developing role of the externally contracted evaluator stood side by side with changing roles nationally and within LEAs. Although it had never been the prime task of HMI formally to service local authority or school evaluation schemes, its day-to-day work often contributed to the process. The continued shift of the role of HMI from local to national level during this second age was enhanced as demands, at national level, for evaluative information grew. The local role of the HMI began to be eroded and replaced by national responsibilities and requests for information on grant-aided projects. There has in recent years been a substantial increase in the 'situation report', the 'HMI discussion document' and the 'national inquiry'. This shift which looked inevitable in the 1970s was being reflected in the 1980s with publicly accessible HMI reports on schools, full LEA reports by HMI and the national curriculum work mandated by the DES.

This trend was also reflected in the increased concern regarding the role of the LEA advisory/inspection services. Discussion papers were produced by the DES and statements ensued regarding the role of the LEA advisers and inspectors and the distinction between the two became increasingly apparent. Their Janus-like role came increasingly under suspicion as questions were raised about the 'independence' of their judgement. Some LEAs began to consider separating out the variety of roles of the traditional adviser and their position *vis-à-vis* systems for local accountability came under some scrutiny.

This second age also heralded a focus on appraisal, a much more judgemental view of evaluation. At first there was a tendency to view appraisal as a process which could be used to eliminate incompetence, as such appraisal has a direct link with accountability. Indeed, much educational time and energy has been used in debating the relative merits of appraisal as 'pure' judgement related to conditions of service and career issues as opposed to appraisal as part of professional development. This very debate has resulted in appraisal activities becoming both defensive and fraught within the 'politics' of industrial action. It is no accident that this coincided with the educational disputes of the mid-1980s and created a temporary diversion within the profession, and an opening for those looking for greater central control. One poignant reflection about evaluation in the context of this second age is that external evaluators were able to make a contribution at a time when those in school appeared unwilling to engage in the process.

As in the first age there were ethical considerations too, including arguments about qualitative versus quantitative approaches, the place of values and procedural ethics such as confidentiality within an evaluation, the strengths of formative evaluation and summative approaches and the impact of the evaluator on the process itself. These theoretical tensions may have hidden the confused understandings about the role of the evaluators, their audience and the political context for such work. Both the 'sponsors' of the evaluations and the evaluators themselves continued to grope for a positive way forward which would cope with the increasing demands for educational judgement.

This second age reflected quickly changing roles and a struggle for control of the curriculum both of which radically influenced the educational agenda. There remains at this stage a confusion about the precise purpose of evaluation. However, there is much to be learned from the two ages described and there is a choice for LEAs between continuing the confusion within their evaluation work or making an explicit decision to move into a third age of 'evidence-based' decision-making. We have seen the increasing demands to make the education service accountable, now enshrined in the new Education Acts. We have come to realize that categorical funding is firmly a part of the educational scene and yet, as with the Ignac Semmel-weis's parallel, many patients, or LEAs' involvement in curriculum decision-making, continue to die despite much evidence pointing to the cause of death.

THE THIRD AGE OF EVALUATION: SYSTEMATIC PROGRAMMES OF LEA EVALUATION

What does the evidence suggest for future local authority evaluation work? The suggestion is that LEAs must enter a third age of evaluation in which they take the initiative and formulate coherent evaluation programmes to meet the specific needs of their future. A second suggestion is that LEAs should design a programme of training and support to sustain their coherent evaluation programmes.

It is becoming increasingly essential that LEAs take control of the educational agenda and develop a range of rigorous and systematic evaluative activities – and turn these into a coherent LEA evaluative programme to support the development of practice and inform decision-makers and decision-making. Put bluntly, the future work of an LEA is only likely to be maintained if there is an accompanying presentation of real evidence of effective performance. This suggests that LEAs have a survival need to develop 'formal' evaluative machinery to support programmes they wish to continue, and furthermore that appropriate staff are trained and supported to implement these activities. Obviously, those who gather the evidence and carry out its subsequent analysis will need specific skills and time to do the work. Policy-makers will need to ensure that the evidence gives direction to the educational system of the future. However useful the evaluation movement has been before, it must now become a fundamental part of both the development and decision-making processes within LEAs. LEAs and schools must begin to work from evidence, not myth.

In developing such an evaluation programme within an LEA another suggestion is that a set of principles agreed by all concerned will be a vital clarifying factor. LEAs must use such principles to inform the formulation of a programme of evaluation which will need to include the bringing together of both appraisal – the judgement of practice – and appraisal – the informing of practice. Without such a clear set of principles to guide future action, confusion could continue to prevail leaving LEAs with disparate and conflicting evaluation work.

A review of the first two ages highlights that much evaluation work in the past has been motivated out of a deficiency model of teachers – identify the bad ones. A further suggestion is therefore that approaches to educational evaluation begin from the assumption that those working within an LEA wish to enhance the quality of the educational experience, and wish to create the conditions where schools and the LEA as a whole can systematically improve that experience for the students. Leading from the above the following principles for evaluation are offered:

(a) that an LEA has a right to know both what is going on in its institutions and the needs of those institutions, the students and the teachers;
(b) that students have a right to well-qualified and skilled teachers whose skills and qualifications will be updated and matched to current and new tasks;
(c) that the LEA has a right to expect staff to be active in refining, developing and expanding their skills and performance;
(d) that whilst an LEA has the right to initiate an evaluation programme, that right is best exercised through supporting the development of local procedures;
(e) that those within the service will need support in developing the evaluative skills required to operate an LEA programme of evaluation;
(f) that the LEA should manage its resources in a way which enables

teachers, alongside others including parents and governors, to take an active part in the determination of criteria to judge and develop performance;

(g) that those being evaluated have a right of access to anything which is written about them and that right also includes a right to respond and a right to appeal;

(h) that staff have a right to expect a negotiated and planned programme of professional development based on feedback on their performance;

(i) that *all* staff within an LEA should be part of the evaluation programme if trust and confidence is to generated.

What is argued here is that LEAs should recognize that there are a number of strands to an evaluation strategy and that each has a distinct contribution to make. Only by clearly identifying the contribution of each strand can LEAs build coherent strategies. Moreover, included within an LEA strategy should be separate evaluation tasks which:

(a) inform the development of classroom practice in order to service the needs of teachers;

(b) judge the performance and effectiveness of individual teachers and schools in order to service the needs of parents, governors and LEAs;

(c) judge the effectiveness of individual LEA programmes or strategies in order to service the needs of LEAs and other paymasters.

There is much to be done to create a programme which is capable of delivering the three evaluatation tasks outlined. A major task is to ensure that there are staff within LEAs with the skills and time to deliver such activities, but the first step is coming to understand the principles as outlined earlier.

In understanding these principles one needs to clarify responsibilities for classroom activity. Embedded within the set of principles is the assumption that the prime responsibility for the delivery of what happens in classrooms is located within the school, indeed with the teacher. By ascribing such responsibility the LEA must ensure that each teacher has the appropriate resources and skills, only then can an LEA reasonably hold teachers accountable. This school focus shifts the traditional mythology and is a prerequisite for evaluation and development.

It will also be important to identify the new roles which staff within an LEA would need to take. In doing so it will be important to recognize the contribution judgement makes to the development process and not just see its purpose as weeding out the incompetent. Following the set of principles each of the three evaluation tasks should become part of a whole programme of support rather than isolated activities.

The first evaluation task is to inform the development of classroom practice in order to service the needs of teachers. There is now some considerable experience both within the UK and abroad which informs evaluation focused primarily on the professional development of teachers. Local authorities should now ensure that it becomes common practice for all professionals to study their practice more formally and more systematically with a view to its improvement. The audience for this work will be teachers themselves. Such work can empower teachers to take ownership of their practice through a greater understanding of their work, rooted in evidence. This form of evaluation may become recognized as an important aspect of a teacher's duties and attention would need to be paid to the skills required to study practice. Consideration must also be given to the most appropriate climate for such work and the kind of help needed to support teachers in such an endeavour. Such evaluation would begin to develop a new theory of practice and, as its audience is the individual teacher, within the context of their school it may be built into appropriate programmes of school improvement. Given the nature of this task it is, of course, best managed at institutional level. Indeed, it may be that such evaluation information may never need to leave the school.

The second evaluation task of judging the performance and effectiveness of individual teachers and schools in order to service the needs of parents, governors and LEAs is perhaps the most problematic for many LEAs. As we saw earlier, there has been a traditional lack of clarity about the role of LEA advisers and inspectors in relation to evaluation and inspection. In many LEAs they have 'inspected by sleuth'. The time has come where LEAs must recognize that there will be evaluation demands which require an 'independent' educational judgement which is outside the school. HMI can never, nor was it intended to, service the needs of LEAs at the level required. The present real demands for accountability mean such work will soon become mandatory. The implications of this are that LEAs will need to develop appropriate staff to validate, monitor and assess the work of teachers and schools. Additionally, such work will require a clarity of criteria for judgement and a clear view of the skills required when working with teachers in such a role.

The third evaluation task, that of judging the effectiveness of individual LEA programmes or strategies in order to service the needs of LEAs and other paymasters, recognizes that within the educational world of the 1980s and 1990s there will be an increasing need for judgements about educational programmes or projects. Policy-making is not about individual classrooms, but about the collective view. Whilst individual schools are responsible for their practice, the LEA is responsible for creating the circumstances where that practice can be developed, and monitoring it within the broader context. The audience and focus of this third strand of evaluation within the local authority must be recognized as being different from the first two. The audience is the educational policy-makers or educational paymasters, be they local or central government. These groups have and will continue to have a right to assure themselves that the money they allocate on behalf of their constituents is being most efficiently and effectively spent. So, the audiences for such work are the paymasters and the purpose is clearly to ensure that resources are being allocated to their maximum advantage. As they face the decision to grant new money or relocate limited resources there is no other rational way of proceeding than that based on evidence. It should be clear that evaluations providing this evidence are owned by the pay-masters and that reporting must be clearly for them. Other benefits from such evaluations must be recognized as secondary. Again, this will mean agreeing clear criteria for success and searching for evidence in relation to those criteria. The implementation of these activities might be performed by task teams of seconded teachers, officers, advisers, paymasters of outside consultants – depending upon the task. They would perhaps best be managed by bringing a variety of perspectives to bear on any particular programme. What is certain is that the work related to these tasks will, as previously, demand both time and skills.

Evaluation is a skilled task. Although recognizing that 'informal' evaluation goes on minute by minute, day by day and term by term within schools, there is a need to become more rigorous in our evaluative study of practice against agreed criteria. There is a need to develop both the clear criteria to work from and the skills of focusing on evidence. There is additionally a need to clarify precisely who within the LEAs can, and should, carry out the important evaluation tasks which face the service, and recognize that each, from differing perspectives, has a part to play in improving the quality of experience. This will demand considerable training of teachers, advisers/inspectors and officers.

It is also important that LEAs learn that the three evaluation tasks require different information and are best serviced by different groups: the location of the first being within schools and about individual professional development; the second being located at LEA level and about organization and performance; and the third being an LEA service function addressing the deployment of resources. These evaluation tasks are likely to demand different approaches, supported by different staff and using different methodologies. No longer can we believe that one evaluation task is able to serve both the complex and various purposes or the variety of audiences which demand evidence.

In conclusion, LEAs must learn that from each evaluation activity must come action. The first evaluation must lead to the development of day-to-day practice; the second must be seen to ensure that individuals and schools are effectively meeting the demands of parents and governors in delivering LEA policy; and the third must enable LEA decision-makers to locate, or relocate, resources to maximize the benefit of educational provision in the community. Without specific action, suggested by the evaluation's evidence, a massive amount of time, energy and resources will continue to be wasted.

Finally the Ignac Semmelweis parallel is informative – he didn't give up, he continued to present his evidence and his analysis. Eventually his colleagues tried his approach and followed his suggestions – the death rate dropped.

2.5
THE LIMITATIONS OF
PROGRAMME EVALUATION
Saville Kushner and Barry MacDonald*

INTRODUCTION AND SUMMARY

Curriculum development has been an active concern of governments for at least thirty years now. For the last twenty years, since it became clear that the task was a difficult one, developments have been monitored by evaluators. The evaluation agenda has expanded in that time, from an initial focus on student-learning outcomes to the study of cases (programmes, schools, individuals) as a better way of understanding the problems and effects of change. Evaluators have become the storytellers and theorists of innovation.

On the whole the early experiences of developers and evaluators alike led them to suggest that central initiatives should give way to local initiatives within a framework of facilitative support. They emphasized, too, that the possession of ideas was a prerequisite of teacher and institutional commitment to their effective implementation. The message was received and understood but, in the rapidly deteriorating economic circumstances of the 1970s, was overwhelmed by other messages offering more persuasive scenarios. The government view, asserted initially in the form of the National Development Programme in Computer Assisted Learning (NDPCAL) (MacDonald *et al.*, 1975) was that only more direct central control of new curriculum sponsorship could ensure that its priorities received due attention from the education professionals. NDPCAL, with civil servants at the helm, was launched in 1973. Since that time, but more dramatically during the period of office of the present government, we have seen the government move to centre stage in curriculum determination, exercising more and more control of development funding, concentrating more and more of that

* First publication.

funding in fewer and larger programmes, and settling for compliance rather than commitment from its weakened local education authority (LEA) and teacher 'partners' in the curriculum enterprise. The organic community metaphors of growth advocated by the educational theorists of curriculum development have been rejected in favour of hard-nosed social engineering. The concept of partnership has given way to the concept of the task force with an unambiguous mission.

Evaluators were among those who foresaw with some alarm this concentration of political power, and feared the threat it could pose to their freedom to inform those who could reasonably be construed as entitled to know what was going on (MacDonald, 1974). It is one thing to tell the story of the entrepreneurial individuals like Lawrence Stenhouse who in the 1960s were enabled by sponsorship to set up their personal stalls in the marketplace of teacher consumerism and ply their curriculum visions. The case for having an evaluator to check on the developers' claims, to help the buyer beware, and to inform the sponsors about what the projects were doing and learning, was fairly straightforward and broadly acceptable in political terms. But it is quite another thing to tell a similar story about programmes where civil servants are in the front line of accountability to government ministers for the successful implementation of politically important curriculum developments. And that is where we are now.

Evaluations have always, by and large, been commissioned by administrators responsible for sponsoring the developments to which the evaluations were attached. That remains the case although it is important to note that contemporary preferences for two levels of evaluation, national and local, mean that the commissioning takes place at the two levels of administrative responsibility for programme enactment. The difference, and this is crucial to the argument of this paper, is that at both levels these administrators have become programme managers rather than programme facilitators. This enhanced responsibility, whilst increasing their need for evaluation as a cybernetic loop, has heightened their sensitivity to bad news about programme development, and has encouraged them to seek more control over both the agenda and the reporting of evaluative inquiry. There can be little doubt that these efforts to control evaluation have been highly successful. The hope that evaluation, carried out by institutions and individuals not implicated in programme responsibility, would help a wide range of audiences to reach informed judgements of the merits of new curriculum directions, that it might help to democratize the processes of curriculum policy-making, has not been fulfilled. The paucity and the blandness of public reports fail to expose the quantity of evaluation now taking place, or the turmoil, disruption, conflicts and contradictions inherent in the processes of systematic planned change. The 'secret garden' survives, but under new ownership. In this paper we will draw upon our own recent experience of evaluation to enlarge upon this proposition, to articulate more precisely the nature of the constraints to which we have drawn attention, and finally to argue the need for alternative sources of programme evaluation sponsorship. Of course we accept the fact that not everyone sees evaluation as primarily a source of credible public knowledge, let alone as a theory of political interaction (MacDonald, 1974, MacDonald *et al.*, 1975). This is a particular view of the evaluator as a democratic agent with privileged access to social service initiatives, and we shall, as our thesis unfolds, refer to other, certainly more widely practised views of the evaluative responsibility. But we cannot be alone in our growing anxiety about authoritarian trends in educational policy-making, or in perceiving a decline in both informed challenge and informed support in relation to the impact of these trends on the experience of schooling. Evaluators have a modest, but important role to play in creating the data base of communal participation in shaping the future of curriculum. That role, we will contend, is no longer acceptable to the managers of curriculum innovation.

We shall begin with an overview of the evaluation process in this context, looking at the relationship between evaluators and sponsors, and at ways in which evaluators typically construe their responsibilities and opportunities. Following that, we shall offer an issues-based analysis of the problems we encountered as independent evaluators of one local project under the aegis of categorical funding, taking the case as illustrative of more general problems associated with that framework. Our concluding section looks ahead to an uncertain future, and explores some strategic possibilities for rescuing this particular public information service from the threat of emasculation.

PROGRAMME EVALUATION – PARTICIPANT AND NOT-SO-PARTICIPANT ROLES

Evaluation is an interrogative activity, intended to yield useful knowledge about social action. 'Useful to whom?' is of course the obvious question. In a democracy such as ours, where ends, means, and perhaps especially priorities are always at issue, utility is problematic. What is useful for some may disadvantage others. Evaluation takes time, and therefore money. In the case of national programmes with action sites spread across the country, we are talking about quite a lot of time and quite a lot of money. To give you some idea, take the case of the Educational Support Grant-funded initiatives in primary science. The DES is paying more than half a million pounds for a four-person evaluation of this programme. Programme evaluation is expensive, and those who can afford it are rarely indifferent to its potential impact. Even if those who pay the evaluation piper don't exactly call the tune, they are not averse to restricting the repertoire. As we have already indicated, the great majority of programme evaluations are, directly or indirectly, commissioned by the executive agencies of central government. Naturally enough they want from the evaluator knowledge that is useful to them about programmes they initiate and manage.

These civil servant managers who commission evaluations are vulnerable to unfavourable judgements of the policies they are implementing or of the ways in which they have chosen to prosecute them. Typically they seek from the evaluator knowledge that will increase their control over programme participants and maintain fidelity of interpretation and action across distributed and distant sites. They also want evaluators to assist development at the local level, to help participants make the most of their piece of the action. They do not want, and will strenuously oppose, policy evaluation of a kind that could embarrass their superiors by raising questions about the validity of the programme rationale. Neither do they want their own performance as managers evaluated, though they may welcome confidential, off-the-record advice. Evaluators, faced with these sensitivities, and not without an interest in their own marketability, tend to adopt one of two roles, both readily tolerable to programme managers. The first is that of ally, auxiliary, or emissary of management, seeking out knowledge that is responsive to the needs and anxieties of those in charge. This is not necessarily a supine role. Evaluators who go along this path can play the part of critic within management circles, can even be a countervailing force within decision-making, exploiting their independence of view to broaden the deliberative frame. At its most influential this can be a power-sharing role, offering the evaluator a seat at the high table of management, albeit at the expense of her credibility as a witness to its transactions, and usually at the expense of her liberty to report them. For some this may constitute a rare opportunity to promote educational values that may be more prominent in the rhetoric of the programme than in the reality of its implementation. Such evaluators may well see themselves as lobbyists for relatively powerless groups in the educational sector – pupils, blacks, women, parents for example. Temporary allegiance to the power structure embodied in the programme as well as to its mission can look like a small price to pay for the chance directly to influence its direction and outcomes.

That is one option. Another, equally acceptable to many sponsoring programme managers, is that of nourishing the grass roots of programme action, more or less defining the programme as a schools-based activity, and providing formative evaluation for those in the front line. What matters most to evaluators who take this path is the contribution they can make to the quality of the programme at the point of delivery, and usable knowledge tends therefore to be defined in terms of the needs of involved teachers. They are teacher rather than manager-allies, and use their privileged access to higher levels of the programme to represent the difficulties faced by teachers in the classroom. With such a singular focus, however, many significant determinants of those difficulties that emanate from programme management remain insulated from evaluative scrutiny. The grass-roots option is in any case increasingly foreclosed to national evaluators by the separate provision of a local level of evaluation, commissioned by individual participating authorities. We shall deal with the problems of evaluation at the local level shortly.

Now, both the evaluation roles we have described are essentially 'insider' roles. They operate within programmes, owing allegiance to different participant groups. They could be called participant forms of evaluation, at best exploiting their independence to educate internal action. This begins to explain why so little evaluative information reaches the world outside. We want to stress, if it is not clear from the way in which we have characterized these roles, that they can and do provide their practitioners with honourable occupations and defensible interpretations of their responsibilities, both in educational and political terms. The programmes are, after all, authorized by elected representatives and managed by public servants. Their legitimacy is not, in that sense, in question.

Or is it? If, as Mcpherson (1973) so succinctly says, a liberal democracy is more than a mere 'mechanism of authorization', and if, which we consider to be evident, categorical funding strategies constitute potentially dangerous concentrations of single-minded power over educational futures, then that 'legitimacy' should be subject to continuously informed and renewed public consent. Programme evaluators have an opportunity, and we would argue therefore an obligation, to play a role in supporting democratic processes of policy formation and accountability. Within the constraints of participant evaluation roles as we have described them, the needs of stakeholders outside the programme are, to put it mildly, de-emphasized. Whether by evaluator prudence, by choice, or by the lure of potent involvement, or by a combination of all three, the end result is that the broad community of citizens concerned about educational change is poorly served by programme evaluation.

Lest it be thought that we are alone, and uniquely presumptuous, in advocating such an obligation, we would remind the reader that Cronbach (Cronbach et al., 1980), undoubtedly the most distinguished academic to specialize in programme evaluation, has reformulated the role as that of 'public scientist', thus harnessing expertise in knowledge construction to the service of public judgement. Although this concept, in our view, overstates scientific authority and ignores the role of evaluators as democratic agents within programmes, nevertheless it represents a way of thinking about evaluation, and about policy-making, that is close to our own. Cronbach has interpreted the role in much the same terms as Cohen suggested might be appropriate for the broader field of applied research in education (Cohen and Garet, 1975), those of improving and facilitating rather than pre-empting democratic discourse about the values and effects of public programmes. For our part, in this country, we have been arguing along similar lines, and trying to embody them in our evaluation practice, since the early 1970s (MacDonald, 1974; MacDonald and Norris 1978; Kushner and Norris, 1980). Under the rubric of 'democratic evaluation' we have attempted in a variety of circumstances to marry the internal demands of programmes for knowledge to serve their private justifications, with external demands for programmes to be justified in the broader court of community judgement. This 'broker' role has never been an easy one to pursue – it has not been popular with our paymasters and we have yet to deliver fully on its promise. Under the new, more authoritarian strategies of innovation that currently dominate the curriculum development scene, we now fear that the opportunities to pursue that aspiration have become restricted to the point of non-viability. To illustrate and substantiate what is for us at least a serious setback to a tradition of evaluation we have spent most of our professional lives cultivating, we turn now to consider a case in point.

CATEGORICAL FUNDING AND PROJECT EVALUATION

Categorical funding of curriculum initiatives, whereby local administrators submit bids to national administrators for money to finance stipulated areas of development, and accept accountability for effective investment, is now a significant feature of the educational landscape. It is essentially a customer/contract relationship between the two levels of administration, through which Whitehall keeps a tight fiscal rein on a necessarily devolved responsibility for action. The money involved may be small in terms of the total cost of schooling, but in circumstances of restrained expenditure it is precious enough to induce competitive tenders and at least formal obeisance to central policy. And central policy no longer operates exclusively through the Department of Education and Science (DES). The utilitarian, vocationalist thrust of policy involves other ministries, such as the Department of

Employment and the Department of Trade and Industry, in curriculum sponsorship. In particular the Manpower Services Commission (MSC), a Department of Employment quango increasingly preoccupied with the politically sensitive issue of youth unemployment, has assumed a leading role in the promotion of curriculum change through its Technical and Vocational Educational Initiative (TVEI). With the Department of the Environment restricting the purse strings of local authority initiatives, development money is heavily concentrated in Whitehall, and administrative professionals at the local level have, in many cases reluctantly, assumed the role of middle managers of earmarked resources.

Two other changes related to contemporary programmes are worthy of note. With the demise of mediating agencies such as the Schools Council in favour of more unilateral political origination of programmes, government ministers are now more closely associated with major programmes and have a correspondingly greater stake in their public success. Conversely, at the local government level, councillors are more marginalized and may even be bypassed as their employees seek to milk the central purse to prop up impoverished infrastructures of school support.

These leaner, more linear structures of command and compliance, unencumbered by compromising negotiations with powerful interest groups, are markedly authoritarian in their management style. They are bigger, less self-questioning, more single-minded in their search for vindicating data, quick to publicize success stories, quicker still to suppress or dismiss bad news from any quarter. The administrators who manage these programmes are under no illusions about the political imperatives that constitute their brief. These programmes, though they may well bear the official status of 'pilot' or 'experiment', and though they may be saturated with evaluation processes apparently designed to establish their worth, are expressions of political conviction rather than explorations of educational hypotheses.

That is the context. Let us turn to the case.

> I do hope that our response to your letter brings us nearer to a resolution of this matter, However I have to add that we would need a written assurance from the Centre for Applied Research in Education [CARE] that no reference is made to the . . . Project in either public or semi-public arenas other than that which is contained within the report of the Evaluation. Therefore if CARE wish to adumbrate upon the contents of the report at some future date in either a semi-public or public arena then approval would have to be sought from the . . . Authority. In the event of the Authority giving such approval it would also reserve the right to be represented at such an occasion.
>
> (LEA official and Director of LAP Project in the Authority)

The evaluation contract to which this item of correspondence refers had been entered into in a spirit of friendly collaboration on both sides. The director of the evaluation and the director of this LAP (Lower Attaining Pupils) project, who commissioned us to do the evaluation, had a shared history of collaborative research and knew each other well. He was familiar with our approach to evaluation, and valued our independent but empathetic perspective on the problems of curriculum development. Despite this favourable background the evaluation was terminated in midstream when it became clear that working relationships with the project management had irretrievably broken down.

The termination, suggested by us and accepted by the project director, was followed by a lengthy, quasi-legal wrangle about who had the right to say what and to whom about the project and about the demise of the evaluation. While this was going on the unexpired portion of the contract was placed with one of the LEA's neighbouring polytechnics. Neither the new local evaluators, nor the national programme evaluators at the National Foundation for Educational Research, nor the DES, who sponsored the programme and provided the money that enabled the LEA to commission the evaluation, made a single inquiry of us as to the circumstances which led to the breakdown. Yet this was the first time in almost twenty years of continuous engagement in the business of curriculum evaluation that members of the CARE group had felt unable to complete a contract. While none of us expected this, or any other independent evaluation, to be conflict-free, the problems encountered in trying to fashion and maintain a viable relationship between ourselves and the project managers were so severe that attempts on both sides to resolve them through negotiation all ended in failure.

It is not our purpose in this paper to explore all the reasons for this failure or to engage in the apportionment of blame. One of the authors (Kushner) who was directly involved in the conduct of the evaluation, is preparing for publication a case study of the experience, which tells the story in some detail and offers an extensive post mortem. Rather we are concerned here to draw upon the experience in order to illuminate issues of generalizable salience to the theory and practice of evaluation in education. These are issues that are more than likely to arise when we evaluate innovations initiated within the framework of categorical funding. The LAP project was one such innovation and, in relation to the difficulties we encountered, we regard it as significant that this was the first time we had undertaken to evaluate a local project operating within the specifications and other requirements of such a programme. We discussed our experience with many evaluators of this and other such programmes. Although terminations have so far been rare (see Baron *et al.*, 1981, and Simons, 1987, however for other examples) the constraints that we will identify command broad agreement among evaluators. We propose to deal with these constraints by grouping them under four headings.

ISSUE 1: 'CURRICULUM DEVELOPMENT IS OFTEN SEEN AS ADMINISTRATIVE ENACTMENT RATHER THAN AS ACTION BY ADMINISTRATORS'

We have already referred to the demise of agencies like the Schools Council which offered a forum for mediating between central government initiative and the needs and initiatives of local authorities and schools.

The professionally representative scrutiny of curriculum policy development such arrangements offered is barely possible under these new funding arrangements. The sources of TVEI, LAP and Records of Achievement lie not in public inquiries or cross-professional consultation. They lie in private discussions at the DES, at the MSC and in the Department of Employment – perhaps in the Cabinet Office. Even the 'Great Debate' had the feel of a false war – a catharsis with no substance. These programmes represent decisions disembedded from due process, leaving their political and ideological assumptions insufficiently challenged.

The result is that the guidelines which attend for example TVEI, read more like substantive prioritizations than parameters for experimentation. Teachers and schools are at the other end of a very long arm that reaches all the way back to the engine-room of politics.

In our LAP evaluation we observed, on a number of occasions, the project managers assuring school teams that they would act as a buffer between schools and the DES – that they would protect experimentation by the teachers. But we also spoke with co-ordinators of school teams and with heads who felt unable to take that leap of faith and who preferred the safety of conservative practice – or the risk of practices which they might not divulge to project managers and which they could not easily, therefore, 'allow' the evaluation to report. Often, this nervousness surfaced when project managers visited participating LAP schools. These managers were also, of course, LEA officials and what could be gleaned or hinted at from their conversations with school heads was read like runes for an indication as to what was expected from 'on high'. Genuine offers to act as a buffer notwithstanding, project managers could not look innocent.

For these and other reasons, teacher teams can easily view categorical funding curriculum projects as the pursuit of preset plans of action rather than as the exploration of alternatives. Equally, and because evaluators find it hard to negotiate data from the teachers at one end, and DES at the other, they, too, are pressurized into looking at these projects as implementation strategies. There was, on our LAP evaluation, a constant demand for formative feedback and a resistance to any kind of overview report. The evaluation was asked to act in a service role – to recognize the 'realpolitik' of the programme and to limit its aspirations. It was an 'all-hands-on-deck' kind of affair. To Stenhouse's (1980) division of curriculum projects into child-centred and content-centred we must now add policy-centred.

ISSUE 2: TEACHERS DO NOT NECESSARILY SHARE THE PROBLEM-DEFINITIONS WHICH UNDERPIN THEIR CURRICULUM PROJECTS

A teacher in a London primary school spoke to us of visits to her classrooms by no fewer than eight official observers in two terms – one for multicultural-ism, one for equal opportunities, another for special education, one an in-house educational researcher, and so forth. The insulation shield has been pierced and the school bell rings visiting hours. Virtually anyone can make a claim on classrooms these days and apply pressure, but the impor-tant point is, of course, that only the government can afford to buy. For some teachers, it must be said, involvement in a programme can provide some insulation from this variety of pressures. 'TVEI', one teacher has been quoted as saying, 'was a chance to stand still and analyse what we were doing' (Fiddy and Stronach, 1987).

Teachers and schools have many reasons for participating in these projects and those reasons are not always consonant with the programme rationale. In our LAP evaluation and in the TVEI evaluation reported by Fiddy and Stronach (1987), there is evidence of these categorical funding programmes being used by educational authorities as remedial strategies for 'lower attaining schools', as it were. Although this is not a new phenomenon (see MacDonald, 1978), offers to participate can be hard to refuse in these impoverished and threatening times. Not only that, but the presence of TVEI or LAP or a major assessment project in a school can often stifle any other curriculum development so that the only way to engage in resource-led innovation is to join the flagship.

In such circumstances teachers often have to rest content with the project passed down to them – to live with official definitions of the problems they are alleged to have. Although a similar charge could be laid at the door of any centrally devised initative, there is now much more of a sense of schools, and individual teachers, receiving 'offers they can't refuse'.

In their overview of the curriculum reform period of the Schools Council, MacDonald and Walker (1976) introduce the term 'curriculum negotiation'.

For them it represented the competing pressures on curriculum developers to justify their products to academic peers on the one hand (who judged them against educational standards) and to teachers on the other (who judged them against criteria like practicability). The same package would be presented (negotiated) to each audience in appropriate terms to ensure, from the former, continued intellectual support (not unrelated to developers' career aspirations) and, from the latter, continued market support. But these developers, as can be inferred, stood outside of these two worlds – in the system, but not of it. Their problem, say MacDonald and Walker, was not whether people understood what they had to say, but whether people wanted to hear it.

In categorical funding programmes there is a similar situation, but with crucial differences. Developers are a more homogeneous group of people – LEA officials, heads, senior teachers, advisers. They are in and of the system – well known by the people they are trying to sell to. They have less chance of camouflage – more need to argue their survival at both ends of the system – nowhere to go if they fail to get the message right and it rebounds. The problem is a variation of the one MacDonald and Walker analysed in the previous decade.

Take the case of one of the LAP schools we were evaluating. They saw themselves as working beyond the LAP rationale – piloting new curricula with pupil volunteers. They saw themselves as programme 'outlaws'. When there were no volunteers they deliberated long and hard before making this known. It was difficult to present what had happened as anything other than 'failure' – in spite of the learning they were gleaning from the event. When they did go public, one of the project managers visited them to try to help out – to discuss the problem. But for the school, all he represented was the symbol of accountability by which their outlaw status would be confirmed. The fear was that he would bring with him criteria of success and failure which related to implementation and not to their autonomous curriculum values.

ISSUES 3: CONTEMPORARY CURRICULUM DEVELOPERS MAY BE CAUGHT UP IN A MOVEMENT RATHER THAN INNOVATION

The following question was raised by Harry Torrance during an in-service training session for teacher teams on the LAP project we were evaluating. It relates to assessment, but is relevant to many features of categorical funding programmes: If, after having developed profiling for two or three years, you find it to be too disruptive or not to have worked, would you feel able to abandon it as a failed experiment?

Of course, underlying that question is a suggestion that there is too much public legitimacy and rhetorical investment behind these developments not to go along with them. If you do decide that profiling is an inadequate educational instrument, are you committing one of the heresies of the contemporary age – anti-modernism? Berger (1974) in presenting his ethical manifesto for researchers of social change argues that 'modernity exacts a high price on the level of meaning. Those who are unwilling to pay this price must be taken with utmost seriousness, and not be dismissed as "backward" or "irrational".' That injunction is appropriate to the political culture we live in at present which embodies at least as much reverence for the future as it does for the past in its social programmes. 'Schools,' said our LEA in its submission for the LAP award to the DES, 'have been unable to grasp the vocational nettle . . . unable to break free from a traditional view of society's expectations.'

The LEA was, of course, searching for the kind of presentation of its bid that would appeal to its prospective sponsor – successfully, it transpired. In order to understand this a little better we might think of the difference between an innovation and a movement.

Both are driven by a sense of mission; both represent attempts at forward momentum; both demand the participation of disciples. But movements have a tendency to use moral compulsion as the driving energy. They tend to rest upon assumptions which are difficult to challenge through formal discourse. There are logics, of course, but beyond logic there is a recourse to arguments that need not be spoken to be understood. 'Our ability to dream goes beyond our ability to explain,' expressed one observer (Heussenstamm, 1973) during a conference, seeking privileged status for the arts. But the claim could well be applied to advocates of categorical funding programmes. It is unlikely that profiling or TVEI would be dropped – whatever its evaluations come up with.

Innovators normally struggle for that kind of institutional security. They are vulnerable because that is their job – to learn about the potential and limitations of ideas by exploring them. So, the Humanities Curriculum Project was adopted or abandoned by teachers who were converts or not – and the arguments were public and vigorous. Nuffield Chemistry became an established curriculum and assessment scheme on the basis of disciplined and empirical claims to validity. The LAP project we were evaluating, while embodying a great deal of experimentation and generating significant learnings about constraints upon change, was part of a programme which carried the *pre-hoc* vindication of political conviction. The programme was 'good' because it was the embodiment of a new and successful idea which emanated from central government. Teachers found themselves caught up in an irresistible movement rather than a (resistible) innovation.

These categorical funding programmes, taken individually, clearly are innovations, however, and the argument is related more to the context of attitudes and expectations in which they collectively exist. We entered the LAP evaluation following experience of evaluating an earlier innovatory project which fitted more into the mould of Schools Council-type initiatives. We spoke to one teacher who was leaving that innovation behind after some experience which she had felt to be largely ineffectual, and looking ahead to participating in TVEI. Hitherto, she explained, she had been accustomed to public attacks on her schools's educational competence, against which she felt there was no easy defence. 'But with our TVEI hats on we'll be seen to succeed.' she said.

Movements have a place in change theory, of course: perhaps the closest model in that literature is Donald Schon's 'shifting centres' model (see MacDonald and Walker, 1976, chapter 1). In this model, the source of the innovation may be ambiguous in its location and in its precise intention – there may not even be a clear definition of the message. It is a model suited to the volatile nature of allegiance, resourcing, political trends and charismatic leadership. It may be hard to pin down in analytic terms, but there is no doubt that it is there, and that it is broadly understood – or intuited.

LAP had a definite source – often, indeed, associated with an individual, Sir Keith Joseph. But the process by which it emerged and through which it was translated into an operational programme to change secondary schooling remains obscure. Indeed, the processes by which its progress and results are monitored and appraised are unclear in spite of there being a national evaluation. The project managers in the LEA we were associated with – though offering themselves as 'buffers' to their teachers – were never (while we were conducting the evaluation) able to penetrate those policy arenas. They were not allowed to attend the steering committee for the programme and they had no direct communication with that steering group. The same is no doubt true for other LEA projects – and yet there was no difficulty in sharing common experiences with LAP teachers from other authorities when visits were made. There is certainly considerable diversity in the LAP and, for example, the TVEI programmes – coupled with a very loose system for monitoring and standardizing the results. In a sense, the 'centres' for the pursuit of vocational curriculum reform are 'shifting' all the time as programmes multiply and redefine their participant constituencies.

But where this diversity compromises the integrity of the 'new vocationalism' remains to be seen. There is a sense in which the movement is sustained less by structures of control and more by a successfully marketed ideology. 'Vocational chic' (Kushner, 1985) is in.

ISSUE 4: HOW MUCH SECRECY IS ESSENTIAL FOR THE SURVIVAL OF THESE PROGRAMMES IN A DEMOCRATIC SYSTEM?

There is always a tension in democratic evaluation between the individual 'right to privacy' and the public 'right to know'. But we have seen that the politicization of these programmes places undue stress on participants who are exposed to potentially punitive consequences for professionally legitimate decisions. For evaluators this can raise, in acute form, issues of fairness to individuals and sensitivity to the consequences of reporting. 'At times,' suggests House (1980) 'evaluators may have to resort to their consciences rather than to their contracts.'

Some evaluators are dissuaded from pressing the publication of features of categorical funding programmes – as did our LAP evaluators, for example, in suppressing all accounts of conversations with the LAP project managers. Where teachers feel themselves – as many did in our LAP evaluation – to be working beyond the preferred direction of the DES, then they feel themselves to be programme 'outlaws'. Doing evaluation can feel like being invited in to the 'outlaw hideout' on condition that its presence is not revealed to the authorities. Project managers, equally, can find it threatening to reveal their allegiances, having to balance patronage from above with credibility from below.

As a result of this, what we are seeing is the gradual disappearance into secretive enclave of crucial programme processes at all levels. We lost policy sources from the very beginning; innovation strategies of LEA leaders are often too sensitive to report; the workings of the infrastructures which support programmes at LEA level are equally sensitive and often lost to confidentiality or conscience; creative educational developments are often secreted away by teachers, fearful of administrative disapproval of deviation. And so it goes on – a litany of anxiety, and the erosion of opportunity to create public knowledge of these programmes.

There are good reasons for this. In our LAP evaluation, in order to document the context of the innovation, we found ourselves evaluating the whole LEA policy of curriculum development. This makes demands on evaluators which outstrip the usually meagre resources available for categorical funding evaluation at the local level. It is all the harder for evaluators who work in schools of education which rely on the patronage of LEAs for students and in-service training resources. McCabe (1986) gives a detailed account of the tensions between the need to survive in a TVEI evaluation and the need to meet the standards expected of a professional research community.

Whether through compliance or through force of circumstance, evaluators can find themselves – as we did – contributing to the endemic secrecy that shrouds the origins and the workings of these programmes. Let us look a little more closely at secrecy.

In the LAP evaluation we were conducting there arose a series of complaints about our activities – allegations of late arrival, low productivity, insensitivity. We found it ever harder to respond to these allegations since there was no direct access to the complainants. For their part, the project managers could not divulge the identity of complainants since they were part of the personal networks of the advisory service. These personal networks are crucial to the functioning of an advisory service which has to operate with an open market and more hidden markets of information. Eventually the evaluation breached the hidden markets – the professional 'gossip' – but only to the point where confidential data could be collected – data which were (and remain) unusuable since they too easily identify vulnerable individuals. The same went for the project managers, though they suffered the added complication of having to reveal their personal thoughts about policy initiatives not yet fully fledged or negotiated with their own authority.

What was happening in this case was that the evaluation was picking up the kind of informal conversations and speculations that characterize any hierarchical system. Such conversations are the lubricants which allow the system's cogs to turn without grinding against each other too abrasively. Gossip can reduce the powerful in the minds of the powerless – it can be used by people to create alliances out of shared grievances, for example. Secret conversations can be comforting and even empowering.

The day an evaluation is commissioned all such private discourses become threatened by possible exposure. And the options are now more restricted. In Schools Council projects, for example, it was usually the case that curriculum developers and project managers came from outside the authority – project venues (conferences and in-service training) were often geographically far off. There were sympathetic ears to be bent without consequence – advice to be sought from outsiders other than evaluators. In categorical funding programmes there are rarely outsiders other than evaluators. Teachers are asked to have an adventure, but to stay at home to do it. It is all too public even without the presence of an evaluator. And participation in a programme can mean the end of old alliances that had proved familiar and supportive. One LAP teacher viewed with trepidation the prospect of his school colleagues learning about some significant difficulties his team was encountering. 'You would begin to get the heebie-jeebies – because you can no longer control what people are saying about it.'

At all levels of programme involvement, therefore, participants feel strongly the need for secrecy and the fear of exposure – of their activities, of their values, of their hopes and anxieties. Evaluators, who must take responsibility for the consequences of what they report, are embroiled in this complexity. In our particular case, we withdrew.

CONCLUDING COMMENTS AND A LOOK AHEAD

Readers familiar with the literature of innovation and evaluation may well be tempted to say at this point 'So what's new?'. The schools system has always been hierarchical and secretive. New curricula have always travelled under an aura of evangelical authority. And case study evaluation, whatever the particular circumstances of curriculum initiatives, has always threatened to 'penetrate the secrecy and so threaten the carefully constructed claims which form the basis of authority' (MacDonald and Walker, 1975). Yes, case study has always been difficult but, with due attention to a reasonable balance between the protection of individual interests and the rights of others to judge the work of those individuals, it has been negotiable. Such negotiation operated in the space afforded by respect for pluralism of interests and values, for the right to dissent without consequence, for choice, voluntarism and growth to be adequately informed. Perhaps crucially, it could work because the bureaucracy, whose most cultivated skills lie in the control of information, kept their distance from the arenas of specific endeavour, and construed themselves as audiences rather than performers.

Basically what we are saying now is that trends in the management of curriculum and particularly in the management of curriculum development, have coalesced into patterns of control which are essentially authoritarian and anti-democratic. The virtual collapse of mediating agencies, a characteristic of the collaborative partnership tradition of post-war management, and the assimilation of local administrators as branch agents of central executives, has created a bureaucratic monolith for the enactment of governing political convictions in curriculum matters. Administrative vulnerability to the exposure of programme failures has correspondingly become acute. Tolerance of independent critique is low. Although there is more funded evaluation of programmes than there has ever been before, and although much of this evaluation is nominally independent, evaluators are largely co-opted into a conspiracy of pretence – that the programmes are educationally and economically sound, that they are going reasonably well, that those who have been drafted by necessity or opportunism within their fold are there by choice and conviction, or have been persuaded subsequently by their merits. Evaluators may know better but they, or their institutions, are more than ever dependent upon the patronage of the implicated, particularly at the local level, where the responsibility for programme impression management is now crucially located. The space for dissent at all levels of involvement has closed down. Democratic brokerage within a programme and the transmission of useful knowledge to the public sphere are not consistent with the requirements of the programme managers who dominate evaluation sponsorship. And evaluation is just as threatening in some respects to those teachers who feel they have no 'right to fail'. Those evaluators who share our broad persuasion about its aspirations will find themselves excluded, or in trouble. This bodes ill for democracy in the matter of schooling. Educational evaluation, in so far as it embodies a promise of impartial and usable knowledge for the enlightenment and empowerment of those who are not party to government action, is in danger of becoming a discreditable activity.

Is there a future for public evaluation? Has the time come perhaps to decline, even in the increasingly rare cases where it is offered on acceptable terms, the sponsorship of programme managers? Before answering that, perhaps we should take a peek at the future, since there are signs that yet another transformation of school management may be in store.

It is June 1987. Mrs Thatcher has achieved a third term of office, and intends to continue the political reform of an educational sector even now in the throes of the most radical redistribution of power since the immediate post-war legislation. Are schools on the privatization agenda, are local education authorities as we have known them on the verge of extinction, will a new partnership of central government, private capital and parent governors take over the 'secret garden'? How far will the logic of the market be applied to the institutionalized experience of the young?

Many of us who work in education, perhaps especially those of us who operate at one remove from direct involvement in curriculum determination, are anxious about such possibilities, taken aback by their boldness, surprised by their apparent electoral viability, bewildered by the speed and confidence with which the props of this scenario are being assembled. In education at least, the ascendancy of the 'new right' has taken us all by storm and, in a sense, changed the problem. Concerned throughout the 1970s to mediate in our various ways the growing centralization of power over the curriculum and the increasing use of that power to control in politically useful terms the knowledge, skills and attitudes acquired by the young, we now face a new prospect, that of statism in reverse gear, fuelled bureauphobia, the theory of public choice, and a keen eye for cost sharing. None of us knows how far or how fast such an ideology will be pursued, or to what extent it will be compromised by prudence or by dissenting counsels – or mediated by party politics. But it would take us into new political territory, perhaps into another country. If so, we may all have to rethink our roles and obligations, not least those of us who work in educational evaluation. Our economy has largely thrived as an offshoot of bureaucratic imperialism, if not its creature. Who will want to spend their voucher on evaluation? Will the bureaucracy, relieved of many of its present burdens, have a renewed interest in evaluative feedback from a devolved system of a new kind? We do not know.

Let not this speculative peek into the future deter us, however, from the here and now, and the very different picture it presents. The manager of the LAP project who accepted our invitation to terminate the evaluation contract commented at one point of high acrimony that democratic evaluation was an 'anachronism'. We take his point, but would assert that his is a short-term view of a democratic society that is presently under great stress as it tries to come to terms with its changing relationship to the rest of the world. John Maynard Keynes wrote in 1930:

> For at least another hundred years we must pretend to ourselves and to everyone that fair is foul and foul is fair; for foul is useful and fair is not. Avarice and usury and precaution must be our Gods for a little longer still. For only they can lead us out of the tunnel of economic necessity into daylight.
>
> (Keynes, 1932)

But it is not for evaluators to pretend that foul is fair and fair is foul. Our task is to demythologize action in ways which facilitate reality-based, broadly participative policy-making processes, because in the longer term that has to be the basis of our collective and individual emancipation. But at this time a heavily implicated bureaucracy – our traditional sponsor – constitutes a disabling source of sponsorship. We must look elsewhere, to others who have been disadvantaged by the present concentration of power and control of information about the consequences of its exercise. Perhaps at the national level of select committees of Parliament, presently hampered by limited access to usable knowledge. Perhaps to local councils, whose knowledge of programmes is too dependent on what their own staff choose to tell them. Perhaps to teacher organizations, as they seek to rebuild their platform. And to the sponsoring charities, who presently tread only in the footsteps of government. Perhaps to multiple sponsorship from diverse sources, splitting the interests and sharing the risks.

Finding alternative sources of funding is not of course a simple matter. Had it been, we would have accomplished it by now. Select committees have no money, local councils prefer to improve their internal evaluative mechanisms. Charities are fearful of accusations of political interference, and have their tax exemption at stake. Our improverished universities seek to placate government, not to question it. This is not the USA, where the checks and balances in education are heavily financed. We cannot look either to the European Commission, despite its increasing role in curriculum sponsorship. Having initially funded a substantial network of programme evaluators in the late 1970s to monitor the first stage of its Transition from School programme. The Brussels bureaucrats showed their contempt for public knowledge by replacing them for the second stage by a small group of hired, in-house reporters.

So it will not be easy. This is hardly the most hopeful of scenarios, but it is not devoid of possibilities. We must work to educate the public, and perhaps particularly politicians, about the difficulties we face. We must stop pretending that all is well, and look to share our perspective, our aspirations and our problems with those whose interests or values are close to our own.

Much will depend on how our democracy responds to further developments of present trends. We certainly should not give up on evaluation, simply because we are dealing with a bureaucracy which Mrs Thatcher once called the most secretive in Western democracies. There is a job to do. Evaluators who can stay in business have the priceless advantage of access to a secret and largely secretive world of significant social action. We must find ways of maintaining that access and of using it to inform all those who have a right to make informed judgements about whether they can entrust children to the care of compulsory state institutions.

REFERENCES

Baron, S., Miller, H., Whitfield, R. and Yates, C. (1981) On the social organisation of evaluation: a case study, in D. Smetheram (ed.) *Practising Evaluation*, Nafferton Books, Driffield.
Berger, P. (1974) *Pyramids of Sacrifice: Political Ethics and Social Change*, Penguin, Harmondsworth.
Cohen, D.K. and Garet, M.S. (1975) Reforming educational policy with applied research, *Harvard Educational Review*, Vol. 45, No. 1, pp. 17–43, February.
Cronbach, L.J. *et al.* (1980) *Toward reform of Program Evaluation*, Jossey Bass, San Francisco.
Fiddy, R. and Stronach, I. (1987) Fables and futures: cases in the management of innovation, in D. Gleeson (ed.) *Inside TVEI: Curriculum Innovation and Technological Change*, Routledge & Kegan Paul, London (in press).
Huessenstamm, F. (1973) Commentary . . . On not exceeding our grasp, in *Evaluating the Total School Art Programme*. Papers presented to the National Art Education Association Study Institute, San Diego, California, April.
House, E. (1980) *Evaluating with Validity*, Sage Publications, Beverly Hills.
Keynes, J.M. (1932) *Essays in Persuasion*, London.
Kushner, S. (1985) Vocational chic: a historical and curriculum context to the field of transition in England, in R. Fiddy (ed.) *Youth Unemployment and Training: A Collection of National Perspectives*, Falmer Press, London and Philadelphia.

Kushner, S. and Norris, N. (1980) Interpretation, negotiation and validity in naturalistic research, *Interchange* (OISF Journal), Vol. II, No. 4, pp. 26–36.

McCabe, C. (1986) The negotiation and familarisation stage of TVEI local evaluation, in R. Fiddy and I. Stronach (eds.) *TVEI* Working Papers No. 1, CARE, University of East Anglia.

MacDonald, B. (1974) Evaluation and the control of education, in B. MacDonald and R. Walker (eds.) *Innovation, Evaluation, Research and the Problem of Control.* Centre for Applied Research in Education, Norwich (paper 1.2 in this volume).

MacDonald, B. (1978) *The Experience of Innovation*, CARE, University of East Anglia.

MacDonald, B., Jenkins, D., Kemmis, S. and Tawney, D. (1975) *The Programme at Two*, CARE, University of East Anglia.

MacDonald, B. and Norris, N. (1978) *Looking Up For a Change: Political Horizons in Policy Evaluation.* Mimeo, CARE, University of East Anglia.

MacDonald, B. and Walker, R. (1975) Case study and the social philosophy of educational research, *Cambridge Journal of Education*, Vol. 5, pp. 2–11.

MacDonald, B. and Walker, R. (1976) *Changing the Curriculum*, Open Books, London.

McPherson, C.B. (1973) *Democratic Theory: Essays in Retrieval*, Clarendon Press, Oxford.

Simons, H. (1987) *Getting to Know Schools in a Democracy*, Falmer Press, Brighton.

Stenhouse, L. (ed.) (1980) *Curriculum Research and Development in Action*, Heinemann, London.

2.6
HMI's INTERPRETATIONS OF
SCHOOLS' EXAMINATION RESULTS*
John Gray and Valerie Hannon

The [fifth-year] examination results, taking into account the ability range of the pupils [were] in the main reasonably satisfactory, except at O level.

(HMI Report on Benfield School, Newcastle upon Tyne)

INTRODUCTION

The 1980 Education Act required schools to publish their examination results; it did not, however, require them to interpret them. As one of the supporters of the legislation maintained in the parliamentary debate, 'examination results speak for themselves' (*Hansard*, 1979). Others were less convinced. 'League tables' and inappropriate interpretations would, they believed, abound. As the Secondary Heads Association (SHA) put it: 'Hospitals are not required to publish annual reports of the proportions of their admissions who, after stated periods as inmates, die. Common sense tells us that such statistics would be a very crude measure of the skill and devotion of hospital staff' (SHA 1980). So why should schools be required to publish equally misleading 'results', ran the argument.

The problem was further compounded by the absence of any publicly agreed procedures for evaluating schools' examination results: earlier controversies had merely served to emphasize the difficulties. Furthermore, there were many who maintained that to confine the evaluation of schools' performance largely to examination results was unduly narrow; a broader, more embracing account was required, if the full range of schools' activities were to be captured and valued.

The publication of reports by Her Majesty's Inspectorate (HMI) on the

* Gray, J. and Hannon, V. (1986) HMI's interpretations of schools' examination results. *Journal of Educational Policy*, Vol. 1, No. 1, pp. 23–33.

individual schools it had visited offered a partial answer to both these concerns. From the beginning of 1983, authoritative and professional judgements on schools' performance were made public for the first time.[1]

HMI's judgements are of central interest because they provide a set of criteria that are publicly visible; as such, they should provide a model for others. They are also important because their observations are placed in the wider framework of the work of the whole school. As former Senior Chief Inspector Sheila Browne put it:

> the basic principle has always been close observation exercised with an open mind by persons with appropriate experience and a framework of relevant principles. HMI's first duty is to record what is and to seek to understan why it is as it is. The second step is to try to answer the question whether or not it is good enough. To do so, HMI uses as a first set of measures the school's – or other institution's – own aims; and, as a second, those which derive from practice across the country and from public demand or aspiration.

> (Browne, 1979)

HMI's involvement in the assessment of schools' examination results, then, would appear to offer some prospect of judgements which are professionally credible. At the same time, since HMI inspectors are themselves recruited from amongst experienced practitioners, their procedures offer some purchase on how the teaching profession might itself judge its performance.

In this article we explore some of the ways in which HMI inspectors have assessed the examination performance of individual secondary schools and ask the question whether they adopt strategies that are equally 'fair' to all schools. Can any school, in other words, given its particular intake of pupils, be seen to be doing well? Or do the procedures run the risk of favouring some kinds of schools at the expense of others?

FRAMEWORKS FOR INTERPRETATION

The view that examination results somehow 'speak for themselves' needs to be challenged. Any set of statistics embodies more or less explicit views about what it is important to present and what requires intrepetation. Such interpretations, in turn, depend crucially on the evaluative frameworks which underly them.

It is not our intention here to suggest in any great detail how a school's examination results *might* be evaluated since such discussions already exist elsewhere (see, for example, Shipman, 1979; Gray, 1982; and Plewis, 1981). Rather, our concern is to explore the broader evaluative frameworks that have been employed and their underlying assumptions.

Over the past three years we have obtained a good deal of experience in understanding how local authorities and schools evaluate their own performance through our work on the ESRC-funded Contexts Project (HR8602). We have worked in a research and/or consultancy role with some dozen local authorities and, as a direct result, have begun to establish the essential features of their evaluative strategies.

From our work to date we discern four basic approaches to the assessment of a school's performance. These can be based on: (a) comparisons with national or local averages; (b) 'pass rates'; (c) comparisons of the school's performance over time; and (d) comparisons with schools with comparable intakes. We shall now discuss each approach briefly in turn.

(a) *National or local averages*: In this approach the individual school's performance is compared with national or local averages for relevant nationally available statistics and its position in relation to them serves as the focus for evaluative comment.

(b) *'Pass rates'*: The focus here is on the percentages of *candidates* who were entered for an examination who 'passed' it. A pass it typically taken as a grade A, B or C at 'O' level; there is more variability as regards what counts as meriting attention at CSE but, typically, candidates obtaining grade 1 are emphasized. Comparisons are often made with the norms for candidates from the relevant examination boards.

(c) *Comparisons over time*: The school's perfomance one year is compare with its performance on the same measures in previous years; trends are noted.

(d) *Comparisons with pupils of comparable ability levels or schools with comparable intakes*: In this approach the school's performance is judged against other schools serving pupils of similar abilities or from similar socio-economic circumstances; it is, in other words, an approach that takes account of the school's context. Although the approach is relevant to all schools, several local authorities, to our knowledge, make particular use of this approach with respect to their 'social priority' schools.

It is tempting to argue that all four approaches should be considered in any overall assessment of a school's examination performance. However, such a strategy is likely to produce certain kinds of inconsistencies which we argue below are unhelpful. The potential conflict between a judgement based on (a) the 'standards' model, which relates judgements to the national average compared with (d) the 'contextual' model, which takes account of intakes, is outlined in Figure A.

In theory, someone who was consistently employing the former model to judge schools' performance would reach a different judgement from

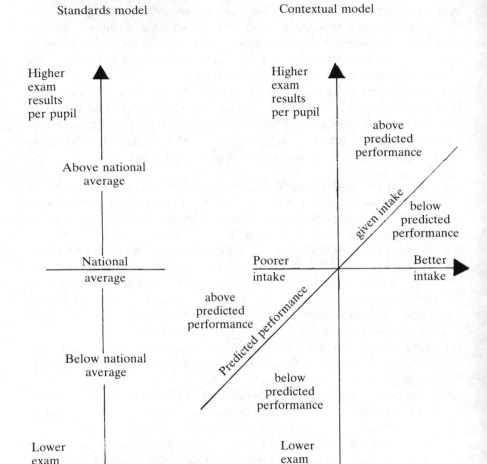

Figure A

someone consistently employing the latter in 50 per cent of the total cases. In practice, given that many schools in both models would be performing around the average, the actual conflicts would probably be fewer in number than this theoretical limit suggests; the example indicates that they would, none the less, occur quite frequently.

THE DATA BASE AND OUR METHODOLOGY

The analyses which follow are based on the set of thirty-five long reports (i.e. those based on 'full' inspections) published in 1983. Schools inspected included those with age ranges 11/12/13–16/18, comprehensive and selective schools.[2] Although the 'short' reports often include comments on schools' examination results, they do not usually provide much by way of supporting evidence. 'Full' reports, in contrast, usually contain one or more pages of appendices, providing summary statistics of examination results and break-downs of grades subject-by-subject. It is, therefore, possible to make some independent checks of the HMI's assessments in the light of the available data.

Since not all the schools for which reports were available contained sixth forms with 'A' level candidates, we confined our study to fifth-year examination results (which included 'O' level, CSE and combined 16-plus examinations). We also confined ourselves, for the purposes of this article, to those sections of the reports which dealt with summary evaluations of the schools' examination results, rather than the detailed breakdowns of the results in terms of individual subjects. The task of determining how HMI inspectors have proceeded is a complex one, even at the level of summary assessments; subject-by-subject comparisons must await further analyses.

WHICH EVALUATIVE FRAMEWORKS DID HMI EMPLOY?

Our reading of the reports enabled us to identify for each of the individual schools which of the four evaluative frameworks outlined earlier HMI was employing. The kinds of comments which contributed to our judgements are outlined briefly below.

Framework (a): National averages

In such evaluations the individual school's performance would be compared with the national average for the same measure. Thus the HMI Inspectors first remarked of Beal High School in the London Borough of Redbridge that nearly 30 per cent of pupils obtained five or more 'O' level (or CSE grade 1 equivalent) passes *and* that this was 'well above the national average'. The comment in respect of the same school that '79 per cent of pupils obtained above grade 4 at CSE or grade A–E at 'O' level in five or more subjects' is also relevant in this respect. Sometimes we found that the way in which such statistics were presented and discussed did not always make the basis of comparison fully explicit but, in such cases, the context usually made the implicit evaluation clearer. At Kirk Hallam School in Derbyshire, for example, the comparison with the national average was left implicit – 'only' nine pupils (6.3 per cent of the year group) gained five or more passes at 'O' level.

Framework (b): 'Pass' rates

These assessments appeared to be based on judgements of the 'success' or otherwise of those who entered as candidates for public examinations. Again some kind of norm was usually implicit; this norm appeared to be the 'success' rates of all candidates who were entered for the examination(s), such as are provided on a subject-by-subject basis in the annual reports of examination boards. At Copley High School in Tameside, for example, the fact that in 1982 'less than 50 per cent of 'O' level entries achieved grades A–C', evoked the negative comment that 'the entry policy may be too ambitious'. The results of Kirk Hallam School for the same year were described as 'disappointing' because '55 per cent of entries achieved grades *below* grade C and most subjects' results were below the norm of the examination boards'. Liverpool Institute for Boys came in for similar criticism. The fact that only 33 per cent of entries for 'O' level in 1981 and 46 per cent of entries for 'O' level in 1982 obtained A–C grades was seen as 'suggesting either that pupils were entered for inappropriate exams, or that the preparation of pupils was inadequate, or both'.

Since many of these comments were essentially about the appropriateness or otherwise of schools' policies for entering pupils for public examination, we also judged comments about the extent to which pupils were 'double-entered' for both 'O' level and CSE examinations in the same subjects to fall into this category as well. Hainault High School in Redbridge, for example, appeared to have had 'difficulty in judging appropriate target exams for pupils'. There was an excessively high double entry for 'O' level and CSE. Ormesby School in Cleveland, on the other hand, was described as having a 'generally sound policy for exam entries. Double entry was avoided unless a strong case was made on educational grounds.'

Framework (c): Comparisons of performance over time

Examples of comments falling into this category included the judgement that Ormesby's results were 'good' and 'showed noticeable improvement over the last three years'; that at Beal the number of 'O' level A–C or CSE grade 1 passes per pupil went up 'from 2.4 to 2.9 per pupil over the last two years'; whilst at Kirk Hallam the overall 'CSE results in 1982 were marginally better than those in 1981 and in some subjects markedly improved'.

Framework (d): Comparisons with pupils of comparable ability levels or schools with comparable intakes

A number of different types of comments, which indicated that the schools' results had been placed in the context of the ability levels of the pupils or catchment area the school was serving, were included in this category. Often this was indicated by a phrase or comment that implied that such factors should be taken into consideration. At Benfield School in Newcastle, for example, the report commented that 'the exam results, taking into account the ability range of the pupils, were in the main reasonably satisfactory, except at 'O' level'. Kirk Hallam's most recent results were described as 'disappointing' but this judgement was qualified by the remark that these results were obtained by the school's 'first comprehensive intake [which] probably included fewer able pupils than might be expected when compared with the national distribution'. The results of the Liverpool Institute were described as 'generally disappointing'; however, the inspectors found the CSE results 'more satisfactory, with the exception of the numbers who were absent or ungraded'. They remark that 'evidence on the ability range of the intake suggests that these [latter absent and ungraded] results were unduly high'.[3]

In making our judgements about which framework(s) were being employed we occasionally found it necessary to infer the approach from relatively brief comments. With respect to making decisions about approaches (a) and (b), relating respectively to 'national averages' and 'pass rates', this was rarely a problem; however, in relation to approaches (c) and (d), relating respectively to 'comparisons over time' and 'comparisons taking account of intakes', we sometimes encountered difficulties. In these latter cases we recorded passing references as evidence that the framework was being employed to a greater or lesser extent.

In Table A we report on the evaluative frameworks being employed by HMI to judge the examination results of the thirty-five schools whose reports we reviewed. From this it is clear that the most commonly employed criterion was that of 'pass rates', which we found to have been used in 86 per cent of our cases. By contrast attempts to evaluate exam results by contextualizing them (i.e. by reference to the ability levels of a school's intake) were found in only 17 per cent of the reports.

Table A   *Incidence of criteria used to judge results in thirty-five schools for which full inspection reports were available*

Criteria	National average	'Pass rates'	Comparison over time	Contextualized in terms of intake
Times employed	23	30	13	6
as percentage of total	66%	86%	37%	17%

Table B, which analyses the combination of criteria employed for each report, reveals a particularly interesting picture. This shows that the context-based evaluative framework was never employed on its own: it was either used in conjunction with all three other criteria (three times), with a combination of 'national average' and 'pass rate' criteria (once), or in conjunction with the 'pass rate' criterion (twice). We have argued above that attempts to combine a 'standards model' (i.e. one based on 'national averages') with a contexts-based framework are likely to lead to inconsistencies. Yet our findings suggest that this is what the Inspectorate did in four out of the six instances in which it appeared to make contextualized judgements.

Table B   *Numbers and combinations of criteria employed in judging results*

	Number of criteria employed	Number of school reports	Totals
	Four		
	(all)	3	3
	Three		
(i)	(Nat. Av + Pass rate + Time)	7	
(ii)	(Nat. Av + Pass rate + Context)	1	8
	Two		
(i)	(Nat. Av + Pass rate)	8	
(ii)	(Nat. Av + Time)	1	
(iii)	(Pass rate + Time)	1	
(iv)	(Pass rate + Context)	2	12
	One		
(i)	(Nat. Av)	3	
(ii)	(Pass Rate)	8	
(iii)	(Time)	1	
(iv)	(Context)	0	12
			35

Table C   *Inspected schools categorized according to intake and nature of criteria used to judge examination performance*

Category of school in terms of ability intake	Number of schools in each category	Number of schools where evaluation of exam results was contextualized
Disadvantaged	5	2
Advantaged	3	1
Average/Unspecified	27	3

We turn now to look in detail at those examples where there was some evidence of contextualized evaluation.

A CONTEXT-BASED MODEL OF EVALUATION

It is perhaps unsurprising that context-based evaluative frameworks were more likely to be brought into play in situations of pronounced disadvantage/advantage in terms of intake abilities.

Table C shows that of the six schools which we found to have had their exam results evaluated in contextual terms, three were clearly identifiable as being at the extremes in terms of the ability of their intake. Of course, the Inspectorate is to some extent dependent on the data which a school makes available. Often, in the absence of accurate information about the prior ability levels and attainments, some informed 'guesswork' is required; but other information that could assist in the process of forming a contextualized judgement (e.g. that the school served a social priority area) is frequently available. This explanation, however, cannot account for the absence of contextualized judgements for, in the majority of reports which we found lacked the contextual dimension, some information about the abilities of the intake *was* available; it was simply unrelated to the judgement made upon exam results. For example, of Range High School, HMI reported that 'on the basis of standardized tests administered in the school, the intake received, while giving a fully comprehensive span, represents an ability range slightly above the national average'. But this fairly precise knowledge was not referred to or, apparently, utilized when the school's exam performance was assessed. Later in the same report, results are judged to be 'very satisfactory' on the basis of data on pass rates, without reference to the known features of the intake.

Other reports in contrast illustrate that, on occasions, HMI does look very carefully at the available information on intake, and takes it into account when evaluating a school's efforts. For example, the results of standardized tests carried out on the intake of Moreton School, Wolverhampton, showed that over the five years preceding the date of inspection the school received a first year intake with significantly lower scores than some 80 per cent of the other secondary schools in Wolverhampton.

The report links this information explicitly to exam results in the following way:

> If these [standardized test] scores are used as indicators of pupils' potential exam success at 16+ one might expect that some two to ten pupils each year would achieve five or more 'O' level grades A–C or CSE grade 1. Using these criteria, pupils' achievements are satisfactory.

The comment exemplifies the context-based model as employed by HMI: a school's exam performance is judged on the basis of whether it performs better or worse than what it would have been reasonable to predict on the basis of the measured ability of the pupils at intake. In the report on Moreton, however, as in all the other cases where a context-based model is employed, such judgements are not allowed to stand alone. Hence, on the basis of pass-rate measures, the O level results are dubbed 'generally poor'. Chelmsford High School, in contrast (the only grammar school in an area of nine other 'comprehensives'), had an intake consisting of 'a very narrow band from the top of the ability range'. A contextualized assessment of performance is presented: 'Public exam results are, in general, highly satisfactory in relation to the intake.'

However, data are then reported making implicit comparison with the national average: 'the mean number of O level grades per pupil was 8.29'. These figures 'show highly commendable results in GCE examinations'. It is interesting to note how these conclusions were reported in the press. An article in the *Sunday Times,* summarizing some findings from HMI reports, describes Chelmsford High School as 'Top Exam School' (Wilby, 1983). The figure of 8.29 'O' level passes is quoted, and there is no reference to the ability of the intake. Arguably, in relation to the kind of selective intake it had received, the school was doing no more than would be reasonably expected. HMI's conclusion on the school must, however, be said to be ultimately standards-based: 'the school enjoys a record of achievement of which it may justifiably be proud'.

A thoroughgoing context-based model of assessment for exam results would permit of the possibility that a school with relatively 'poor' results (i.e. in terms of comparisons with national averages and pass rates) could none the less also be said to enjoy a record 'of which it might justifiably be proud'. We found, however, a marked difference between the language employed in the description of the performance of disadvantaged schools as

Table D *Summary evaluations of the exam performances of three advantaged and three disadvantaged schools*

School	Intake description	Exam performance summary
Advantaged schools		
Chelmsford High	'Intake consists of a very narrow band from the top of the ability range.' 'Certain that the majority of the pupils are from relatively prosperous homes.'	'Highly commendable' 'Highly satisfactory'
King Edward VI	'Apparent that there are few pupils with serious learning difficulties and many with above average potential.'	'Very good'
Beal High	'Rather more of above average academic aptitude than below.' 'Significant numbers for whom a high academic expectation is entirely appropriate.'	'Very good' 'Generally sound' 'A good degree of success'
Disadvantaged schools		
Moreton	'Intake with significantly lower [VR] scores than some 80 per cent of the other secondary schools in Wolverhampton' serving area 'suffering multiple and intense deprivation.'	'Satisfactory'
Ruffwood	In LEA with 'the highest proportion of disadvantaged children in socio-economic terms'. This is 'reflected in the ability range of the school population, which is skewed downward. Average attainment on entry is about one year below the national average.'	'In about all cases satisfactory rather than good'
Benfield	'Three-quarters of pupils from inner city areas in which there is considerable deprivation.' 'Full ability range, but pupils of below average ability are over-represented. The proportion of pupils with a reading age of less than nine years on entry has averaged 10 per cent over the past seven years.'	'In the main reasonably satisfactory except at 'O' level'

against that used in relation to schools clearly identified as advantaged. In table D we compare the summary evaluations of exam performance in respect of three advantaged and three disadvantaged schools. The contrast is clear. Irrespective of the degree of deprivation, disadvantaged schools have merited no more than a 'satisfactory' to sum up their performance.

Now it could be, of course, that the inspectors had not, in fact, visited any 'disadvantaged' schools whose performance merited higher praise than this; but it seems odd that this should be the case with these three disadvantaged schools and yet not apply to even one of the three advantaged ones. And we wonder what the inspectors actually meant when they commented of Benfield's exam results that the 'exam results were, in the main, reasonably satisfactory *except* at 'O' level' (our italics)? Did they mean that the school's CSE results were 'reasonably satisfactory'? Equivocal evaluations of this kind abound in the reports.

None of these pieces of evidence is fully convincing as regards the HMI's use of contextualized approaches to evaluation. However, the genuine assimilation of such a model should result in the language of excellence being as frequently applied to disadvantaged schools as to more advantaged ones. This does not appear up to now to have been the case.

DISCUSSION

In the introduction to this analysis we quoted former Senior Chief Inspector Sheila Browne's (1979) comments on the criteria HMI employed to answer the question whether or not a school's performance was 'good enough'. To recap, 'as a first set of measures [they use] the school's own aims and, as a second, those which derive from practice across the country'. Browne was, of course, referring to the whole spectrum of a school's aims, objectives and activities, and not just those which lend themselves to public examination. Furthermore, in our experience to date, secondary schools rarely set out explicitly their objectives in the field of public examinations. If we were to impose an interpretation upon their aspirations in this area, however, we suspect it would take the form that:

(a) they would wish their performance to be *at least as good* as that of schools with comparable intakes of pupils; and
(b) they would hope to improve it over the years.

Such objectives would, of course, correspond to the third and fourth criteria we identified HMI employing, namely comparisons over time and the contextualization of performance.

In practice, we have found that, to date and in the reports we have examined in detail, HMI has placed emphasis on the second set of measures to which Browne refers. Whilst our four categories of criteria do not exhaust those employed, we found that in no fewer than thirty-four of the thirty-five schools comments were made in terms of criteria that made reference to standards 'derived from across the country', either based on national averages, pass rates (see Table B) or both. In contrast, only sixteen of the thirty-five schools were evaluated in terms of what we take to be the school's 'own aims', namely comparisons over time, on a contextualized basis, or both. Whilst nineteen of the thirty-five schools were evaluated exclusively in terms of a model based on national averages, pass rates or both, just one school was evaluated exclusively in terms of the alternative, on comparisons over time or context (again see Table B).

Furthermore, whereas Browne's comments would lead one to suppose that aspects of both sets of approaches would be used, in the group of reports we have examined here we found this to be the case in fewer than half (fifteen out of thirty-five). In brief, a standards-based approach seems to have predominated.

We asked in our introductory remarks whether HMI had developed an approach to evaluating school's examination results which was equally fair to all schools. We indicated that, given the demonstrably strong relationship between schools' intakes and subsequent outcomes in terms of exam results (see for example, Gray and Jones, 1983; Rutter *et al.*, 1979), a standards-based approach could not achieve this objective. In so far as our analysis has suggested that HMI has, in practice, adopted such an approach, we must conclude that schools are unlikely to be treated on an equal footing. Indeed, it follows logically that the less favoured a school is in terms of the ability levels of its intake, the more likely it is to receive a relatively less favourable evaluation.[4]

In conclusion, we have found very considerable variation between reports on individual schools in respect of which combinations of evaluative approaches were employed, and what supporting evidence was provided for their judgements. We have not attempted to address in this paper the question of how much weight should be attached to schools' examination results as against other forms of achievement, nor how HMI appears to us to have balanced these in its reports. However, we find it a matter for concern that, on the single dimension of examination results, three schools in our sample were evaluated in terms of all four criteria identified, but twelve were evaluated exclusively in terms of one. A more rigorous and consistent application of an agreed framework, from the professional body best placed to operate it, would surely be of service to the schools inspected, and ultimately to the school system as a whole.

ACKNOWLEDGEMENTS

The research reported in this article was supported by a grant to the Contexts Project from the Economic and Social Research Council (HR8602). We are grateful to the ESRC for their support but wish to emphasize that we alone bear responsibility for the views and interpretations offered here.

NOTES

1. It is interesting to note, in this connection, that until 1855 Inspectors' Reports had been circulated to every teacher holding a Certificate of Merit. As Ball remarks, these reports were at the time almost the only means by which a progressive teacher could find out what was going on in education (Ball, 1983. p. 222). We are indebted to our colleague Jean Rudduck for drawing Ball's work to our attention.
2. The thirty-five schools were as follows: Applemore; Archbishop Sancroft; Beal; Benfield; Chapel-en-le-Frith; Chell; Chelmsford; Chipping Norton; Copley; Fartown; Gateacre; Hainault; Keswick; Kettlethorpe; King Edward VI; Kirk Hallam; Liverpool Institute; Madeley Court; Moreton; New Heys; Old Hall; Ormesby; Our Lady's; Piggott; Prince William; Range; Reepham; Rowena; Ruffwood; Stalham County; St Kevin's; Thomas Becket; Wadebridge; Wheathampstead; Wrenn.
3. It may be, however, that in the case of *very* disadvantaged schools there is some qualified recognition of the need to take account of a school's particular circumstances.
4. Interestingly, we found the fullest interpretation of a school's results, taking account of its intake, in a 'short' report rather than a 'full' one. Archbishop Tenison's School is part of the Inner London Education Authority and, as a direct consequence of the Authority's policies, undertakes analyses of its examination performance broken down in terms of the ability levels of its pupils; these are presented in some detail in the HMI's report on the school.

REFERENCES

Ball, N. (1983) *Her Majesty's Inspectorate*, Education Monographs VI, Institute of Education, Birmingham University.
Browne, S. (1979) The accountability of HM Inspectorate, in J. Lello (ed.) *Accountability*, Ward Lock, London.
Gray, J. (1982) *Making More Sense of Examination Results*, supplementary material to Block 6 of Course E364, Curriculum Evaluation and Assessment in Educational Institutions, Open University, Milton Keynes.
Gray, J. and Jones, B. (1983) Towards a framework for interpreting examination results, *Sheffield Educational Research Current Highlights*, No. 5, pp. 1–4.
Hansard (1979) *Parliamentary Debates*, 5 November, HMSO, London, p. 100.
Plewis, I. (ed.) (1981) *Publishing School Examination Results: A Discussion*, Bedford Way Papers, Institute of Education, University of London.
Rutter, M., Maughan, B., Mortimore, P. and Ouston, J. (1979) *Fifteen Thousand Hours*, Open Books, London.

Secondary Heads Association (1980) You cannot treat exams as important and then try to suppress the results, *The Times Educational Supplement,* 12 December, p. 2.
Shipman, M. (1979) *In-School Evaluation,* Heinemann, London.
Wilby, P. (1983) An inspector calls, *Sunday Times,* 5 June.

2.7
WHAT CAN EXAMINATIONS
CONTRIBUTE TO SCHOOL EVALUATION?*
Harry Torrance

INTRODUCTION

Recently John Gray and Valerie Hannon have taken HMI to task for not contextualizing its analyses of examination results in its (now public) reports on schools (Gray and Hannon, 1985, paper 2.6 in this volume). They argue that data on pupil ability have to be taken into account in any discussion of a school's examination results. It is a familiar enough argument from the field of school effectiveness research and one I will outline in a little more detail below. However, in conflating the interpretation of examination results with the evaluation of schools, Gray and Hannon, even in the act of critique, draw attention to only one aspect of the evaluative process and run the risk of conferring legitimacy on a very narrow activity.

MacDonald (1976, p. 87), following Stake (1967) among others, draws our attention to the difference between assessment and evaluation: 'The purpose of assessment is to make statements about the recipients of an educational service . . . their actual and potential accomplishments . . . The purpose of evaluation . . . is . . . to make statements about the educational service.'

He goes on to suggest that assessment can only be part of any overall attempt at evaluation, and that assessment techniques designed to discriminate between individuals (norm-referenced) rather than describe what each had actually learned (criterion-referenced) would be unhelpful even to this limited role. MacDonald's distinction is useful in itself and also because it reminds us of how important it is to define the focus of our concern in any discussion of evaluation. This is not as straightforward as it might appear,

* Torrance, H. (1986) What can examinations contribute to school evaluation?, *Educational Review*, Vol. 38, No. 1, pp. 31–43.

since the components of any discussion will overlap considerably, or even be subsumed, one within another. In this paper I intend to discuss the use of examination results in the context of evaluation. During the course of the paper, attention will be drawn to the difficulties which might be encountered in using various assessments and examinations in evaluative exercises. In particular, the discussion will focus on assessments which are presented in the form of examination results (essay papers, multiple-choice tests, etc.) and assessments which some would claim can aid the interpretation of examination results (attainment on entry to secondary school and the like). I also intend to draw a distinction between school evaluation, discussed more often than not in the context of accountability, and curriculum evaluation, which is much more concerned with development – what to *do* about the conclusions drawn. Towards the end of the paper, however, I want to suggest that such distinctions, and indeed the distinction between assessment and evaluation itself, while beneficial to any analysis of the current role which examinations play in evaluation, may not be so helpful in the context of school development. Indeed, the advent of widespread school-based examining in GCSE may provide the mechanism for a proper integration of individual assessment and educational evaluation.

THE DEBATE OVER EXAMINATION RESULTS

It is the 1980 Education Act in particular which has brought examination results so explicitly into discussions of school effectiveness and evaluation. The compulsory publication of results rests on the assumption that results are indeed worth publishing – that they are a valid indicator of school performance and that the public in general, parents in particular, have a right to know about results and make comparisons across schools. Elliott (1981a) argues that only a vocal minority of parents are solely or even mainly interested in examination results. And yet it seems that schools do take examination success extremely seriously and point to their local communities as the source of the pressure for 'results' (DES, 1979). It may be, of course, that the pursuit of examination success brings benefits for the school and the individual teacher in terms of the control of pupils, career advancement and the like, with pressure from the local community being used as a convenient scapegoat for the pursuit of rather narrow educational aims. But such a crude interpretation seems unlikely. Rather a combination of pressures and policies will bring about a more, or less, exclusive concern of secondary schools for examination success (see Kushner *et al.*, 1983; Torrance, 1984a). However, the publication of results clearly focuses attention at national level on examination results as the main measure of performance.

Recently, we have seen this manifested in the continuing comparison of comprehensive and selective schools (e.g. Marks *et al.*, 1983) and in local authorities dithering over a return to selective secondary schooling (e.g. the *Guardian*, 10 November 1983), as well as in HMI reports.

The debate and the dithering revolve around how to interpret examination results. And in this respect, a number of authors have cautioned against straightforward comparisons across schools. In particular, Shipman (1979, p. 87), anticipating the Act, devoted a major chapter of his 'do-it-yourself manual' – *In-School Evaluation* – to the interpretation and presentation of examination results and writes: 'The valid interpretation of examination results depends on allowing for factors outside actual teaching that might account for changes across the years or between subjects, or between a school and others.'

In particular, Shipman draws attention to pupils' attainment on entry to secondary schools, and their socio-economic circumstances, as crucial variables. The argument is that the higher the measured attainment of pupils on entry, and the more middle class their background, the more likely will it be that examination success will be achieved. The task is then to ascertain whether the school did as well as, better than, or worse than, it could have been expected to. Other factors relating to school and departmental examination entry policies and the like are also clearly relevant here. Likewise Gray has played a leading role in the development of school effectiveness studies and has recently discussed similar issues in an Open University teaching text (Gray, 1982a) . . .

So examination results are being published and are being used in evaluative exercises. Further, that use is being endorsed – with apparently appropriate cautions – by leading observers of and commentators on the debate about school effectiveness. And yet there are clearly problems with such use, problems with the validity and reliability of the various assessments and examinations themselves, and problems with the utility of the exercise anyway, even supposing that it is indeed valid. This last point springs from the overlap between discussions about school effectiveness and educational evaluation. Schools may be shown to be more or less effective in terms of examination results (a narrow enough measure of educational performance to be sure, and a highly criticized and possibly even outdated one, cf. Burgess and Adams, 1980) but that still begs questions about particular courses, and about how schools might become more effective in this and other areas. This will be my focus in the latter part of the paper. For the moment, however, I want to consider whether the results of examinations, even set in a context of previously measured attainment, can be treated as unproblematic in themselves. A large body of statistical and interpretative evidence suggests that they cannot.

THE RELIABILITY AND VALIDITY OF EXAMINATION RESULTS

As long ago as the 1930s, research evidence was being presented which cast considerable doubt on inter-marker reliability in examination marking. Hartog and Rhodes (1935) demonstrated among other things that passing or failing an examination could vary according to who marked a particular paper. Other studies over the years have continued to cast doubt on the accuracy of examination marking. Ingenkamp (1977, p. 14) in his international review writes: 'By 1970 a stage had been reached when traditional oral and written examinations had been shown to be neither objective nor reliable: their content validity was jeopardized by subjective influences, predictive validity was low, and the marking of different examiners could not be compared.' More recently still, and with regard to GCE in this country, Murphy (1978) found that although agreement among examiners was generally good, variation could still occur in large measure. And variation itself varied with subject, type of response required (e.g. essay) and the number of parts to the examination. Murphy also reminds us that inter-marker reliability is but one aspect of the overall reliability of an examination. Not all examinations comprise 'traditional' essay questions of course, and partly in response to criticism levelled at such examinations, papers involving multiple-choice items and the like have come to be introduced. But Ingenkamp (1977, p. 48) is not particularly optimistic about their value either: 'We can only say that the state of research on this important question is extremely disappointing. Many efforts are made to promote the use of objective tests in examinations, but we know little about their validity.'

Beyond this, a candidate's final grade will also be affected by the method of grading which an examination board uses, and very small variations in marks can result in large variations in grading. The boards themselves have drawn attention to the problem and the Joint Matriculation Board (1983) in commenting on their 'A' level results for 1982, show that a minimum of 16 marks out of 196 separated grade D from grade B in Mathematics, while 9 out of 200 separated D from B in English Literature. Their pamphlet goes on to state that: 'The percentage marks required to take a candidate from grade D to grade B ranged from 2.9 (of a maximum of 340) for Chemistry Syllabus A to 9.5. (of a maximum of 200) for Sociology' (p. 8). Casting our net a little wider still, when considering the comparison of examination grades across schools, we also need to consider whether grades are comparable not just within boards, but across boards. Various investigations of comparability were initiated when CSE was first introduced and Nuttall (1971, p. 11) reported, for example, that 'the evidence from the 1965, 1966 and 1967 studies considered together forms a sound basis for concluding that there is very little cause for concern about mean grade standards . . . and only mild cause for concern about grade 1 standards'.

Six years later, however, in a study investigating CSE and GCE, Wilmott (1977, p. 10) concluded that 'some apparently considerable variations in the subject grading standards of the CSE and GCE examining boards have been found'. This conclusion was qualified by numerous methodological caveats and latterly it is in fact the methodological discussion which has begun to take precedence. Leading writers in the field are beginning to wonder whether it is actually possible to compare results across boards and across time, let alone whether such work would reveal further variation. After looking at various cross-moderation models and practices, Goldstein (1982, p. 116) concludes: 'This review has been generally critical and pessimistic about the utility of various equating and comparability methods in use . . . if reasonable comparability is simply not possible, perhaps we should be asking whether attempts to achieve it should not be abandoned.'

THE RELIABILITY AND VALIDITY OF ABILITY TESTS

On the input side too, the picture is by no means as clear cut as an invitation to make use of tests of ability might lead us to believe. The validity and utility of testing the attainment and ability of children at 11+ was undermined almost as soon as it became widely practised after the 1944 Education Act, from both psychological and sociological perspectives (see, for example, Watts, Pidgeon and Yates, 1952; Vernon, 1957; Floud and Halsey, 1957; Goldstein and Levy, 1984, provide a more up-to-date review of available tests while Haney (1984) reviews eighty years of American debate – and more recently litigation – on these issues). Currently, as testing young (and not so young) children on a regional and national basis becomes more widespread again, it is proceeding nevertheless on an *ad hoc* basis. Thus our cautions with regard to the marking and administration of examinations, and the comparison of like with like, would also seem relevant to attainment testing. The recent SSRC-funded evaluation of testing in local authorities seems to bear out our doubts. Steadman and Gipps (1983) report that different local education authorities (LEAs) use different tests in different ways for different purposes, often tests which 'informed opinion' would regard as 'seriously out of date'. They suggest that it is the symbolic role of testing which is crucial – LEAs, and schools, being seen to do something about standards – rather than its actual validity or utility, and conclude that 'even given well-designed tests which are correctly administered and scored, the pluses of testing are more evident when individual children are tested to guide their education, and the minuses are more evident when groups are tested to serve administrative and/or political purposes' (p. 10). None of which would surprise devotees of evaluation literature and reminds us of MacDonald's (1976) distinction between assessment and evaluation.

If we now move on to review briefly one or two interpretative studies of testing, we find that detailed observation of the test situation also raises serious questions about the validity of the enterprise. Mehan (1973) working in the context of a major American socio-linguistic investigation, studied the response of children to language testing, and in particular looked at the sorts of mistakes they were making. He points out that children can answer incorrectly for many reasons, particularly when they interpret the question in a different way to that which the test designer and administrator intended. He challenges the assumption that test takers will respond uniformly and unambiguously to the test and suggests that 'Conventional testing techniques cannot determine if a child's wrong answers are due to his lack of ability or are due to his equally valid alternative interpretations' (p. 129).

In short, misunderstanding can all too easily arise, even assuming, and it is a big assumption, that children will try hard and give of their best in an unusual setting which might be construed as uninteresting and/or unimportant. They may even try to do badly if they understand the consequences of success in terms of separation from friends, and so on. All of these problems might be realized and compounded by differential administration of the test itself. To return again to the UK, Stierer (1983) reporting on an ethnographic study of testing also carried out under the auspices of the SSRC evaluation, confirms the variation of test administration across LEAs, schools, and indeed individual teachers. He writes:

> It is obviously difficult to ensure uniform testing conditions across large numbers of schools and classrooms . . . these variations . . . where standardized scores are taken seriously, by teachers, schools and LEAs . . . call into question the way in which scores on a standardized test are achieved and then related to the population.
> (Stierer, 1983, p. 11; for the full report see Gipps *et al.*, 1983)

Nor are such issues only relevant to the testing of young children prior to or on entry to secondary school. The interpretation of examination questions is as significant a problem as the interpretation of test items. When issues of question choice, essay response and so on are brought in, knowing what it is that is actually being tested becomes especially difficult. Wilmott and Hall (1975, p. 120) suggest that

> the taxonomic content of an item would appear to be not so much a property of the question itself, but a property of the learning experiences of the candidates answering the question. Under these circumstances, it would seem to be a difficult, if not impossible, task for an examiner to write an item which would test the same ability in all candidates.

And this remark itself takes as read the general difficulties surrounding the design of valid examinations. Interestingly enough, the examination boards themselves are now taking seriously criticisms of the one-off final paper as well as trying to make sure that the one-off final paper is as valid as possible in its own terms. Claims that certain aspects of a course can only properly be examined during the course, and that a wider sample of examined work would in any case give a more reliable result, have led the boards to introduce many schemes involving coursework assessment and the like. This in turn however adds to the problems of variability of practice and interpretation across schools, teachers and individual children (AEB, 1981; Torrance, 1985a).

So the use and interpretation of examination results is by no means as straightforward as even well-informed commentators might lead us to believe. Of course, we must beware of condemning techniques of assessment simply because they are not perfect – striving for what is reasonable in the circumstances seems appropriate enough. But by the same token, we must then beware of making use of the results of such measurements in anything other than the most cautious of discussions. To return to Shipman (1979), it would seem that we have identified many 'factors outside actual teaching that might account for changes across years or between subjects, or between a school and others'. All of which is not to suggest that test scores or examination results are simply distributed by chance. Clearly patterns do emerge and recur, particularly with regard to their distribution across social classes. As Gray (1982a) demonstrates, measures of verbal reasoning and social class do 'give quite good predictions of how well schools will subsequently do in terms of public examination results'. But if examination results are not distributed randomly, they could certainly be distributed erroneously, across both individuals and social classes. This of course leads us into the area of class and cultural bias which I simply want to note, then leave to one side.

For the purposes of the current discussion – the comparison and evaluation of results across individual pupils and individual schools, and indeed the evaluation of schools in terms of their results – it is sufficient to note that the data under consideration are not particularly valid or reliable.

TESTING AND CURRICULUM EVALUATION

To take matters a little further, it is also interesting to note that, even if our measures of input and (particularly) output were to be relied upon, they would still leave us wondering exactly what pupils had or had not learned, and what we might do about it. They would not be a great deal of use, in other words, in the context of (curriculum) evaluation, as opposed to a fairly crude notion of accountability. We have already noted that MacDonald (1976) suggested criterion-referencing might be more helpful than norm-referencing. A few years earlier Wiseman and Pidgeon (1970) were convinced that this was the case. Their (apparently, and at that time) definitive review of the American literature of the 1960s called for curriculum planning and development by the clarification and specification of measurable objectives. The measurement of these objectives would then provide the basis for evaluation and review:

> existing instruments may not provide a measure of the precise objectives in which the teacher is interested . . . and . . . they have been developed for the most part to assess and to compare the abilities of individuals. Curriculum evaluation involves a quite different approach to the problem of assessment . . . In this kind of assessment, the concern is rather with the overall performance of a group of pupils.
>
> (Wiseman and Pidgeon, 1970, p. 47)

Over recent years, the vocabulary, if not the practice, of teaching by objectives has certainly established a 'beach-head' (as MacDonald, 1979, put it) in English schools; not least because a number of examination boards have adopted it, particularly with regard to injecting some rigour into Mode III submissions. For example: 'It must be possible to observe and measure all of the objectives . . . Centres should remember that there are a number of objectives which are valid on educational grounds but which cannot be observed and measured objectively and cannot therefore be assessed' (NREB, 1981, p. 32). How teachers interpret such instructions is another matter of course. One who has worked on a Mode III submission to NREB commented: 'this form we have to fill in . . . drove everybody crackers . . . it was difficult to find the wording of what the board were after' (Torrance, 1982, p. 44).

The Southern Regional Examinations Board is another which adopted an objectives model of syllabus development in the early 1970s. But their experience has also been that of a poorly understood initiative misapplied by hard-pressed part-time subject panels. Jones (1983) shows how the language of objectives was applied to existing syllabuses without any change in the syllabus, and indeed, that the objectives which were produced by at least one panel were 'largely based on objectives written for another board' (p. 90).

For the most part then, the design and administration of examinations remains inappropriate even to the sort of task which measurement-oriented evaluators would wish them to perform. We could persevere of course, and recent reviews such as that of Black and Broadfoot (1982) urge us, among other things, to do so. It is argued that well-designed criterion-referenced tests would be relevant to and useful in the 'modern classroom', particularly with regard to monitoring the progress of individual children. But as we have seen, valid and reliable tests are hard to come by and very difficult to design, and the conflation, not to say confusion, of diagnostic testing with criterion-referenced curriculum evaluation could still cause problems. Black and Broadfoot do in fact make a good deal of the broader process-oriented perspectives on evaluation but then we have Steadman and Gipps (1983), among many others, to remind us that once developed, a test may be used in many different ways.

It seems that you cannot have it both ways – tests in the classroom and ruminative reflection at the governors' meeting. The logic of measurement, of course, is to develop different tests for different purposes but we are left to ask who would do this and where would the money come from.

Until recently the gap – if indeed there is one – was being filled by the APU . . . But this in turn begs questions about curriculum control. The APU originally claimed to be in the business of taking 'snapshots' of current practice; now, at least some of its researchers are happy to acknowledge that they are likely to have a major impact on the curriculum and that this will be no bad thing (Harlen, 1984). More recently still, the Secretary of State for Education has talked of a national testing programme being introduced. We should not be surprised, of course; many authors have maintained that tests and examinations have always influenced and indeed controlled the curriculum in this country (e.g. Broadfoot, 1981) . . . MacDonald (1974) has argued that the clarification of objectives is an inherently political activity, while even in terms of a narrower educational debate the objectives model of curriculum development and evaluation has its critics. Thus Stenhouse (1975, p. 83) for example, maintained that 'the objectives approach is an attempt to improve practice by increasing clarity about ends. Even if it were logically justifiable in terms of knowledge – and it is not – there is a good case for claiming that it is not the way to improve practice,' while Parlett and Hamilton (1972) [have argued that] test-based evaluation simply does not provide enough relevant and useful information on which decisions might be based.

EVALUATION AND THE DEVELOPMENT OF THE EFFECTIVENESS OF SCHOOLING

This brings us back to the use which might be made of examination results. While the suggestions of Shipman (1979) and Gray (1982a and 1982b) might help schools to defend themselves against ill-informed attack (an important enough aspiration) and might even encourage some schools to think in terms of reviewing aspects of curriculum and pedagogy if results turned out to be worse than could be predicted, they do not in themselves provide much of a basis for such a review. This is the case whether results are reviewed as a whole or department by department. Results *per se* provide too little information, too late. Changes of teaching method or methods may be made from one year to another, but if enacted in too mechanistic a fashion, if improving results is the only yardstick, then such changes are likely to derive from strategic suspicions of what 'the board is after', rather than from any overall consideration of educational aims and provision. So examination results may tell us a little bit about what has happened, but not how or why. As Davis (1981, p. 13) suggests, 'the *improvement* of the object of evaluation usually requires some degree of *understanding* which, in turn, depends on appropriate data and information' (original emphasis). To be fair, Gray (1982b) acknowledges this and Shipman (1979) reviews many other aspects of a school's work besides examination courses. Shipman also alerts us to means and methods of evaluation which go beyond examination results – observations by colleagues, review by interested outsiders, and the like – but he says little about how these might actually be accomplished and used.

Other writers have made similar observations about utility and responsibility in school evaluation. Debates over democratic, illuminative and responsive evaluation at programme level have their corollaries at the level of the individual school. As MacDonald has put it:

> It is the duty of the school to provide the best possible opportunities for learning consistent with its circumstances. This should be the basis of a school accountability model – a process rather than a product model . . . the 'process' in the process model refers to the process of educational critique.
>
> (MacDonald, 1978, pp. 138 and 143)

and Simons:

> We need to know not so much what pupils can be demonstrated to have learned . . . rather what transpires in the process of learning and teaching, the outcomes we could reasonably expect from such transactions and the strengths and weaknesses of educational provision . . . evaluation on process lines allows schools to demonstrate and to account for what they can reasonably be held to be accountable for, i.e. creating the opportunities for children to learn and for the quality of provision.
>
> (Simons, 1981, pp. 119 and 130)

MacDonald and Simons outline various quasi-practical steps which schools may take along the road to process evaluation – they should initiate the process of review themselves; they should start small and probably privately, collating easily accessible data on staff qualifications, resources, quantity and range of textbooks and the like before starting to think about the issues which such data might raise, and how the issues might be pursued. But we are still left to wonder how data on pedagogy and the realization of curricular intentions would be gathered. We are left with the feel of a defensive review carried out by an already overworked deputy head (just as she might pull a 'seriously out of date' test from the back of her cupboard once a year). Even presuming that schools have overall policies and curriculum review committees and the like, the learning and teaching that Simons talks about is still essentially organized at departmental and classroom level. In saying this, I may be running the risk of focusing attention too narrowly on 'nitty-gritty' academic problems, but it seems appropriate to start any overall review of practice by thinking more systematically about those problems which will be given (unsystematic?) attention in any case. Elliott (1981b) and Broadfoot (1981) have made similar points, suggesting that it is in their day-to-day dealings with departmental colleagues and pupils that teachers feel a sense of responsibility and accountability.

TOWARDS SCHOOL-BASED EVALUATION

So what might school-based, process-oriented evaluation look like? I have argued elsewhere with specific reference to Mode III, that school-based examining can provide the context for self-evaluation initiatives within the individual school, as well as being a mechanism which could be used across schools (Torrance, 1984b). Involvement in Mode III work of itself presupposes some dissatisfaction with existing provision, a review of curriculum and assessment methods, and continuing meetings to discuss teaching and learning within the department, as well as marking and moderation with teachers from other schools. In the context of Mode III, of course, involvement is voluntaristic. Yet the spread of teacher-assessed elements in many Mode I examinations, in both CSE and GCE, suggests that the mechanism – the forum of discussion and the stimulus to action – will now encompass many more teachers than those who might have previously wished to become involved in curriculum development and evaluation. National criteria for GCSE suggest this trend is now very well established.

In the longer term it is still not clear what GCSE examinations will look like, but it does not seem likely that teacher involvement in assessment will diminish, quite the reverse (Torrance, 1985b; Nuttall, 1985). Indeed, at

least one examination board secretary is canvassing for a broader involvement of teachers in regional accreditation networks (Macintosh, 1982) while
the Oxford Delegacy, anticipating interest in Records of Achievement (or
Profiles) is pressing ahead with the development of a 'certificate of achievement' which seems certain to involve teachers more widely in the board's
procedures (OCEA, 1983). Continuing developments with regard to Records of Achievement possibly organized on a formative, tutorial basis
rather than as some arbitrary summative statement, could bring pupils and
their parents into the dialogue about means and ends in education. It is in
this way then, that routine assessments of individual pupils' work, and
routine meetings to moderate grades, can connect with broader evaluative
questions of what it is reasonable to expect individual pupils to achieve, what
it is reasonable to expect individual teachers and departments to provide,
and how might the quality of provision be improved. In turn, and going
beyond MacDonald's and Simons's brief, such reflection could also raise
questions about the *quantity* of provision – about resource allocation on a
local and national scale.

There could be problems of course. Many teachers do not want to become
'examiners' in any narrow sense of the word and are very wary of coursework assessment schemes. Clearly, unwilling conscripts are not likely to wish
to devote more time than they absolutely have to to an activity which they
regard with suspicion (see Torrance (1985b) for a more detailed account of
some of the problems inherent in the extension of school-based examining).
At the same time, making the most of current subject-based mechanisms
may not be particularly helpful in the context of an overall school evaluation. The strength of the English department's review system may depend a
good deal on the number of pupils they have to examine and the teaching
team which has therefore to be created, as well as a particularly helpful
moderator. The weakness of the History department's review could be
caused by a reverse set of circumstances. Furthermore, all the problems of
validity and (particularly) reliability which were outlined previously might
be said to be compounded by school-based examining and evaluation.

There are two issues involved here really – first whether pupils' final
results can actually be relied upon, and second, whether teachers' reflections upon them and upon the course – their self-evaluation – can be relied
upon. The first is of less direct concern to our argument than the second,
though it is still important, not least because teachers themselves take the
need for cross-school comparability very seriously (Torrance, 1985a). This
in itself is a starting point, and previous studies have suggested that local
groups of teachers can produce reliable results (Schools Council, 1967). In
this respect they would be acting little differently from a team of external

examiners who might meet under the auspices of a chief examiner to agree marking criteria and grades. National comparability is another matter of course but then, as Goldstein (1982) has remarked, if comparability across more controlled test situations is so difficult to achieve, perhaps users should simply 'make allowances for different standards . . . (with) . . . the onus for a valid interpretation of the examination results (resting) with the user rather than with the present somewhat shaky comparability procedures' (p. 117). The point would seem to be that as school-based examining spreads more widely, so does the experience of marking and moderating work, and thinking about the relationship between work set and work produced. Experience, good or bad, will raise issues for debate as well as contribute to actual practice. Problems of validity and reliability can thus be confronted on a local and regional scale through the accessible 'technology' of discussion and argument, open to scrutiny rather than shrouded in statistics.

In similar fashion, self-evaluation already takes place informally and more or less intuitively in the context of school-based examining. The impetus for action derives from, and the locus of action resides in, the individual teacher within the departmental structure. The proper assessment of pupils' work demands attention to the context in which the work was produced, the nature of the task and so on. The many facets of evaluative inquiry are therefore already present. Individual teachers set work, mark work, and are in a position to observe whether and in what respects a particular project or assignment has been successful. Thinking about why it has or has not been successful and how it might be improved goes beyond the immediate classroom task, but there is little reason to suppose that teachers would knowingly deceive themselves. In discussions with colleagues, they would in fact have most to gain from as objective an evaluation as possible, in order to 'get it right' or at least make it 'work better' next time around. Whether that evaluation remains at the level of informal chat rather than becoming more systematic and focused is the real concern.

Thus, just as evaluation is still interpreted in too narrow a fashion, so too are assessment and examinations. In reality, schools and examination boards are casting their nets far wider than might be commonly supposed in an attempt to produce more flexible and valid assessments of pupils' work and in so doing, are creating the conditions in which focused, useful and effective self-evaluation can be pursued. Such an evaluation strategy would build on existing activity rather than simply adding to it and ought to be responsive to need – both within the school and within the community. In starting with an examination focus, such self-evaluation is likely to have an immediate relevance with regard to the instrumental pursuit of 'results' yet almost certainly lead to wider reflection about overall provision. Similarly, while 'going public' with internal departmental discussion is hardly appropriate, the writing of reports, the setting of homework, the examination of coursework by moderators, and so on, means that a good deal of the assumptions with which a department and a school operate are open to scrutiny – albeit fragmented and *ad hoc* – at the moment. School-based examining ought to mean that this at least remains the case, and perhaps is more coherently organized.

To return to the opening argument with regard to HMI reports and school effectiveness, the logic underpinning the improvement of HMI reports is the improvement of information for decision-making (by government and/or citizen, e.g. individual parents choosing schools). All well and good, but as I have indicated that task is both difficult and narrow. To improve schools we need to build dialogue about *curriculum*. Thus just as the reliability and validity of examination results can be confronted through discussion and debate – recognizing the uncertainty of the enterprise – so too can broader questions of educational evaluation and the quality of educational provision. In this respect the key question becomes not so much given examination results how might we best interpret them, but given examination courses (and particularly teacher involvement in assessment) how can we best organize them to promote self-evaluation and the improvement of educational practice.

REFERENCES

Associated Examining Board (1981) *Combining Teacher Assessment with Examining Board Assessment*, AEB, Aldershot.

Black, H. and Broadfoot, P. (1982) *Keeping Track of Teaching*, Routledge & Kegan Paul, London.

Broadfoot, P. (1981) Towards a sociology of assessment, in L. Barton and S. Walker (eds.) *Schools, Teachers and Teaching*, Falmer Press, Lewes.

Burgess, T. and Adams, E. (eds.) (1980) *Outcomes of Education*, Macmillan, Basingstoke.

Davis, E. (1981) *Teachers as Curriculum Evaluators*, Allen & Unwin, Sydney.

DES (1979) *Aspects of Secondary Education*, HMSO, London.

Elliott, J. (1981a) How do parents judge schools?, in J. Elliott *et al. School Accountability*, Grant McIntyre, London.

Elliott, J. (1981b) Teachers' perspectives on school accountability, in J. Elliott *et al.*, op. cit.

Floud, J. and Halsey, A. (1957) Intelligence tests, social class and selection for secondary school, *British Journal of Sociology*, No. 8, pp. 33–9.

Gipps, C., Blackstone, T., Steadman, S. and Stierer, B. (1983) *Testing Children: standardised testing in local education authorities and schools*, Heinemann, London.

Goldstein, H. (1982) Models for equating test scores and for studying the comparability of public examination, *Educational Analysis*, Vol. 4, No. 3, pp. 107–18.

Goldstein, H. and Levy, P. (1984) *Tests in Education*, Academic Press, London.
Gray, J. (1982a) *Making More Sense of Examination Results*, Open University Press, Milton Keynes.
Gray, J. (1982b) Publish and be damned? The problem of comparing exam results in two inner London schools, *Educational Analysis*, Vol. 4, No. 3, pp. 47–56.
Gray, J. and Hannon, V. (1985) HMI's interpretations of schools' examination results. Paper presented to British Educational Research Association annual meeting, Sheffield.
Haney, W. (1984) Testing reasoning and reasoning about testing, *Review of Educational Research*, Vol 54, No. 4, pp. 597–654.
Harlen, W. (1984) The impact of APU science work at LEA and school level, *Journal of Curriculum Studies*, Vol. 16, No. 1, pp. 89–94.
Hartog, P. and Rhodes, R. (1935) *An Examination of Examinations* Macmillan, London.
Ingenkamp, K. (1977) *Educational Assessment*, NFER, Windsor.
Joint Matriculation Board (1983) *Problems of the GCE Advanced Level Grading Scheme*, JMB, Manchester.
Jones, A. (1983) *The Perception and Implementation of Examination Syllabus Objectives*, Department of Education, Southampton University.
Kushner, S. *et al.* (1983) *Decision-Making in the Secondary Curriculum*, Open University Press, Milton Keynes.
MacDonald, B. (1974) Evaluation and the control of education, in B. MacDonald and R. Walker (eds.) *Innovation, Evaluation, Research and the Problem of Control*, Centre for Applied Research in Education, Norwich.
MacDonald, B. (1976) Who's afraid of evaluation?, *Education 3–13*, Vol. 4, No. 2, pp. 87–91.
MacDonald, B. (1978) Accountability, standards and the process of schooling, in A. Becher and S. Maclure (eds.) *Accountability in Education*, NFER, Windsor.
MacDonald, B. (1979) Hard times – accountability in England, *Educational Analysis*, Vol. 1, No. 1, pp. 23–44.
Macintosh, H. (1982) The prospects for public examinations in England and Wales, *Educational Analysis*, Vol. 4, No. 3, pp. 13–20.
Marks, J., Cox, C. and Pomian-Srzednicki, M. (1983) *Standards in English Schools*, National Council for Educational Standards, London.
Mehan, H. (1973) Assessing children's school performance, reprinted in M. Hammersley and P. Woods (eds.) (1976) *The Process of Schooling*, Routledge & Kegan Paul, London, for the Open University.
Murphy, R. (1978) Reliability of marking in eight GCE examinations, *British Journal of Educational Psychology*, No. 48, pp. 196–200.
North Regional Examinations Board (1981) *Handbook for Mode 3 Examinations*, NREB, Newcastle.
Nuttall, D. (1971) *The 1968 CSE Monitoring Experiment*, Schools Council Working Paper 34, Evans/Methuen Educational, London.
Nuttall, D. (1985) Evaluating progress towards the GCSE. Paper presented to British Educational Research Association annual conference, Sheffield.
Oxford Certificate of Educational Achievement (1983) *Newsletter*, No. 1, Oxford Delegacy.
Parlett, M. and Hamilton, D. (1972) Evaluation as illumination, reprinted in D.

Tawney (ed.) (1976) *Curriculum Evaluation Today*, Macmillan Education, Basingstoke.

Schools Council (1967) *Teachers' Experience of School-based Examining*, Schools Council Examinations Bulletin 15, HMSO, London.

Shipman, M. (1979) *In-School Evaluation*, Heinemann, London.

Simons, H. (1981) Process evaluation in schools, in R. McCormick (ed.) (1982) *Calling Education to Account*, Open University Press, Milton Keynes.

Stake, R. (1967) Toward a technology for the evaluation of educational programs, in R. Tyler, R. Gagne and M. Scriven *Perspectives of Curriculum Evaluation*, AERA Monograph series on Curriculum Evaluation No. 1, Rand McNally, Chicago.

Steadman, S. and Gipps, S. (1983) Teachers and testing: pluses and minuses. Paper presented to British Educational Research Association annual conference, Institute of Education, London.

Stenhouse, L. (1975) *An Introduction to Curriculum Research and Development*, Heinemann, London.

Stierer, B. (1983) Reading tests in the classroom: a case study. Paper presented to the British Educational Research Association annual conference, Institute of Education, London.

Torrance, H. (1982) *Mode III Examining: A Study of Experience.* Centre for Applied Research in Education, Norwich.

Torrance, H. (1984a) Teachers, pupils and exams, in J. Schostak, and T. Logan (eds.) *Pupil Experience*, Croom Helm, London.

Torrance, H. (1984b) School-based examining: a mechanism for school-based professional development and accountability, *British Educational Research Journal*, Vol. 10, No. 1, pp. 71–81.

Torrance, H. (1985a) *Case Studies in School-based Examining*, Department of Education, University of Southampton.

Torrance, H. (1985b) Current prospects for school-based examining, *Educational Review*, Vol. 37, No. 1, pp. 39–51.

Vernon, P. (ed.) (1957) *Secondary School Selection*, Methuen, London.

Watts, A., Pidgeon, D. and Yates, A. (1952) *Secondary School Entrance Examinations*, Newnes, London.

Wilmott, A. (1977) *CSE and GCE Grading Standards*, Schools Council Research Studies, Macmillan, Basingstoke.

Wiseman, S. and Pidgeon, D. (1970) *Curriculum Evaluation*, NFER, Slough.

CONDUCTING EVALUATION — GATHERING AND ANALYSING DATA

INTRODUCTION

In this section of the reader we move on to look at actual ways of 'doing' evaluation. The section begins with a paper which offers very short, sharp accounts of the 'dos and don'ts' of evaluation for beginners. For all Stronach's brevity and ruthless pragmatism (Chapter 3.1), when it comes to designing and surviving evaluation the advice he offers is sound.

The following four papers attend to the particular methods of inquiry which evaluators might use. These papers do not in any respect cover the full range of evaluation methods, which can be used, neither do they provide the kind of detailed introduction that novice evaluators unfamiliar with educational research methods might need. There are of course plenty of existing texts that provide a more comprehensive range of methods which can be used in evaluation studies. Here we have chosen to include a selection of papers which are concerned more with qualitative than quantitative approaches, and which illustrate some of the practical issues that arise in applying qualitative data collection methods in evaluation studies.

In particular we have chosen to give special attention to papers discussing interviewing – Stenhouse (Chapter 3.2), Jones (Chapter 3.5) and Powney and Watts (Chapter 4.4 in Section 4). This has allowed us to penetrate one technique in some depth, whilst illustrating issues which are in many cases equally applicable to other techniques (e.g. observation). As Stenhouse argues in the first of the series (Chapter 3.2), interview and observation are by no means mutually exclusive. Walker's paper (Chapter 3.3) then attends to a range of techniques in addition to interview and observation, particularly the use of questionnaires and documents, while May and Sigsworth (Chapter 3.4) offer some interesting reflections on the immediate feedback and formative use of observational data. Jones (Chapter 3.5) is a helpful complement to the earlier paper because of her particular focus on issues to do with analysing rather than just collecting interview data. She offers some practical guidance that should be a great help to anyone faced with this often daunting prospect. The final three papers in this section attend to a key issue which has exercised evaluators for some time but which is still not widely enough discussed in the educational community at large – the *ethics* of evaluation. Many arguments have raged over the validity and reliability of evaluation and over the criteria which we implicitly or explicitly bring to judging the worth of an educational activity – how we decide what counts as 'good teaching' – and they are likely to become sharper still as teacher appraisal schemes develop and are introduced more widely. A further extension of this debate is the issue of the extent to which evaluation data and overall judgements can and should be made public. On the face of it, as MacDonald argued in Chapter 1.2 and reiterated in 2.5, the public has a 'right to know' what goes on in the education service and how its rates and taxes are spent. And certainly, *if* evaluation *is* to be conducted, the 'democratic' model would seem the most appropriate one to pursue and develop – leaving the DES or the MSC to evaluate themselves, 'bureaucrati- cally', would leave knowledge and power concentrated in very few hands indeed. Yet, as Pring argues (Chapter 3.6), there may be occasions when it would be best to leave delicate educational processes in peace. Without doubt, at the present time, there are many TVEI and Record of Achieve- ment project teachers who feel they've no sooner said hello and goodbye to their local evaluator before the national evaluators arrive, not to mention HMI and the meta-evaluators! (cf. Pennycuick, 1986). Chapter 3.7 demon- strates how one national evaluation has tried to take on board ethical issues, while Adelman and Alexander (Chapter 3.8) reflect on how such issues can shade into those of basic integrity, when institutional structures are really not adequate to the task of using, as opposed to conducting, evaluation democratically.

REFERENCES

Pennycuick, D. (1986) *TRIST Meta-evaluation Project: Interim Report,* University of Sussex.

3.1
PRACTICAL EVALUATION*
Ian Stronach

INTRODUCTION

My starting point is a desire to help the majority of local TVEI evaluators who feel they have little training or experience relevant to the task. They are in the same position as I was a few years ago – an experienced teacher, ignorant of evaluation and vocational education, and unable to be honest about it to the project and the schools (it pays to be modest about your incompetence). So what would be helpful? I thought I would offer highly specific and prescriptive advice. This would be opinionated, and often inappropriate, wrong, or nonsensical. But it might clarify evaluation design and practice issues as evaluators tested their own ideas against it, and it might create more reflection by being controversial and specific than an abstract waffle about methodological or ethical issues. At any rate, that's the intention.

STARTING UP

1. Ignore the literature on research and evaluation. You haven't time to shop around for methods or 'models'. Anyway, most articles are too abstract to be useful – and will leave you with a style rather than substance. They're holiday reading.
2. Plan your evaluation on a commonsense appraisal of your own resources (time, skills, personal strengths), the most pressing demands on you from the project (if any, sometimes projects need to be helped to ask questions), and the emerging issues from your fieldwork. Go for penetration rather than coverage. Don't underestimate the relevance of

* Stronach, I. (1986) Practical evaluation, in D. Hopkins (ed.) *Evaluating TVEI: Some Methodological Issues*, Cambridge Institute of Education.

your teaching experience or local knowledge – the ability to talk to students, staff, project workers, to understand subject, department and timetable issues is central.

3. Get to know the project as an educational rather than an administrative event – don't get too distracted by the bureaucratic scenery, bizarre though it may be. That means: ask educational questions – what does student-centred learning mean in school or subject X? What acts of negotiation take place in profiling and what kinds of knowledge are created and exchanged? How do students 'integrate' work experience into their formal and personal curriculum? What classroom interactions represent an equal opportunities policy in action? How is 'relevance' defined in TVEI curricula? (A non-educational example of a question – what percentage of students find 'work experience' worth while?)

4. Get to know the substantive areas, like hi-tech and profiling. That also includes project activities and their origins and sponsorship as ideas, other TVEI projects' activities in relevant areas, and parallel projects like Records of Achievement. Some innovations are second or third time round – look for old evaluation reports. Develop a comparative knowledge in key areas so that you can locate your project's practices against that background and generate new issues for further research (e.g. CGLI 365 profiles have been evaluated several times before: work experience schemes have been sorted into various types). Let these other projects be your library. Learn economically – attend workshops, use the phone, tap other evaluations and projects. Read as little as you can get away with.

5. Generate key questions and foci about your project, based on all of the above. Be creative – take chances with ideas, look for meanings as well as opinions (what is TVEI like – modernization in the Third World, the obelisk in 2001 AD, a monetarist attempt at educational theory, a new currency?).

6. Be a source of researched information and judgement about project activities. Let that source be independent of project political influence, but collaborative in terms of inquiry and interpretation.

7. The intellectual 'start-up' problems are easy compared with the diplomatic ones. Rule one: be seen – visit schools, talk to teachers informally, attend residentials, ask everybody what the issues are, what the evaluation ought to be doing.

8. Be tactful. Break the ice before asking to observe classrooms. Explain offers of anonymizing or negotiating data. Negotiate your way into the project from the top down (head, heads of department, TVEI co-ordinator, TVEI teachers). Negotiate and clear your data in the reverse

order to protect informants. Remember that although your job seems a nightmare of uncertainty, incompetence and vulnerability to you, it looks like paid leave to them.

9. Staff will tacitly accord you an equivalence in the hierarchy (= scale 2, scale 4, deputy head, adviser, UFO). What they tell you will be influenced by that equivalence. Erode it – try to become acceptable in steering groups and staffrooms.

10. Accept your vulnerability and refuse to become paranoid about it (but bear in mind that just because you're not paranoid doesn't mean that they aren't out to get you . . .). Evaluation may threaten project 'image', LEA accountability to MSC, the co-ordinator's career, the head's autonomy, the teacher's privacy, and so on. Everyone has more power than you, but not necessarily more influence. Expect unfair criticism, and listen to it – understand its political undercurrents as well as its ostensible meanings, without assuming that the former subsume the latter. So for example:

(a) Work for an acceptance of the evaluation's independent role. Set up an evaluation steering group to advise you and protect your integrity. Try to widen membership beyond LEA and MSC. An outsider may assist your independence.

(b) Spend much longer than you think you need explaining who you are, who you work for, in what way you're independent, where the data goes, what rights informants have over it, and what your specific intentions are. Never assume that written introductions will have filtered through, been read or understood.

(c) Persuade the project that you need to learn to evaluate just as much as they need to learn to innovate. 'Trial and error' is a mutual condition.

(d) Accept that projects and especially co-ordinators are often under intense pressure to 'deliver'. Image and PR are a necessary part of that. Resist the feeling that you are 'truth's representative on earth' – don't work against their PR so much as on their private ability to distinguish image from real development. And don't be cynical about the co-ordinator – he or she has more sleepless nights than you.

(e) Be honest. The dangers are without limit. Three common ones – pretending to understand when you don't (loss of face); exaggerating the reliability and significance of your data (loss of 'science'); tempering judgements to suit political winds in or out of the project (loss of nerve). Allow research questions to include a testing of your own initial assumptions and values, not simply build on them.

(f) Watch your time. After the initial bliss of 'no bells' comes the anxiety of a job that doesn't seem to have an end. This kind of self-disciplined work is as hard for ex-teachers as ex-pupils. Two rules of thumb: make fieldwork plans and divide them by two: and double the time for analysis and writing up. Getting the data is often quick and relatively easy (e.g. three days on tape-recorded small-group interviews on work experience); but transcribing, analysing and writing-up is slow and difficult (say three weeks on that task, including some teacher/co-ordinator/employer follow-up).

(g) Keep sane by talking to other evaluators. Your greatest error will be commonplace. Avoid experts: look for the evaluator who 'cocked up' something last term that you're going to look at next term.

DESIGNING AND DOING

1. Abandon the idea that other evaluators may be expert. People often do better evaluation first time around than fifth time because they're more creative, better at talking to kids, more industrious – whatever. There are experts *about* evaluation, but not expert evaluators.

2. Evaluators play their own version of 'Tinker, tailor . . .' in order to decide what to be when they grow up. Most ambitions centre on anthropologist or scientist as role model, and on beggarman and thief (respectively) as ethical model. The scientist appropriates data without negotiation, is 'objective', does surveys, determines correlations and norms, and tries not to contaminate the data. The anthropologist asks permission to use data, negotiates about interpretation, is inter-subjective (well, subjective), does case studies, draws out understanding, and tries not to go native.

3. Avoid these role models. Help evaluation break its academic chains. Both styles are unhelpful to project development (too little, too detached, too late).

4. Acknowledge two of the central myths of evaluation – the myth of audience, and the myth of decision-maker. Accept the need to create debate within projects (often project workers and teachers have no time to think ahead, no mechanism for meeting, no incentive to contribute, no desire to rock the boat, etc.). Also promote broader debates about project issues (like student-centred learning, vocationally relevant curricula, management of innovation). There is a need to act *inside* the project, analysing and reporting, influencing change, 'contaminating' data; and a need to stand *outside* the project, placing its activities in

comparative and critical perspectives. So do both: be a double agent, and be open about that duality. Defend the duality – change is a research strategy. Reject claims that you have betrayed neutrality or objectivity; both are imposters.

5. Be a double agent in another sense: not just 'inside and outside' the project, but also formative and summative in your strategy. That means working out a short-term evaluation strategy that will also contribute to a long-term summative goal.

For example:

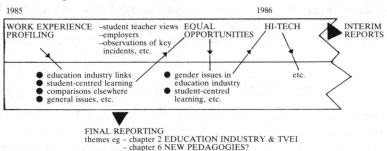

6. Here's another example, linking an inside approach to an outside goal, taking a developmental process to an eventual summative account:

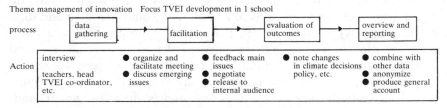

The dilemma, of course, is to include the evaluation's role in the summative account. The potential bonus is richer data, some natural 'experimental' knowledge (what happens if . . .?), and an impact on the project.

7. Finally, a highly condensed version of a comparative approach:

THEME: PROFILING

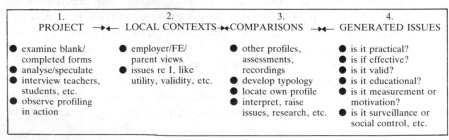

Forced into boxes like that, the process is mechanical – but no sequence is necessarily implied. Much 'to-ing' and 'fro-ing' between 1, 2, 3 and 4 is likely in working out new questions and testing their significance against old and new data.

An example of the above strategy would be to take Murray Saunders' interesting idea of TVEI as 'enclave' within a school [Saunders, 1986] and to identify the other types of 'host' relationship. Impressionistically, there's the 'exile' model, with TVEI banished to the periphery. And there's the *Mutiny on the Bounty* model where the school took the money and ran. What else? Surely there's a *Marie Celeste,* a project floating aimlessly and empty around somewhere? How could these types be better characterized?

8. There is nothing comprehensive or prescriptive in the above illustrations. Work out your own strategy for promoting development while retaining a critical overview of process, outcome and context. The tension between 'inside' and 'outside' role can also be productive in limiting some forms of bias – not least the bias of the spectator who thinks he really understands – and in giving new insights. The evaluation role will also always be problematic, difficult to take for granted, and exposed to reflexive questioning.

9. Developmental evaluation should be a set of practices, not a 'method-in-action': case study, history, dialogue, natural experiment, survey, comparative analysis and social critique may be components but should not be determinants.

Those practices should go beyond information and opinion. Evaluation must conceptualize the project, pick out the ideas and examine the concepts and intentions behind it. At the workshop it was the tea-lady who asked the best question – 'What does TVEI stand for?' Other questions might include: 'What kind of economic theory underlies TVEI rationales?' 'How are educational principles and vocational practices reconciled?' 'If there's a Bad Thing called vocationalism, is there a Bad Thing called educationalism?' If we never ask questions like these, we may end up knowing everything about TVEI except what it means. The project must not become the silent centre round which debate revolves: 'If evaluation uncritically accepts project definitions, and follows the assumptions and boundaries of the project, then it begins to discuss the meaning of the project from inside the project's understandings' (Stronach, 1981).

As a workshop participant playfully suggested, evaluators should 'subvert the project by taking it seriously'.

Developmental evaluation, therefore, should aim to create a critical dialogue both within and about the project. Evaluation should be both a mirror and a window. It should aim for action as well as reflection, and see action as a form of research. Nor should evaluation privilege groups like decision-makers or teachers. When Peter Holly (1986) lumps teachers and students together in arguing for a 'professional' model for evaluation, he is making a powerful ideological move on behalf of teachers, but not necessarily on behalf of students. Evaluation should not privilege such groups by making them into a tacit 'bottom line' but should be informed by a radical scepticism about all values, including its own. Above all, it should not take detachment to be a virtue: 'But to look in order to know, to show in order to teach, is not this a tacit form of violence, all the more abusive for its silence, upon a sick body that demands to be comforted, not displayed?' (Foucault, 1976, p. 84).

10. That's getting a bit grandiose. Some practical tips to conclude this section:

   ● draw up evaluation plans in conjunction with the project; expect to change them;
   ● keep a record of everything, dated, filed, accessible;
   ● keep a diary of emerging issues, impressions, feelings, embryonic interpretations – very useful at all reporting stages;
   ● allocate enough time for each piece of evaluation work so that you have a reasonable chance for knowing more about it than the participants (or, more usefully, knowing differently about it);
   ● commission outsiders, if you lack specialist expertise in an area and really need it;
   ● leave plenty of time for the report-writing stage, it's the worst one: a common failing – too much data, no time to process it;
   ● don't forget how ill-informed and over-prescriptive this is, especially in relation to the particular context of your evaluation.

REPORTING

1. Writing reports feels like sitting an exam without being quite sure what the question is, but in the knowledge that the world will read and mark your paper according to an unpredictable whim. The mental blocks, the mad desire to postpone writing for more research, or for another cup of coffee, is normal. In fact, there's a consolation if you're a beginner – it gets worse later on.

2. People who read evaluations either say they are too long to read, or they are too short to believe. The best bet is a report as short and condensed as you can make it (with detailed justification tucked away in appendices).

The biggest temptation is to display your productivity in the number of pages. Resist it.

3. Decide in advance what debate you're trying to influence, or who you are writing for, and what would be the most effective format and style (but this of course may not be exclusively the evaluator's decision). Where length is unavoidable, as in a case study (e.g. student/tutor interactions in profiling or work experience debriefings), provide a summary of the main issues.

4. Follow negotiating procedures to the letter. Try to get full clearance of reports so that other TVEI projects and evaluations may benefit from them.

5. Look for a general theme, or metaphor, that will carry your main point without distorting it too much, for example, if the report were about the management of innovation you might find that the project had moved from the role of researcher (let's make up our own profile), to that of guinea pig (let's test the CGLI 365 profile), or vice versa.

6. Follow up reactions to your reports (you may have to create reactions by begging teachers to read and criticize them for you). Try to get a cross-sectional view – there may be a lot to learn from the distribution of criticism, as well as from its content. Ask what the report ought to have been like. What questions were ignored or inadequately addressed, what the assumptions and values of the writer appeared to have been, and so on. And remember that there's (almost) always a next time.

7. Local evaluation in TVEI runs at over £350,000 p.a. It is the largest component in the evaluation budget. There is no reason why it should not also be the most productive.

8. Good luck.

REFERENCES

Foucault, M. (1976) *Birth of the Clinic*, Tavistock, London.

Holly, P. (1986) Professional evaluation, *Cambridge Journal of Education*, Vol 16, No. 2.

Saunders, M. (1986) Developing a large scale 'local' evaluation of TVEI: aspects of the Lancaster experience, in D. Hopkins (ed.) *Evaluating TVEI: Some Methodological Issues*, Cambridge Institute of Education.

Stronach, I. (1981) Beyond dispute, Clydebank Evaluation. Jordanhill College of Education, mimeo.

3.2
THE CONDUCT, ANALYSIS AND REPORTING OF CASE STUDY IN EDUCATIONAL RESEARCH AND EVALUATION*
Lawrence Stenhouse

On the road toward science, social philosophy has lost what politics formerly was capable of providing as prudence.

(Jurgen Habermas, *Theory and Practice*)

Researchers have turned to case study in the face of the difficulties which have been encountered in attempting to apply a classical scientific paradigm of research to problems in which human behaviour, action or intention play a large part. Experiment in the physical sciences depends heavily on the control of variables. As we move through the life sciences to the behavioural and social sciences, the control of variables becomes increasingly difficult. The classic response to this difficulty (Fisher, 1935) is to attempt to randomize the effects of uncontrolled variables so as to tone them down into a kind of white noise in the background of observed experimental effects. This process of allocating experimental treatments to subjects by chance rather than by judgement enables the researcher to use the mathematics of probability to calculate how far differences between observations of the experimentally treated subjects and the others may be 'significant'. This strategy is the basis of the use of inferential statistics in experimental design (see Glass and Stanley, 1970) . . .

The results of investigations [based on this logic] are actuarial, describing trends or distributions in broad populations. We can readily calculate the distribution of heights of adult males in Britain, but that gives us little idea of how tall the man we're about to meet off a train will be. . . When our need is

* Stenhouse, L. (1982) The conduct, analysis and reporting of case study in educational research and evaluation, in R. McCormick (ed.) *Calling Education to Account*, Heinemann Educational Books, in association with The Open University Press, London.

to act or to devise a policy, such research techniques guide us only to the extent that the action, treatment or policy must be the same for every case we meet.

In all social arts, such as education, the practitioner aspires to modify his actions to meet the characteristics of particular cases. He or she diagnoses the case before treating it. In such situations practitioners need to know the broad trends which can be expected as responses to treatments but equally importantly the pattern of variation across cases. Medical practitioners and researchers have long recognized this and have reported individual cases which illuminate the incidence and treatment of particular conditions. One may say that the reporting of cases improves the practitioner's judgement by extending his or her experience and by treating experience more reflectively and more analytically. In my own experience there were within the Humanities Project, for instance, three styles of case study as applied in education which I shall call action research, evaluation and naturalistic research. All shade into each other.

The action research element is based on the close study of individual classrooms involved in the action of the project. From this study are derived hypotheses concerning the important variables in teacher behaviour which seemed to affect the quality and progress of student discussion. There is analysis across cases but the emphasis is not on extrapolating findings in the project as generalizations applying to a target population. Instead the teacher is urged to investigate his case by acting experimentally in it and monitoring effects. The research is applied by the user to his case rather than generalized by the team to a population of schools. Using research means doing research. This strand of experimental case study is developed in John Elliott's *Ford T Project* in Jean Rudduck's *Small-Group Work in Higher Education* (1978) and *Learning to Teach through Discussion* (1979) and by Robert Wild (1973) and Stenhouse *et al.* (1982) in *Problems and Effects of Teaching about Race Relations*. It is generally addressed to teachers.

The evaluation element is centrally concerned with gathering evidence which enables people to make judgements about the project in reflective or deliberative settings. Where action case studies invite action responses, the evidence gathered and presented by an evaluation supports decision-making, either by individuals or by groups. Examples can be found in the main publications from the Humanities Curriculum Evaluation Project (e.g. Hamingson, 1973; MacDonald, 1978; Verma, 1980), the first of which was called *Towards Judgement*. Other examples are Parlett and Hamilton's *Evaluation as Illumination* (1972) and an American trend characterized particularly by the work of Robert E. Stake (1967, 1972a, 1972b), who writes of evaluation in terms of 'portrayal' of cases and suggests that it should be responsive to the case rather than imprisoning the study of cases in preordinate categories. More recently Barry MacDonald has taken up again the theme of democratizing judgement which was broached in the Humanities Project and distinguished autocratic, bureaucratic and democratic styles of evaluation (MacDonald, 1974). The democratic style, clearly preferred by the author who chose those terms, rests heavily on case studies presented in forms that make them accessible to a wide public.

This general tradition of evaluation has been well publicized and widely applied at varying standards of quality. It always involves case study, and I would regard it as characteristic of evaluation as opposed to research that the case in point – be it policy, programme, institution or individual – be identified (not anonymized). The tradition of evaluation is exemplified by MacDonald's work in *Understanding Computer-Assisted Learning* (UNCAL, 1975), and *Careers Guidance Observed* (currently supported by DES and EEC [Final Report 1983]).

Independently of this growth of case study work in evaluation, there is a classic case-study tradition. In Britain this includes Hargreaves's *Social Relations in a Secondary School* (1967) and Lacey's *Hightown Grammar* (1970). In America Smith and Keith's *Anatomy of Educational Innovation* (1971), Harry Wolcott's *The Man in the Principal's Office* (1973) and Alan Peshkin's *Growing up American* (1978) are exemplars. All of these studies are in a style that goes back to the Chicago School in sociology. A particular characteristic is the use of participant observation as a research strategy. The participant observer conducts his research by joining a social group, participating to a greater or lesser extent in its activities in order to achieve an understanding of the meanings and perceptions of its members, but retaining a degree of detachment as an observer and recording observations and conversations.

The participant observer role was forged in ethnography when Western anthropologists studied preliterate societies by living in them. The term for this kind of case study most commonly used in America is 'school ethnography'. The term is coming to be used loosely, but at its most precise it probably implies penetration of the *culture* of a group by participant observation (Wolcott, 1980). The technique of participant observation demands aptitude, theoretical training (since theory is important to the maintenance of the observer role while participating) and long-term fieldwork, certainly extending over months.

The characteristic nuance which evaluation contributes to case study work is caught in Walker's phrase 'condensed fieldwork' (Walker, 1974). Evaluation runs to the pace of the events it studies and the demands of sponsorship.

A portrayal of a case is needed and time allows only a few days in the field. The classic participant observer strategy is not available on such terms (though some condensed case workers do describe themselves as participant observers). The conditions of condensed fieldwork radically alter case study and require us to rethink its rationale and validity. But that strategy also offers the possibility of bringing case study within the range of opportunity of the majority of researchers who cannot see the prospect of laborious long-term studies in the classic mould.

Case studies based on condensed fieldwork are currently being undertaken in a variety of settings in evaluation and in research. The two fields are not always easy to distinguish. When a research is commissioned by a sponsor who asks that it provide evidence on which to judge a specific issue or policy or programme or institution, we are pretty sure it is evaluation. When a research can be seen to relate to an issue of understanding or interpretation conceived as contributing to our state of knowledge about education, we can see that it needs no name but research. However, there are many instances where the distinction is not easily drawn.

There are, moreover, common fieldwork problems in both research and evaluation and these can perhaps best be reviewed by picturing them in a real situation, say, the study of a school.

In the tradition of condensed fieldwork what is the researcher's task in the school? In a project on 'Library Access and Sixth Form Study' in which I am currently engaged (to take an example) he will have not more than twelve days' fieldwork. Most of the time will be spent on interviewing – in this case teachers and students, but in some cases parents, employers or former pupils. Some time will be spent in observation. For my part I may give the librarians of the two institutions I am studying clerical assistance for a couple of days so that I can observe the activity in the library, and I shall also in one case spend time in the public library used by the students. Records will be collected of a kind called by the Webbs (1932) 'documents', that is, records made by the schools to serve their own purposes rather than the purposes of research. Some quantitative indices will be recorded: data on the library holding, borrowings, physical space, budgets and so forth [see Rudduck and Hopkins (1984) for the final report of this project].

Typically, interviews will be tape recorded. Those with staff who have their own rooms will be conducted in their rooms: those with other staff and students will be conducted in a room allocated to me for fieldwork interviews. Rooms I have used include: a stockroom, a medical room, a librarian's side-room, a spare lounge and a parents' waiting room. I never sit facing the interviewee: always side by side, generally angled towards each other. The interview starts with securing the right to record and undertaking to return an anonymized transcript of the interview for clearance. Its purpose is described as trying to capture a sound picture of the school in the voices of the people who work in it. The interview will be a one-sided conversation in which I speak relatively little. In the present project my purpose will be to consider with the interviewee the growth and limitations of the capacity for independent study as students move up the school and into the sixth form with some emphasis on the role of access to books and other library resources.

Observation is not in the classic sense participant observation, though superficially it has a participant appearance. Sitting working at such a paper as this in a public library, I am privy to the fact that three fourth formers, who came in to look up a reference to an author in *Who's Who*, chance upon Ringo Starr and look up and copy out the four Beatles' entries. Or I notice which boys engaged in study in the library do not look up when girls walk in, and I find I know some of them from interview.

Documents collected include prospectuses and school hand-outs, syllabuses and reading lists, library publications, perhaps minutes of staff meetings, perhaps photocopies of essays.

Quantitative indices include demographic and budgetary data on the school, library holdings and data on use, dimensions of the library, number of seats, tallies of users, and so forth. In some circumstances time-series analysis or routine testing is appropriate. *Middletown* and *Middletown in Transition* (Lynds, 1929, 1937) are good stimulants to imagination in descriptive statistics: Tukey's *Exploratory Data Analysis* (1977) is thought-provoking on presentation. The statistics used in surveys and experiments conducted on samples need rethinking when one wants to apply them to cases.

These descriptions of fieldwork practice are not meant to offer a model: on the contrary, they are intended to throw up dilemmas or problems. Among the most crucial of these are: observation versus interview; data versus evidence; explicit versus covert research; and the participant roles available.

I lean towards interview rather than observation. As has been explained above, this is partly because I feel that the conditions of condensed fieldwork preclude classic participant observation. But that is not the whole story. The people I interview are participants and they are observers of themselves and others; my object is to provide in interview the conditions that help them to talk reflectively about their observations and experience. It is their observations I am after, not mine. There is, of course, the possibility that at some points the interviewee is out to deceive the interviewer, and we must take account of the truism that we are all self-deceiving.

(That is, of course, what a major concern of historical criticism is about.) I find these problems less intractable than the dominance of the researcher's eye.

At the same time it must be recognized that interview is often dependent upon observation. When you ask: 'Do you think the siting of the library is an important factor?' or hazard to the librarian: 'I suppose you have to keep them in order from time to time', it is either observation or experience that lies behind your question. In the end, perhaps the issue is: is observation used to test interview or interview used to test observation? The first position is likely to be taken by those who see themselves as trying to establish facts: the second by those who see themselves as trying to disclose meanings.

Whether one's attitude to information will be to use it as data or as evidence (the distinction is mine rather than generally current) is an important issue. When we use information as data we hope to process it as 'comparable' or standardized. Generally this means stripping information of context and treating it analytically. When we use information as evidence, we try by critical selection to present an interpretation which we claim is tenable: the test is that we achieve a synthesis which carries meaning and rings true without violating the tendency of the larger store of information from which our selection is drawn. In both cases we reduce information and attempt to control distortion.

The choice between explicit and covert styles of research is partly a matter of ethics and partly a matter of validity. There are those who believe that research with human subjects should not be conducted without their consent and understanding and this points to an explicit approach. The urge towards more covert strategies comes from those who fear that the responses of subjects who understand the research in which they are involved will be influenced by this knowledge. Such influence will, it is claimed, distort the data they provide for the researcher and hence reduce the validity of the research. Whether this is a cogent argument or not must depend heavily on the research problem and on the style of interpretation to which the researcher aspires. My own stance is the ethical one, perhaps the more easily adopted because I am working with fellow professionals in education as subjects. In so far as this limits the problems and the modes of interpretation accessible to the researcher; those limitations are generally acceptable to me. But I find acceptance the easier because the limitations do not constrain me too much.

A problem of particular force for the researcher in schools or similar institutions is the narrow range of participant roles available. In some social situations it is relatively easy to become a member of the group being investigated, but in the classroom there appear to be only two truly participant roles available – that of teacher and that of pupil. Normally each classroom has only one teacher: normally the researcher cannot be mistaken for a pupil. Even when we include in the school community ancillary staff such as caterers, caretakers, lab technicians and secretaries, the role opportunities for participant observers are strictly limited. Most observation in educational institutions is non-participant and at the same time explicit. The observer thus influences the behaviour observed, if only marginally, but does not enter fully enough into the pattern of interaction for his own experience of participation to become admissible as evidence.

Of course, with the growth of research work by serving teachers, we are finding more fully involved and natural participants turning to observation. The promise and the difficulties of this teacher-as-researcher stance in the classroom have been well explored in the Ford T Project (Ford T, n.d.) and in its follow up – the Classroom Action Research Network (CARN, 1977–80). Less well documented so far are the problems of studying, not one's own classroom, but one's own institution. A number of excellent pieces of this kind of work now exist, mostly in the form of master's theses, but it takes a good deal of discretion and power to conduct such a study successfully. The main problem is that social and political life in schools as elsewhere depends heavily on the unspoken agreement and the hidden cards. Studies which open the process in a particular school to scrutiny do not merely put personal relations at risk: they shift the balance of power.

Such important issues in fieldwork as have just been discussed need to be taken into consideration in planning case study research and ought then to inform sensitivity in its execution. The problems of record-keeping are less a matter of sensitivity than of efficiency. It is on them that the plans of many case study researchers are wrecked.

The essence of the problem is this. Since the fieldworker in case study does not much simplify or attenuate the information he will gather by preordinate decisions, he will have a great deal of information to handle. His first problem is to record this information, his second to organize the record for use and his third to use the record to write a report.

So far as interviews are concerned the choice is between tape recording and taking notes. I use a tape recorder if I can: it protects the interviewee against misrepresentation, it captures the vividness of speech, it preserves a full record. Working within the context of projects which are fairly generously funded for secretarial support, I have been fortunate enough to be able to get full transcriptions of interviews. When this is not possible, tapes need to be carefully indexed, and selected portions should be transcribed and each annotated with a contextualization. When interviews are not taped, it is a good idea to make notes on paper divided into two columns – one column being used for a running contents list or minutes of points made, the other column being reserved for verbatim quotation.

Notes on observations (like interview records) should always be dated and a time record should be kept in a margin. Sketches or photographs may be useful. A considerable problem in observation is its relation to inference, and the observer should cultivate a considerable depth of insight as to the individual characteristics of his observation and the degree and style of inference involved.

My name for the total collection of information as organized for use – interview, observation and document – is the 'case record' (Stenhouse, 1977). The good organization of this record is crucial for writing up. It should be carefully indexed. Photocopies of the record can be used to cut up and sort under different topics (record the page number on each piece!). Another possibility is to colour-code margins using a different colour for each section or chapter of the report. Meticulous attention to such detail makes an enormous difference when the job of writing up has to be faced.

There is not enough experience of the problem of writing up this kind of material in contemporary educational research. The examples to turn to are clearly historians. For present purposes a good starting point is to consider the use of narrative, vignette and analysis. Such styles as these can, of course, be blended.

Narrative, as a form of presentation, has two great strengths: it is simple and direct to read and it is subtle. Its simplicity and directness is partly due to its being within a convention of representing the natural world that is thoroughly established and that most readers meet in the nursery, but it is also partly because, as compared with analysis, the narrative form constrains the author from presenting his own logic in the teeth of resistance from the story. He does not drag the reader on to the territory of his own mind, but rather goes out to meet him. The subtlety of narrative lies in its capacity to convey ambiguity concerning cause and effect. In telling a story the author does not need to ascribe clearly causes and effects. Rather he may select from the record an array of information which invites the reader to speculate about causes and effects by providing him with a basis for alternative interpretations. Hexter (1972) has some interesting observations on storytelling written from the point of view of a historian. In case study of the kind we are discussing, narrative lends itself to the treatment of the history of institutions and of the biography of individuals as well as to reportage of transactions such as meetings or the course of events observed.

A vignette has the status of a sketch as compared to a fully worked picture. Inevitably interpretative, it is founded on the act of selection of a subject for the vignette which in itself constitutes an interpretation, and the illumination of the observation, situation or event by the selection of features whose meaning is determined by the author's interpretative stance. The art in the hands of a master can readily be observed in the extended scene settings in Bernard Shaw's plays. The element of interpretation in vignettes does not necessarily rule out ambiguity if the writer is skilful.

Analysis, by contrast with narrative and vignette, debates its points explicitly, wherever possible reviewing evidence. Analysis may be couched in the concepts of the people in the case, but often its conceptual framework is contributed by its author and draws on systematic theory – in our field generally from the social sciences – in which the concepts chosen by the author are anchored. Analysis is, viewed in one light, much cruder than narrative or vignette, but it is more explicit. This tends to mean that, though it is difficult to understand at times, it is also less easy than narrative to misunderstand, and also that it favours the search for precision in terminology and in theory. Whereas the words of narrative are crowded with their connotations and derivations those of analysis tend to be starker, denotative in the light of their definitions.

An important issue in all reports of case study is the conception of reality they reflect. The sort of issue involved can be illustrated by contrasting two typical viewpoints. In one of these reality is seen as factual or at least consensual. In order to establish what *really* went on we use 'triangulation' taking bearings on the issue by using evidence from different sources to cross-check. From another viewpoint there are multiple realities, for the world in which reality is to be located is that of the perception of participants and the meanings they ascribe to them. The point is well illustrated in Karel Capek's novel. *The Cheat*, in which a single character is seen successively from different points of view.

Interesting problems for both the use of case records and the writing of reports are set by multi-site case study research. In the United States the National Science Foundation project, Case Studies in Science Education, directed by Stake and Easley (1978), was based on case studies of twelve different cases, each written up by the fieldworker who handled the case. The overview attempted to generalize across the cases. This work, though it shows some evidence of our lack of a tradition in this genre, is nevertheless of great interest. In the project on Library Access and Sixth Form Studies, mentioned above, the fieldworkers in a twenty-four case study are contracted to produce indexed case records rather than case studies, and the overview will be based on this less refined data.

The emergence of multi-site case study as a style of research raises interesting issues. What would earlier studies based upon sampling look like if they were analysed, not within the conventions of the classical statistical tradition, but as a collection of cases? Could one look towards a national archive of case records? There is certainly much of promise in research based on interpretative case study though some of its disciplines still need to be thought through.

A crucial issue in the development of case study research is the role of theory in educational thinking. There is a sense in which no thinking is entirely free of theory, but there are types of research in which theory is seen as the crucial product – notably the sciences – and other types in which theory is a groundwork on which a different kind of interpretative effort is built – notably history and criticism.

Popper (1959, p. 27) begins his *Logic of Scientific Discovery* with this simple statement: 'A scientist, whether theorist or experimenter, puts forward statements, or systems of statements, and tests them step by step. In the field of the empirical sciences, more particularly, he constructs hypotheses, or systems of theories, and tests them against experience by observation and experiment.' The press is towards predictive generalization: the result is a hierarchy of generalizations, the more circumstantial and testable deducible from those that are more abstract and general (and consequently more difficult to test directly). Much theory in the social sciences is rather distant from this conception, but it aspires towards it and one can see that theory in social science which met the criteria suggested for the physical sciences would be accepted by most social scientists. Zetterberg (1965, p. ii) suggests that 'the quest for an explanation is a quest for theory'; and yet in half a dozen books concerning explanation in history (which I have consulted in the space afforded by the preceding semi-colon) I find no reference to theory in the indexes. The fact is that there is an alternative, interpretative style of explanation:

> We do explain human actions in terms of reaction to environment. But we also explain human actions in terms of thoughts, desires, and plans. We may believe that it is in principle possible to give a full causal explanation of why people think, desire or plan the things they do in terms of their past experience or training, or perhaps in terms of the working of their bodies. But, even if the latter proposition is true, it still does not follow that explanation in terms of thoughts and desires has been rendered superfluous, or that it has been 'reduced' to cause-effect explanation.
>
> (Gardiner, 1961, p. 139)

This is still too simple, but it cannot be refined here. Suffice it to say that there is an interpretative, rather than theoretical style of explanation of human action, that it can at times use ambiguity as a spur to speculation and that its generalizations will contain the qualifier *often*, or *probably*

(Habermas, 1974, p. 45), not *other things being equal*. Thus their soundness may be the subject of discussion or discourse but their refutation will be by informed judgement and not by proof.

In history, judgement is informed by virtue of the quality of the historian's 'second record' (Hexter, 1972). This second record which he brings to the 'first record' of documentary sources in order to interpret them is a specially tutored experience: an experience of, say, eighteenth-century diplomatic practice or fifteenth-century agriculture.

In the matter of educational case study, theoretical interpretation would appear to be most applicable when the interests of the researcher are in social science rather than in education. Such an interpretative framework is alternative to a strong second record, and rests on generalizations across from other studies of human behaviour in institutions. It may, of course, contribute new insights concerning educational behaviour. A historical style of interpretation would be more open to the researcher, the richer his or her second record of educational experience, and it would in its turn offer to enrich the experience of the reader, being accessible to those who have experience of education.

There is an interesting line of thought to be followed up concerning the application of these two styles of case study to practice or action; for theory in the context of social science approximates *episteme* while interpretation in the light of a second record approximates *phronesis*. Such an identification leads us to the heart of the dilemma underlying one of the most famous recent attempts to relate theory and practice, that of Habermas, who points to Vico towards the opening of his own discussion:

> Vico retains the Aristotelian distinction between science and prudence, *episteme* and *phronesis:* while science aims at 'eternal truths', making statements about what is always and necessarily so, practical prudence is only concerned with the 'probable'. Vico shows how this latter procedure, precisely because it makes lesser theoretical claims, brings greater certainty in practice.
>
> (Habermas, 1974, p. 45)

Interpretative descriptive case study of the kind which has been given centre stage in this paper is deeply concerned with practice. It appeals to the experience of participation in education rather than to technical theory and holds to the vernacular because it recognizes 'the task of entering into the consciousness and the convictions of citizens prepared to act' (Habermas, 1974, p. 75). It aims to strengthen judgement and develop prudence.

REFERENCES

Carn, (1977–80) Annual Bulletins, 1–4, Classroom Action Research Network, Cambridge Institute of Education.

Fisher, R.A. (1935) *The Design of Experiments,* Oliver & Boyd, Edinburgh.

Ford, T. (n.d.) Materials from the Ford T Project (booklets) obtainable from J. Elliott, Cambridge Institute of Education.

Gardiner, P. (1961) *The Nature of Historical Explanation,* Oxford University Press.

Glass, G. and Stanley, J.C. (1970) *Statistical Methods in Education and Psychology,* Prentice-Hall, Englewood Cliffs, N.J.

Habermas, J. (1974) *Theory and Practice,* Heinemann, London.

Hamingson, D. (ed.) (1973) *Towards Judgement: The Publications of the Evaluation Unit of the Humanities Curriculum Project 1970–1972,* Norwich Centre for Applied Research in Education, Occasional Publications No. 1.

Hargreaves, D. (1966) *Social Relations in a Secondary School,* Routledge & Kegan Paul, London.

Hexter, J.H. (1972) *The History Primer,* Penguin, Harmondsworth.

Lacey, C. (1970) *Hightown Grammar: The School as a Social System,* Manchester University Press.

Lynd, R.S. and Lynd, H.M. (1929) *Middletown: A Study in Contemporary American Culture,* Harcourt Brace, New York.

Lynd, R.S. and Lynd, H.M. (1937) *Middletown in Transition: A Study in Cultural Conflicts,* Constable, London.

MacDonald, B. (1974) Evaluation and the control of education, in B. MacDonald and R. Walker (eds.) *Innovation, Evaluation Research and the Problem of Control,* SAFARI, Interim Papers, CARE, University of East Anglia.

MacDonald, B. (1978) *The Experience of Innovation,* Vol. 2 of the revised edition of the publications of the Humanities Curriculum Project Evaluation Unit, Norwich Centre for Applied Research in Education, Occasional Publication No. 6.

MacDonald, B. and Kushner, S. (1983) *Final Report of the 'Cargo' Evaluation,* Centre for Applied Research in Education, Norwich.

Parlett, M. and Hamilton, D. (1972) Evaluation as illumination: a new approach to the study of innovatory programmes. Occasional Paper of the Centre for Research in Education Sciences, University of Edinburgh, October 1972. Reprinted in D. Hamilton, D. Jenkins, C. King, B. MacDonald and M. Parlett (eds.) (1977) *Beyond the Numbers Game: A Reader in Educational Evaluation,* Macmillan Education, Basingstoke, pp. 6–22.

Peshkin, A. (1978) *Growing up American,* University of Chicago Press.

Popper, K.R. (1959) *The Logic of Scientific Discovery,* Hutchinson, London.

Rudduck, J. (1978) *Small Group Work in Higher Education,* Society for Research in Higher Education, London.

Rudduck, J. (ed.) (1979) *Learning to Teach through Discussion,* Norwich Centre for Applied Research in Education, Occasional Publication No. 8.

Rudduck, J. and Hopkins, D. (1984) *The Sixth-Form and Libraries: Problems of Access to Knowledge,* British Library.

Smith, L. and Keith, P.M. (1971) *The Anatomy of Educational Innovation,* Wiley, Chichester.

Stake, R.E. (1967) The countenance of educational evaluation, *Teachers' College Record,* Vol. 68, pp. 523–40.

Stake, R.E. (1972a) An approach to the evaluation of instructional programs (program portrayal vs. analysis). Paper delivered at the AERA Annual Meeting in Chicago, 4 April.

Stake, R.E. (1972b) Responsive evaluation. Mimeo, Center for Instructional Research and Curriculum Evaluation, University of Illinois, Urbana-Champaign.

Stake, R.E. and Easley, J. (1978) *Case Studies in Science Education. Vol. 1 The Case Reports. Vol. 11 Design, Overview and General Findings,* Center for Instructional Research and Curriculum Evaluation and Committee on Culture and Cognition, University of Illinois, Urbana-Champaign. Reprint, US Government Printing Office, Stock Nos. 038 000 00377 1, Washington, DC.

Stenhouse, L. (1977) Exemplary case records: a proposal to the Social Science Research Council.

Stenhouse, L., Verma, G.K., Wild, R.E., Nixon, J., Sheard, D. and Sikes, P. (1982) *The Problems and Effects of Teaching about Race Relations,* Routledge & Kegan Paul, London.

Tukey, W. (1977) *Exploratory Data Analysis,* Addison-Wesley, Wokingham.

UNCAL (1975) *The Programme at Two,* Norwich Centre for Applied Research in Education.

Verma, G.K. (ed.) (1980) *The Impact of Innovation,* Vol. 1 of the revised edition of the publications of the Humanities Curriculum Project Evaluation Unit, Norwich Centre for Applied Research in Education, Occasional Publication No. 9.

Webb, S. and Webb, B. (1932) *Methods of Social Study,* Longmans Green, London.

Walker, R. (1974) The conduct of educational case study: ethics, theory and procedures, in B. MacDonald and R. Walker (eds.) *Innovation, Evaluation Research and the Problem of Control,* SAFARI, Interim Papers, CARE, University of East Anglia.

Wild, R.E. (1973) Teacher participation in research. Conference document, project on problems and effects of teaching about race relations.

Wolcott, H. (1973) *The Man in the Principal's Office,* Holt, Rinehart & Winston, New York.

Wolcott, H. (1980) How to look like an anthropologist without actually being one. Paper at Annual Meeting of the American Educational Research Association, Boston. Available on audio tape from AERA (session 28.01: Alternative conceptions of qualitative educational research).

Zetterberg, H.L. (1965) *On Theory and Verification in Sociology,* Totawa, NJ, quoted in D. Harvey (1973) *Explanation in Geography,* Edward Arnold, London.

3.3
TECHNIQUES FOR RESEARCH*
Rob Walker

In this chapter I shall look more closely at a range of techniques that might be used in educational research. These techniques will not be described fully as accounts are available in other places; the intention here is to add to conventional descriptions those characteristics of each technique that are relevant to problems of doing educational research in the context of application and practice.

I have chosen to present this chapter in terms of three headings. The first section I have labelled 'Interviews', and have used it to include techniques which are not strictly speaking interviews, but which share generic characteristics with the interview, like questionnaires. Second, I shall look at observational techniques, including the use of video and photography which may be considered extensions of human observation methods. Third, in a section I have called 'Intraviews', I will consider the use of documentary sources that speak from within the institution or from the viewpoint of the people who are the subjects of study – looking at diaries, log books, narratives and timetables.

INTERVIEWS

In essence the interview relies on the fact that people are able to offer accounts of their behaviour, practice and actions to those who ask them questions. The interview is, in this sense, a method or a group of techniques specific to the social and human sciences. It includes a wide range of techniques, from the structured questionnaire through to the 'unstructured' conversation, but all hinge on the assumption that people are, to some

* Walker, R. (1985) Techniques for research, extracts from chapter 4, R. Walker, *Doing Research*, Methuen & Co.

Questionnaire 1

Name..

Date..

Please try to give an answer to all the questions. Underline the answer you think applies.

1. Did you learn anything new?
   nothing/a little/some/a fair amount/a lot

2. Did you find the session interesting?
   interesting/acceptable/boring
   Can you give a reason? ....

3. Did you understand what you were supposed to do?
   fully/sufficiently/vaguely/not at all

4. Did the teacher talk?
   too much/enough/too little

5. Did you need any help from the teacher?
   none/a little/some/a fair amount/a lot

6. Were you able to get the help you needed from the teacher?
   straight away/after a little while/after some time/after a long time
   If you had to wait for help, or never got help, can you give a reason? ....

7. Did you ask for help from outside your group?
   frequently/occasionally/not at all

8. Could you find all the things you needed?
   all of them/most of them/some of them/a few of them/none of them

9. Were you interrupted by other people outside your group?
   frequently/occasionally/not at all

10. If you were delayed was it caused by?
    *going out/unable to talk to teacher/someone coming into the room/
    unable to concentrate/lack of equipment/any other reason*

Here is a space for you to write any other comments about the session. You may continue on the other side if you wish.

Analysis sheet for first questionnaire

1. Did you learn anything new?

nothing	a little	some	a fair amount	a lot

2. Did you find the session interesting?

interesting	acceptable	boring

3. Did you understand what you were supposed to do?

fully	sufficiently	vaguely	not at all

4. Did the teacher talk?

too much	enough	too little

5. Did you need any help from the teacher?

none	a little	a fair amount	a lot

6. Were you able to get the help you needed from the teacher?

straight away	after a little while	after some time	after a long time

7. Did you ask for help from outside your group?

frequently	occasionally	not at all

8. Could you find all the things you needed?

all of them	most of them	some of them	a few of them	none of them

9. Were you interrupted by other people outside your group?

frequently	occasionally	not at all

10. If you were delayed was it caused by?

going out	unable to talk to teacher	someone coming into the room	unable to con- centrate	lack of equip- ment	any other reason

(Browning, n.d., pp. 6, 7)

degree, reflective about their own actions, or can be put in a position where they become so. Implied in the notion of interviewing is a notion of the subject as a researcher, that is as someone able to offer reflective accounts and to test these against experience.

This feature of the interview has brought it to prominence amongst advocates of the teachers-as-researchers 'movement', for it places a degree of authority on the subject and to some extent at least takes for granted that the account that is given has truth value.

Questionnaires

The questionnaire may be considered as a formalized and stylized interview, or interview by proxy. The form is the same as it would be in a face-to-face interview, but in order to remove the interviewer the subject is presented with what, essentially, is a structured transcript with the responses missing. The questionnaire is like interviewing by numbers, and like painting by numbers it suffers some of the same problems of mass production and lack of interpretative opportunity. On the other hand it offers considerable advantages in administration – it presents an even stimulus, potentially to large numbers of people simultaneously, and provides the investigator with an easy (relatively easy) accumulation of data.

Questionnaires are often thought of as mainly applicable to large samples and as demanding rather superficial levels of questioning, or at least questions that are carefully honed to give preordained determined answers. They may also be used in more localized and intimate settings. A group of teachers in the Ford Teaching Project used questionnaires to investigate the conditions of learning among nine to twelve-year-old pupils (Browning, [presented above, pp. 226–227]) . . .

. . . When questionnaires are used in small-scale intimate settings they can be used with a sense of risk that would not be possible when they are used for collecting responses from large samples through direct mailing or by making use of trained interviewers. This is possible because in face-to-face contact there are opportunities for cross-checking, fast turn-around of information and generally a higher redundancy in communication than is present when the researcher faces large quantities of anonymous returns. This is perhaps why many of the standard texts on questionnaire design, while they offer much advice that is appropriate, are sometimes pitched at a level of precision that is inappropriate for the designer of a small-scale study.

In a small-scale study it may be appropriate to break the rules of questionnaire design, for instance by asking taboo questions and by making considerable use of open-ended questions. As an example, Barry Mac-

Donald and I once organized a weekend conference which was designed to collect what we called 'professional life histories' of a group of twenty teachers who had been involved, one way or another, in curriculum innovations:

When we sat down and asked ourselves what we'd like to know about you, these were some of the questions we asked.

Is your background working class or middle class?

....

In politics do you lean to the left/centre/right?

....

Do you have any strong religious beliefs?

....

How do you feel about the raising of the school leaving age?

....

If you had the power to change one thing in the education system, what change would you bring about?

....

Do you see yourself as a career teacher?

....

Is promotion important to you?

If you weren't in teaching how would you prefer to earn a living?

....

Do you think teachers are, or could be, an important influence on the lives of the children they teach?

....

The intention here is very different from the intention that lies behind a multiple-choice questionnaire designed for large-scale mail distribution. The questions are 'real questions' in that we could only guess the kind of answers we might receive and did not know quite what to expect. The intention was not simply to ask questions in order to secure answers for later analysis but rather to set signposts, to indicate a tone, to set going a line of thought and analysis. Given that we were to spend a weekend with the respondents pursuing questions of motivation in relation to curriculum innovation, we wanted from the start to indicate that we were interested in certain kinds of data. In this sense the questions were as important as the answers.

Once the size of the sample expands and communicative redundancy becomes reduced, so questionnaires have to become more precise and carefully tested. It is however still possible to retain some of the open-ended quality of the small-scale questionnaire, if this is desired, by linking it to other information. For example, in a study of science curricula in eleven school districts in the USA, Stake and Easley (1977) designed questionnaires which were mailed out to a sample of a thousand or so people and which managed to incorporate case-study material. The assembled 'scenarios' from the drafts of the case studies, tested these in site-visit interviews, and then wrote them into questionnaires, as in the following example:

Scenario Y: Personal bias in teaching

The National Science Foundation has been explicit in including social studies or sciences along with mathematics and science in its definition of science education. This definition provided the opportunity to investigate two issues that are of special interest in the social sciences. First, it was desirable to investigate how the scientific method of inquiry is perceived as applied to social studies and the prevalence of its use. Second, perhaps more than the other two disciplines, social studies include topics of potential controversy and possibly are more prone to contamination by personal bias.

A conversation between the teacher and students in an American history classroom is the setting for this scenario. Four groups were asked to respond to the scenario: social studies teachers in grades 7 through 9, social studies teachers in grades 10 through 12, high school seniors and parents of high school seniors.

Extract from the questionnaire

Please consider the following situation:

At Metro High School, Mr Robinson's American History class is studying immigration and the settlement of America, noting particularly how immigrants have influenced the growth of their city. Here is dialogue midway through Monday's class:

MR ROBINSON: After the Irish immigration of the 1840s and after the importation of Chinese laborers, what other waves of immigration occurred? Sally?
SALLY: Europeans around 1890 and then again after World War I.
MR ROBINSON: Good, I guess that's when we got our Polish jokes – right? (no one laughs) Well, let's see. What sort of long-time trend are we studying?
SHERMAN: People coming to America.
MR ROBINSON: Why did they come, Tammie?
TAMMIE: To come to a country with freedom.
DOUG: (sarcastically) Like freedom to pick cotton.
MR ROBINSON: Well, let's think about that. Some of the early colonists *were* seeking freedom. Were the Chinese who came after the Civil War seeking freedom? (no answer) What were they looking for? (no answer) What were the Irish looking for?
WENDY: Food!
MR ROBINSON: Food more than freedom? Let's make a list of possible reasons for immigrating, then consider each one.
ERIC: My dad says we should be studying how to send them back where they came from rather than how they got here.
MR ROBINSON: Okay, that's an idea. After we make our list of reasons for immigration, let's figure out who wanted the immigrants here and who didn't want them. And then let's decide whether I should be sent back to Africa or Europe.

Mr Robinson is asking questions about history and joking about it. What is your reaction to his teaching style?

- It is fine for some teachers to teach this way. It gets their attention.
- I find it offensive.
- I don't mind, but he is not likely to get the job done.
- Other (fine in principle but not in this case).
- Other (please indicate).

Do teachers and students talk like this in your school(s)?

- Yes, lots do.
- Yes, a few do.
- No.
- Other.

Mr Robinson seems reluctant to accept the idea that most immigrants came to America seeking freedom. Let us suppose that this is a bias of his. How important is it for social studies teachers to keep their biases to themselves?

- They should recognize their biases and keep them to themselves.
- They should speak honestly as to how they feel on matters.
- They should tell how they feel, but present alternative views too.
- Other.

Suppose Mr Robinson was leading up to a critical analysis of the free enterprise system. Suppose he intended to say that the system was dishonest, that it was cruel in the way it imported cheap labor from foreign lands to work in this country. Do you feel that it would be inappropriate for Mr Robinson to acquaint the students with his conclusions about the free enterprise system in early America?

- It would be right, in fact it is his responsibility to be frank.
- It would be all right as long as he indicated his value-orientation.
- It is ethically proper, but he would be foolish to do so.
- It is wrong for him to use his position for teaching those things.
- Other (please explain).

Some parents believe that certain topics should be left out of science and social studies courses, topics such as evolution of the species, human reproduction, and family attitudes and customs. Some parents want such things taught, and of course, want them taught well. We need to find out how you feel about *using federal funds* for development of teaching materials that include such controversial topics.

- Federal funds should never be spent on such development.
- It is all right to spend federal funds this way if it will not cause trouble.
- It is important to provide federal support for such development.
- Other.

In what ways have budget cuts in your district *seriously* affected the social studies curriculum? (Check one or more)

- We have not had budget cuts recently.

- The social studies curriculum has not been seriously affected in any way.
- Classes have been larger in size.
- Needed and highly qualified teachers have been 'let go' and not replaced.
- We have more teaching from textbooks, less with materials or in the field.
- No longer can we provide a textbook for each student individually.
- The in-service training program has been cut back substantially.
- Other (please indicate).

As you look at social studies courses in your high school and elsewhere, you probably see things that concern you. Please check those things that you consider to be major problems. (Check as many as you wish)

- Too much emphasis on facts, not enough on concepts.
- Too much emphasis on concepts, not enough on facts.
- Too much emphasis on teaching about personal values.
- Not enough emphasis on teaching about personal values.
- Not enough qualified teachers.
- Belief that teachers teaching the same course should teach the same things.
                        (Stake and Easley, 1977, pp. 75–80)

   This approach to questionnaire design promises to provide a form of integration between 'qualitative' and 'quantitative' forms of data, though you should be warned that Stake and Easley's experience was that such integration was harder to achieve than they thought. First, it proved difficult to extract scenarios from case study data: they almost always had to be rewritten in order to make them usable questionnaire items. Second, in analysing the resulting data the responses to the questionnaires did not easily fit with the case study material, or at least did not provide the kind of straightforward corroboration or refutation of the case studies that might have been expected.

   In relation to case studies questionnaires can be used to provide a stimulus to the reader. For example, I followed a descriptive case study of the work of a team of school advisers (inspectors) with a questionnaire, written for those who were the subjects of the study, in order to go beyond the descriptive account and begin the interpretative process. This questionnaire was therefore designed to be speculative and analytic, to go beyond the data I had available, and to draw those who were the subjects of the study into the work of interpreting it.

The observational work of LEA inspectors and advisers

Questions to the advisory team on the basis of the descriptive and narrative accounts (extracts).

3 The adviser in the classroom

3.1 Advisers have to guess at what is hidden from them more than they can observe directly. Each glimpse of a classroom becomes shorthand for a set of extrapolations derived from experience.
Comment

Test: When were you last surprised by something you saw happen in a classroom?

3.2 Eve and Colin both put a major stress on their presentation-of-self in managing their relationships with schools, through dress, appearance, editing of what they say and their behaviour.
Is this typical adviser behaviour?
Example

What considerations do you take into account when:

(a) visiting a prestigious secondary school;
(b) attending an interview for a secondary headship;
(c) running an in-service course at the teachers' centre;
(d) visiting the university;
(e) attending an Afro-Caribbean evening at a primary school?

6 The nature of the system

6.1 I have taken the view that the system is characterized by being simultaneously hierarchical and loosely connected. That is to say that each adviser enjoys a high degree of autonomy but suffers a degree of isolation (and fears of being ineffectual). The adviser has little power but a good deal of influence.
Comment

6.2 The main currency in which advisers deal is information. What is significant is not what they know but how much and when. The information they have access to is largely trivial, but they have it before anyone else and that creates the base for their political power within the system.
Comment

Test: Is gossip important to you?

6.8 A formal assertion.
The culture of the system is one in which individual autonomy survives within an overall hierarchy. The cost for the advisers is a degree of isolation (as felt from within), and of inefficiency and ineffectiveness (as peceived from without). The causes are deeper than the management system level and relatively unaffected by changes in the management structure. Attempts to exert greater control over advisers, and to create more efficient management structures have only a limited effect before the high entropy level inherent in the system reasserts itself.
Comment

This questionnaire was intended to go beyond what I knew. It was not designed to obtain answers to questions I had derived from theoretical speculation but was part of an attempt to test out my own interpretations derived from observation and interviews. In this sense it was the precursor to a first draft of the report. Writing to a select audience of knowledgeable people allowed me to break many of the rules and conventions of questionnaire design.

The face-to-face interview

This might seem a strange term to use, but I have been describing ways of using questionnaires that are primarily qualitative, and which take the form of written conversations; a form of structured correspondence if you like. In order to distinguish this from conversational interviews I have adopted the term 'face-to-face interview', though in doing so I immediately have to qualify it, for there are those who would claim that posture, seating position and the angle at which interviewee and interviewer face each other is crucial. Lawrence Stenhouse (1982, paper 3.2 in this volume), for example, has advocated sitting side by side rather than face to face as if to symbolize the fact that interviewee and interviewer together face a common task, rather than confront one another. Others find this creates communication difficulties and that people facing one another talk more freely and fluently, given the support of non-verbal signals . . .

Just as questionnaires may be more or less highly structured, so interviews may be more or less planned in advance. Here, as in discussing questionnaires, I have tended to concentrate on unstructured interviews because these tend to be poorly accounted for in standard texts, while structured interviews are fairly thoroughly described elsewhere.

An early decision that faces most interviewers is how to record. It is tempting to use tape recording in order to obtain the fullest and most accurate record; on the other hand many people find tape recording intrusive and cumbersome. Barry MacDonald and Jack Sanger have given an exhaustive account of the advantages and disadvantages of recording as opposed to note-taking (MacDonald and Sanger, 1982) . . .

What is particularly interesting is that the comparison reveals that tape recording and note-taking emerge not simply as alternative techniques for achieving similar ends, but as really quite different ways of going about doing research. I suggested that Stake and Easley (1977) found something similar when they attempted to marry questionnaire techniques with descriptive case study, and tape recording and note-taking, too, turn out to be more different than they at first seem. They each imply a different kind of relationship between the researcher and the task and between the researcher and the subject, and a different conception of the nature of the task. Thus parallel studies carried out using the two different approaches would be likely to be less similar than might be predicted in advance. Note-taking draws the researcher into interpretation early in the study and in one sense makes the researcher more of a person in the eyes of the subject. Tape recording lends itself to a recessive style on the part of the researcher, disguising the interpretative process by burying it in the editing and selection of extracts from transcripts. Of course at later stages in the study these positions can be altered and reversed, but initially each technique provides this initial impetus or inclination. Selection is partly a matter of personal preference, partly a question of fitting the technique to the task or to the nature of the setting.

Behind much of this discussion is a view of the interview as an arena for negotiation between the researcher and the subject . . . Interviews can be conceived as data-collection devices which attempt to capture the responses of people to questions that are carefully standardized and intended to be minimally interventive: the image is one of skimming from the subject's consciousness a series of statements, views or attitudes. Anyone who has been interviewed, even on trivial topics (such as which television programmes they watched last week), will know that the interview is a rare enough event for it to leave a mark on the interviewee. You find yourself rethinking what you said, aware of the gaps between what you wanted to say and what you are able to say. When interviewed on deeper topics, such as how you see your work, or relationships within the family, or your feelings about death, the effect is more marked. The interview both opens up areas of dialogue in taken-for-granted areas of your life, and at the same time, perhaps because of the conversational asymmetry in the relationship between the interviewer and the interviewee, fails to offer a sense of closure. As a result the interviewee typically emerges from the interview with a feeling of being left stranded. It is the researcher who goes away with the data to rework it in his or her own fashion, to gain satisfaction from making it make sense, and who indeed has the context to do so.

David Tripp has argued that the interview ought to provide more coherence for the subject. It should (for social science reasons) attempt to understand, take on board and explore what the interviewee's questions are as well as pursuing only the interviewer's agenda:

> Thus an attempt to record what someone thinks on a particular question must also include the attempt to discover how that question and its relevant features is placed in the worldview of the interviewee, that is in the interviewee's rather than the interviewer's terms. In this regard it must be equally important to the

interviewer to learn what questions are important to the interviewee, as it is to learn the answers to questions considered important by the interviewer. One way of achieving this is to allow the interviewee, at the very least, joint responsibility for structuring the interview in terms of the progress of questions, in content, kind, sequence and number. One is thus dealing with questions of power: the extent to which power is equally shared, or in this case, the symmetry of the communication.

(Tripp, 1983, pp. 4–5)

For the interviewer alert to the issue it is not difficult to frame the interview in ways that at least provide the opportunity for reflection and processing within the interview itself. For example, pausing at intervals and asking the interviewee to recapitulate and to summarize, or even offering summaries and asking for an assessment of your own understanding; explaining initially what your intention is and asking for critical responses; leaving tapes with the interviewee to allow him or her to listen back to what was said and to comment on it; corresponding with people after an interview. All these things are possible and may be appropriate in some instances. They relate in part, as David Tripp argues, to a more complete understanding, but also at a procedural level to problems of exit. The word in itself comes as a surprise. We are familiar with problems of access, and research texts tend to discuss access problems and how they might be overcome at some length. Less often do we talk about making exits, either at the level of the interview or at the level of the study.

Taking the interview in this direction does of course have serious implications in terms of staffing. Most large-scale projects are unable to think of the interview in such terms because they operate on the assumption that interviewers will be relatively low-status people with specialized interviewing training but without a grasp of the essential research questions. In such terms it is necessary to develop a view of the interview that is predominantly technical: that is to say, a view that sees the interview as a technique in which people can be trained, and which is transferable from one project to another without too much difficulty.

For most student projects it is not feasible or appropriate to hire interviewers. They tend to be small-scale, one-person projects in which the student does pretty well everything, and most of it on his or her own. It makes sense therefore to make full use of the strengths and advantages of the situation, rather than to attempt to mimic techniques that are really only appropriate to large-scale studies. The problem is compounded by the fact that it is the work of large-scale studies that mostly informs textbook writers. The difficulty, I think, is in drawing a line between the standards set and the questions raised by professional research and making full use of appropriate techniques . . .

It follows that students and novice evaluators need to be prepared to argue the case for what they do, and not simply to do it. This in turn demands a high level of self-awareness and reflexivity, not so much at the personal level (though that too may be necessary) but at an academic level. You have to ask yourself: What am I doing? Why? How do I justify it?

With every interview and every question it may be necessary to run a second record through your head which asks you these questions. The difficulty is doing this without losing a grip on the interview itself. Once you seem mechanical, unrelaxed, unsure or manipulative you may lose rapport or, more important, trust.

OBSERVATIONS

In the previous section I have tended to overlook the importance of fitting the technique to the task and instead have leapt to discussion of the techniques *per se*. In part this is a consequence of the position I argued earlier, that techniques may search for problems rather than be rationally selected on the basis of a carefully framed formulation of the task. The same may sometimes be true of observations; that is to say, observation may lead to an awareness of a researchable problem rather than strictly following the formulation of the problem . . .

Fitting the technique to the task and the task to the problem is crucial but often overlooked by enthusiastic researchers. Doing research is frequently seen to be essentially a question of collecting, processing and interpreting data. The necessary prior phase of getting a definition of the problem that provides you with challenging yet feasible research tasks is sometimes neglected, or rushed by in haste. Perhaps this is why so many retrospective accounts of research return to discuss this crucial phase of the process, for it is only when it is too late and the die has been cast that its significance is realized.

Part of the problem concerns the generation and creation of topics and problems. This established, the next phase is to frame the problem as a series of research tasks, which is far from easy and perhaps the phase where creativity and experience enter most strongly. It is certainly the case that it is in this phase that many of the later problems to emerge concerning the selection of methods and techniques will be determined. So, in trying to fit techniques to tasks it may be necessary to rethink the progress of the project to date, and to work back through the tasks and the way they have been defined, to the problem and the way it has been generated. Before the 'research', as a practical process, has begun, it is surprising how many things have been decided, how many options have become closed and how narrow has become the researcher's thinking. Boehm and Weinberg (1977) offer a checklist for deciding what kind of observation system to use, and their first question is: 'For what purpose was the system developed?' followed by the corollary question: 'Does the stated purpose match your goal?' These are perhaps obvious questions – so obvious that their significance and import-ance may be overlooked. There is always a temptation, at this stage in research, to choose techniques off the shelf so as to avoid the frustration and work involved in developing new ones. The trouble is that techniques may have factors built into their assumptions that make them inappropriate or distort the task to a point where it no longer relates to the initial problem. Research tends to be very effective in providing answers to the questions that no one is asking.

In interviewing there is at least the opportunity for dialogue; for people to challenge or question your questions. In observing, whether in using check-lists or cameras, it is rather more tempting to let the technique become a justification in itself, and for the purpose and intention to fall from view. Perhaps this is sometimes a good thing and liberating for the research. Certainly most people will experience phases in a study where this happens, though perhaps they do not always notice it happening until the point comes to write up the study . . . However, it helps to start questioning the gap between technique and task, task and question from the start; the more the dialogue can be sustained, the further the research will reach in the end.

Observing, I suggest, puts particular stress on the observer to be asking such questions. It is in this sense a technique that internalizes the interview, constantly putting the observer in the position of relating what is observed to questions that are primarily questions of meaning and intent. This is just as important for the 'qualitative' observer, who can get lost in notebooks full of inconsequential shorthand, as it is for the research technician armed with checklists and category systems.

Observation systems

There are currently a wide variety of observation systems available for classroom use. They have been usefully summarized by Simon and Boyer (1970) and by Galton (1978). You should be warned, however, that these volumes consist of catalogues of available instruments and give little indica-tion of the purposes to which they may be put, or of the likely meaning of the data they provide. In order to pursue such questions it is necessary to put the instruments back into a context of use, either by searching the literature for more detailed accounts of their development and application or by trying them on a pilot basis.

The checklist provided by Boehm and Weinberg (1977) provides some help in quizzing the catalogues and is reproduced here:

Checkpoints for determining the appropriateness of an observation system

Checklist   *Comment*

1. For what purpose was the system developed?
   Does the stated purpose match your goal?

2. Are the conditions for observer reliability met?
   A: Behaviors to be viewed are
   sufficiently specified so as to be:
   Mutually exclusive (do not overlap
   each other).
   Exhaustive* (all behaviors of
   concern for the given problem, can
   be classified).
   B: Categories are sufficiently narrow
   so that two or more observers will
   place an observed behavior into
   the same category.
   C: Is observer interpretation
   necessary or not?

3. What type of system is employed?
   A: Category system: every unit of
   behavior observed is categorized
   into one of the categories
   specified.
   B: Sign system: selected behavioral
   units, listed beforehand, may
   or may not actually be observed
   during a period of time.

4. Are appropriate sampling procedures employed?
   A: The procedure for sampling
   behaviors is systematic:
   Time sampling: occurrence or
   non-occurrence of behaviors within
   specified uniform time units.
   Event sampling: event recorded
   each time it occurs.
   B: Is the procedure feasible?
   How do you sample individuals to
   be observed?
   In what period of time?
   Is the desired detail possible given
   the number of individuals and time units?

C: What is the coding system like?
Do tallies or codes require
memorization? If coding required,
is code indicated on the record
form?

D: Are the behaviors to be viewed
representative?
How many behaviors are to be
viewed?
Over what period of time?
Using how many subjects?

5. Are the conditions for validity met?
Are the behaviors you observe relevant to the inferences you make?
Have sources of observer bias been eliminated?

*Optional, depending on purpose of particular observation.

(Boehm and Weinberg, 1977, pp. 58–9)

It may also be useful to refer to a checklist developed by Millman (1981) at this point, for though his list was developed as a retrospective critical tool it raises questions about need, market, sizes and kinds of effects, causation, audience, durability, generalizability, statistical significance, legality/ morality/enjoyability, cost, future availability/improvements/costs, comparative significance and overall value. Evaluators will recognize these

Action checklist for aggressive behaviour

| | Time interval (minutes) | | | | |
Behaviour	0	5	10	15	18
Personal physical attack					
Taunting/ridicule					
Threatening					
Destruction of another pupil's labours					
Usurping property					
etc.					

Alternatively, the checklist could be set out as follows:

Behaviour	No. of occurrences
Personal physical attack	
Taunting/ridicule	
etc.	

(Hook, 1981, p. 82)

items as deriving from Scriven (Scriven and Roth, 1977), and they may seem too product- and market-oriented for some researchers. Nevertheless, the questions are for the most part valid and useful and should not be passed by too readily.

To return to the problem of selecting suitable observational systems for research, it may be helpful to group the maze of existing techniques. The grouping most frequently used is between checklists, or sign systems, and category systems. Checklists provide a series of items which can be recorded as present or not present in a particular classroom, usually on a time-sampling basis. They are therefore useful for making comparisons across a number of classrooms in terms of the relative presence or absence of phenomena, resources or behaviours.

Colin Hook provides some interesting examples of checklists used by teachers in different research projects. One is an attempt to record aggressive behaviour in class (p. 240).

Other examples include a checklist devised by a woodwork teacher to document pupil skills, and another used by a geography teacher attempting to evaluate a fieldwork project:

Checklist for woodworking skills

Behaviour	Satisfactory	Unsatisfactory
Chisels trench		
Saws down a line		
Uses marking gauge		
Explains what is face side and face edge		
Uses try-square		
Sharpens chisel or plane iron		
etc.		

Checklist for field excursion

Activity	Stop 1	Stop 2	Stop 3
Sketching scenery			
Examining vegetation			
Photographing scenery			
Making field notes			
Gathering samples			
Taking measurements			
Drawing sketch maps			

(Hook, 1981, p. 82)

Other checklists might pay attention to the availability and/or frequency of use of materials and resources (say, in art studio, science lab, or in a nursery/reception class). Alternatively it might record the frequency and occurrence of laughter or of co-operation.

Simple checklists are relatively easy to construct; more sophisticated systems do not pull items from the air but through a long period of testing select and sort them on a statistical basis . . .

The line between checklists and category systems is not an easy one to draw. I prefer to keep the term 'category system' to refer to systems that, unlike checklists, use a relatively small number of items, each of which is more general than a typical checklist item, but which attempts to use the system to maintain some sort of more or less continuous record. The system you will find referred to most often is Flanders Interaction Analysis (Flanders, 1970), which is basically a ten-category system for recording teacher–pupil talk. Using the Flanders system requires the observer to code, each three seconds, what category best fits classroom talk at that time. At the end of an observation you come away with a record of the lesson in terms of a string of coded numbers which allow certain kinds of analysis of teaching style to be carried out. There are numerous variations and elaborations of the Flanders method available, many of which are to be found in Simon and Boyer (1970) and in Galton (1978) . . .

Observation for description

It is not easy to think of the right term to place in opposition to systematic observation. The obvious term, unsystematic observation, is not accurate except in a very limited sense and carries prejudical overtones. Broadly what I am concerned with here is observational techniques that remain close to the natural observations made by teachers and others as part of their routine work. A lot of this observation goes on; pupils observe teachers, teachers observe pupils; teaching practice supervisors, inspectors, school psychologists and heads all have a considerable investment in observation. They tend not to make their methods and techniques explicit, though increasingly there is pressure on them to do so.

What I am concerned with here are ways of strengthening this kind of 'natural' observation rather than introducing add-on systems or replacements – which is what I would argue techniques like Flanders do.

One method increasingly used is to tape record or videotape lessons in order to provide the basis for extending or elaborating 'natural' observation. This offers some of the same understanding that slow motion and stop-frame analyses of sporting highlights provide for the enthusiast. Experience suggests though that the method on its own is inadequate and that techniques need to be brought to bear in order to understand this new reality. One useful suggestion is provided by David Ireland who, with Thomas Russell, attempted to start teachers researching their own teaching by having them audiotape some of their lessons. They suggest using a method of pattern analysis to begin making sense of what they discovered:

> Pattern analysis is a techniques for looking at what happens in classrooms. One of its most constructive applications is its use to provide 'feedback' which is otherwise not readily available to teachers. Pattern analysis is an 'open-ended' technique, rather than a preconceived set of categories for analysis. It is amenable to a variety of different points of view and is probably most useful to teachers who have already indentified particular aspects of their teaching which they wish to examine.

Some examples of patterns

A. To every student response, the teacher replied with the phrase. 'OK, very good'.
B. When the teacher proposes an idea, the students elaborate it.
C. When the teacher asks students to read a book, students may choose from several titles.
D. Virtually all questions are asked by the teacher.
E. When the teacher records responses on the board, the responses are recorded in precisely the language used by the students.
F. When students propose an idea, the teacher elaborates it.
G. When students make no response, the teacher never waits more than three seconds before speaking again.
H. After the teacher speaks, a student speaks; then the teacher speaks again, then a student, and so on.
I. The teacher often sits behind the desk when speaking to the entire class.
J. To every student response, the teacher replies by saying 'Yes, . . .' but . . .'
K. Students usually wait to speak until the teacher calls on them.

Pattern analysis: the basic technique

1. Tape record a class, and then transcribe word for word a small portion of the tape. (For example, five minutes of the class, or enough of the tape to fill three of four pages of paper.)
2. Read through the transcript, looking for patterns . . . regularities of behaviour, forms of interaction which occur over and over again.

State these patterns in descriptive terms. It is important to avoid interpretative language which goes beyond the data and assumes knowledge of thoughts and intentions. We try to avoid interpretative language because it introduces values and judgements about what is happening.

For example, if a teacher had a regular way of using words of praise, say what that regular way is, but do not assume that the praise was intended or that the words actually had the effect of praise on students. In short, at this stage it is enough to describe behaviour patterns. Interpretation of patterns is a second stage in the use of pattern analysis.

A note on recording: It's best to use a cassette tape recorder with an automatic level control. Locate the recorder closer to students than to the teacher . . . the teacher's voice is always the loudest. Try the recorder when the classroom is empty to make sure it is working; it's very disappointing to make the effort of recording, only to find that the tape is blank or inaudible.

(Ireland and Russell, 1978, p. 21)

This approach may be used in a number of ways. Anyone with an interest in socio-linguistics will find in the examples given here starting points that might be readily translated into detailed and systematic research studies. On the other hand the level and style of analysis suggested may be sustained and a closer grip kept on the immediate professional issues of teaching, learning and classroom organization.

The same is generally true of videotape recording. In the early days of video use in classroom research the technique was applied to problems that remained from previous research. That is to say, videotape made it possible to solve some of the long-standing problems of inter-observer reliability, of selectivity and of validity that remained from previous decades of research effort (for example in the work of Biddle and Adams, 1971, and Kounin, 1970).

Other problems were of course created by videotape, or at least made worse, namely those involving the reactivity of the subjects and interference effects stemming from the intrusiveness of the technology.

Recently, however, researchers have begun using videotape in ways that are more suited to its own potential strengths and weaknesses, rather than using it to solve other people's problems. One major development has been in the making of documentary films; in research, video has been used not only to record, but for its interactive effect: that is to say, making virtues out of the very things that in conventional terms appear weaknesses. Hull and Rudduck, for example, have used videotape to record discussion-based teaching in a school where it is an established approach in order to replay it to children in schools where such an approach is being introduced as an innovation (See Rudduck, 1981). Such a process short-circuits to some extent the intermediate process of interpretation, and creates a novel role for the researcher as a manager of the research process rather than as solely responsible for 'doing research'.

Once the step is taken to invoke and involve the interpretative response of others, rather than seeing this as essentially the researcher's task, then a range of possibilities opens up. Photographs, for example, long unused in observational research because of the problems of subjectivity and bias associated with the taking and processing of pictures, provide a more acceptable stimulus once selectivity becomes part of the subject of the research. [Two photographs taken in fairly rapid succession show just how selective the process can be.] A slight shift in angle, the inclusion or exclusion of contextual information, the choice of one split-second rather than another provide similar pictures open to very different interpretations.

This very weakness of the photograph as data can be turned to a strength when it is used to elicit responses or to communicate complex messages. Often in applied studies what has to be communicated to people is not a processed and unambiguous set of findings, but rather some portrayal of an event. If, for example, you are asked to evaluate a conference or a course, or to look at a novel teaching programme, part of the task may be to replay events to the people involved to get them thinking and talking reflectively. In this kind of situation the photograph may well have a place and a role to play. What is important about the picture is determined, in part at least, by what people say about it . . .

The ambiguities that are intrinsic to the visual record are a consequence of the complexity of information that images contain. At the same time photographs, films and videotape are the result of a series of selections that derive from the nature of recording systems and the actions of the recorded. Erickson and Wilson argue that, in viewing visual and audio-visual records it is important to bear this selection and editorial process in mind:

> It is important to keep in mind that any kind of documentary is essentially a case study. No documentary case study, whether reported through the medium of print or through an audio-visual medium, is a full account of what actually happened in everyday life. All case studies are highly selective accounts, and any selection from life reduces its complexity and involves an interpretative point of view. Selection of what is to be included in the account focuses the attention of the viewer or reader on what the film editor or writer considers to be the key aspects of the happenings portrayed. The key aspects are foregrounded, while other aspects are backgrounded. In the written case study, this is done through variation in descriptive scope, detail and emphasis. It is done in the audio-visual document by variation in camera angles, framing, pointing of the microphone, and in the cutting and sequencing of the shots. What is judged salient and given emphasis in the document depends on the editor's descriptive theory of the events being described. In edited documentaries editorial selection points the viewer directly to the main message of the film or tape and to interpretative patterns for viewing and for reflecting on what is there to be seen and heard. Having one's visual and auditory attention directed one way or another is an intrinsic part of the experience of viewing edited documents.
>
> (Erickson and Wilson, 1982, p. 6)

While acknowledging that audio-visual media have been used to collect information in the context of experimental studies, Erickson and Wilson, in what is one of the most useful surveys of the field, declare their preference for audio-visual techniques as an extension of participant observation and they suggest projects which lend themselves to this approach:

> Audio-visual documentation involves the recording of the finely shaded details of everyday life in a setting. The record permits the researcher and the researcher's audience various kinds of vicarious 'revisiting' at later points in time. Because settings of social life are so complex and their details are so numerous, the ability to revisit an audio-visual record enables us to compensate for our limited human information processing capacities and to discover, after the fact, new aspects of meaning and organization that we did not realize at first. Audio-visual documentation and analysis is a research procedure that is essentially similar in its underlying logic to that of participant observational fieldwork. . . .
>
> (Erickson and Wilson, 1982) . . .

INTRAVIEWS

While the interview is based on the assumption that it takes two to tell the truth, the intraview hinges for its effect on the power of introspection. I have included in this section those techniques that depend on the researcher using his or her own experience and subjectivity as the key instrument. The problem is essentially one of being objective about what is essentially subjective – not so impossible a task as it might seem, but one which may draw the researcher to traditions of thought in the arts rather than in the sciences.

In some respects much research data already exists in the system. People keep diaries, schools (in Britain at least) keep log books and, in the US, yearbooks. There are school magazines, notice boards, timetables, staff documents, letters and circulars to parents, pupil records. All contain material which may give insight into the individual's experience of school.

Finding such documents is one thing, stimulating their creation is another. Attempts to organize pupils in keeping diaries have been both highly successful and virtual failures. Some the successes have become literary works or popular fiction (Bel Kaufman's *Up the Down Staircase* and Herb Kohl's *36 Children*); others have become research classics (Royston Lambert's *The Hothouse Society*, for example, which consists almost entirely of letters written by children in residential schools).

It is difficult to give advice on how to collect and use such material, though it is important to try, where possible, to integrate diary accounts with interviews, other documents (Bel Kaufman has some excellent examples), or observational data. Mary Louise Holly has provided a useful handbook for teachers on 'keeping a professional diary' which includes some examples (Holly, 1984).

School log books are not always easily accessible though many from old (or closed) schools find their way into local libraries or public record offices. Ronald Blythe includes extracts from the school log book in his study of an English village, *Akenfield* . . .

Recently reports from HMI have become available, though it remains to be seen how informative or useful these are likely to be, or how much they become used . . .

School timetables, while not strictly intraviews, are a valuable source for curriculum analysis, especially in the secondary school, and indeed there are sophisticated techniques available for timetable analysis in terms of use of space/time/staffing and resources (e.g. Johnson, 1980). Combined with budgets and lists of stock (particularly textbooks) and examination syllabuses, such information can be used to get an insight into ways in which organizational and curricular issues connect, and sometimes clash. Such detailed case studies are, however, relatively rare.

SUMMARY

In this chapter I have indicated a wide range of techniques that might be drawn on in carrying out a research project. These techniques have not been discussed in great detail, nor do they comprise an exclusive list of available research tools. It is important not to lose sight of the intent and purpose of the project, or to design complex and demanding research or evaluation studies that might drain energy better put to other purposes. In educational research, perhaps more than in any other area of social and human research, the context of use should never be subsumed to questions of a technical kind. The temptation is to let technical questions displace educational questions. It is a temptation that needs to be resisted.

REFERENCES

Biddle, B. and Adams, R. (1971) *Realities of Teaching*, Holt, Rinehart & Winston, New York.

Boehm, A. and Weinberg, R. (1977) *The Classroom Observer: A Guide for Developing Observation Skills*, Teachers College Press, New York.

Browning, L. (n.d.) *Team-Based Action Research*, Ford Teaching Project, Cambridge Institute of Education.

Erickson, F. and Wilson, J. (1982) *Sights and Sounds of Life in Schools*, Institute for Research in Teaching, College of Education, University of Michigan, Ann Arbor, Michigan.

Flanders, N. (1970) *Analyzing Teacher Behaviour*, Addison-Wesley, Reading, Massachusetts.

Galton, M. (1978) *British Mirrors: A Collection of Classroom Observation Instruments*, School of Education, University of Leicester.

Holly, M. (1984) *Keeping a Personal–Professional Journal*, Deakin University Press, Geelong.

Hook, C. (1981) *Studying Classrooms*, Deakin University Press, Geelong.

Ireland, D. and Russell, T. (1978) Pattern analysis as used in the Ottowa Valley Teaching Project, *CARN Newsletter*, No. 21, Cambridge Institute of Education.

Johnson, K. (1980) *Timetabling*, Hutchinson, London.

Kounin, J. (1970) *Discipline and Group Management in Classrooms*, Holt, Rinehart & Winston, New York.

MacDonald, B. and Sanger, J. (1982) Just for the record? Notes towards a theory of interviewing in evaluation, *Evaluation Studies Review Annual*, No. 7, pp. 175–98, Sage, Beverly Hills.

Millman, J. (1981) A checklist procedure, in N. Smith (ed.) *New Techniques for Evaluation*, Sage, Beverly Hills.

Rudduck, J. (1981) The effects of systematic induction courses for pupils on pupils' perceptions of innovation, SSRC Final Report, Grant No. HR6848/1, Centre for Applied Research in Education, University of East Anglia.

Scriven, M. and Roth, J. (1977) *Evaluation Thesaurus*, Edge Press, Point Reyes, California.

Simon, A. and Boyer, G. (eds.) (1970) *Mirrors for Behaviour*, Research for Better Schools, Philadelphia.

Stake, R. and Easley, J. (1977) *Survey Findings*, Case Studies in Science Education, Booklet 15, University of Illinois, Urbana.

Tripp, D. (1983) Co-authorship and negotiation: the interview as an act of creation. Paper for Australian Association for Research in Education annual conference, Adelaide.

3.4
TEACHER–OUTSIDER PARTNERSHIPS IN THE OBSERVATION OF CLASSROOMS*
Nick May and Alan Sigsworth

In recent years, the growth of collaborative teaching has given many teachers the chance to plan together, work together, and discuss their experience together, but for the majority of teachers the practice of teaching still remains a very private affair – apart from the visits of 'official' observers (teaching practice tutors, advisers, HMI). Partnerships with official observers are not really feasible given the one-off nature of many of the visits and the status of the visitor. The situation we studied was very different: an outsider and a teacher tried to build a working relationship over time that would foster mutual learning, and where the authority of the outsider, to whatever degree it existed, would be faced and managed so that it did not constrain the mutuality of the learning.

What can be achieved through such partnerships, and what do they entail?

An outsider/observer may be able to see a classroom more coolly and comprehensively than the person who is teaching can see it. First, the teacher is likely to have preconceptions about pupils and events that make it difficult to look at interaction in the classroom as a source of data. Second, teaching generally requires continuous, active engagement and there is rarely an opportunity for the teacher to stand back and reflect – or if there is, the teacher, by taking the role of observer, moves out of the action. The outside partner offers, as one teacher put it, 'a second pair of eyes'. He or she gathers evidence through observation to illuminate a problem or concern

* May, N. and Sigsworth, A. (1983) Teacher–outsider partnerships in the observation of classrooms. Adapted with the permission of SCDS Publications from *Teachers in partnership: four studies of in-service collaboration*, ed. J. Ruddock, Longman, York, 1982.

that the teacher has identified as worth exploring. Through discussion, the outsider helps to analyse and interpret the evidence, thus deepening the teacher's understanding of some aspect of his or her teaching.

A partnership, as we conceived it, consists of one or more cycles of meetings. A cycle consists of a pre-observation discussion, then a series of observations followed by post-observation discussions. During the *pre-observation discussion* the teacher nominates the focus for observation, which may be any aspect of classroom life that the teacher finds problematic or interesting. During the *observations* the teacher's responsibility is, as usual, for the children's learning. The outsider's responsibility is to attempt to record observations which he or she thinks will inform the subsequent discussion. Techniques other than observation – for instance, interviewing – may sometimes be needed to supplement the evidence gathered through observation. During the *post-observation discussion* the teacher and the outsider consider the data – usually in the form of 'field notes' – that the outsider has gathered to support the close analysis of particular episodes. The sequence of observation/post-observation meetings then continues until the teacher feels that the focus has been sufficiently explored or that another, perhaps more important, aspect of the classroom situation emerges that needs to be explored.

The partnership approach to in-service activity has a range of possible benefits. First, it offers teachers the professional satisfaction, even excitement, of conducting an inquiry into aspects of their own teaching. Second, it counters the sense of isolation often felt by teachers in schools where travel problems make it difficult for them to get to after-school in-service meetings held at a distance, and where there are difficulties in securing cover to release teachers to attend in-service events held during the school day. Third, it offers a relationship with someone outside the teacher's everyday professional group: this can be important both in helping the teacher to see that what he or she is doing is worth while and in translating thought into action (a teacher may have ideas that routine prevents from being implemented: the partnership with the outsider may provide the necessary break with routine).

In order to indicate the problems and possibilities of the partnership approach, we discuss below the various stages of the activity, using the experience of the experimental partnerships as a source of information and illustration.

FINDING PARTNERS

The outsider

For our experiments, college or university-located outsiders were used but there are alternative possibilities. One would be to establish a consortium of teachers and others within which partnerships might be developed. LEAs which have a system of teacher-advisers may find this kind of activity well suited to the teacher-adviser role, and it would surely provide a sound basis for the teacher-adviser to develop professional working relationships with colleagues in local schools. There is also the possibility of teachers acting as observers for each other in their *own* school.

The outsider does not need to be seen by the teacher as an expert in the content of what is being taught. One teacher felt that lack of expertise regarding lesson content was not important: that the visitor was there to 'observe the children and see how they react to the stimulus presented and how they interact with each other'. Both partners agreed, however, that familiarity with the age group of pupils being taught was helpful, and that what the outsider *must* claim is an expertise in classroom observation. This is not an expertise that needs to be burdened with esoteric technology: experience of classrooms, judgement as to what constitutes appropriate evidence, familiarity with basic techniques of data gathering, sensitivity, and a capacity to be unobtrusive – these are the hallmarks of a good outsider-partner. In addition, both outsider and teacher need to share a respect for formality in the structuring of their relationship through the definition of roles and responsibilities . . .

Also, we think it important that the teacher enters the partnership willingly. The pressures which might act to make a teacher join a partnership unwillingly are many – and the effects relatively easy to predict: for example, a conscript teacher might offer a spurious focus for observation or engineer events so as to render any real problem unobservable. Such defensive strategies would seem legitimate in circumstances where it was against the teacher's real wishes to be involved.

PRINCIPLES OF PROCEDURE

Partnerships are not easily realized, mainly because they are dependent on teachers and outsiders establishing a relationship that is likely to be different from what either of them is used to. One relationship that may be called to mind by the suggestion of observation is that between teaching practice tutor and student: there, the tutor is regarded as an authority figure by virtue of his or her maturity, role as assessor, familiarity with a range of classroom practices and, possibly, by knowledge of the content of the student's teaching. The one-sided relationship tends to generate anxiety in students who, understandably, may seek to parade strengths and disguise weaknesses. It was our concern to try to minimize the pressures that spring from such status-differentiated relationships so that there would be more chance of creating conditions which would support open dialogue and contribute to genuine learning and development. However, some teachers acknowledge that at first the partnership *had* reminded them of the tutor-student relationship they had known in pre-service training:

> It wasn't as horrific as I was expecting it to be. I imagined it was going to be a little like college and a tutor coming in, a final assessment for TP, that sort of thing. The night before you came I sat there and I was a bit concerned about what I was going to do and what you were going to do and what we were going to talk about.

The first problem, then, was to find a way of explaining the outsider's role so that the 'spirit of teaching practice past' did not intrude on the relationship. The 'consultant' role was not a good analogy in that it emphasized expertise and implied a responsibility for diagnosis and prescription. In our partnership the teacher, by defining the focus for the outsider's observation, has already made some sort of diagnosis of the teaching situation: and as to prescription, we believe that the right of determining an appropriate course of action lies with the teacher, even though he or she might use the data supplied by the outsider to guide action. What the outsider contributes is what the teacher cannot easily do – provide evidence that will support the close analysis of events and interactions in the classroom. It is essential that the outsider does not use the occasion to make authoritative criticisms of practice or offer authoritative proposals for the improvement of practice. Thus, while the status of the teacher and the outsider are equal during the partnership, the teacher retains control over the future direction of the partnership and over any subsequent action in the classroom.

In order to ensure that the nature of the partnership is seen in similar terms by the teacher and the outsider, a contract may need to be agreed. This is the 'contract to guide the partnership' which we used:

> With the intention that the partnership be based on equal and shared responsibility, the following is agreed:
>
> 1. *Focus of observation*: to be chosen by the teacher and discussed until the outsider feels that the brief is understood and that it is clearly enough articulated to shape the observation. The focus may be refined or redefined by the teacher as appropriate.
> 2. *Method of observation*: to be discussed by the two partners in terms of suitability to the chosen focus and any constraints of the classroom situation.

The method may be refined or modified, as appropriate, during the course of the partnership.

3. *Observational record*: to consist of non-judgemental notes made by the outsider, preferably in a carbon-copy notebook so that sets of notes are immediately available for both the teacher and the outsider to study.

4. *Post-observation discussion*: to be conducted as soon as possible after the observation. The outsider has the responsibility for making a summary of this discussion so that it is possible for both partners to recall, at their next meeting, where they had got to in their analysis and interpretation of the data presented in the observational record.

5. *Formative or summative discussion of procedures*: at any stage during the partnership, either partner should be free to take the initiative in calling for a review of the way that the partnership is working.

6. *Confidentiality*: the outsider guarantees to regard the observations, the observational records, and the discussions and summaries of discussion as confidential information.

CHOOSING A FOCUS AND A STRUCTURE FOR THE INQUIRY

In the first pre-observation meeting the shared task of the teacher and the outsider is to agree a focus for observation and a structure within which to work. Discussion of the focus is important in order to establish a common understanding of what it is the teacher has in mind. And in reaching towards a definition of a problem or concern, the teacher may well sharpen his or her sense of the situation and perceive relationships among events which had not, until now, seemed significant.

Suitable topics are those that can be defined in fairly unambiguous terms and examined through the somewhat limited resource of an observer. It is helpful if the focus is not on the actions of the teacher ('I didn't feel as though *I* were being watched, and I could forget that you were there') but on what goes on around the teacher. These were some of the topics chosen in our experimental partnerships:

(a) the non-participation of four seven-to-eight-year-olds in the class drama lessons;

(b) lack of space in a reception class of twenty-six five-year-olds;

(c) the problem of integrating two handicapped children into the life of the class;

(d) whether children were really learning anything in a maths lesson.

Some topics proved difficult to handle, either in themselves or in terms of the circumstances of the partnership. The choice of topic needs to take into account the amount of time that the outsider can spend at the school, and on what days the visits can be made. For example, the outsider partner concerned in topic 3 had a timetable at the college where he worked which restricted his visiting to the same day each week; moreover, the school was about an hour's drive away, and he did not have time to respond properly to the topic which really demanded a series of observations of the class engaged in different activities at different times during the school week. Retrospectively we realized that this focus should have been renegotiated.

Topics 1 and 2 proved to be well suited to the partnership approach – indeed, topic 2 was effectively managed within one meeting: the outsider began his observation by drawing a ground-plan of the classroom and entering on it all the furniture other than the movable tables used by the children, eight of whom were constructing a giant collage which was laid out on four of the tables. He then spent the remaining eighty minutes observing how the children moved about the room and the ways in which they used the available space. In this way, he and his partner were able to identify a 'dead area' in the classroom as a basis for a reorganization of furniture and equipment. For topic 1, the two partners planned several sessions: first, an observation of a drama lesson to check whether the teacher's view of the situation could be substantiated; interviews with the four children (the outsider planned to hear them read – a familiar activity for the children and one in which visitors were sometimes involved anyway – and to talk to them about drama at the end of the reading); additional observations of drama lessons in which some variables were changed (for example, size of group and dramatic situation). In the event, the interview was non-productive. The teacher commented to the outsider afterwards:

> I should have realized that they would be much more likely to tell me because they know me better. You were a relative stranger . . . In an effort to please they will often say what they think we want to hear rather than express what they feel. They were like that when I first had them.

Overall, the outcome of the partnership was that the teacher found that the children were more likely to participate actively and with enjoyment when they could work in a sub-group and in half-class (the headteacher agreed to take the other half of the class while the teacher worked with the remaining half on drama): 'These two weeks have gone well for the children. It might be that every time the class splits they have a super time – and the act of observing them could become unnecessary. More room, less accidental pushing about by the children.'

A suitable focus is one which can easily be shaped into an intelligent and straightforward structure for inquiry. In all the partnerships that were formed, the methods used are available to anyone familiar with classrooms and with an understanding of the protocols of observation – judging where to place oneself, knowing how to remain unobtrusive, being competent to record information without disrupting what is going on. No sophisticated observation schedules were employed – partly through inclination and partly because such approaches were not called for by the topics identified for observation. We were confident that significant insights could be culled from the commonsense picture of classroom processes which a committed and sensitive observer can build up. In this way, the theoretical partialities of some observational schedules can be avoided. Thus we sought in our observations to reflect the classroom as a mirror: any refractions of the image, we felt, were more correctly introduced by the teacher, or by the outsider and the teacher in their discussion of the observational record.

OBSERVING, AND MAKING AN OBSERVATIONAL RECORD

One of the functions of the pre-observational discussion is to reaffirm that the partnership is about reflection and not action: it is understandable if hard-pressed teachers, on finding another adult in their classroom, are tempted to use him or her as another pair of hands rather than as another pair of eyes. We would argue that the way of looking at classroom interaction that is generated through involvement in a partnership is likely to serve the teacher *after* the partnership is over, whereas the help that is given by a temporary teaching assistant is bound to end with the disappearance of the assistant.

However, the outsider may need to offer a token participation in the task of teaching in order to allay the curiosity of the children. One partner, trying to maintain the purity of a non-participant observer, was asked by one small child whether he was writing a letter to his mummy! Another found that even allowing the children to write in his carbon-interleaved notebook took some of the mystery out of his role. The kind of participation that is functional is where the outsider comes to be seen by pupils as the person to call on to hold the free end of a piece of string or to unjam the scissors!

During the observation the outsider must accept the discipline of the contract and ignore events and interactions that do not bear on the agreed focus for observation. Moreover, he or she is committed to making non-judgemental observations – as well as to writing legible notes . . .

From the continuous wash of interaction and activity that characterizes a classroom, how does the outsider select what is worth observing? Here, judgement is important – the kind of judgement that grows out of close familiarity with, and curiosity about, the world of classrooms. We cannot offer guidelines – but we can reproduce an extract from one of our observer's field notes. In this partnership the teacher partner was concerned about how the children responded to the task she set them in maths lessons and how they actually arrived at the 'answers' in their books. There were over thirty six-year-olds in the class and the teacher was unable to observe because she was kept busy at her desk checking the work that individual pupils brought to her. In this lesson the task was to measure objects. It was agreed that the outsider should observe individual pupils. The extract reproduces his notes on two boys.

> Boy engaged with – grey trousers, fawn shirt with shoulder and sleeve epaulettes – How wide is your drawing book? Offers card (coin) to adjacent boy. Talks about what other boy is doing. During this time intermittently completes 'Tuesday June 19th'. Turns card face upwards – gets up looks around – goes to T's desk returns with rubber; sits down. Watches boy stacking plastic egg cartons. Head on elbow watches girl at table. Adjoining boy takes egg boxes away. This seems to signal movement to subject – goes to tray rack, picks up egg cartons – returns with them to table – has now written 'My d'. Re-sorts cuisennaire rods in box on table. Now sorts four small cards and selects one containing word 'coin'. Now has written 'Mr dr' – goes off – returns with rubber – erases 'r' – extends writing to 'my dra'; watches two children pensively – resumes writing. Completes 'My drawing'. Obs. discontinued.

> *Boy in red and blue,*
> Obs. begins. Has written 'The black domino box is' – goes off to T's desk – then returns and passes out of range of observer. Observer wanders about, boy not to be seen (toilet?). Returns after interval of six minutes. Observer asks 'What are you doing?' Child: 'I can't think of word' – silence. Writes 'six' in box – Did he measure the box? converses with a girl – returns to papers: 'Now I got it' (girl has shown him 'black dominoes long' on reverse of sheet) – completes 'the black dominoes box is six dominoes long'. Goes off with paper. Returns and announces 'I'm going to do a puzzle now' – Goes to puzzle cupboard – selects puzzle – and settles on carpeted area.

So far we have only thought of a written observational record but it would be possible to use video recording. We were, however, reluctant to introduce a camera in the early stages of a partnership because we felt it was more obtrusive and consequently more intimidating for the teacher. One advantage would be that the teacher and the outsider would have equal access to the information on which their post-observation discussion would be based; at present, the notes, although shared with the teacher, are a more subjective record of the observer's perceptions than a video film would be and in some sense remain 'the observer's'.

USING THE OBSERVATIONAL RECORD

It is, of course, important that the post-observational discussion takes place as near the observation as possible. The goodwill of the headteacher may be needed to ease the teacher's timetable to make this possible. (The head of the school in which one of our outsiders worked was able to release the teacher partner from assembly, which was held in the afternoon, so that she could discuss the observation with him.) Or the goodwill of the teacher may be called on if he or she has to give up free time during the lunch hour or after school in order to take part in the post-observation discussion.

The observational record is likely to be used mainly to reconstruct events which the teacher does not have access to. For example, the fieldnotes reproduced above were used by the outsider as an *aide-mémoire* when he described what he had seen (topic 4):

> OUTSIDER: He'd written 'the black domino box is'. Then he went off to teacher's desk and then he returned and this was when he passed out of my range. He went behind me. About half a minute after he'd disappeared I got up and wandered about to see where he'd gone. He was quite distinctive in his bright red and blue but I couldn't find him and then he returned after six minutes. At this point he smiled at me so I said: 'What are you doing?' And he said 'I can't think of a word', and then there was silence, and then he wrote 'six'. Again I thought: Did he measure the box? I didn't see him measure it: it was on the table all the time when he'd gone off on this errand, wherever it was. Well, then he conversed with the little girl in a sort of pale brown . . .
>
> TEACHER:No, he probably couldn't think of the word 'black dominoes' . . .
>
> OUTSIDER:He talked to her and he said: 'Now I've got it' and the girl had shown him that 'black dominoes long' was, in fact, on the reverse of the work sheet.
>
> TEACHER:Actually I had shown them twice.
>
> OUTSIDER:It might have been that he actually measured it, but I certainly didn't see him do it. Then he completed 'dominoes long'. So we then had 'the black domino box is six black dominoes long', and then he went up with his paper and said: 'I'm going to go a puzzle now.' He said that with a great jubilation and went to the puzzle cupboard, took a puzzle, and settled on the floor.

The teacher found the evidence . . . offered her a different view of her classroom and provided a basis for thinking how she might reorganize her teaching in order to get feedback about how individual children were working. Such notes might also be used, of course, to help the teacher and the outsider plan the next sequence of observation.

In another setting, the outsider's reconstruction of the lesson served as a stimulus to release the latent knowledge of the teacher. Here, the focus was the constraints imposed on the teaching and learning by the lack of space in the classroom (topic 2). Having offered a reconstruction, the outsider's role was to sustain the teacher's flow of reflections:

> TEACHER: I mean, really I suppose in some ways I'm not utilizing it to its best because originally that area taken up by the doll's house was meant to be my sort of craft/paint area, which was the reason for the old carpet, because I had easels

there so they could paint on the old carpet, and it didn't matter, and they were nearer the sink. But then that was a problem because it wan't big enough for more than two, and then it was going to be a glueing area, then I realized I needed a place to put all my stuff for collage work. I think I really ought to do something about that area.

OUTSIDER: Yes, well, what's it possible to do? You need all that stuff.

TEACHER: The trolleys are another thing that – whether I move those and put them underneath the shelves on the carpet area or not . . .

OUTSIDER: I wondered about that. Do they all sit on the carpet for stories and things?

TEACHER: Yes, and some of them lean on the shelves.

The brainstorming continued, and through talk the teacher was able to move towards a solution to her problem.

At another time, field notes were used to answer specific questions: there was a lot that the teacher wanted to know about the behaviour of the four pupils who didn't seem to be enjoying drama (topic 1):

TEACHER: Did they appear to talk to any of the others when they were planning and deciding who was going to lead, who hold the torch?

OUTSIDER: Tracey I noticed talking to the leader in her group, at the torch stage. I remember her talking to . . .

TEACHER: I am pleased that Tracey was so active because she wasn't last week – although she has been attentive in everything else we have done, keen to join in stories. I mean, it just made me wonder, so I was pleased to see her taking an active part . . . it was only her second session of drama. What about Diane, because she doesn't relate to the others terribly well?

OUTSIDER: I didn't notice her talking.

TEACHER: And I don't think she would talk of her own accord unless somebody actually asked her a question. And then she might not answer.

OUTSIDER: I didn't notice her talking, nor John either. Although he did act out having the torch later on. I noticed Tracey and Mary talking, but not talking within the role, just chatting.

The effect of these exchanges (which continued beyond the pasage quoted above) was to reaffirm the teacher's perception of the low level of participation from Diane and John, to modify somewhat her view of Mary, and to suggest that her concern about Tracey's lack of engagement last lesson was probably more to do with it having been Tracey's first-ever drama class than with an antipathy towards drama.

The partners should recognize that the relationship may take a little time to develop and until they learn how to make use of detailed observation, the field notes may seem of doubtful value and the post-observation discussion may lack bite and depth. The teacher quoted above commented:

I did feel (at first) a little irritated that we weren't getting anywhere and that I didn't know what you thought. I felt the discussion was airy-fairy. But subsequent discussions were better. I felt we got more honest with each other and less wary. But your notes were very helpful – I can't make those sorts of observations when I am teaching. They amazed me the first time; you noticed so many things that I just missed completely. At first I thought they weren't going to be any good: 'Diane waves her hand about'! I thought: 'Well, she often does!' But when you read them through you can build up quite a picture, especially when you compare them week by week.

ADVANTAGES AND SHORTCOMINGS OF THE APPROACH

It is clear that if a realistic focus for observation can be agreed and a respect for the principles of procedure maintained, then partnerships can provide evidence to help the teacher rethink important aspects of teaching. Sometimes, however, it may not be easy for the teacher to see exactly what action to take even though he or she has, as a result of the partnership, acquired a deeper understanding of the situation. This is how the teacher quoted above felt: 'I think we have brought to light things that were probably there anyway but which I have overlooked or hadn't noticed. But even now I don't know how we use those things to make drama more pleasurable for the children.' But the experience was worthwhile for this teacher: she had embarked on the partnership almost as a conscript – 'I started off quite negative' – but her commitment had grown as she saw that she was learning – 'I ended up being very positive about it all'. Moreover, she had picked up, in a relatively short time, a habit of trying to look more closely at what was happening in her classroom.

The teachers who took part valued in particular the chance to engage in a focused discussion of practice with someone who was, in career terms, a neutral professional. Some of the teachers in our study, for example, had felt a keen sense of isolation in what was a small village school:

> I think particularly at the moment we have very few courses that we can go on and, if there are, they are too far away. In a small school you can't really go on them. You can be in a small school for years and never see an adviser. There's no outside person ever coming to give you that bit of a lift really, to make you feel that you're *not* isolated. There is someone there to give you a boast with this. I think it's very useful.

Outside partners have other advantages over inside (teacher colleague) partners. First, they can make teachers feel more in touch with the world outside their own classrooms: teachers sometimes have no sense of how what they are doing compares with work in other schools; they may think that they are idosyncratic, failing, old-fashioned, and so on. Two of our partners talked about this:

OUTSIDER: I think it's an endless problem for people with reception classes in schools built about this time – and older schools – where they're nearly always in a room that's designed either for a general purpose or for kids sitting down, being taught in rows.

TEACHER: Well, it's nice to know that it's not just my problem. You get to the state when you think 'Perhaps it's me!' So when you hear somebody else chewing it over and finding a problem, then you think: 'Well, I'm not so bad after all.'

A second advantage is that contact with an outsider whom the teacher comes to respect can serve to extend the teacher's thinking: the outsider represents an alternative reference group and therefore offers some leverage for action. The teacher quoted above, in a post-observation discussion, identified the kind of ideological constraint that frequently blocks routes to the solution of problems. She was quick to see the way in which images of 'good teaching' instilled during her training were still so powerful that they could lead her to maintain a set of practices that were in fact at odds with her personal preference and professional judgement:

I suppose really the answer is, you know, to stop thinking about the way you've been trained, to stop thinking in 'areas'. When I was at college it was the late sixties/early seventies – it was very much the thing: you've got to have areas – you've got to have a maths area, an activities area, and your quiet area. So, you know, it's very hard to get your mind off that.

As a result of this discussion with the outsider she felt able to rethink the notion of areas and to organize her classroom in a way that helped her to make the best use of her limited space.

If the partnership is to be successful, the teacher must know that there is some prospect of it lasting for at least several meetings. If the partnership is short, then the teacher's suspicion of the outsider's motives may not fully wear off:

It depends whether it's a one-off thing, you know – what sort of time that person would come out for. If it's a once-a-year sort of thing people think: 'Oh, Crikey and it would fall by the wayside . . . If you were having someone in regularly that you knew and chatted to, you'd learn to forget that they were there (in the classroom, observing). You wouldn't think they were there to judge. They would be just part of the classroom. It's when people just pop in occasionally that I think problems occur.

What we cannot know is how realistic it is for people like our outsider partners both to find time for such activities and to discipline themselves so that they do not behave like the judge, assessor or expert.

One aspect of our work disappointed us. We were not able, as we had hoped, to speculate with any confidence about what the likely outcomes of the partnership approach might be on a school as a whole. In a large school, an outsider–teacher partnership could probably remain private and contained. In small schools we felt that partnerships *could* even change the climate for the worse: where communication among the three or four teachers is already open and easy, the privacy of the teacher–outsider relationship *could* restrict the freedom of internal talk and cause friction. In both our schools, teachers tended to talk about their partnerships with each other and in this way defused any potential tension.

SUMMARY

1. The starting point for this study was the question: what contribution can an outsider make to the professional development of teachers?
2. The approach that we developed is characterized by the idea of partnership in the observation of classrooms.
3. There is the matter of finding the right outsider. In this study the outsiders were from a college and university but there may be other potential partners, such as teacher–advisers.
4. The essence of partnership is that the teacher defines a focus for the outsider's observation; the outsider's responsibility is to gather evidence which the teacher and the outsider can discuss as a basis for modifying practice. The sessions of the partnership should comprise:

   (a) *a pre-observation discussion* at which principles of procedure are agreed, the focus is clarified and practical matters are worked out – such as what kind of data will be most useful to the teacher; how the data are to be gathered; where the observer is to place him/herself;
   (b) *observations*;
   (c) *post-observation discussions* based on the observational records made by the observer.

5. It is not always easy for teachers to choose something that is of real concern *and* to invite an outsider to examine the situation in which the problem manifests itself. Teachers need to be confident.
6. Not all concerns, however real and pressing, lend themselves to exploration through a series of short observations. Ideal are topics which offer an unambiguous and narrowly defined research focus and which can be explored mainly through observation of classroom events and interactions.
7. It seems that few teachers have visitors in their classrooms who are not either 'learner' teacher or authority figures associated with the tasks of assessment or judgement and it is, therefore, difficult for teachers to see a visitor as a research partner.

8. The outsider is not there to make definitive judgements on the teacher's practice in the classroom or to make authoritative recommendations but to help the teacher to see how the careful analysis of evidence from his or her own classroom may help the teacher to develop a strategy for responding to a problem.

9. Some of the concerns which teachers might feel about inviting an outsider into their classrooms might be allayed by the outsider's commitment to confidentiality as an important procedural point.

10. It is important that teachers enter into partnership willingly, and with curiosity and confidence. Conscripts can easily protect themselves from learning about their own classrooms by identifying 'safe' unproblematic topics for observation.

11. The partnership, provided that it is extended over time, can counter the sense of professional isolation felt by many teachers.

12. Contact with a trusted outsider gives the teacher a point of reference outside his or her school and this can be helpful in legitimizing changes of approach.

3.5
THE ANALYSIS OF DEPTH INTERVIEWS*
Sue Jones

A great deal more has been written about methodologies of qualitative data collection than about those of data analysis. This is not particularly surprising. The analysis of qualitative data is a highly personal activity. It involves processes of interpretation and creativity that are difficult and perhaps somewhat threatening to make explicit. As with depth interviewing there are no definitive rules to be followed by rote and by which, for example, two researchers can ensure that they reach identical conclusions about a set of data.

The difficulty of explication should not, however, lead to the extreme of mystification. Indeed a great deal of qualitative data analysis is rather less mysterious than hard, sometimes tedious, slog. In this chapter I shall attempt to describe and explain the kinds of processes I go through when I analyse qualitative interview data. There is no intention to be prescriptive, but rather to offer a personal account of a personal process, in sufficient detail to enable those who are interested to try something similar to do so.

GROUNDED THEORIZING

The analysis of qualitative data is a process of making sense, of finding and making a structure in the data and giving this meaning and significance for ourselves, and for any relevant audiences. As with data collection methodologies, the way we do this and the kind of structures we look for in the data depend on the purpose of inquiry and what we see as the underlying purpose of qualitative research. As with depth interviewing, therefore, my starting point is a concern to understand the world of the research participants as

* Jones, S. (1985) The analysis of depth interviews, in R. Walker (ed.) *Applied Qualitative Research*, Gower.

they construct it. As Psathas (1973, p. 12) argues, the key issue for social research is 'whether the results of an inquiry fit, make sense and are true to the understanding of ordinary actors in the everyday world'. It is a concern which is intensely practical. Theory which is 'grounded' (Glaser and Strauss, 1967) in the concepts and theorizing of the people it is about is likely to 'fit and work' as the basis for explanation and prediction.

I know I cannot empathize with the research participants completely. I also know that I am likely at some points to set my understanding of their 'concrete' concepts – those which they use to organize, interpret and construct their own world (Diesing, 1972) – within my own and/or audience's concepts and frameworks that are different from theirs. When I do this, however, I try to be clear that I am doing this and why, and to ensure that this 'second level' of meaning retains some link with the constructions of the research participants. This is because of my concern to avoid what Lofland (1976) calls 'undisciplined abstraction', leading to concepts which bear little relation to the social world that they are supposed to refer to, either because they are not apparently based in any empirical research, or are wondrously elaborate edifices of theory based on very little empirical research. As Lofland (1976, p. 11) argues, 'an empirical science is constructed . . . out of the interplay of data and perplexed perception that *gives rise* to concepts yet contains and *constrains* them by a context of concrete empirical materials'.

I am trying to do this whether I am doing 'academic' research without a direct research client, or research commissioned by clients. My audience is different. When it is an academic one I am likely to make more references to existing theory within that audience, and I use words like concepts, models, theory and so on, relatively freely whereas I might be more circumspect with certain clients to whom they might smack of 'ivory tower' academicism. With some commissioned research I may also be less concerned with moving beyond a relatively concrete or substantive analysis of the data than for an academic audience. I am still however, theorizing and cannot but do so.

As Bulmer (1982) points out, there is a tendency among the commissioners of policy-related research, whether in government or other organizations, to see it as primarily concerned with the gathering of 'facts' – objective information on the basis of which informed policy decisions about specific policy problems can be made. Researchers undertake this information-gathering activity against the specific brief of their clients, and in analysing and reporting their findings are required also to be objective, impartial and descriptive. But the analysis of data about the social world can never be 'merely' a matter of discovering and describing what is there. The very process of deciding 'what is', and what is relevant and significant in 'what is', involves selective interpretation and conceptualization. As Bulmer (1982, p. 38) also points out, 'There is a constant interplay between the observation of realities and the formation of concepts, between research and theorizing, between perception and explanation.'

STRUCTURING THROUGH CATEGORIES

I start off with [audio] tapes or, if for some reason the interview was not taped, the notes about the interview made immediately afterwards. I also have the notes that I make after each interview which are not detailed records of what went on but rather more general comments on the nature of the interaction. They cover such things as: whether the interview seemed to go well; if not why not; how distracted, comfortable, nervous, confident, relaxed, wary and so on, the interviewee (and I) had been; whether I felt I had, or had not, managed to get behind the person's legitimating scripts; whether there were any particular parts of the data that did not quite ring true and why. In short, I note any factors about the place, time and relationship with the inteviewee that seem likely to be important to take account of when I come back to the data. I make these notes because otherwise it is all too easy to forget these additional contextual data which can so importantly affect the interpretation of the interview content.

I sometimes have transcripts [typed up from the audio tapes]. They are a help in managing the data and holding on to the detail which can be missed by selective jottings from the tape. However, it is important that reading the transcripts does *not* become a substitute for listening to the non-linguistic data on the tapes: emphasis, mood, intonation and so on that crucially elaborate meaning. Transcribing tapes does, of course, take a long time, and is expensive if someone else is paid to do it. Thus I usually code the data directly from the tape. Since this is typically done in considerable detail I do not feel particularly concerned that I am going to miss key data by not having transcripts.

Like many qualitative researchers a great deal of my analysis is concerned with 'coding' the data into categories. The quickest and easiest way to do this is to decide upon your categories in advance and simply go through the data putting the appropriate sections of data into the particular categories they illustrate. However, while it is in principle possible to do this and still remain sensitive to the unanticipated categories which derive from the concepts of the research participants, in practice it is difficult to do so. The data all too easily become structured with the a priori definitions of the researcher in precisely the ways that data collection methodology was intended to avoid.

Thus, Glaser and Strauss (1967) argue, in *The Discovery of Grounded Theory*, that theory about the social world which 'fits and works' is that which is generated inductively from the data. Categories emerge out of the examination of the data by researchers who study it without firm preconceptions dictating relevances in concepts and hypotheses beforehand. The problem with this, if taken literally, is that categories do not just 'emerge' out of data as if they were objectively 'there' waiting to be discovered. As Kaplan (1964, p. 133) points out: 'We always know something already and this knowledge is intimately involved in what we come to know next, whether by observation or any other way. We see what we have reason of seeing.' Different persons, with different perspectives and different curiosities about the area of investigation will inevitably find different categories with which to structure and make sense of the data. Furthermore, in commissioned research, the clients of the research will also have their own theories, even if sometimes inchoate and relatively implicit. They will inevitably bring these to bear when confronted with the framework of the researchers' conclusions to respond to and evaluate. To ignore them is merely to increase the likelihood of the researchers' analyses and conclusions being ignored themselves.

Nevertheless, the enormous influence and attraction of Glaser and Strauss's (1967) ideas in the literature of social research lies within the perspective discussed earlier, that is, in their stress upon building understanding about the social world which is firmly grounded in the concepts and theories of the persons inhabiting and acting in it. Thus I try to develop my conceptual categories from the crucial base of the categories and concepts of the research participants. However, in comparing and contrasting and bringing them together I will inevitably formulate broader superordinate or 'sensitizing concepts' which are not identical to the former, and also reflect my own and/or my audiences' research relevances. (See Diesing, 1972, on the nature and relationship of concrete and sensitizing concepts in qualitative theory development; also Glaser, 1978, on a similar substantive/ theoretical concepts distinction.)

In doing this I am also inevitably making connections, as carefully and as explicitly as I can, with the concepts and theories I already have about the area of investigation, in ways which can confirm, elaborate, modify or reject them. I also make connections with what I understand to be the concerns and preconceptions of any research clients. By this I do not mean just what is set down in a final brief, but what I believe (and have usually put some energy into finding out) to be the typically more complex, less neatly organized set of ideas and interests they have about the topic. I would expect to take these into account in any debriefing and report.

Although I do not start with a list of categories into which the data are to be slotted, thinking about these and the broad question taken into the research represents the 'focusing' I will do before starting the detailed analysis. I prefer to listen to the tapes of each interview at least twice: the first time to get a sense of the whole interview, its themes and dynamics; the second time to examine the data in more detail. Then I begin to 'map' the interview, using the technique of cognitive mapping.

MAPPING THE DATA

Cognitive mapping is a method of modelling persons' beliefs in diagrammatic form. It was developed in the context of action research and consultancy, as a tool to enable clients to make explicit, explore, and work through their thinking about a particular problem in order to devise ways of handling it (see Eden, Jones and Sims, 1979, 1983). However, I have also used mapping extensively in analysing interview data that was not part of an action research project.

In mapping we are listening for, and seeking to represent, persons' explanatory and predictive theories about those aspects of their world being described to us. A cognitive map comprises two main elements: persons' concepts of ideas in the form of descriptions of entities, abstract or concrete, in the situation being considered; and beliefs or theories about the relationships between them, shown in the map by an arrow or simple line. An arrow represents a relationship where one thing leads to, or is explained by, another; a simple line represents a connotative, or non-causal link. So the following statements taken from an interview may be coded as shown:

Our ability to carry out additional desirable policies rests in part on our making best use of current resources on current policies. We cannot carry out additional

decision just   +   fundamental waste
on a gut basis → of resources on \ −
                            current policies

    +   make rational +   make best use of   +   our ability to
adequate   → and accurate   → current recources → carry out add-
information   decisions   on current policies   itional desirable
                                                                            policies

Note   X + Y : X leads to Y; or
                        an increase in X leads to a decrease in Y
                        a decrease in X leads to a decrease in Y

            X − Y : X leads to the opposite of Y / a reduction in Y;
                        or
                        an increase in X leads to a decrease in Y
                        a decrease in X leads to an increase in Y

desirable policies if there is fundamental waste of resources on current policies. This means being able to make rational and accurate decisions based on adequate information, not decisions just on a gut basis.

This is the simplest form of coding, one which those trying out the method often find helpful to begin with. However, more complete coding takes account of the way in which the particular meaning of an idea for a person is elaborated through its contrast, explicit or implicit, with some psychological alternative (Kelly, 1955). For example, the notion of 'being bored' only makes sense because there is some implied opposite notion, of say, 'being interested', although it is important to note that different persons may have very different opposite poles and thus different personal constructs; perhaps 'bored . . . excited' or 'bored . . . happy'. They may, furthermore, use either of these constructs at different times, depending on the situation they are in. Persons do not, of course, always express explicit discrete alternatives, but when they do these can be coded for, and furthermore the opposite poles can sometimes legitimately be inferred. The above quotation was chosen because it is a good example of expressed bipolar constructs. We could record the statements, now, as follows:

	make rational and accurate	make best use of . . . fundamental	our ability to carry out
adequate information . . .	+ decisions . . . → decisions just on a gut basis	+ waste of current → resources on current policies	+ additional → desirable policies

Note: Dots separate discrete alternative poles or indicate 'void' poles where the alternative has not been made explicit. Concepts without dots are monotonic concepts where the inferred poles are 'an increase in', 'a decrease in' respectively. A + ve sign between constructs indicates a relationship between similar-sided poles. Thus, for example, 'make rational and accurate decisions' leads to 'make best use of current resources on current policies' while 'decisions just on a gut basis' leads to 'fundamental waste of current resources on current policies'.

A −ve sign would indicate a relationship *across* poles so that the first pole of a construct 'A' would lead to the second pole of a construct 'B' and the second pole of construct 'A' would lead to the first pole of construct 'B'.

I code the interviews on large sheets of paper so that each interview, as far as possible, is coded on to one sheet. If there is not enough space I simply attach further sheets. At the end I therefore have a map of the whole interview in front of me. It is often untidy, bitty, but a map that I can make sense of, and it is worth noting that the skeleton rules for coding outlined above are often elaborated with additional personal conventions by others who use the technique. What is important is the use of mapping as a tool to help understand the way in which the interviewees make sense of their world

– attributing meaning and significance through explaining and predicting the consequences of events, for themselves and/or others.

Whilst I am coding I also make a great many notes, some on the map itself, others on separate sheets which I then clip on to the map. For example, the use of lines to represent relationships between constructs clearly omits the verbal and non-verbal data which elaborate the particular strength, or tentativeness, or subtle qualification, of beliefs about these relationships. Where it seems important to do so, I therefore put these data in. I may put words along an arrow or draw heavy or dashed lines to indicate emphatic or tentative assertions, add question marks to represent questions and so on. I have no firm conventions for this activity because I do not wish to become bound up in an elaborate system of rules for coding. I underline or ring constructs or groups of constructs that seem to be particularly significant to the person, including those, for example, that seem to express strong preferences or values, and note why I am making the inference.

I comment on any apparent contradictions in the data, thinking about whether, for example, they reflect genuine inconsistency, or apparent inconsistency that is in fact reconciled by underlying beliefs, a change in thinking over the course of the interview, or indeed greater honesty later in the interview. I make notes about any data that feel more like legitimation than sincere belief, why they seem to be of this kind, and what inferences I can justifiably make about them. I note where I seem to have influenced the data by misreading significance and 'over-probing' in a certain direction or, on a second hearing, seem to have missed clues which I should have probed further. I continually jot down ideas that spring to mind about the significance and implications of the data for my research interests, including connections with existing theory. If there is a research client I record those things which are likely to be particularly pertinent to him and which I could expect to comment on in any report. I also note connections with and implications for previous interviews I have looked at and future ones I am going to analyse. I make a tentative list of possible categories.

At the end of this process I thus have a map and a series of notes that represent my inferences and interpretation of the data. At this point I look at the map as a whole, and draw out the clusters of constructs and relationships that seem to form the substantive categories in the data based on the 'concrete' concepts of the respondent. I also note other categorizations that reflect my own ways of organizing the substantive categories in accordance with my own research relevances. These further categorizations may well change as I examine the rest of the data. Finally, I produce a summary diagram of the categories and their relationships which I use to help me relate interview to interview when I put the analyses together.

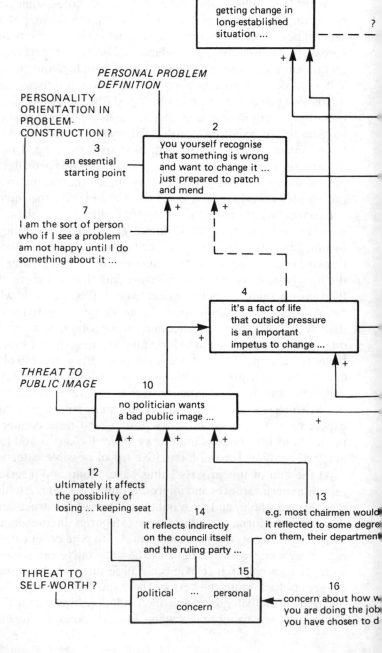

Figure A

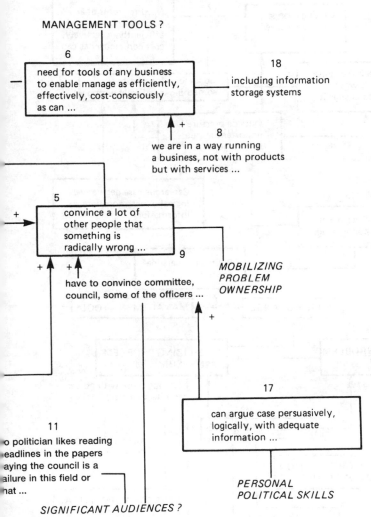

MANAGEMENT TOOLS ?

6

need for tools of any business
to enable manage as efficiently,
effectively, cost-consciously
as can ...

18

including information
storage systems

+ **8**

we are in a way running
a business, not with products
but with services ...

5

convince a lot of
other people that
something is
radically wrong ...

9

have to convince committee,
council, some of the officers ...

*MOBILIZING
PROBLEM
OWNERSHIP*

+

17

can argue case persuasively,
logically, with adequate
information ...

11

o politician likes reading
eadlines in the papers
aying the council is a
ailure in this field or
hat ...

*PERSONAL
POLITICAL SKILLS*

SIGNIFICANT AUDIENCES ?

ure A A cognitive map of the transcript on page 273, illustrating what an initial
ategorization might look like. Numbers are merely arbitrary identification
odes used to identify constructs and often differentiate between interviewees.
Blocked constructs represent potential category labels from the constructs
of the interviewee, subsuming as the content of the relevant category those
onstructs traced back from these until another category label is reached, and the
ubordinate category related in the way. Thus, for example, the category indicated
by construct 10 would contain constructs 10, 12, 13, 14, and the subordinate
ategory indicated by construct 15, containing construct 16. Concepts in capitals
ndicate potential 'second order' categorizations, grounded in those of the interviewee but nevertheless reflecting my own perspectives and research interests
and no doubt other researchers with different perspectives and interests would
ind different categories). Dashed lines and question marks indicate tentativeness
n inferences and interpretations that I would expect to come back to or require
urther evidence for and my maps typically have many of these as I code.

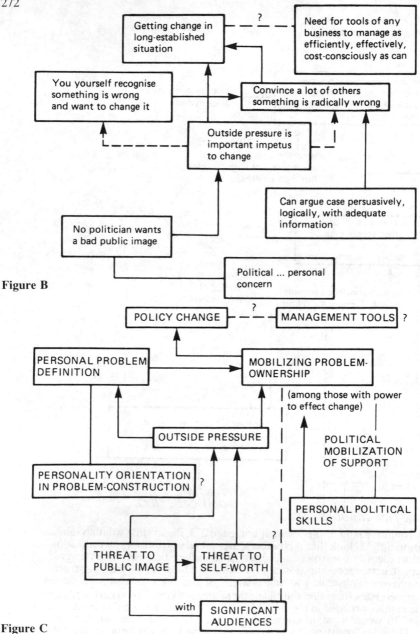

Figure B

Figure C

Figures B and **C** show examples of 'summary' diagrams that illustrate the category relationships that might be built from the map in Figure A. One would of course expect both categories and their relationships to be elaborated and modified in the light of the related data in the rest of the interview.

To give an example of this process, see Figures A, B and C which relate to part of an interview with a local politician concerned with exploring his perceptions of his role. It sets out part of the answer to a question asking him to elaborate further on the factors he saw as important in trying to effect 'change in a long-established situation', a concept he had used previously in the interview.

To get change in a long-established situation an essential starting point it seems to me is that you yourself recognize that something is wrong and want to change it, you are not just prepared to patch and mend. I suppose I am the sort of person who if I see a problem I am not happy until I do something about it. Then, of course, you have to convince a lot of other people that something is radically wrong. You have to convince committee, council and some of the officers that something is radically wrong. Obviously you have to be able to argue your case persuasively, logically and with adequate information. This is actually another question that we ought to look at at some point. We are in a way running a business, not with products but with services and we need the tools of any business, including information storage systems, to enable us to manage as efficiently and effectively and cost-consciously as we can. Anyway, in getting change, it is a fact of life that outside pressure is an important impetus to change. No politician wants a bad public image. No politician likes reading headlines in the papers saying that the council is a failure in this field or that. Most chairmen, for example, would feel that it reflected to some degree on them, on their department and certainly it reflects indirectly on the council and on the ruling party. Ultimately of course, it affects the possibility of losing or keeping your seat. But it is also a personal concern as well as a political concern about how well you do the job you have chosen to do.

COMPARISON AND INTEGRATION

I go through this process with each interview and then I bring the resultant analyses together. With the help of the summary diagrams, I locate the categories that have similar labels and then compare the content of the categories, putting together the categories that seem to go together because they are about the same topic and/or illustrate a particular conceptual theme. I sometimes use computer software, specifically designed to assist with the analysis of cognitive maps (e.g. Jones, 1981; Eden, Smithin and Wilshire, 1980), but it is important to point out that the process is not computer-dependent and this chapter concentrates on manual analysis. In the latter I literally cut up the maps, using photocopies but retaining the original, and put the categories next to one another. The process of comparison will usually result in further categorization, such as finding superordinate concepts that bring together similar categories and perhaps further sub-categorizations beneath these.

The superordinate conceptual categorizations may be very closely related to the original concrete category labels and/or comprise those that particularly reflect the client's relevances and/or go further in conceptualization to employ wider theoretical concepts. Thus to give one example, the notion of 'significant audiences for performance in a problem' is one that emerged for me as an important theme in interviews with local government members and officers. This was grounded in my understanding of what they construed as significant to pay attention to in performing their role but also reflected my own way of bringing together and conceptualizing their constructs.

As Glaser and Strauss (1967) point out about their constant comparative method of analysis, this process of comparison (albeit somewhat different from their method) is one which very soon leads to ideas about the dimensions and properties of the category, including its relationship with other categories and including the differences as well as the similarities between people's constructions. Thus, to continue the above example, the broad category 'significant audiences for performance in a problem' can be mapped out through a range of different types of audience, significant for a variety of different reasons to different individuals. Here exploration of the relationships between concrete categories perceived by the individuals is important. For example, several interviewees may express a concern about the importance of 'good . . . bad public image' but they may differ in what they see as the particular consequences for themselves and the factors facilitating or inhibiting this image. Throughout the process of comparison and integration I continue to make yet further notes, my commentary on what I am doing and why. It is these notes, with the data they refer to which, finally, form the basis of any research report and/or debrief.

INVOLVING CLIENTS

I usually write for any clients a traditional report, with quotations from the data, but I also refer to and include, in appendix form, maps of the categories and their contents on separate pages. I also provide summary diagrams of category labels and the relationships between them. I do not always put in all the data in each category. This is contingent upon the amount of data and the degree to which I feel justified in regarding some idea as so similar that it is not a distortion to remove the repetition and retain one chain of beliefs as representative of the beliefs of a number of the respondents.

The process of mapping I have described can be used by researchers for themselves alone. Maps can also, however, be used to involve the client in the data in a way that a few isolated quotes cannot. In most qualitative research the client is heavily reliant upon the summary interpretations of the researcher, with little direct access to the data. Yet clients will have their own interpretations of the particular significance of the findings to themselves. The good researcher will take account of what he or she understands to be the concerns and theories of the client about the research arena. Yet the process of building meaning and significance in the data is a dynamic activity of *direct* interaction with the data, and maps can offer more opportunity for this direct interaction than most typical research reports.

It is obviously the case that the maps produced by a researcher do not comprise 'raw data,' but those which have been modelled and organized in a particular way. It is also the case that some clients are inclined to prefer brief summaries and recommendations from a researcher than become involved in the detail of the data underlying these. Nor do researchers always want clients to become involved in detailed examination of the data. Nevertheless maps do enable clients to explore considerably more of the language and theorizing of respondents than can possibly be captured in selected quotations. Indeed, the maps can be used as a strong tool of detailed evidence and backing for a researcher's interpretations and conclusions. More contingently, clients can be invited to make their own interpretations of the data in a relationship where neither they nor the researcher have sole proprietary 'rights' to interpretation. They can become involved in 'negotiations' about particular meanings and significances.

MANAGING COMPLEXITY

Cognitive mapping is not, of course, the only method for carefully and systematically analysing qualitative data. To take a very simple variation on the methods explored in this chapter, one may choose to categorize the data, not coded in maps, but in sentence form. Thus, for example, one may listen to the tapes and write down the content of categories collected as statements on different sheets of paper, or cards. As statements occur later on in an interview that seem to relate to an earlier category, these too are entered on to the relevant sheet. Alternatively, if working with transcripts, the categories in which one wishes to place sections of data can be marked by the side of them in the margin and the pieces cut out and aggregated later. While doing this, one can also simultaneously make notes about the relationships between categories as they are being constructed and additional notes of the kind described earlier. Categories collected in this way will be compared and the process of comparison will lead to the development of further conceptualization. This is a perfectly 'good' and thorough way to analyse qualitative data and one I have used.

It is perhaps worth noting at this point that, as Marshall (1981) points out, the debate within quantitative content analysis about the appropriate unit of analysis – whether it should be a word, phrase, sentence and so on – seems an unnecessary one. We find relatively easily 'chunks of meaning' and these may vary considerably in length. Not only is the debate unnecessary, it also seems inappropriate. Meaning is given by context. Words in isolation from their particular context of associated, elaborating beliefs are indeed meaningless. To make them meaningful researchers have to 'put back' the context from their own, and perhaps very different, framework of beliefs.

However, since this has been essentially a personal account, I should perhaps finish by explaining why I find myself repeatedly returning to cognitive mapping as a technique, despite the fact that it is sometimes a laborious and tedious process. First, rather than distancing me from the data, I find that the discipline of mapping leads to an intense immersion in them. Second, I am helped by the confidence I have in the theoretical basis for the technique, provided by personal construct theory. Third, I find it easier to develop grounded concrete categories and their relationships in this way. Fourth, and perhaps most important, mapping helps me with the complex '*Gestalt*' of data. We need to 'fracture' the data in order to grasp and manipulate them; but the process of doing so by parcelling them into separate categories during coding makes it difficult to retain a sense of the relationships between the various elements in the data. I find that a map of a whole interview helps me to manage and also to retain the complexity of interrelated data better than if I follow a method which, for example, involves separating the data out as I proceed. In doing so I hope it also helps me retain and respect something of the unique 'wholeness' of unique persons' views of the world (e.g. Diesing, 1972, on holistic research).

Yet this has been a personal account and other people will inevitably find their own ways of managing and retaining complexity and *Gestalt* in data. There are many different methods that researchers can construct for themselves, all variations on the same themes of breaking down and building up analytic structure in the data. We can make some judgements about these as being more or less thorough, systematic, careful, non-pre-emptive, reflective, and so on, but some categorical determination of a 'best' method seems quite inappropriate. Finally, we all build and use the routines and tools with which we find, often through trial and error, we are most comfortable and which help us best make sense of the way other persons make sense of their realities.

REFERENCES

Bulmer, M. (1982) *The Uses of Social Research: Social Investigation in Public Policy Making*, Allen & Unwin, London.

Diesing, P. (1972) *Patterns of Discovery in the Social Sciences*, Routledge & Kegan Paul, London.

Eden, C., Jones, S. and Sims, D. (1979) *Thinking in Organizations*, Macmillan, London.

Eden, C., Jones, S. and Sims, D. (1983) *Messing About in Problems*, Pergamon, Oxford.

Eden, C., Smithin, T. and Wiltshire (1980) Cognition, simulation and learning, *Journal of Experimental Learning and Simulation*, Vol. 2, pp. 131–43.

Glaser, B.G. (1978) *Theoretical Sensitivity*, The Sociology Press, Mill Valley, California.

Glaser, B.G. and Strauss, A.L. (1967) *The Discovery of Grounded Theory*, Aldine, Chicago.

Jones, S. (1981) Listening to complexity – analysing qualitative marketing research data, *Journal of the Market Research Society*, Vol. 23, No. 1, pp. 26–39.

Kaplan, A. (1964) *The Conduct of Enquiry*, Chandler, San Francisco.

Kelly, G.A. (1955) *The Psychology of Personal Constructs*, Norton, New York.

Lofland, J. (1976) *Doing Social Life*, Wiley, New York.

Marshall, J. (1981) Making sense of a personal process, in P. Reason and J. Rowan (eds.) *Human Inquiry*, Wiley, Chichester.

Psathas, G. (1973) *Phenomenological Sociology: Issues and Applications*, Wiley, New York.

3.6
CONFIDENTIALITY
AND THE RIGHT TO KNOW*
Richard Pring

INTRODUCTION

Evaluation of what happens in schools requires access to information and the right to report on what is observed so that different people – employers, parents, curriculum developers – can be better informed. But this may not in all cases be in the best interests of the teachers and the children. Moral problems arise concerning the *right* of researchers and evaluators to know what they need to know for their particular purposes. Some of these moral problems can be anticipated, and safeguards established, through a code of conduct, but such a code must remain fairly general and can be no substitute for moral responsibility on the part of the evaluator and for appropriate relationships of trust between evaluator and teacher.

THE SOURCE OF THE PROBLEM

There is a lot of criticism, quite understandably, of the secrecy with which the affairs of public institutions such as schools, local education authorities, or government departments and committees are conducted. There is a need for more openness to ensure that decisions are made in an informed manner and that these institutions are properly accountable to the people they serve. To many therefore there is a prima facie case for claiming the 'right to know' and for the exercise of this right through a more thorough evaluation of schools and other institutions. Often this right is insisted upon even when the subsequent inquiry and revelation are said to damage the people or institu-

* Pring, R. (1984) Confidentiality and the right to know, in C. Adelman (ed.) *The Politics and Ethics of Evaluation*, Croom Helm.

tions into which the inquiry is made. The problem is a complex and difficult ethical one – the right of some to know versus the right of others to preserve a degree of privacy even in matters that affect the public good. In what follows I shall do no more than examine what 'the right to know' means and indicate why, in any programme of evaluation, it should be made conditional upon the realization of other values.

THE RIGHT TO KNOW

Broadly speaking, ethical theories (and therefore the way issues are tackled from an ethical point of view) tend to fall into one of two camps. First there are those that stress the intrinsic value of particular activities, irrespective of the consequences. Secondly, there are those that judge the value of what is done much more by reference to the consequences. Of course, most ethical positions have (and must have) a bit of both, but there are differences of emphasis, and these differences seem particularly relevant to consideration of the ethical problems in evaluation, and in particular to the respect to be attached to confidentiality.

The insistence upon 'rights' falls very much in the first kind of ethical position. When the Americans asserted that all men had an equal right to life, liberty and the pursuit of happiness, they appealed, not to the beneficial consequences of having such a right acknowledged, but to self-evident principles. And indeed the view that certain rights are 'natural', and as such can be appealed to in any criticism of society's actual laws, practices, and institutions, has been a popular aspect of political argument. In the context of education, we hear frequent talk of the rights of various groups – parents, children, teachers, employers. Furthermore, since the extent of this talk is often inversely proportional to the extent of agreement about these rights, we can presume that often it is an appeal to rights which, because not recognized, are somehow there 'in a state of nature', existing whether agreed upon or not.

The current concern for accountability has, as one might expect, resulted in many 'natural right' types of claim. When we ask why schools should be more accountable to parents, taxpayers, professional colleagues, children, employers, the answer often is that these bodies have certain rights – natural rights in that they are not written into any laws or rules and have not been agreed upon and in that they 'arise from' the particular social relationships that exist between the agents of schooling on the one hand and these different groups on the other. Thus parents, by virtue of special responsibilities for their children, claim special rights which are often not fully recognized by schools. Roughly these rights might be of two kinds: first the right to have more information about what happens in schools; secondly, the right to intervene in the light of that information. I, as a parent, *feel* that I ought to be fully informed about what happens to my children in school. I also *feel* that if I do not like what I am told, I ought to have certain powers to help me change what I do not like. It is a short step to transform such feelings into talk about rights.

On the other hand such rights, claimed on behalf of parents, employers, administrators, professional bodies must be set against the other rights claimed by teachers as professionals. First, they would claim, as in the case of priests or doctors, the right not to release information that has been gained in pursuit of their professional tasks. Secondly, they would claim the right to pursue their own judgement and therefore draw upon the special insights afforded by experience and training. Perhaps such rights, arising from the professionalism of teachers, would not be held to be 'natural ones', but they often seem preciously like them since professionalism in the context of teaching is ill-defined, without any agreed code of conduct or set of obligations.

A major problem that I see therefore in the current interest in making schools and teachers more accountable lies precisely in the rather foggy area of establishing rights and obligations, where there is no agreement on what these are and where there is no well-established social tradition that can be appealed to. In the absence of either, we are left with some sort of appeal to natural rights with all the problems that that entails, for 'rights' (especially 'natural rights') are most certainly what in current philosophical language might be called 'an essentially contestable concept'.

I talk of it as 'an essentially contestable concept' because:

(a) the meaning of 'rights' is disagreed upon and indeed contested;
(b) these disagreements incorporate fairly fundamental differences of view about what is of value;
(c) there seems ultimately no way of settling these differences.

Hence, arguments about 'rights' so often contain appeals to different political or moral values. And this was never so true as in the present assertion of rights by parents or by the taxpayer or by any group of people – the rights both to know more about schools and to intervene where what is known is not liked.

In one sense, 'right' is not 'essentially contestable'. There are certain logical features of its use that any competent speaker of the English language implicity subscribes. And indeed a great deal of philosophical literature has marked out these characteristics – the nature of the relationship between rights and duties, the classification of different kinds of rights, the function of claims to certain rights, the connection between rights, responsibilities, freedoms, and so on. To say, for example, that somebody has the right to something implies that there is some rule that establishes mutual obligations. If A has a right to X then somebody else has an obligation to make sure that A is not prevented from having X. Rules may be explicit in a legal system or they may be implicit in a social custom or a widely shared traditional way of behaving. But where there are no such laws and no such agreed understandings, it is difficult to make sense of there being rules establishing mutual obligation; and thus the claim to there being 'rights' prior to such agreement seems a spurious one. Rights are not the sort of thing that can be observed. They do not hang around the world, as it were, waiting to be discovered. Hence, many of the current claims to have a right to know or to intervene [are assertions of a political or moral position and], the different definitions of right that reflect them seem *essentially* contestable. 'The right to know' is often a false claim, since there are rarely such established rights, either in legislation or in social practice. It is therefore much more a slogan, a part of the rhetoric which might however result one day in the establishment of such rights. 'Right' is essentially contestable not in its broad formal features but in the substantive claims made under its banner.

These considerations are particularly relevant to some of the claims made on behalf of curriculum evaluation. MacDonald [1976, Chapter 1.2 in this volume] distinguishes between bureaucratic, autocratic, and democratic evaluation, and there has, since then, been no doubting the anxiety with which some evaluators wish to be seen in the democratic camp. Few of us indeed would wish to be called bureaucrats or autocrats, since these words have a pejorative ring to them. But upon analysis what characterizes the democratic evaluator seems to be the recognition of the basic right to know. As MacDonald explains, 'the key concepts of democratic evaluation are "confidentiality", "negotiation", and "accessibility" ', but 'the key justificatory concept is the right to know'. It should be noted that the key justificatory concept is not that of making the system a happier one, or of promoting better education, or of enabling [pupils] to learn more efficiently, or of respecting the aspirations of parents. It may be of course that 'democratic evaluation' or 'providing an information service to the whole community' might promote these worthy aims. On the other hand it may not. But whether it does or it doesn't would not matter to the democratic evaluator, as described, since the right to know is basic – indeed it is *the* key justificatory concept.

My hesitation in readily joining the democratic camp is that I cannot, for reasons given above, see how the 'right to know' is 'basic' or is a 'key justificatory concept'. To repeat what I said, in the absence of agreed social norms or rules that encapsulate such rights, then it is difficult to see what form of existence they have. And clearly there are no such agreements – except, by definition, amongst 'democratic evaluators'. This is not to say that a democratic mode of evaluation cannot be justified. Quite clearly it may be defined for a variety of reasons as the most appropriate means of achieving certain valued ends. But that is not the same as asserting the *basic* right to know. To justify the right to know as a means to an end raises the ethical questions about evaluation in a quite different way. It allows room for the bureaucrat, and even for the autocrat, since, having got rid of basic rights, it can approach each situation more pragmatically, less dogmatically.

One kind of argument is however worth attending to. John Stuart Mill in his essay 'On liberty' argues thus for preserving and extending freedom of discussion:

> the peculiar evil of silencing the expression of an opinion is, that it is robbing the human race; posterity as well as the existing generation; those who dissent from the opinion, still more than those who hold it. If the opinion is right, they are deprived of the opportunity of exchanging error for truth; if wrong, they lose, what is almost as great a benefit, the clearer perception and livelier impression of truth, produced by its collision with error.
>
> (Mill, 1859, p. 142)

Of course, the accessibility of information is a precondition of discussing properly any opinion. There is on Mill's argument a prima facie case therefore for establishing the right to know as somehow a basic one, *if* either the eradication of error or the sharpening up of what is true is held to be of value – as indeed it *must* be by anyone who seriously engages in some particular inquiry. The intellectual life has its own peculiar virtues – not cooking the books is one, being properly informed is another. There are no absolute certainties, and thus, faced with the continual possibility of self-deception or of wrong conclusions, one should welcome rather than spurn the well-informed critic. The peculiarity of Mill's argument lies in its pointing to necessary conditions of the proper pursuit of inquiry, *and* the necessary value attached to inquiry by anyone who is seriously asking these questions. The 'right to know' may not exist, like mountains and rivers, independently of the social rules that man has created and that established mutual relationships of obligations and rights. On the other hand, such social rules must necessarily be agreed upon where getting at the truth is a valued activity.

Why then do I still hesitate to concede this basic right? There are several reasons. First, the right to know seems most defensible where the connection between such a right and the sincere pursuit of disinterested inquiry is clear. But not always is there such a clear connection. People engage in inquiries for a variety of reasons – some to confirm their prejudices (and is it not the case that false theories can be confirmed, given enough information to choose from?), others to pursue their small vendettas, yet others for undesirable political ends. The information industry is as much the servant of *interested* parties as it is the servant of those who in a disinterested way are keen to know more.

Would I be prepared to concede the 'right to know' to someone whose motives I had good grounds to suspect or whose record in misinterpreting what is known is notorious? Where such doubts about the right to know remain, I cannot see it as a basic right – the *key* justificatory principle, requiring no appeal to further more fundamental principles. It may be conceded in particular cases precisely because of the arguments that Mill puts so cogently. But such concession, if made wisely, would be weighed against other considerations.

A lot in practice rests on these considerations. Under the misguided belief in the right to know – the right not only of oneself but also of the wider public – schools have been observed, teachers and pupils interviewed, classroom conversations and activities minutely examined, and all reported upon to the public at large, [irrespective] of the consequences to that school or to those teachers and pupils. It is an ethic of absolute rights, rather than an ethic of consequences. The answer to this, of course, is not to deny the right to know, but to see that right as something that needs to be established in particular cases. Its establishment, of course, will require the acceptance of a set of rules that incorporate that right, as well as obligations upon which it is made conditional.

CONDITIONS FOR GRANTING 'THE RIGHT TO KNOW'

The acceptance of certain obligations upon which the concession of the right to know is made conditional, provides the main reason why I cannot see that right as basic – as so self-evident that the person, group, or institution should immediately expose himself or itself to the public gaze. And what these obligations are – how they are formulated – would depend upon the circumstances. None the less, certain general principles might be suggested for general airing. Let us test these through a particular example.

In Britain the Social Science Research Council agreed to fund a three-year study by the University of London Institute of Education (Gipps and Goldstein, 1983) into the effect of the monitoring of achievement in schools on the educational system. The object of the study was to assess the influence of testing programmes on schools and on educational policies at local and national levels, but it would have a particular interest in the effects of the work of the Assessment of Performance Unit. The Assessment of Performance Unit, like the National Assessment of Educational Performance in the USA, is concerned with monitoring pupil performance across the country in different curriculum areas on a light sampling basis, but unlike National Assessment of Educational Performance it is firmly rooted in a government department and therefore more vulnerable to the influences of central government. In pursuing this interest the study was to evaluate the 'political' context of the APU programme – 'how researchers, professional groups, local education authorities and other special interest groups have reacted to the APU, and how the APU committees and research teams function'. It would also focus upon the effect of APU and local education authority testing programmes on the school system.

In pursuing this research, the team wished to monitor discussions of some of the working and steering groups. How should those groups have responded to this request? First, there is no doubting the importance of some research of this kind – not because of any basic right to know (I repeat, the very conception of 'basic rights' is meaningless in the absence of particular agreements, and it is the getting of agreements that is precisely at issue), but because of the possible consequences to social welfare of the work of such bodies as the APU. Hence, in general terms the importance of discussion of these issues should be recognized and the essential condition of such discussion – viz. the availability of relevant data – acknowledged, and indeed that exactly is what the Department of Education and Science agreed to.

But there is a world of difference between such general approval and its detailed application. Ethical arguments, despite impressions given in undergraduate courses, rarely arise at the general level, but only in their detailed working out. That cruelty is wrong might generally be agreed upon; that this or that particular action is cruel, or that, if cruel, it is permissible in extenuating circumstances, is where the disagreement arises. It is in relating the general principle to the concrete case, and in deciding upon the exceptions, that moral disagreement really bites, and it is the sort of disagreement therefore that ethical considerations need to get to grips with. Hence, the ethical questions in this instance concern not the right to know as such, but how much should be accessible and under what conditions. And, in sorting this out, one is not acknowledging natural rights; rather is one negotiating what the reciprocal rights and obligations *should* be.

Let me suggest therefore certain general considerations that might provide some formal framework of principle within which details might be decided – and let us think of it, too, in the context of a particular group whose work is being monitored. What obligations should they wish to see placed upon the 'researcher' or 'evaluator' upon which the right to know would be conditional?

1. The researcher would set out clearly the *kinds* of knowledge that he wanted. It is of course impossible in research to anticipate all kinds of information that you want, but the continuing opportunity to renegotiate the terms of contract (of agreed rights and obligations) could be secured.
2. The researcher has an obligation to show, throughout the research, his 'papers' – i.e. the data collected (*or selected*) and the interpretation of that data.
3. The researcher, both at the beginning and throughout, would be open to cross-examination by the group about the research – its main objectives, its research methodology, its political implications, the data it collects and the interpretation upon that data. Such an obligation arises particularly from the ill-conceived nature of some research, and from the often-prevailing but naïve philosophical view that 'knowledge' is a sort of datum not in essence affected by the style of research, its main purposes, or its underlying political motivation.
4. The researcher is obliged to incorporate in his findings the reply, if any, of those researched.

The above considerations were a development of my first reason for hesitating to concede the right to know as basic. In a few words, that reason is that the connection between making available all that is relevant on the one hand and disinterested inquiry on the other is not in all cases simple and straightforward. And accessibility to available knowledge therefore is by no means a natural right but has to be established as a worthy aim, after the wider implications of knowing have been scrutinized. All this, of course, should be set against the argument of Mill which makes a prima facie case of openness rather than concealment.

There is however a second reason closely connected, and to some extent touched upon, in principle 3 above. The slogan 'the right to know' suffers not only from the essentially contestable nature of 'right' but also from the ambiguities surrounding the word 'know'. Knowledge does of course refer to those sets of beliefs that are not only true but that one has good grounds for believing. The right to know must include the opportunities to put on a firmer footing one's beliefs and to rid oneself of whatever is false. The right to know would require the best possible conditions for thorough critical scrutiny of what is believed. Only that, as one might argue, which has survived such criticism is worthy of knowing – for anything else may not be knowledge at all, only the delusions of a fanciful imagination. On the other hand, what we know is expressible in propositions, and ultimately in bodies of knowledge or interrelated sets of propositions that are the product of particular inquiries. To have knowledge requires understanding and understanding often requires in turn a grasp of the interconnections that relate one part of the picture to another. It also often requires some participation in those very inquiries in terms of which that 'knowledge' is to be understood. Forgetting this, one is in constant danger of confusing the possession of blobs of so-called knowledge with knowing itself. This is, of course, a difficult matter to be clear about. But at least it means this – that the exposure to particular facts or to particular statements or to a selection from the data can so easily distort an understanding of what then is made public, for it removes that which is to be known from the context in which it must be understood or from the process to which it is logically related as product. It is for this reason that I would want to link the right to know with a reciprocal obligation to permit enlargements and explanations from those who are researched. The sum of what we know is more than the sum of atomic propositions, corresponding to a range of atomic facts. It involves interpretation, theoretical assumptions, reference to the peculiarities of context. And these therefore must be as explicit as possible in what is publicly revealed.

The final reason for hesitating to concede, without further justification, the right to know is that so often the exercise of such a right would clash with other values which prima facie seem as, or indeed more, fundamental. It is a mistake, in the attempt to be more systematic in ethical thinking, to look for some hierarchy of principle, duties, or values, such that just one supreme principle remains as the ultimate court of appeal – whether it be the maximization of happiness or obedience to some authority or some form of enlightenment. On the contrary, there is a range of different values and principles and prima facie duties. And it is the character of the moral life that where there is a clash of such values and principles there is no 'higher-level' set of principles to appeal to in order to resolve that clash. Examples of such a clash would be where keeping a promise can only result in hurting a person. There is no rule of thumb for resolving the difficulty, just as there is no way of quantifying the seriousness of the promise and the degree of hurt.

Respect for another person is of course a very general principle, so general in fact that it is safely without much content. On the other hand, it indicates a general orientation towards the other person, a recognition that he is a centre of conscious life and feeling, an acceptance of his responsibility for what he does, and a determination to protect and to support that life. It is reflected in a range of lower-level principles such as not betraying trust, trying not to hurt, keeping promises, and (more positively) helping him to accept responsibility for his actions. It, is not difficult to see how 'the right to know' can so easily clash with this general principle of respect. First, it can require an intrusion into the private life of the individual. Secondly, it could mean betraying trust and confidence. At this point we have to consider, albeit briefly, the interests of the individual weighed against those of the public.

PRIVATE AND PUBLIC INTEREST

The distinction between the private life and the public life of an individual is a difficult and blurred one, just as Mill's distinction between public and private morality, essential to his principle of liberty, becomes exceedingly fuzzy when analysed in detail. On the other hand, however blurred the boundaries there do seem to be clear cases of activities on each side of the boundary. Nose-picking after 10 p.m., no matter how repulsive some may find it, would be part of Blogg's private life, and he would quite understandably resent the publication of this in the daily papers. Whereas, *if he were a teacher*, his advocacy of corporal punishment of his inability to spell correctly would be, quite rightly, of public interest. The right to know would need to attend to this distinction which quite clearly it does not in a lot of journalism. I say 'attend to' on purpose, because where exactly the distinction is drawn between the public and the private is not possible to say in advance of particular cases. But that there is a distinction to be made does put restrictions upon 'the right to know'.

Furthermore, this distinction does become more difficult to define given the political context of decisions which affect many people. That I willingly concede. There is a close connection between making people and institutions more accountable and political questions about the distribution of power and control. And it would be wrong to treat the ethical issue between the right to know and confidentiality in a totally apolitical manner. That is why in matters of considerable political concern, such as the work of the APU, the case for complete openness of committee deliberations should be made at the earliest stages of discussion and the area of confidentiality limited quite explicitly. The balance in other words between competing ethical principles, and between the private and the public, must relate to the political significance of the authorities or institutions being evaluated.

TRUST AND CONFIDENTIALITY

The betrayal of trust raises more significant issues which are just as complicated. Clear cases of betrayal of trust are where a promise is broken. There is of course something very peculiar about the obligation to keep promises. Where that obligation is not recognized the very meaning of 'making a promise' disintegrates. And furthermore little value can be put upon promises where it is understood that promises can be broken should the person promising, upon reflection, believe that this would be for the general good. Keeping promises would seem to be a prima facie duty. However, the trust that is built up between evaluator and the people evaluated, on the basis of which information is given and intelligence gained, is rarely made explicit in actual promises. It is much more a matter of implicit trusting with information, putting oneself in a vulnerable position. This respect for the other person as vulnerable and as having entered into a relationship of trust puts considerable constraints upon the evaluator however much public importance he attaches to the information he has.

It is out of respect for this particular value, as against the 'right to know', that as far as I can see so much attention has been given in recent literature to 'negotiation'. The particular difficulties of spelling this notion out in practice have been well analysed by Helen Simons (1977) in 'Building a social contract: negotiation, participation in condensed field research', in particular the difficulties in protecting the person being evaluated even after faithful adherence to agreed procedures of negotiation. Somehow a contract is not enough. Such a contract has to be suffused with a spirit of respect for the other that can never be captured in a contract alone.

I am not in a position to develop this aspect of the problem. There is something odd about the idea of negotiation. It is a metaphor taken from business, and like all metaphors it plays its part but has its limitations. Particularly, however, it seems odd in an area where matters of truth and falsity are concerned, and there does at times seem to be some confusion between negotiating the release of 'knowledge' and negotiating what that knowledge consists in. To follow that particular point is beyond the scope of this paper, but it touches upon the main topic because the right to know, if established, would be limited by, amongst other things, the principle of not betraying trust and confidence. Certainly this would be most directly applicable to the release of information. But it could also be extended to interpretation put upon that information. What must one agree to, or 'negotiate', prior to making public one's evaluation, in order to keep within the bounds of confidence – the information given, the sense given to the information, the conclusions drawn? What certainly is clear from Helen Simons's account is that the further one extends the notion of confidentiality and the consequent obligation to negotiate, the greater must be the constraints in establishing any right to know. I would have thought that confidentiality had a strong claim where one is concerned with the release of basic data, obtained for example in interview or as a result of trust. But it has a much less formidable claim as soon as one moves away from that to interpretation and to drawing conclusions.

None the less, the word 'negotiation', inadequate metaphor though it may be, does remind us once again that drawing the boundary between the right to know and preserving confidentiality cannot be seen outside a political context – outside, that is, of a context in which power and influence are exercised over people. In the last section I referred to the prima facie case for limiting the area of confidentiality in areas of considerable political significance such as in the work of the APU. Knowledge is an important ingredient in the balance of power, and 'negotiating' contracts with an evaluator can be seen as a sort of 'trading' in political power which in many cases will be a consequence of a shift in the distribution of knowledge.

This does none the less pose very real problems for the evaluator when he takes seriously the ethical context in which he pursues his inquiry. I have throughout this paper failed to distinguish clearly between research and evaluation, and yet this may be an important distinction for our purposes. Evaluation studies, unlike central cases of research, are concerned not so much with theory-building or generalization as with a grasp of the particular and with improved practice and it could be seriously affected if particular episodes, interactions, relationships, and differing perceptions which constitute 'the particular' get omitted from the record. There is a prima facie case for more access to detail in evaluation studies than there is in much research. In other words, there are limits to how much negotiation is acceptable if the aims of the evaluator are to be achieved and this would need to be taken into account in drawing up any code of practice or principles of procedure.

CONCLUSIONS

In this paper I have examined briefly the force of the notion 'the right to know'. I share the view that, all things being equal, openness, availability of relevant information, and public criticism are, as Mill argues, good for getting rid of error as well as for sharpening one's perception of the truth. To that extent there is a prima facie case for establishing a right to know. But such rights do need to be established – they are in no way basic. And to establish them requires some examination of the consequences of establishing such a right in particular cases. Maybe the right to know all (or this or that) will lead to undesirable results. Maybe it will clash with other principles such as confidentiality. The main thing however is that, as in most moral matters, whether the right should be given and over what area it should be extended need to be argued in the context of particular cases.

REFERENCES

Gipps, C. and Goldstein, H. (1983) *Monitoring Children*, Heinemann, Educational, London.

MacDonald, B. (1976) Evaluation and the control of education, in D. Tawney, (ed.) *Curriculum Evaluation Today: Trends and Implications*, Macmillan, London.

Mill, J.S. (1859) On liberty, published in M. Warnock (ed.) (1962) *Utilitarianism*, Collins, London.

Simons, H. (1977) Building a social contract: negotiation and participation in concerned fieldwork research, in N. Norris (ed.) *SAFARI: Theory and Practice*. CARE Occasional Paper No. 4, University of East Anglia, Norwich.

3.7
ETHICAL GUIDELINES*
PRAISE (Pilot Records of Achievement in Schools Evaluation)

INTRODUCTION

These guidelines are intended to clarify the role of the national evaluation and spell out the procedures that the evaluation team will adopt to protect individuals whilst respecting the public right to information about the pilot schemes. The guidelines are set as answers to questions that participants might wish to ask.

WHAT IS THE PURPOSE OF THE NATIONAL EVALUATION?

1. The national evaluation is required to evaluate the progress and results of the Records of Achievement Pilot Scheme on behalf of the National Steering Committee (RANSC), which will be responsible for drawing up draft national guidelines. The evaluation team will pay particular attention to the objectives and issues identified in the DES statement of policy, but will also be sensitive to other issues and concerns that emerge during the study.

2. The evaluators will respond to requests for feedback from the pilot schemes and individual schools that participate in the evaluation study, in so far as these requests are compatible with 1 (above).

3. It is also anticipated that the general progress of the pilot schemes, and the evaluation, will be of interest to the wider educational community. We are developing plans for dissemination.

* PRAISE, (1985) Ethical guidelines, 2 pp. project guidelines for schools, national evaluators and local evaluators.

WHO ARE THE EVALUATION TEAM?

The team comprises a group of researchers from the Open University School of Education and Bristol University School of Education. Their names, university base and involvement are as follows:

Dr Patricia Broadfoot, Bristol, Co-Director, part-time;
Phil Clift, OU, part-time;
Tim Horton, OU, part-time;
Mary James, OU, Research Fellow, Deputy Director, full-time;
Bob McCormick, OU, part-time;
Sue McMeeking, OU, Research Assistant, full-time;
Professor Desmond Nuttall, OU, Co-Director, part-time;
Dr Barry Stierer, Bristol, Research Associated, full-time.

HOW WILL THE EVALUATORS SEEK ACCESS TO INFORMATION?

1. The evaluators will seek reasonable access to the work and personnel of participating LEAs and schools, including pupils. Access to parents and employers will be sought where appropriate.
2. The evaluators will treat all relevant interviews, meetings, oral and written exchanges with participants (including DES sponsors) as 'on the record', unless specifically asked to treat them as confidential.
3. Where practicable, and providing the permission of participants has been sought, oral data will be tape recorded and transcribed. In the case of interviews, copies of transcriptions will be returned to participants who will be given a period of fourteen days in which to amend them, if they so wish.
4. When information is sought from pupils, or when pupils are observed, the school will be invited to decide whether it is appropriate to seek the permission of parents.
5. The evaluators will seek reasonable access to relevant documents of pilot schemes and schools. However, they will not examine or copy files, correspondence, or other internal documents without explicit permission.

HOW WILL THE DATA BE STORED?

1. Where feasible, data will be entered into microcomputers for data-base and textual analysis.

2. Participants will be given access to any identifiable personal data held on computer files, in line with the Data Protection Act 1984.
3. All data, including data on disc, will be kept in archives at the Open University and Bristol University. Only members of the evaluation team will have access to these. They, and the project secretaries, will undertake to treat all data as confidential until release has been agreed with participants.
4. Data of a personal nature, e.g. pupil records, will not be kept longer than is necessary for the purpose of the study.

HOW WILL THE INFORMATION BE REPORTED?

1. Evaluation reports can be expected to contain three elements: description, interpretation and judgement. Criteria for judgement will be made explicit.
2. Consortia and LEAs will be identified, but case study schools will be given fictitious names. Individuals will be referred to by role descriptions or pseudonyms. While this does not guarantee anonymity it reduces the likelihood that individual schools, teachers and pupils will be identified.
3. Information to be used in general summaries, which involve no specific detail about individuals or groups, will require no special clearance.
4. Permission will be sought for the reporting of statements (quotations, etc.) that might identify individuals. They will also be invited to comment on the accuracy, relevance, and fairness of any report concerning them. A period of twenty-one days will be allowed for participants to respond to reports in this way.
5. The evaluators will seek to improve reports in the light of such comments. However, participants will have the right to make a short written response to any report concerning them if they disagree with its contents.

3.8
THE INTEGRITY OF EVALUATION*
Clem Adelman and Robin Alexander

THE CHALLENGE OF THE INTEGRITY CRITERION

Despite the general inadequacies of the processes of decision-making and management [which our research into colleges of higher education has identified], and despite the inconsistencies which they demonstrate, they do – after a fashion – work, at least in respect of some people and some decisions. For while the processes seem not wholly consistent with those political and intellectual ideals which one might assume would be combined nowhere if not in a west European higher-education institution – democracy, value-pluralism, academic autonomy, the pursuit of truth – they are in fact the norm, rather than the exception, and tend to be reinforced in the maintained sector of higher education by key interests like local authorities and the [Council for National Academic Awards, CNAA]. In terms of the external forms in the educational ritual they produce results: courses are planned, validated and implemented; students are recruited, taught, examined and awarded degrees. In terms of the underlying curricular and educational meanings of these rituals one might be considerably less convinced, for this would be to invoke a set of criteria for judging the worth of educational ventures which might be somewhat at variance with those of expediency and instrumentality.

But . . . we cannot avoid these alternative criteria, for evaluation is about valuing, and educational evaluation is doubly value-laden. If it is to have any use other than as a purely cosmetic device for satisfying the demands of a validating body, or for servicing the power requirements of institutional oligarchies, evaluation has to be accepted as challenging, uncomfortable,

* Adelman, C. and Alexander, R. (1982) The integrity of evaluation, from Adelman, C. and Alexander, R. *The Self-Evaluating Institution*, Methuen & Co., London.

untidy and potentially disturbing to an institution's equilibrium. For evaluation must exist, at least in part, to expose and clarify value issues – the varieties of educational goals and priorities for educational programmes, and the varieties of criteria for judging the quality and effectiveness of these programmes (see House, 1973).

This being so, evaluation must be seen both as problematic in its own terms and problematic for the context of management and decision-making in which it is set. For ultimately, it seems to us, while an evaluation must be useful and should provide practical support to teachers, course planners and administrators, it must meet a further criterion, that of *integrity*. The kernel of the evaluation 'problem' is a basic concern with knowledge and truth, and the 'integrity' criterion is, simply, an imperative which in an academic institutional context an evaluator can no more ignore than can the historian or scientist. The problem for institutional evaluation is that the integrity criterion has somehow to be upheld in the face of strong contrary pressures and constraints – time, limited resources, organizational problems, for example, but above all the risk of evaluation's use, abuse or neutralization to further or protect individual or sectional interests . . .

[In particular] *there is little doubt that plurality is a fact of institutional life* to which the integrity condition for evaluation demands attention. It is not merely a plurality of values, such as is inherent in all educational ventures: what is a 'good' course, an 'effective' lecturer, a 'successful' student; what is the best way to train teachers; what sort of qualities does a good teacher need; how should a teacher-training course relate to educational change – by producing a teacher who conforms to and perpetuates established norms and practices or one who works to change them? And so on. The plurality goes beyond such matters of opinion, it includes 'fact' as well as value: it concerns the basic status of the information on which decisions are made. Formal evaluation has been defined (Cronbach, 1963; Stufflebeam, 1971) as the 'provision of information for decision-makers' and the essence of its justification as a distinct activity is that such 'information', systematically gathered and presented, is inherently more 'reliable' than hunch or belief, and the decisions made are therefore more likely to be right, or at least can be defended (tautologously perhaps) as 'informed'.

FACT OR VALUE? A NOTE ON EVALUATION METHODOLOGY

What then is the status of information presented as a result of formal evaluation processes? What claims can legitimately be made for data gathered by means of techniques available to evaluators which cannot be made with such assurance about judgements rooted in experience and common sense? The answers involve a discussion of methodology more detailed than we can offer in a [chapter] concerned mainly with the institutional context of evaluation, and in any case there are available numerous excellent discussions of methodology *per se* . . . But institutional practices in relation to management and innovation have a critical connection with ideas about what constitutes valid evaluation and about what sort of evaluation evidence can be relied upon, to which we must devote some attention.

One of the difficulties here is the extent to which the methodological scene is depicted in terms of polarities; the 'illuminative' method of Parlett and Hamilton (1972) [chapter 1.4 in this volume], or the 'responsive' procedures of Stake (1976), or the 'curriculum criticism' of Mann (1978) and Eisner (1979), on the one hand, are presented as standing in a mutually exclusive relationship to the objectives-referenced methodologies of, say, Tyler (1971) or Gagné (1972) or Bloom, [Hastings and Madans] (1971).

The protagonists themselves in this debate have usually been careful to identify the extent of shared territory and the polarities are as often as not set up by writers of textbooks or teachers of evaluation concerned to restructure the arguments in terms amenable to the outsider. Moreover, while a 'research community' can achieve, on the basis of its members' depth of engagement with the issues as specialists, a reasonable sophistication in methodological discussion, this is less likely where institutional evaluation is concerned. Here, the 'community' comprises the institution's inhabitants, very few of whom, if any, will have made evaluation methods their central academic or professional interest; they are, after all, contracted as staff or admitted as students to devote their time to other areas of concern, challenging enough in themselves. Consequently, institutional discourse about evaluation is conducted very much at the commonsense level, with communication facilitated by the ready use of dichotomies. Here are three on which we can comment briefly:

1. 'Pure' research is contrasted with 'impure' evaluation. Institutional evaluation cannot be controlled or experimental, and judged by mainstream research standards it may appear to be 'contaminated', *ex post facto* and methodologically imperfect. It takes place in working educational settings, is subject to practical and political constraints and is usually conducted by non-specialists. Clearly the legitimacy of conclusions from an evaluation study needs to be demonstrated, but criteria for legitimation applied to social science research are not necessarily the most apposite for institutional evaluation studies. Methodology as such is perhaps less significant here than what is claimed for and done with the

'findings'. If factual accuracy is claimed, then it is right to scrutinize an evaluation study's methods and conclusions in these terms, checking on sampling, statistical treatment and so on; not a few evaluation studies would fail this test. However . . . the role of an evaluation conducted as a part of an institution's continuing process of debate and development indicates that other criteria can be invoked.

2. A study is either 'objective' or 'subjective'. In everyday discourse 'objective' and 'subjective' usually appear as mutually exclusive categories, incorporating the assumptions that objectivity is an absolute, that it is achievable and that it is a higher plane of thinking and being than 'mere' subjectivity. Without entering what we recognize to be an intellectual minefield, we would suggest that at least an awareness that it is a minefield needs to pervade institutional discussion on such matters. For example, do not 'subjective' values and perspectives inform 'objective' as well as interpretative methods; how else do we decide on which test items to include or omit, what words to put in our semantic scale? Perhaps the methods of analysis are more 'objective' in that they have been publicly devised and corroborated, and are therefore open to external scrutiny, but what goes into the original evaluation instrument may well be as rooted in 'subjective' views of knowledge, learning, development and behaviour as what goes into an interview schedule; 'Under the rug of technique lies an image of man' (Eisner, 1969).

3. Studies are 'scientific' or 'unscientific'. By this judgement the methodology of the physical sciences is seen as providing the only legitimate route to the truth, and other approaches are judged not in terms of their distinctive claims but in terms of their failure to be 'science'. The judgement perhaps reflects a view of science as the rational pursuit of indisputable facts and immutable laws about the 'real' world, which contrasts with the vagaries of intuition and common sense on the one hand, and on the other with artistic endeavour as the construction of internal, private worlds which cannot be publicly demonstrated to correspond with the real world 'outside'. Again, the scope for disputing the assumptions here is extensive; those concerning the nature of reality, for instance, have kept philosophers in business for centuries. Or again, scientists as well as artists might wish to dispute the implied view of their activities; both groups might wish to argue that in different ways each seeks truth and in pursuit of it offers statements which are open to verification, falsification or some form of external critical judgement; that each uses personal intuition and imagination as well as the publicly accepted procedures, theories and forms; that creativity and rationality enter both scientific and artistic judgements and acts. Some would

question the assumption that scientific knowledge, unlike artistic expression, produces final, unchangeable 'truths', and would point to the
way that many apparently convincing scientific theories are eventually
disproved or substantially modified:

> Those among our theories which turn out to be highly resistant to criticism,
> and which appear to us at a certain moment in time to be better approxima-
> tions to truth than other known theories, may be described, together with the
> reports of their tests, as the 'science' of that time. Since none of them can be
> positively justified, it is essentially their critical and progressive character – the
> fact that we can argue about their claim to solve our problems better than their
> competitors – which constitutes the rationality of science.
>
> (Popper, 1972, p. vii)

Others – not least physical scientists – might be sceptical of the claims of
the human sciences, from which evaluation draws most of its methodology, to constitute a science at all, at least in terms of the vocabulary of
laws, proof, causality, and so on. The grounds for this objection might be
not only the methodology of the human sciences but the complexity of
human behaviour. At this point they might be more inclined to commend
the artist's concern to expose and explore the subtlety, diversity, richness
but essential elusiveness of the human condition than the social scientist's
attempts to superimpose on it categories and models; the artist's concern
to portray rather than the social scientist's urge to explain: 'The soul
wanted what it wanted. It had its own natural knowledge. It sat unhappily
on superstructures of explanation, poor bird, not knowing which way to
fly' (Bellow, 1971, p. 5).

Thus, beneath the prepackaging of everyday discourse about evaluation
methods, are issues which in exploration become more, rather than less,
complex. But because evaluation is a practical activity the issue seen as most
pressing is not so much 'which methods have the soundest theoretical basis
in terms of their claims to produce a valid picture of events?' but 'which
method will work best?' The contingent problems are those of resources,
time, expertise and acceptability. A simple feedback questionnaire with a
small number of closed responses is much more convenient than, say, a test
or scale requiring computerized analysis, or open interviews which need to
be transcribed from audio tapes (in itself a lengthy and tedious process)
before analysis can begin. Some methods require a financial and human
investment which is just not available in many institutions. A crucial
difference between research-oriented evaluation, as in the funded project
[in our research], and institutional course evaluation, as [in our second case
study] is that the latter has to be done quickly in order to be fed into decision-
making while the course component is still warm: time is a major factor.

Then there is the matter of acceptability: staff and students are most likely to participate in an evaluation which makes minimal demands on their time, and which will not expose their individual weaknesses to public scrutiny . . .

Is it sufficient to take a thoroughly pragmatic view of evaluation methodology as is implied above? If we do so, evaluation becomes a more marketable commodity, to teachers and administrators alike. Some might argue, for example, that the debate about scientific method has little application to the murky and methodologically questionable field of evaluation. They might argue further that the invocation of such matters, however one views scientific method, weakens the claim of practical evaluation in two respects: firstly, because most evaluation fails to meet the observational and experimental criteria of the inductive method; secondly, because the Popperian position [quoted above] produces a relativism which provides a respectable justification for those who oppose all evaluation but the private and self-referenced in that apparently it makes the *ad hoc* intuitive 'theory' as sustainable, in the absence of convincing evidence to the contrary, as that achieved more systematically.

However, the pragmatist's position is as open to abuse in institutionally contextualized evaluation as the relativist's; the fact that such evaluation is generally decision/policy directed makes the status of the information it provides of some significance for those affected. Either way, then, methodology matters.

At the root of the debate is the fundamental question: 'What is the basis of our claim to know?' with the related questions concerning the nature of 'truth' and how we may approach it, of the nature and validity of empirical inquiry, 'proof' and 'evidence' and the provability of causal relationships.

If one accepts that an evaluation combines a purportedly accurate *description* of an educational circumstance with a *judgement* of its worth, one has to consider the status of descriptions and judgements in general. A description is a linguisitic or otherwise symbolic representation of the external world and there are, to say the least, competing views about the point (if there is one) at which language and the external world might coincide. And a judgement of worth is ultimately an expression of personal value, an ethical statement rooted in individual beliefs and experiences, and as such cannot claim to be true or false. So educational evaluations are value judgements based on what are debatable pictures of a 'real' world of courses, teaching and learning, and evaluators may need to accept that there can be no 'objectivity', only various degrees of subjectivity, and that the nearest they can get to an 'accurate' observation is to have private observations publicly tested and corroborated so that there is a measure of agreement that we have all seen the same thing, more or less. (Cf. Habermas, 1970: 'Objectivity is the consensus of subjectivities.')

If one's view of evaluation is of a process of feedback at the individual teacher level, if all one wants to undertake is a purely private activity, then objectification remains an academic issue, and one's judgements, or value judgements do not have to be justified. But once evaluation becomes the concern of more than one teacher, once it is used to inform policy decisions which will affect students, teachers and courses at the institutional level, we have an obligation to ensure that such evaluation is as well founded, conceptually, as possible. And if, once one explores its epistemological basis, all evaluation can be shown to be of intrinsically limited reliability, certain policy implications seem to follow concerning how we should evaluate, how we should use evaluation findings, and how the process should be controlled.

Firstly, an evaluation programme methodology derived from a single discipline will compound its limitations and potential distortions. There is relative security to be gained from a stance of considered eclecticism deliberately drawing on contrasting methodologies.

Secondly, it would seem essential, particularly where decision-making is to be based on evaluation 'findings', to 'cover' one method by another – to use alternative ways of representing and interpreting the educational encounter(s) in question with a view to juxtaposing them and exploring the extent of match or mismatch (cf. the 'triangulation' principle developed in the Ford Teaching Project (Adelman, 1981; Elliott, 1976)).

Thirdly, it is important to recognize that while, methodologically, different perspectives or 'definitions of the situation' gained through 'triangulation' might seem equally valid, in practical institutional terms such definitions are more likely to be in competition. Moreover, the competition is an unequal one, and certain definitions may well be seen to 'matter' more than others – the teacher's more than the student's perhaps, or the administrator's more than the teacher's. The extent to which a plurality of views is permitted to be significant in evaluation is a function of the power structure of the institution. In this case the evaluator may feel that to preserve methodological integrity he has to redress the balance, to over-represent some views, to act perhaps, in Elliott's words, as 'underdog's advocate' (Elliott, 1977).

Fourthly, given what can be shown to be the rather shaky status of the 'objective fact' in evaluation methods, we might feel more favourably disposed towards overt subjectivity, more prepared to value the intuitive judgements of ourselves and others as much as the 'scientific' findings of evaluators, more inclined to see such intuitive judgements as evaluation data of potentially comparable validity to the findings of formal evaluation studies. Equally, it might be argued that we should be very cautious in the way we make decisions on the basis of evaluation 'findings'; does the data really justify the decision?

Finally, if we are prepared to evaluate then perhaps we should also be prepare to submit our evaluation practices to the same critical scrutiny as our courses receive.

These conditions are required to maintain the integrity of institutional evaluation methods, caught as they are between the unattainable perfectionism of these who advocate an all-or-nothing research 'purity' and those who argue that precisely because this is unattainable, anything goes as long as it produces usable information. We believe there to exist a legitimate middle ground for the methodology of institutional evaluation . . .

A CLASH OF EPISTEMOLOGIES

It will be perceived that this view of evaluation methodology contrasts markedly with the view required by the production-line model of curriculum development . . . which we saw to be implicit in much current practice in the maintained sector of higher education, possibly reinforced by CNAA requirements. It will also be recognized that if evaluation knowledge is regarded as provisional and tentative, this has important implications for policy-making generally, not just for those areas of policy evolved from systematic evaluation studies. For all decisions rest on evaluations of some sort, on situational appraisals, on attempts to base decisions about what ought to happen on the best possible information about what is happening or what is likely to happen. *If the status of 'facts' gained from systematic evaluations using established methods can be shown to be in a fundamental sense questionable, how much more so may be the sorts of information on which most day-to-day institutional decision-making rests?* By this view policies can most usefully be regarded as hypotheses, theories or predictions.

Policy formulation and institutional decision-making ought to be subject to an approach analogous to scientific inquiry, namely, one of constant critical examination using the experience of implementing policy as a means not of proving, whatever the cost, that the policy was right but as a means of testing its validity, strengths and weaknesses. Similarly, a course submission to a validating body is not a master-plan to be 'implemented' but a hypothesis, the best available perhaps, which restates a particular problem (e.g. that of training teachers) and offers as a solution, a practical *theory* of instruction to be tried out, modified, used to refine the analysis of the problem itself as well as the solution, and so on.

However, the parallel between scientific inquiry and policy formulation/ implementation can be pursued only up to a point, as Lubasz (1981) has pointed out. The trial-and-error approach requires some degree of consensus over standards, techniques and criteria for judgement among the community concerned; while in an educational institution this is achievable in procedural and organizational matters, it is more difficult where questions of curriculum purpose and content are concerned since these are inherently questions of value. Moreover, in a bounded, hierarchical educational institution, values are as likely to be positional as educational and the criteria for judging recommendations, decisions and policies will reflect individual and group views of what is fair and just.

Our analysis suggests a likelihood of conflict between the prevailing 'epistemology of management', with its emphasis on consensus, finality, proof, stability and efficiency, and our 'epistemology of educational evaluation' with its emphasis on value-pluralism, hypothesizing, change and the improvability of educational thought and practice. This is likely to be most acute in those institutions which adopt a more strongly scientistic, mechanistic approach to management, or an authoritarian one, and which underscore this by compartmentalizing the related functions of educational management, innovation, development and evaluation. The conflict will be less in institutions prepared to blur the organizational and conceptual boundaries and which allow elements of the 'epistemology of evaluation' to inform styles and processes of management.

ACCOUNTABILITY, EVALUATION AND THE MANAGEMENT OF INNOVATION: MATCH AND MISMATCH

The character and force of management and evaluation epistemologies within educational institutions, and the degree of congruence or conflict between them, is not simply a matter of style but a matter of human consequence . . . The extent to which an evaluation agent or agency acknowledges institutional pluralism has consequences for the sort of methodology that might be used. Similarly there is an interdependent relationship between the strategies used to bring about innovation and the approach to evaluation, and between each of these and the prevailing accountability relations within an institution . . .

Management involves the everyday decisions which regulate actions and information within an institution with the intention of maintaining continuity and stability. Essentially management maintains the nature of the accountability relationships within the institution. Attempts at innovation may lead to change, to adjustment or to neither, but whatever its consequences, attempts at innovation introduce instability in some parts of the institution's systems. To regulate the introduction of innovation, the institution devises more or less complex and visible strategies for staging, delivering and monitoring the progress of the innovation. Evaluation – judging the worth and effectiveness of the innovation and its consequences – may be contemporaneous or it may follow on later after attempts at implementing the innovation. The range of evaluation approaches that may be adopted is directly dependent upon the accountability relationships and the strategies for innovation that the institution prefers and practises.

The relationships between management, strategies for innovation and evaluation are complex. One could discuss them simplistically in terms of match and mismatch between the three activities but as soon as one begins to give reasons for the match and mismatch, the complexities of these interrelationships are revealed. These three institutional activities have different histories of development reflected in the differences in the literature that is cited in each case. The body of knowledge, including that derived from research, that may be utilized by management, has been developing for at least eighty years, whereas the knowledge about the very idea of 'strategies of innovation' are more recent . . . Evaluation, in the sense that it is used [here], is an even more recent field of study than management and innovation, only emerging with any coherence in the 1960s. The ideas and practices of evaluation and the development of strategies of innovation are poorly understood compared to those relating to management, and one of the intentions of [our research was] to enhance understanding of these three institutional activities and to foster discussion about their interrelationships. In times of stability or minor adjustment, the rhetoric/reality discrepancy in management practices may be unimpressive. However, when an institution wishes or is forced by external circumstances to bring about change internally, then the reality of the accountability relationships is displayed in the strategies employed to conduct the course of the innovation.

Trying to manage innovation has built-in contradictions. Management thrives on stability and predictability; innovation introduces uncertainty, it de-skills, and it produces relative instability. Strategies of managing innovation to bring about the desired changes can be planned and seen through with minimum deleterious consequences for human freedom and dignity. Unfortunately, perhaps partly due to ignorance of the interrelationship between these three activities, the strategies and their means of delivery are more often destructive of freedoms and lead to some degree of degradation of institutional life. There seem to be remarkably few managers in higher education with the imagination and verve that are required to develop and implement strategies of innovation whilst preserving human freedoms and dignity.

IDEAL TYPES

Accountability

In [our work we identified] five 'ideal types' of accountability relationship within educational institutions (adapted from Alexander, 1980). These were:

1. Managerial
2. Consultative
3. Mutual culpability
4. Professional autonomy
5. Proletarian

Both [of the case studies in our research] illustrate a 'consultative'/ 'managerial' mixture, with the stricter 'managerial' relationship asserting itself at points where evaluation produced threatening data . . . Also . . . the more straightforward 'managerial' tradition of the polytechnic world into which, by virtue of their new affiliation with CNAA, both institutions moved, contrasted markedly with the culture of collegiality (Wyatt, 1977) of the former colleges of education, though we must emphasize that mutuality was only one element in that culture, a commitment or aspiration held by significant groups within the institutions, but sometimes at variance with the 'consultative' relations represented by the formal decision-making arrangements. Universities . . . are really institutions-within-institutions, or semi-autonomous states within a federal structure. That federal structure is bureaucratic and managerial/consultative, but at the department level one can find examples of all types of accountability relationship (Moodie and Eustace, 1974). Generally, at this level the 'professional autonomy' ethic is very powerful, and there is little evidence of collective action or mutual culpability, though there may be a semblance of mutuality in the *form* of departmental academic decision-making, or alternatively a sometimes rather toothless managerialism. In most cases, however, the individual's professional autonomy will be assumed. It is interesting in this context to compare the parallel ambience of the unions concerned. The university teachers' union, AUT, upholds individual autonomy and has had some difficulty in mobilizing members to act collectively over matters like salaries at times when, as until very recently, their autonomy and security remained unthreatened: for many, the latter were more precious than salary comparabilities across the binary line. The now defunct college of education union, ATCDE, had a pronounced collegiality, verging on the genteel . . . this contrasted starkly with the polytechnic/further education union, ATTI, with which ATCDE merged during the 1970s reorganization and cutback of teacher education to form the present NATFHE. In ATTI, as now in the enlarged NATFHE, the battle-lines between employer and employee were clear and unbridgeable, and of the three former unions it most resembled its industrial counterparts. Undoubtedly there was congruence between management, accountability climate and union ethos in each case, though the direction of the influence is hard to establish.

The accountability relationships that are considered in what will follow are those that we term 'managerial', 'consultative' and 'mutual culpability' . . . The other two ideal types, 'professional autonomy' and 'proletarian', are not considered in relation to innovation strategies and evaluation. 'Professional autonomy' in an extreme form is manifest when academics declare themselves and the discipline they represent as sacrosanct, accountable only to themselves and their own criteria of worth. In its extreme form, 'professional autonomy' has no common ground at all with institutional self-evaluation, which of course is premised on *collective* endeavour, relationships and responsibility. 'Proletarian' accountability relationships have been described as part of the life, for instance, of the Chinese communes and within such Western institutions as the free universities of Berlin and London, which emerged in the late 1960s. At its roots, 'proletarian' accountability considers that the student has the capability and responsibility to define and negotiate what is to be the content and form of his curriculum. This form of institutional epistemology requires considerable or even absolute consensus over the aims and values underpinning institutional practices, and over the educational worth of these practices. 'Proletarian' accountability produces a form of public self-criticism of the worth of one's activities in relation to these ideals. This is so unusual in the West and most other parts of the world that we have no direct experience of such practices. In our experience the practices most resembling the 'proletarian' type, apart from the free universities already mentioned, were the school meetings held by A. S. Neill at Summerhill and the 'Moot' held at Countesthorpe College in the 1970s (Bernbaum, 1975).

Managing innovation

We take our three types of management of innovation strategies from Bennis *et al.* (1976). In our thinking about the institutions with which we were involved as evaluation agents and in our studies of other institutions, we find that the ideas of Bennis *et al.* seem best to fit analysis. The three terms for the types refer to strategies for effecting planned educational change. The strategies indicate procedures for the formulation and adoption of innovation. Implementation of these three approaches is through the maintenance of continuity of accountability relationships by management.

'Power-coercive' strategies rely on the political/administrative system for their effectiveness. They involve statutes, include legislation, political press-ure groups and election, as well as using guilt and shame as legitimate means of furthering ends. Power-coercive strategies may be effective in the stages of formulation and adoption of innovation, but implementation which requires changes in norms, roles and relationships is difficult to achieve by this approach.

'Empirical-rational' strategies assume that man is reasonable and will act in some rational way. The knowledge presented during the formulation, adoption and implementation stages of the innovation would be seen by the adopters as 'objective', based upon research that is itself unbiased in terms of interest groups. However, the question of the redistribution of power in the system is not usually taken into account and the continuance of the current structure is taken for granted. It may be that systems adopt empirical-rational strategies especially at the innovation and perhaps adop-tion stages, when knowledge does not threaten members' status.

'Normative re-educative' strategies regard the question of how the client understands his problems as of central importance. The problem of innova-tion is not a matter of supplying the appropriate technical information but rather a matter of changing attitudes, skills, values and relationships. In the normative re-educative approach a change agent works with the client. The change agent seeks to avoid manipulation of the client by bringing the values of the client into the open and by working through value conflicts in a responsive manner. The change agent may concentrate on improving the problem-solving capabilities of a system by developing and fostering the institutionalization of problem-solving strategies and processes (institution-al self-study, perhaps leading to institutional self-evaluation'). Another approach is to release and foster growth of awareness in persons within a system. This approach is based on the belief that persons are capable of creative action if conditions are made more favourable.

The conduct of evaluation

The set of principles and procedures for conducting the evaluation that the evaluation agent or agency may use are adapted from MacDonald (1976)

[Chapter 1.2 in this volume]. These are 'bureaucratic', 'democratic' and 'autonomous' (termed 'autocratic' by MacDonald).

The bureaucratic ('hired hand') evaluation matches the control in power-coercive institutions. The bureaucratic evaluation agent serves the needs of senior administration. The democratic ('honest broker') evaluation meets the needs of normative re-educative institutions where access and response to information is available to all members.

The autonomous evaluation entails the use of evaluation 'experts' with esoteric knowledge of how to conduct 'objective' evaluations. The autonomous evaluation agent takes attempts by any staff to influence the procedures or content of the evaluation as introducing a form of 'contamination' to the design and thus, to an extent, as making the evaluation invalid. The criteria of validity to which the autonomous agent or agency expresses allegiance aspire to be universalistic: the generalizable findings of research conducted via methodologies having some extent of claim to 'objective' or 'scientific' status. The relationship between these generalized findings and methodologies and the specific issues or problems of a particular institution do not become a basis for discussions about 'validity' or 'objectivity' with the evaluation agent.

As the agent or agency claims immunity, through context-free methodology and claims for the 'truth' and generalizability of research findings external to those of the specific cases in the institution, we term this type of evaluator 'autonomous'. Note, however, the strong reservations we have expressed about such claims in respect of evaluation earlier in this chapter, and how we come to define an evaluation's integrity (i.e. autonomy) in a way which places rather greater emphasis on its acknowledgement of the plurality of goals, perspectives, perceptions of reality and truth in educational institutions, and the way these are position-related rather than random, and rather less emphasis on supposedly context-free truth or objectivity claims.

MATCHING

If there is consonance between accountability relationships, strategies of innovation and the principles and procedures used by evaluation agents or agencies, then the following typology emerges:

	Accountability context	Innovation strategy	Evaluation strategy
Type 1	Managerial	Power-coercive	Bureaucratic
Type 2	Consultative	Rationale empirical	Autonomous
Type 3	Mutual culpability	Normative/ re-educative	Democratic

What kinds of innovations are these institutional Types 1–3 capable of? We suggest that Type 1 institutions, for instance, could introduce new programmes and courses of study and would do so ensuring that organizational components like the academic department, the committee structure or the status and power of individuals would be maintained. Goals such as crossing the established boundaries of knowledge, regrouping staff, or rotating positions of power and authority tend not to be within the ambit of institutions of Type 1. Senior management would tend to prefer an evaluation agent or agency which could be trusted or required to raise topics and issues and choose modes of investigation in such a way as to maintain the status quo, i.e. bureaucratic evaluation.

Type 2 institutions collect information pertinent to their development needs. The information to be collected is predominantly that required by the senior managers on the basis of what they define as the future needs of the institution. Agendas emerging from the collection of such information may be discussed in committees or other bodies which other members of staff may attend. The committees which are elected through 'democratic' processes may engage in deliberations leading to some form of decision, eventually, but the top decision-making forum, perhaps chaired by the head of the institution, faculty, department or course, gives the concluding and final decision on earlier deliberations. We have already mentioned the role of the autonomous evaluator in Type 2 institutions.

We believe Type 1 and particularly Type 2 would encompass the majority of educational institutions.

Institutions of Type 3 are very unusual. Between us we know of few educational institutions which we consider could be placed as this type. In Type 3 institutions the overriding goal of accountability relationships and strategies of innovation is improving the quality of the educational experiences for both students *and staff* (on the assumption that learning is socially embedded and conditioned, and therefore the situation of staff and the quality of institutional life are powerful influences on, and thus matter as much as, the learning experiences of students). The introduction of innovation which brings about change and adjustment may mean that changes in occupational role, formal organizational structures and the epistemological bases of academic activities are necessary to the pursuit of ways of implementing innovation in ways most beneficial to the institution's activities. The rigid continuity of academic positions, structures, salary differentials and knowledge boundaries might need to be replaced by the establishment of relations which relate to developments arising from the evaluation.

Given the involvement of staff in the strategies of innovation and the mutual culpability acknowledged by the management, the form of evaluation in Type 3 would acknowledge the 'right to know' of all members of the institution and would be responsive to issues arising across the institution. The principles and procedures of the evaluation agenda would then be close to those expressed by MacDonald (1976) as 'democratic' . . .

This use of ideal types and our attempts at matching must be treated with caution. Models invariably oversimplify, they

> impose a seeming rationality and order, and a network of logical and reciprocal relationships, on areas of human activity frequently characterized by irrationality, disorder, illogic and *ad hoc*ery . . . They tend to imply a static relationship between categories, aspects or elements where such relationships are in reality dynamic and constantly changing through time and space.
>
> (Alexander, 1980)

We might add that it would be strange indeed in a discussion of evaluation in educational institutions which made so much of the complexity of institutional life, of plurality, of multiple perspectives and levels of meaning and explanation, of incongruence between word and deed, claim and action, and so on, if we ended by encapsulating all this complexity in three types of institution and three dimensions of institutional life (Wildavsky, 1979). The models are intended to be suggestive rather than conclusive, and in particular to serve to emphasize two central arguments of this present chapter. Firstly, that the integrity of the evaluation process (an elusive goal in itself) is, in institutional evaluation, critically dependent on aspects of institutional life which conventionally fall outside the boundaries of methodological discussion, management and innovation styles and procedures, and accountability assumptions and relations; and these aspects demand attention by those developing evaluation programmes and procedures. Secondly, that notwithstanding this institutional or contextual reinterpretation of the methodological 'problem' in evaluation, that problem, even as reinterpreted, remains at root a substantially epistemological one, since all decision-making (not merely formal evaluation) rests on claims to know.

REFERENCES

Adelman, C. (1981) On first hearing, in C. Adelman (ed.) *Uttering, Muttering*, Grant McIntyre, London.

Alexander, R. (1980) Towards a conceptual framework for school-focused INSET, *British Journal of In-Service Education*, Vol. 6, No. 3.

Bellow, S. (1971) *Mr Sammler's Planet*, Penguin, Harmondsworth.

Bennis, W., Benne, K., Chin, R. and Corey, K. (1976) *The Planning of Change*, Holt, Rinehart & Winston, New York.

Bernbaum, G. (1975) Countesthorpe College, In A. Harris, M. Lawn and W. Prescott (eds.) *Curriculum Innovation*, Croom Helm/Open University Press, London/Milton Keynes.

Bloom, B., Hastings, J. and Madans, G. (1971) *Handbook of Formative and Summative Evaluation of Student Learning*, McGraw-Hill, New York.

Cronbach, L. (1963) Course improvement through evaluation, *Teachers' College Record*, No. 64.

Eisner, E. (1969) Instructional and expressive objectives, in J. Popham, E. Eisner, H. Sullivan and L. Tyler *Instructional Objectives*, Rand McNally, Chicago.

Eisner, E. (1979) *The Educational Imagination*, Macmillan, London.

Elliott, J. (1976) Preparing teachers for classroom accountability, *Education for Teaching*, No. 100.

Elliott, J. (1977) Conceptualizing relationships between research/evaluation procedures and in-service education, *British Journal of In-Service Education*, Vol. 4, No. 1.

Gagné, R. (1972) Curriculum research and the promotion of learning, in R. Tyler, R. Gagné and M. Scriven *Perspectives on Curriculum Evaluation*, AERA monograph, Rand McNally, Chicago.

Habermas, J. (1970) *Towards a Rational Society*, Beacon Press, New York.

House, E. (1973) *School Evaluation: The Politics and the Process*, McCutchan, Berkeley.

Lubasz, H. (1981) Popper in Utopia, *Times Higher Education Supplement*, No. 477.

MacDonald, B. (1976) Evaluation and the control of education, in D. Tawney (ed.) *Curriculum Evaluation Today*, Macmillan, London.

Mann, J. (1978) Curriculum criticism, in G. Willis (ed.) *Qualitative Evaluation: Concepts and Cases in Curriculum Criticism*, McCutchan, Berkeley.

Moodie, G. and Eustace, R. (1974) *Power and Authority in British Universities*, Allen & Unwin, London.

Parlett, M. and Hamilton, D. (1972) *Evaluation as Illumination: A New Approach to the Study of Innovatory Programmes*, Centre for Research in the Educational Sciences, Edinburgh.

Popper, K. (1972) *Conjectures and Refutations: The Growth of Scientific Knowledge*, Routledge & Kegan Paul, London.

Stake, R. (1976) Programme evaluation, particularly responsive evaluation, in B. Dockrell and D. Hamilton (eds.) *Rethinking Educational Research*, Hodder & Stoughton, London.

Stufflebeam, D. (ed.) (1971) *Educational Evaluation and Decision-Making*, Peacock, Hasca.

Tyler, R. (1971) *Basic Principles of Curriculum and Instruction*, University of Chicago.

Wildavsky, A. (1979) *Speaking Truth to Power: The Art and Craft of Policy Analysis*, Little, Brown & Co., Boston.

Wyatt, J. (1977) 'Collegiality' during a period of rapid change in higher education, *Oxford Review of Education*, Vol. 3, No. 2.

REPORTING EVALUATION

INTRODUCTION

In the earlier sections of the reader much stress has been placed on the practical utility of evaluation studies. Everyone involved in education can potentially benefit from considering the findings of evaluations of the activities in which they are involved. Here the practical difficulty is how to communicate evaluation reports most effectively to those who might be in a position to act upon them. There are plenty of instances where carefully conducted and well-intentioned evaluations have had little or no impact because very few people other than the evaluators ever got to know about them.

Alkin (Chapter 4.1) provides a constructive and helpful analysis of some of the strategies that evaluators can consider to enhance the impact of their evaluations. Inevitably this debate brings us back to the role of the evaluator and issues such as the negotiation of evaluator–contractor relationships. Jenkins (Chapter 4.2) provides examples to illustrate the pitfalls that lie before even experienced evaluators when it comes to reporting their findings. His work highlights in particular not just the issue of effective 'communication' but the way in which the political perspective of the sponsor provides an inescapable context for the interpretation of both the findings and the methodology of an evaluation.

In the current climate of educational change it is clear that many educational innovations and experiments are acted upon, in terms of their impact on future policy, well before they are formally completed. The movement from the TVEI pilot schemes to a national extension of TVEI long before the evaluations were completed, is one well-known case in point. This puts even more importance on the recent emphasis on formative reporting in evaluation as well as summative reporting. The evaluator who delivers a major evaluation report six months after the end of an educational pilot scheme may find that his or her audience has already moved well beyond the point where the report could have any impact at all, though this is not to suggest, as Kushner and MacDonald have reminded us in Section 2, that the public good cannot also be served by accurate 'post mortems'.

Fiddy, Loose and Stronach (Chapter 4.3) in their exchange of correspondence provide an illustration of a very different approach to reporting evaluation findings. Here is an informal exchange of ideas shortly after one part of an evaluation study. One of the key participants in the innovation which is being evaluated is brought into a formative dialogue about the evaluation findings, in a way that promises to have a realistic opportunity of influencing his thinking and the project's future development.

The demand for quick feedback from evaluations has to be tempered by the danger of oversimplified interpretations of evaluation data. Powney and Watts (Chapter 4.4) highlight the need to reveal some of the hidden constraints that can often strongly influence the data that is presented. Continuing our particular focus on interviewing they illustrate problems of interpretation in relation to the reporting of interview data. In particular they stress the need for those attempting to make sense of such data to have some understanding of the context in which it was collected, the procedures used by the interviewer in both eliciting the information and in analysing and reporting it.

Jenkins paper (Chapter 4.2) illustrates the fact that the reporting of evaluations is frequently influenced by ethical and political considerations. Many of the papers here and throughout the volume point to the need to anticipate such difficulties in advance and have a planned and agreed strategy for dissemination and reporting prior to embarking upon any evaluation study. They also point to the need to consider a wide range of approaches to reporting evaluations in order to attempt to reach the very different audiences who could benefit from considering the findings that emerge during and at the end of evaluation studies.

4.1
EVALUATION: WHO NEEDS IT? WHO CARES?*
Marvin C. Alkin

Evaluation: Who needs it? Who cares? What kind of strange title is this for a paper in an evaluation journal? Surely, we are all aware of and convinced of the value of evaluation. Yet, how often have we encountered situations when a study is completed by an evaluator amidst the claims of his colleagues that he has indeed performed one of the finest evaluation endeavours to date – the research design, statistical methods and quality of data were beyond reproof. Despite the evaluation community's hopeful expectations, the 'technically perfect' evaluation apparently had absolutely no effect on the programme's decision-makers or upon the decisions made. No one apparently needed it, no one apparently cared.

To understand why it is even of concern whether the evaluation is ultimately utilized in decision-making one must recognize the distinction between 'evaluation' and 'research'. This author has for some years felt that it was important to recognize the distinction between studies designed primarily to add to the body of knowledge (research) and those designed primarily to provide information for decision-making (evaluation) (Alkin, 1973a). Thus, while the comment 'even if the results of a study were not utilized, its redeeming feature is its intrinsic value and its contribution to the corpus of knowledge' is appropriate as a statement for a study designed primarily as research, it is *not* appropriate for an evaluation study. In short, in an evaluation it is important if someone 'needs' the evaluation and someone 'cares'. As Weiss (1972) has aptly stated, 'The basic rationale for evaluation is that it provides information for action. Its primary justification is that it contributes to the rationalization of decision-making.'

* Reprinted with permission from *Studies in Educational Evaluation*, Vol. 1, No. 3, Alkin, M. Evaluation: Who needs it? Who cares? (1975), Pergamon Journals Ltd.

UTILIZATION OF EVALUATION FINDINGS

In the example just presented, what might have caused this breach between evaluator and decision-maker – a technically 'perfect' evaluation with no impact on subsequent decisions? Further, how can an evaluation be considered to be of highest quality by evaluators and yet be of no use to decision-makers? What factors limit the potential utilization of evaluation information in decision-making?

For purposes of categorizing those things that perhaps determine the extent to which evaluation findings will be utilized, I will consider four sets of factors in this paper. They are:

(a) the decision-maker/decision process;
(b) the programme and social context;
(c) the nature of the evaluator; and
(d) the evaluation process/evaluation report.

I began the process of identifying these factors and discussing them in earlier reports. In particular, exploration of the motivation and reward system for decision-makers was considered in an article in *Planning and Changing* (Alkin, 1973b). In the same article the various contextual questions were considered and discussed. In a more recent publication, a monograph published by the Center for the Study of Evaluation (Alkin *et al.*, 1974), a number of the evaluator and evaluation report factors were considered in an empirical study which examined evaluation studies performed under a particular programme sponsored by the US Office of Education. Other authors, primarily outside the field of education, have also begun to deal with the topic of utilization of evaluation findings. In particular, the work of Weiss (1972) and of Riecken (1972) are noteworthy. A book edited by Caro (1971) also contains some excellent selections. More recently, studies by Bernstein and Freeman (1975) and by Patton *et al.* (1975) have shed additional light on an understanding of problems related to the utilization of evaluation findings.

Decision-maker/decision process

The first question of all is who is the decision-maker? For whom is the evaluation report? One of the major factors impeding the utilization of the evaluation findings is the improper initial recognition of who makes what decisions. One of the major distinguishing characteristics of an evaluation in contradistinction to a research report is an initial concern for identifying the decision-maker or decision audience that is intended as the prime recipient of the evaluation report. If a study is completed with *no* particular decision-maker or decision audience initially identified as its recipient, it is possible for the study to provide valuable new information about the nature of an entity, but it is not likely to lead to related decisions. Alternatively, it may be possible for a single study to attempt to meet the information needs of many decision-makers or decision audiences, but in all likelihood no one will be served well in such a situation.

Even when a decision-maker has been identified, it is important to recognize that each individual has his own value system and that the extent to which evaluation findings become utilized will be a function of philosophical orientation, political ambition, personality make-up and who knows what else. The nature of decision-making and the characteristics of decision-makers that provide indication of the likelihood of utilizing evaluation information have been explored by a number of researchers and theoreticians including Carlson (1965), Wirt and Kirst (1972), Braybrooke and Lindblom (1963) and Johnson (1970). Moreover, Weiss (1972) has pointed out the necessity of early identification of potential users of the evaluation information as well as the selection of appropriate issues of concern.

Sieber (1972) has added an interesting insight to an understanding of decision-maker practitioners. He derives three strategies of planned educational change with each strategy based upon the image of the practitioner: as a rational man, as a co-operator, or as a powerless functionary. Each of these images, no doubt, necessitates a different evaluation strategy.

This comment leads us to a second factor to be considered – 'What is the decision purpose?' At the outset of a commissioned evaluation, there is usually a purpose in the mind of those who commissioned the study. Sometimes there are even possible decisions that will occur based upon the information to be presented by the evaluation report. While intentions can be modified, the surest predictor of likely utilization is still an intended utilization at the outset of the project. In instances where there is a lack of decision purpose, where decision-makers contracting for evaluation reports do not have in mind an intended usage of that report and a decision purpose, then it is not likely that evaluation relevant to decision-making will take place, nor that utilization will occur.

Sometimes there is no intention that a real decision will take place; the evaluation has been contracted with a different purpose in mind: either no decision is intended or the decision intended has been predetermined prior to the initiation of the evaluation project. Let us consider within this category four different types of situations:

(a) window dressing;

(b) legal requirements;
(c) public relations;
(d) professional prestige.

In the first instance, evaluations are sometimes commissioned purely for purposes of *window dressing*, or *post hoc* justification of decisions that have already been made. In some instances the future decision is already positive and the evaluation is intended, in the words of Suchman (1967), as either eye-wash ('an attempt to justify a weak or bad program by deliberately selecting . . . those aspects that "look good" '), or whitewash ('an attempt to cover up program failure or errors by avoiding any objective appraisal'). Sometimes, according to Suchman the evaluation is intended as an attempt to torpedo ('provide a rationale for doing away with the program regardless of its effectiveness'). This is relatively easy to do since no programme is perfect and, if one is so intentioned, areas of programme deficiency can be noted in almost any evaluation report.

Sometimes, evaluations are commissioned simply to maintain compliance with *legal requirements* by another agency. For the programme director, continuance of his programme is the primary goal and consequently he may fear that a negative evaluation or an evaluation which points out any deficiencies will result in a reduction of funds or even a total curtailment of the programme. Thus, the evaluation is not looked at by him with a sympathetic and eager-for-information posture. In such instances, where the evaluator is hired by the programme director and not by the external agency, the intention is usually to do the utmost to assure that the evaluation is solely a pro forma exercise designed only to meet legal requirements.

Often an evaluation is commissioned simply as a *public relations* gesture where the intent may be to demonstrate the objectivity of project personnel by the mere fact that they have commissioned an evaluation. What is important in the eyes of the decision-maker is the *commissioning* of the evaluation and not the potential results that may emerge. In fact, given their preference, most decision-makers who commission evaluations with such intentions in mind would far prefer (after the initial publicity has taken place) that the evaluator float away and never again be seen by mortals. Enough frivolity, let me proceed.

The final category of evaluation report commissioning in which no decision is intended, I have referred to as *professional prestige*. Occasionally, administrators view themselves as 'men on the move' and all decisions and actions taken are seen as serving this master objective. Thus, to build a reputation as an innovator, it is necessary to have commissioned at least one evaluation to demonstrate one's own recognition and awareness of this new innovative procedure. If the results of the evaluation demonstrate the success of the 'innovative' programme that the administrator has started, all is well and good: otherwise, it is enough simply to have commissioned an 'innovative' evaluation whose results will likely not see the light of day.

As a final comment in this section on decision-makers and decision processes, let us assume that the best of all possible worlds exists and that a real decision is likely at the conclusion of the evaluation report. In that instance, it is imperative that the evaluator be aware of the kind of decision that is intended.

Dexter (1966) has noted that while it may be unwise for the evaluator to state explicitly the client's ulterior motives for commissioning the evaluation, the evaluator none the less should attempt to determine whether such motives exist. Only then is the evaluator able to determine whether to take the assignment, and if so, to understand his or her potential difficulties. There is a great deal of communications research offering potential transfer value to evaluation-utilization research. One such study which provides amplification for the above point was performed by Greenwald (1965) who examined the effects of prior commitment on behaviour change after a persuasive communication. Among subjects who had a strong prior commitment against a position favoured by the persuasive communication, Greenwald found that while the communication significantly modified the attitude, it did not modify behaviour. One would have to wonder about the results of a similar study extended to an educational evaluation situation.

Programme and social context

The characteristics of the programme and the nature of the contextual setting in which it rests are 'apparently' important factors in determining the potential utilization of evaluation studies in decision-making. I have said 'apparently' because it is almost a truism among researchers to consider these variables as being important, yet the research evidence at this point cannot be considered as particularly well organized. It is my belief that the nature of the programme and the characteristics of the programme staff are essential elements in the set of interactions that will determine the potential utilization of evaluation data. In my current research studies on the utilization of evaluation findings, I have been considering factors such as the organizational constraints, the formal and informal structure of the organization, and the nature of competing groups within the organization.

Outside the organization itself, I believe that the political alignments of the various external interest groups are a decisive determiner of utilization/ non-utilization. The importance of the characteristics of the community (socio-economic status, other demographic traits) which the programme serves were investigated in an earlier study (Alkin *et al.*, 1974).

Patton *et al.* (1975) listed five sets of characteristics of organizations that they felt might influence utilization of evaluation report findings. These were:

1. The constraints of decision-making in national bureaucratic organizations.
2. New and innovative agencies vs. older, established agencies.
3. Communication patterns in organizations.
4. Level in the organization where evaluation is done.
5. The degree of politicization of the organization.

The extent to which these and other programme and social context variables affect the utilization of evaluation findings in decision-making is not yet clear. Ferman (1969) has noted that 'the influence of the social context is important and shapes some of the considerations of logical inquiry . . . These conflicting networks of self-interest and values are important data to be considered in any evaluation . . . the same considerations often influence the utilization of the findings of an evaluation.' In an excellent article dealing with problems involved in the utilization of information, Deats (1974) concluded that information transmission and utilization occur within the context of a social system involving social interactions and perceptions which significantly influence utilization. While these and a great number of other contentions point to the importance of social context in the content of evaluation information, there is a paucity of research data.

Nature of the evaluator

Who is so naïve among us as not to recognize that who we are as evaluators, our past reputation, our organizational affiliation, and – oh yes – our personality traits, have a great impact upon the extent to which someone 'needs', 'cares', or utilizes the evaluation report that we produce? Bernstein and Freeman (1975) and Alkin *et al.* (1974) have investigated evaluator characteristics in relationship to quality of evaluation report and ultimate utilization of those findings in decision-making. Bernstein and Freeman reached some conclusions on the most important characteristics of evaluators *vis-à-vis* organizational affiliation and academic background, but their study was limited primarily to the consideration of evaluation quality (under a limited definition of quality) rather than a consideration of utilization findings. Alkin *et al.* (1974) explored a group of variables that they called the evaluation context. Included in this group was the distinction between internal and external evaluator. The results pointed out the necessity for more careful definition of what constitutes internal and external evaluation.

Patton *et al.* (1975) noted that perhaps the most important utilization factor is the personal human factor of an interested and committed evaluator (especially when accompanied by an interested and committed decision-maker).

> Where the personal human factor emerges, where some individual takes direct, personal responsibility for getting the information to the right people, evaluations have an impact. Where the personal factor is absent, there is a marked absence of impact. Utilization is not simply determined by some configuration of abstract factors; it is determined in large part by real, live, caring human beings.

Archibald (1970) confirmed the importance of the reputation and legitimacy of the evaluator as an important factor in the potential utilization of evaluation findings. Ashburn (1973) would apparently agree, citing the perceived nature of the individuals involved in the evaluation system as one cause of the credibility gap regarding evaluation.

Evaluation process/evaluation report

The nature and characteristics of the evaluation report including the process engaged in during the course of the evaluation are important elements related to the ultimate utilization of evaluation findings. For purposes of discussing this issue, I have conceived six subheadings for discussion, as follows:

1. Attention to appropriate goals.
2. Technical credibility.
3. Report comprehensibility.
4. Report timeliness.
5. Scope of recommendations.
6. Evaluator relationships.

Attention to appropriate goals

In part, the issue of attending to appropriate goals has been considered in a previous section under the heading of Decision-maker/decision process. It is, however, such an overarching question that it must be considered as well in the discussion of the characteristics of the evaluation process. After all, in looking at the evaluation report, what could be more basic than the question of the congruity of the goals and objectives measured and examined by the evaluator with those considered to be of interest by decision-makers and decision audiences. Far too many studies are conducted dealing with issues splendidly isolated from the educational policy issues at hand. The lack of appropriateness of goals used within an evaluation is, undoubtedly, a more important reason for the lack of utilization of evaluation results than any other characteristic of evaluation reports.

I have discussed in another source (Alkin, 1975) the nature of the process that evaluators must undertake in order to clarify who will be making what kinds of decisions within the decision structure as well as to clarify the extent to which other agencies will be receiving, and intending to utilize for decision-making, the evaluation information presented in the report. It is important to seek clarification and agreement from all parties involved, prior to the collection of any data, that the goals being employed in the evaluation are those which are considered relevant for the programme at hand. There is substantial agreement on this point. Bend (1970) attributes many evaluation difficulties to initial misunderstanding of and lack of agreement upon the 'objectives, activities, and outputs of the evaluative research project'. Bosco (1971) has an interesting article geared to administrators in which he has as his purpose instructing administrators on how to manage educational evaluation so as to maximize their usefulness. One major piece of advice provided to administrators is that they must take care to ensure that the information collected is relevant to the decisions they must make, with particular attention to those factors which will really make a difference when the decision is made. Perhaps Bosco is correct, and the key to greater utilization is more instructions to administrators on the potential uses of evaluation.

Technical credibility

Technical soundness or credibility in the way the evaluation was performed is not the *sine qua non* of evaluation utilization (evaluation reports which are by no means technically well done have in many instances been pointed to as the basis for decisions which have been made). On the other hand, lack of attainment of technical credibility provides the first, easy, and instinctive means for the dismissal of the conclusions of an evaluation report when a decision-maker wishes to forgo making decisions logically related to those conclusions. That is, failure to attend to technical soundness in an evaluation report provides decision-makers with the most basic of reasons for dismissal of the report. Even the least technically sophisticated of decision-makers (who could not normally distinguish a multiple R from a 't' test) suddenly emerge as technical wizards able to find methodological flaws in evaluation results not to their liking. An alternative tactic is for decision-makers to obtain someone (another consultant?) who can and will willingly (in part to build their own professional prestige) find those flaws. Apparently, one of the best conscientious defences against non-utilization of evaluation findings is a technically sound, methodologically credible study.[1]

One of the areas of threat to the credibility of evaluation findings is a set of factors which in large part are beyond the control of the evaluator. I refer here to what I will call 'programme controlled factors'. There are ways in which programmes operate and function that severely inhibit the nature of the evaluation that can be conducted. For example, one must be concerned that the programme be initially established in a way that would even make an evaluation possible. There are instances where the policy established by decision-makers with respect to the nature of the programme – who will be in it, the assignment/non-assignment of teachers – virtually assures that a technically credible design cannot be attained. In these instances, there is great likelihood that the evaluation is doomed at the start. Flanagan (1970) has asserted that administrators must use comprehensive, rigorous procedures in making the decision to try out an innovation. Advanced planning is the key to successful implementation and ultimately to successful evaluation.

In addition to the way in which a programme is conceived and initially organized, the way in which it is operated may also destroy the technical credibility of the evaluation. Where the programme is implemented unevenly across classes or schools, and perhaps even with variations in the procedures utilized by programme personnel, doubts may again be raised about the credibility of the evaluation based, not upon the deficiencies of the evaluator, but on programme operational problems beyond his or her control. Sometimes, also, reliance on programme staff for assistance in the collection of routine data, the administering of instruments, or even providing time to be personally interviewed may all provide sources of potential breakdown in the data collection that are partially beyond the responsibility of the evaluators.

There are other factors related to technical credibility that are more dependent upon the particular skills and knowledge of the evaluator. Obviously, the evaluator's ingenuity in devising an appropriate design is of vital importance. Despite the clear distinction between research and evaluation, the use of experimental designs is highly desirable in order to provide for the strongest possible inferences related to the measurable outcomes of programmes. But failing this, the evaluator must select the strongest design possible given the situation.

Another area of potential technical deficiency of evaluation is the quality of the data collected. In part, data quality can be improved in terms of its potential utilizability to decision-makers by the evaluator engaging in the process of initially simulating the possible findings of the study. I have engaged in this process with decision-makers by providing simulated findings based upon data sources being proposed in order to determine from decision-makers at the outset of the process (prior to data collection) the adequacy of these sources for the potential decisions that might be made. In essence, this pre-data-collection activity involves considerable interaction between evaluator and decision-maker in which the evaluator attempts to determine the extent to which various data items would be considered convincing evidence for decisions. I firmly believe that one important element related to increasing the utilization of evaluation information is the reaching of agreement at the onset of a study on the kinds of data which would be considered acceptable if presented at the end of a study.

Of course, there are other issues related to the production of quality data. The question of selecting the appropriate measuring instrument is always an essential element in producing a technically competent study. Issues related to the extent to which the instrument selected measures the desired objective of the programme is a standard measurement question which is dealt with in most, if not all, textbooks. Likewise, the debate about the relative virtue and appropriateness of standardized tests vs. criterion-referenced tests is also a topic that has been dealt with effectively in prior literature (Popham, 1975; Millman, 1974; Harris, Alkin and Popham, 1974).

Another descriptive attribute of an evaluation report is the data analysis procedures used. Bernstein and Freeman (1975) paid particular heed to the technical sophistication of the data analysis procedure used by evaluators. I am personally not convinced that technical sophistication *per se* is a prime concern for evaluators (after all, evaluations should not be attempts at mathematical magic or exercises in esoterica).

Report comprehensibility

The evaluation report must be in language understandable to the decision-maker. Since decision-making is, in practice, a very diffuse process, frequently including lay community and other decision audiences, evaluation reports face a severe test. The reports must, on the other hand, be simple enough to be understood by the technically unsophisticated yet rigorous enough to withstand the tests of technical credibility.

This twofold dilemma of both credibility and comprehensibility offers an imposing task for would-be evaluators. How can a report on the one hand be easily understood by non-technical persons yet have sufficient technical credibility that it is not easily dismissed as unworthy of utilization? Sometimes (or do I mean usually?) those engaged in the process solve the dilemma by ignoring the potential utilization question and simply prepare the evaluation reports in a format appropriate for reading by their academically oriented colleagues. Thus, the evaluator–researcher has at least heightened his or her own reputation with colleagues even if no decision is to come of the evaluation.

Weiss (1972) has made a number of recommendations for improving the effectiveness of evaluation reports:

(a) presentation (of the report) must be clear and attractive;
(b) the implications of evaluation findings must be fully considered;
(c) many audiences require evaluation reporting procedures other than bulky written reports; and
(d) recommendations and other positions taken by the evaluator should not be presented in a lukewarm manner but, rather, advocated forcefully.

I have found it helpful to combine a fully documented report with short readable 'executive summaries' and oral presentations of findings. A typical format that I have been using recently consists of short executive summaries at the beginning of the evaluation report. (Typically, this section of the report is printed on a different-coloured paper for ease in dealing with it and to ensure that those not interested in a full report treatment do not get 'mixed up' in the full body of the report.) Usually a single page is used for each predetermined decision question, with the summary filling no more than one page and with each question starting a new page. Each page of the executive summary begins with a predetermined statement of the decision question and a short paragraph elaborating the nature of the question. Another paragraph summarizes the findings related to that specific question with a reference to the pages of the complete report in which a more extensive treatment of the findings may be found. This assures the reader that the simple statement of findings has been substantiated in a technically credible fashion elsewhere and enables him to examine the full procedure if he wishes. Finally, the last item on the executive summary page is a listing of the recommendations (if any) with reference to the pages in the full report in which they are formulated and justified.

In more comprehensive evaluation reports, I have included a technical appendix that presents detailed analyses, instrumentation, etc., which were felt to be too much for the main body of the report. Thus, the report has sections presenting various degrees of technical complexity depending upon the needs of the particular reader.

I have found this procedure to be helpful in attaining greater utilization of evaluation findings: although it should be noted that the value of this format and procedure has not been tested empirically. Weiss (1972) would agree that this is an important area worthy of further research. In her list of evaluation procedures identified as particularly important for study, she had discussed 'the effective presentation of findings and dissemination of information'.

Report timeliness

Another important evaluation report attribute related to potential utilization of evaluation findings is its timeliness. Ammunition received after a battle is over, food provided to a person dead of starvation, and evaluation reports received after a decision has been made are of equal worth. They each represent degrees of worthlessness.

An evaluation must provide the information that a decision-maker needs before the decision is made. Despite the obvious, this is most frequently neglected. For example, most evaluation reports are presented to governmental agencies at the conclusion of the school year (naturally, this is so since end-of-year student-achievement data must be included). Unfortunately, this does not correspond well with government budget-making cycles. Most decisions about the funding of programmes for a subsequent year have already been made by the time that evaluation reports are received.

This factor was noted as a possible cause of the lack of utilization of evaluation findings for federal decision-making related to project funding (Alkin *et al.*, 1974). In essence, the projects had already been funded for the next year prior to receipt of evaluation reports. Thus, there could be little likelihood that evaluation information would be utilized in this important area of decision-making.

On the other hand, in the same study, evaluation information was considered to be of value by local decision-makers, for whom the evaluation reporting was timely. Clearly the timeliness of reports is an important factor in ultimate utilization for decision-making.

Scope of recommendations

Another characteristic of the evaluation report that has been suggested to us by Patton *et al.* (1975) is the 'scope of recommendations for change'. They suggest that essentially bureaucratic organizations are slow to accept findings that require massive reorganizations of the system and that evaluation findings which in essence present minor modifications are more likely to be adopted in subsequent decisions. With these statements, a caveat must be offered – there are unique decision contexts which would increase rather than decrease the probability that recommendations of major scope would be utilized and accepted in subsequent decisions (e.g. a new administrator who would relish the opportunity of demonstrating the relative prior inefficiency by making major changes).

Evaluator relationships

The worth and ultimate utilization of evaluation findings and reports can be greatly affected by the personal relationships developed between evaluator and decision-maker. Evaluation involves far more than the presentation of reports (albeit credible and comprehensive reports).

The simple fact is that even the scientific endeavour of performing the evaluation of programmes rests heavily for its success on the relationships built between individuals. To the extent to which school staff, decision-makers, and others engaged in the programme that was evaluated came to trust and respect the integrity and honesty of the evaluator, the likelihood of utilization of findings is increased. Likewise, the absence of basic tensions and/or antagonism between participating parties is also an important element in evaluation success (i.e. utilization). Rodman and Kolodny (1964) expressed concern about the evaluator/decision-maker relationship and argued that role differences as well as the formal social organization of the programme are the principal causative factors in the development of a strained relationship between the evaluator and the practitioner decision-maker. Forehand (1970) is so concerned about the nature of the relationship that he has argued that an evaluator/decision-maker dichotomy should not be discussed but rather one must contemplate a unified decision-making process.

As simplistic as these comments about the importance of relations between individuals appear to be, they none the less warrant inclusion. Frequently, we become so involved in the technical and mechanistic aspects of evaluation that the non-scientific human relations questions are ignored – all to the detriment of effective evaluation.

REALISTIC PERCEPTIONS OF UTILIZATION

The argument goes that: 'evaluation has no impact upon decision-making, so why bother doing it? A simple examination of the evaluation literature finds very few instances where the findings of evaluation were adopted and led to a set of concurrent programme decisions.' The point we must make (and we are reminded of it by Patton *et al.*, 1975) is that judgements of utilization/non-utilization cannot be made based upon the extent to which evaluation findings are *totally* accepted and implemented. It is naïve to assume that no information existed prior to the conduct of the specific study which had been commissioned. Rather, evaluation findings must be viewed as an additional source which will hopefully affect the decision in part. Patton *et al.* (1975) noted in their study on the evaluations of twenty health programmes that 'none of the impacts described was of the type where new findings from an evaluation were directly and immediately used in the making of major, concrete program decisions. The more typical, in fact, was one where the evaluation findings provided additional pieces of information.' In essence, a more realistic perception of evaluation utilization rests upon the use of the evaluation information as an element in the making of complex decisions.

> The view of evaluation research that emerges in our interviews stands in stark contrast to the image of utilization that is presented as the ideal in the bulk of the evaluation literature, or at least, the impression with which that literature left us. The ideal held forth in the literature we reviewed earlier is one of major impact on concrete decisions. The image that emerges in our interviews is that there are few major, direction-changing decisions in most programming, and that evaluation research is used as one piece of information that feeds into a slow, evolutionary process of program development. Program development is a process of 'muddling through' and evaluation research is part of the muddling.
>
> (Patton *et al.*, 1975)

WHO NEEDS IT, WHO CARES?

It is true that decision-makers involved in the process of educational improvement have a need for information. Evaluators provide information in the belief that it will lead to rational (e.g. data-based) decision-making. Although this sounds like an effective relationship, it implies some rather simplistic assumptions on the part of many evaluators. First, the mere presentation of data is not alone likely to improve decision-making. In addition to presenting technically credible evaluation reports related to appropriate goals, it is necessary that evaluators pay heed to appropriate methods of information presentation so that the right person gets the proper information at the proper time and in the proper format. Moreover, the complexities of decision context and social context in which programme decisions are ultimately embedded require that evaluators become more fully aware of these factors. Evaluators will be better prepared to provide the right kind of information if they understand who the decision-makers are, the decisions they make and the constraints upon their decision-making. Also, it is essential that we maintain a proper perspective on the potential role that evaluation might play in making an impact upon decision-making and not become frustrated by attaining minor impacts only. Finally, in considering these factors, perhaps it is important as evaluators that we learn to distinguish those situations in which the context and decision factors are so predetermined that it can be inevitably said that no one needs it and no one cares. Finally, I would urge that evaluators make more judicious selections of where and how to apply their evaluation talents.[2]

NOTES

1. Of course, the 'best' defence against non-utilization is performing an evaluation which produces favourable results in line with a decision that someone in authority wanted to make initially.
2. The work upon which this publication is based was performed pursuant to a contract with the National Institute of Education, Department of Health, Education and Welfare. Points of view or opinions stated do not necessarily represent official NIE position or policy.

REFERENCES

Alkin, M.C. (1973a) Evaluacion: investigacion o praxis? *Educacion Hoy*, Asociacion de Publicaciones Educativas, Ano 111, No. 17, Colombia, Bogota.

Alkin, M.C. (1973b) Evaluation and decision-making, *Planning and Changing, A Journal for School Administrators*, Vol. 3, No. 4.

Alkin, M.C. (1975) Framing the decision context, *AERA Cassette Series in Evaluation*, American Educational Research Association, Washington, DC.

Alkin, M.C., Kosecoff, J., Fitzgibbon, C. and Seligman, R. (1974) Evaluation and decision-making: the Title VII experience, *CSE Monograph Series in Evaluation No. 4*, Los Angeles Center for the Study of Evaluation, University of California.

Archibald, K. (1970) Alternative orientations to social science utilization, *Social Science Information*, Vol. 9, No. 2, pp. 7–34.

Ashburn, A.G. (1973) Credibility gaps and the institutionalizing of educational evaluation functions, *Planning and Changing, A Journal for School Administrators*, Vol. 4, No. 1, pp. 18–28.

Bend, E. (1970) The impact of the social setting upon evaluative research, *Evaluative Research*, AIR, pp. 109–128.

Bernstein, I.N. and Freeman, H.W. (1975) *Academic and Entrepreneurial Research*, Russell Sage Foundation, New York.

Bosco, J. (1971) The role of the administrator in the improvement of evaluation studies, *Education*, Vol. 92, No. 2, pp. 70–74.

Braybrooke, D. and Lindblom, C.E. (1963) *A Strategy of Decision*, The Free Press, New York.

Carlson, R.O. (1965) *Adoption of Educational Innovations*, University of Oregon Press, Eugene.

Caro, F.G. (ed.) (1971) *Readings in Evaluation Research*, Russell Sage Foundation, New York.

Deats, T. (1974) Moving and using information, *Teachers' College Record*, Vol. 75, No. 3, pp. 383–93.

Dexter, L.A. (1966) Impressions about utility and wastefulness in applied social science studies, *American Behavioral Scientist*, Vol. 9, No. 6, pp. 9–10.

Ferman, L.A. (1969) Some perspectives on evaluating social welfare programs, *The Annals of the American Academy of Political and Social Science*, No. 385, pp. 143–56.

Flanagan, J.C. (1970) Administrative behaviour in implementing educational innovations, *Education*, Vol. 90, No. 3, pp. 213–20.

Forehand, G.A. (1970) Curriculum evaluation as decision-making process, *Journal of Research and Development in Education*, Vol. 3, No. 4, pp. 27–37.

Greenwald, A.G. (1965) Effects of prior commitment on behaviour change after persuasive communication, *Public Opinion Quarterly*, Vol. 29, No. 4, pp. 595–610.

Harris, C., Alkin, M.C. and Popham, W.J. (eds.) (1974) Problems in criterion-referenced measurement, *CSE Monograph Series in Evaluation No. 3*, Los Angeles Center for the Study of Evaluation, University of California.

Johnson, G.H. (1970) The purpose of evaluation and the role of the evaluator, *Evaluative Research*, AIR.

Millman, J. (1974) Criterion-referenced measurement, in *Evaluation in Education: Current Applications*, McCutchan Publishing, Berkeley, California.

Patton, M.Q., Grimes, P.S., Guthrie, K., Brennan, N.J., French, B.D. and Blyth, D.A. (1975) *In Search of Impact: An Analysis of the Utilization of Federal Health Evaluation Research*, University of Minnesota Press, Minneapolis.

Popham, W.J. (1975) *Educational Evaluation*, Prentice-Hall, New Jersey.

Riecken, H.W. (1972) Memorandum of program evaluation, in C.H. Weiss (ed.) *Evaluating Action Programs*, Allyn & Bacon, Boston.

Rodman, H. and Kolodny, R.L. (1964) Organizational strains in the researcher–practitioner relationship, *Human Organization*, Vol. 23, No. 2, pp. 171–82.

Sieber, S.D. (1972) Images of the practitioner and strategies of educational change, *Sociology of Education*, Vol. 45, No. 4, pp. 362–85.

Suchman, E.A. (1967) *Evaluative Research: Principles in Public Service and Action Programs*, Russell Sage Foundation, New York.

Weiss, C.H. (1972) Utilization of evaluation: toward comparative study, in C.H. Weiss (ed.) *Evaluating Action Programs*, Allyn & Bacon, Boston.

Wirt, F.M. and Kirst, M.W. (1972) *The Political Web of American Schools*, Little, Brown & Co., Boston.

4.2
CHOCOLATE CREAM SOLDIERS: SPONSORSHIP, ETHNOGRAPHY AND SECTARIANISM*
David Jenkins

Northern Ireland is a very particular place. Not only do a number of terms at least relatively unproblematic in Britain (like 'policing' or 'political education') pose unique problems over here, but the whole society is shot through with a phenomenon of particular interest to the ethnographer, battles over crucial definitions. Social research in any aspect of life infiltrated by sectarianism is likely to place the researcher in an arena for conflict between antithetical accounts. When an armoured pig ran into Catholic youths in the Bogside it was immediately processed for public consumption by both sides: the Royal Ulster Constabulary (RUC) press statement spoke of a 'road accident'; *Republican News* hinted at psychopaths on the loose. The most familiar recent example, outside education, of conflicting definitions must surely be the H-Blocks hunger strikers, variously held to be suicidal criminals or murdered martyrs. The educational researcher is caught in a not dissimilar cross-fire.

Schools arguably respond to 'the Troubles' in one of three ways; some implicitly declare school to be 'time-out' and keep community issues off the curriculum; others teach from the local subculture, reflecting its values in a way that is implicitly sectarian; a third group sees the curriculum, particularly in social and cultural studies, as having a critical or reconstructionist potential.

This report concerns an evaluation study directed by the author and Father Sean O'Connor, a Jesuit priest who had strayed purposefully into the North, crossing the symbolic border at some unguarded point. The study

* Jenkins, D. (1984) Chocolate cream soldiers: sponsorship, ethnography and sectarianism, in R. Burgess (ed.) *The Research Process in Educational Settings: Ten Case Studies*, Falmer.

was a broadly ethnographic account of the Schools Cultural Studies Project (SCSP), sponsored by DENI (the Department of Education, Northern Ireland) and the Joseph Rowntree Charitable Trust (JRCT). The study was commissioned in 1977 and was dramatized on public hoardings as a high-risk exposure of a high-risk programme; independent, issues-based, methodologically eclectic with its commitment to 'illuminative portrayal', and likely to be close-up, possibly to an unnerving extent. Its enigmatic title, *Chocolate Cream Soldiers*, was borrowed from Shaw's *Arms and the Man*. The original 'chocolate cream soldier' was a pacifist who found himself inadvertently in a war zone; 'chocolate' is intended to suggest the quaker Rowntree Trust, 'cream' the curriculum task force, and 'soldiers' the Northern Ireland problem. Like the report itself, the title had a somewhat mixed reception.

It is probably useful to sketch something of the Schools Cultural Studies Project itself. The original funding proposal, by Professor Malcolm Skilbeck, sought to use schooling in a concerted attempt to blunt the edge of sectarianism in Northern Ireland schools by using the curriculum system of its secondary schools as an instrument of cultural change. Its novel features *vis-à-vis* current models of curriculum development were that it was *school-based* (thus valuing selective adaptivity rather than proposing a 'course of study' to be tested by teachers); premised on a philosophy of *'cultural reconstructionism'* (and thus, ambiguously, believing that the Province's teachers, erstwhile 'naïve bearers of the sectarian culture' could become, virtually overnight, 'cultural change agents'); and *open* (thus committed to painful self-analysis and seeking to promote a general unfreezing of attitudes).

Although Skilbeck's original funding proposal stressed analytical processes, and envisaged a community-wide cultural critique (with education an important part of, rather than monopolizing, the exercise), subsequent changes in the leadership of the project led to a redefined more restrictive brief, with the production of curriculum material and a common teaching strategy acquiring a central emphasis. Hooked into the Schools Cultural Studies Project pedagogy was a version of the 'values clarification process', by which the project hoped its teachers would avoid using the classroom as a platform for sectarian indoctrination. It thus echoes Lawrence Stenhouse's Humanities Curriculum Project which also put controversial issues on the secondary school curriculum, but espoused a different solution to the underlying problem in so-called 'neutral chairmanship'.

THE EVALUATION CONTRACT

Much of the discussion leading up to the final version of *Chocolate Cream*

Soldiers hinged on the initial contract. The main issue was whether groups other than the evaluators had proprietorial rights over the data rather than a point of view that we were committed to listen to. Yet the notion that there was an agreed initial contract itself became cloudy, even ambiguous; the surviving document is the proposal, said by some parties to have been modified in discussion. Even the proposal was not without some internal inconsistency and unfortunately might (viewed in retrospect) have disguised the extent to which non-recommendatory reports might none the less be implicitly judgemental. It was, however, quite clear on the independence of the evaluation. As presented to the consultative committee and Schools Cultural Studies Project teachers, the stance of the evaluators was characterized as follows:

(a) *independent*, the project allowing reasonable access and accepting the final report, although negotiated for fairness and accuracy, would be the responsibility of the evaluators, not the project team or the consultative committee;
(b) *non-judgemental*, not making crude recommendations but seeking instead to write an issues-centred portrayal, collecting judgements rather than making them;
(c) *methodologically eclectic*; although broadly working in an illuminative tradition, the evaluation team would gather survey data and perhaps employ measurement techniques in relation to some of the more crucial objectives;
(d) *responsive*, trying to assess the audiences for its reports and what questions they wanted answered, rather than simply posing its own;
(e) *short, sharp, intensive*, writing up quickly while hot.

At the meeting called so that project teachers might endorse or reject the proposal for an evaluation, the evaluators' 'sales pitch' was constructed around ten reasons why the teachers might legitimately *not* want the evaluation. The teachers, to their credit, agreed to co-operate. ('You've been honest with us; we'll be honest with you.') The evaluators were also open about secondary agendas. We wanted hands-on experience for a group of MA students studying programme evaluation. We also wanted to press the chosen model (the close-up issues-based portrayal) in circumstances that would test it to the limit.

THE EVALUATION IN RETROSPECT

In the event it went ahead. Yet those who took part in it, sponsored it, and underwent its scrutiny, felt in general to have been a little bruised by the experience. The final report, *Chocolate Cream Soldiers*, has been lauded, denounced, suppressed, surreptitiously circulated, methodologically attacked, ethically condemned, cited as exemplary practice, and humanly criticized. What happened? What, if anything, went wrong? This chapter is an attempt to reflect on the discomforting experience of the exercise. In particular it takes the view that ethnographic research in educational settings, particularly in an 'evaluative' role, cannot treat its methodology as if it were abstractable and separable from more complex problems of role performance, and the need to generate 'understandings' *in situ*. Lying behind this issue is a more general snare, the evolution of a rhetoric of research methodology that claims spuriously to 'guarantee the findings'. Yet threats to the validity of an account at times feel more like the familiar problem of trying to 'tell the truth' in ordinary social life. The worries expressed about *Chocolate Cream Soldiers* barely touched upon technical matters like 'triangulation' or the basis upon which we had selected 'quotable quotes' from the mass of interview transcripts. It focused rather on the evaluators' 'value position', whether we had demonstrated 'bad faith', or whether we were politically bright enough to anticipate and appropriately forestall potential 'adverse' consequences. A crucial series of episodes surrounded our attempts to 'negotiate' with the sponsors and subjects of the report concerning its accuracy and fairness; the unambiguous emergence of an unacknowledged political agenda characterized these negotiations.

Politically, and in terms of its stylistic aspirations, the ethnographic style of evaluation (also called 'naturalistic', 'illuminative' or 'portrayal') (Shaw, 1978; Hamilton *et al.*, 1977) has been reasonably well documented recently. The aim of such evaluations, broadly, are to portray innovative programmes in action. Such portrayals tend to be intimate, analytic, emotive, concerned with processes and performances as well as effects, but tending to use issues as advance organizers. *Chocolate Cream Soldiers*, within this tradition, was not overtly theoretic and aspired to a balance of 'thick description' and analysis. But the evaluators were also attracted to Elliot Eisner's (1972, 1981) notion that the tools of literary criticism might make a legitimate contribution to alternative evaluation. Concepts like 'tone', 'irony' and 'paradox' moved nearer the centre. The evaluators also accepted the appropriateness of 'portrayal of persons' in evaluation reports, and were prepared to experiment with wit and humour as heuristic devices for 'getting inside' situations characterized by conflicting definitions and inner tensions. Perhaps not surprisingly, this was often misunderstood, and parts of *Chocolate Cream Soldiers* were widely perceived as flippant.

The evaluators' reports (two interim reports, *Chocolate Cream Soldiers* and the digest, *Chocolate Drops*) (Jenkins, O'Connor *et al.*, 1980a, 1980b) evidenced considerable sympathy for the Schools Cultural Studies Project, which has been facing bravely one of the most intractable social and cultural problems in Western Europe, recording that 'the great success of the Project can be simply stated; it introduced sharp issues into the curriculum of Northern Ireland schools, and has produced many many examples of courageous, high-risk, and seemingly successful probing. In other words, there does seem to have been an unfreezing.' Yet some slightly disturbing aspects were highlighted: the personality-dependence of the innovation, oscillating wildly under its changes in directorship, unchallenged in the Rowntree predilection for trusting people rather than ideas; the regression back towards a non-adaptive first-generation curriculum project ('centre-peripheral' rather than 'school-based') increasingly 'technologizing' its problems in a flight from direct confrontation with the sacrosanct (even SCSP's 'value-clarification process' appeared in a curious technical guise as a value-free heuristic); the over-concentration on the five-year 'course of study' (which was neither envisaged nor financed in the funding proposal) in a way that encouraged an assimilative rather than a critical response.

Some problems, too, arose out of the ambiguous political image of SCSP, perceived variously as a 'state sell', 'the educational wing of the Alliance Party', 'the soft under-belly of English liberalism', or even 'in a republican corner'. Certainly Malcolm Skilbeck's early formulations (built into the funding proposal to Rowntree, but to some extent subsequently reneged on) envisaged a community-wide attack on the problems of cultural reconstruction in the Province, spearheaded through the school curriculum. The teachers, it was supposed, were to become 'change agents' through a kind of shoe-strap self-enhancement with the self-lift coming through a commitment to analytical processes. But their 'diagnosed' starting point, in the Skilbeck scheme, was as 'naïve bearers of a sectarian culture'. Their working situation was held to be substantially infiltrated by unexamined social meetings; only by considerable reflexivity could they avoid failing by default. The subcultures, *as represented in the schools*, seemed to Skilbeck to be ideological, militant, aggressive, and highly reproductive, although thin and translucent, lacking complexity and internal diversity.

The evaluators saw themselves as portraying the project holistically, disclosing its perceived meanings, inner tensions, natural history, and educational issues, but also contributing to an analysis of the 'logic of the problem', particularly the role that might be played by schooling. In charting what turned out to be the rather deviant natural history of the innovation, we felt able to generalize tentatively concerning personality-dependent innovation. But our stance was important for another reason; since the evaluation claimed to be non-judgemental in any strong sense of that term, its own value position (that is, the basis of its adjudication) did not have to be 'on the line'. Indeed, when pressures grew we took the view that a project, and a department, and a trust, so unequivocally committed to a liberal intervention might adequately and legitimately be chastened, as appropriate, *by confrontation with their own rhetoric*. Yet our comment on DENI's geographical carve-up (that gave Skilbeck, at the New University of Ulster (NUU), Derry and the north of the Province, and Queens' John Malone and his project Belfast and the South) was not appreciated by those who held that the notion of 'liberal critique' did not properly extend to criticizing the sponsors ('statements should be deleted that in the view of the Management Committee might be detrimental to the Department, the Trust or the Project'). Yet, astonishingly, a project 'blunting the edge of sectarianism' in Northern Ireland had been established in a way that gave it no presence in Belfast, and only an equivocal toehold in Derry where it has been taught almost entirely by schools in the Catholic sector. The relative acceptability (after what might euphemistically be described as 'soundings by local community entrepreneurs') of the Derry materials in the Creggan rather than the Waterside is clearly of public interest; yet the evaluation team was all but instructed not to present its data.

RELATIONSHIPS WITH THE SPONSORS

Relationships with the sponsors became increasingly brittle over time. In December 1979 an international workshop was held at Girton College, Cambridge, to review the use of naturalistic inquiry in educational evaluation.[1] Most of those at the workshop admitted to major problems with sponsors or clients at one time or another. The first source of discontinuity appeared to be the unexpected difficulty in 'targeting' evaluation data to the information needs of the decision-maker. Certainly DENI wanted from the evaluators recommendations and supporting evidence of a kind that would allow them to adjudicate whether the Schools Cultural Studies Project merited further funding. The second discontinuity was the perceived gap between programme evaluation, with its invitation to concentrate on a putative solution, and policy-related research, which allows independent access to the logic of the problem. *Chocolate Cream Soldiers*, from the sponsors' point of view, offered the worst of both worlds, claiming the right to comment upon policy and the underlying logic of the problem, but not offering the policy-makers much by way of 'indicators' against which they might 'measure' success. Ethnography, in other words, becomes what Paul Atkinson called a kind of 'surrogate theory', offering description rather than analysis or recommendation.[2] Even the concentration on issues is sometimes seen by the administrators as a kind of fence-sitting. We were consequently perceived as appealing over the heads of the sponsors to some 'hidden audience', perhaps academic peers, perhaps the population at large, perhaps the verdict of history.

THE TALE OF TWO MEETINGS: 1 COLERAINE

The edginess of the relationship between the evaluators, the project and the sponsors can most readily be exemplified by two meetings. Both of these concerned the report, *Chocolate Cream Soldiers*, which appears to have taken the sponsors by surprise. It was regarded as over-personal, even hurtful, lacking decorum, and naïve about its own predictable consequences. An affronted management committee requested to meet the evaluators on 5 November 1979, two hours after high noon. Sean O'Connor and I had been excluded from the immediately prior morning session. The agenda indicated an afternoon session 'in the presence of Professor Jenkins'. It was a long time since things had looked this formal.

The first snippet of news came from the New University of Ulster's Professor Hugh Sockett over a lunchtime beer. According to Hugh, the morning had been inconsequential ('They haven't a clue how to handle an issues-centred portrayal. I keep telling them what kind of report they have got.') Hugh saw the morning meeting as 'nitpicking' and 'preoccupied with procedures'.

At the private dining room lunch, due to a symbolically apt oversight by the university catering department, the visitors had not been provided with knives.

Chairman Tom Cowan (ex-DENI) opened the afternoon session briskly, putting the meeting on a short fuse. The management committee had concluded a 'long complex discussion' in the morning. The 'major points of conclusion' were that *three copies only* of the report were to be circulated, to those the committee were 'duty bound' to supply (the University, the JRCT and the DENI). Any wider circulation would have to be 'subject to two conditions', the 'deletion of references to individuals unless agreed', and the deletion of statements that in the view of the management committee might be 'detrimental to the Department, the Trust, or the Project'.

I felt unable to endorse this suggestion. It had been made clear from the start that the evaluation team, not the Trust, the Project or the Department would be responsible for the products. I reminded the meeting of the 'contract'; the evaluation was offering to negotiate, not the fact of a report, but its content, mainly for accuracy and fairness. But Tom Cowan held that the evaluation's known view of itself notwithstanding, there had been no 'agreement'. Besides, the management committee *per se* could not deliver on such a contract. He felt we were back to the legal position that sponsors 'buy' an evaluation. (Cowan: 'I have worked for the Department for more years than I care to remember. Every single word I have written has been their property.') He claimed that, as a general principle, every report is 'the property of those that sponsor it'. Hugh Sockett, on the other hand, felt that copyright had not been surrendered. Professor Joe Nesbitt (NUU) said that he did not suppose the university, in any particular sense, to have been 'party to a contract'. NUU had however, joined in a decision to fund an avowedly *independent* evaluation ('I don't think we should have the intention of interfering'). The rest was a matter of 'occasional phraseology' which could safely be left to the writers.

I responded that the evaluation team did not need to be taught lessons on the sensitivity of the exercise. On the other hand, the principle that the sponsors can claim automatic protection from detrimental comment seemed a weak one. The evaluation saw the conduct of the sponsors as lying within its legitimate range of interests. Nicholas Gillett of JRCT agreed. The report's probing was useful ('I would be worried if the report were so bland that it worried nobody'). He himself had found it 'sharp and readable' (a letter saying just that was already on the table). Hugh Sockett capped the point: 'If *Chocolate Cream Soldiers* does not raise suspicions, then it ain't worth reading.' At this point Joe Nesbitt vigorously shook his head, but said nothing. But SCSP Director Alan Robinson was still unhappy. He did not 'want *Chocolate Cream Soldiers*, unrevised, landing on the desk of an uncommitted headteacher in Belfast'. He had also exhibited slight defensiveness with Hugh Sockett, sitting bolt upright, arms folded, as Hugh used his 20:20 hindsight to indicate what SCSP should have done. Sockett added that one problem that the evaluators had missed concerned the 'high-risk funding'. It was 'amazing' that the university had touched SCSP in the first place. SCSP exhibited 'something unusual: a conservative Department of Education in partnership with an avowedly radical funding body'. That these unlikely bedfellows got together at all was 'a comment on the depth of the problem'. ('I don't know what Hugh was driving at there,' confided Professor Nesbitt afterwards, 'the Department are far from conservative and some people might suppose that in one sense quakers are conservative.')

Suddenly Tom Cowan comes in line with the Trust. The evaluators have produced a 'worthwhile report', if somewhat 'jargon-ridden' and a bit of an 'insiders' document'. Circulation will be to the trial schools, the project and evaluation teams, professional developers/evaluators likely to find it of practical interest, and the sponsors. It can also be used as part of the NUU in-service award-bearing programme, but it should not, without further thought and negotiation, go into general circulation. The Rowntree representative, Nicholas Gillett, keeps up the Trust's recessiveness to the end, although putting his weight behind the eventual 'reconciliation'. Both sides fibbed that the original clash was a misunderstanding, a trick of the shifting light. It was a big step for the evaluation; although doubtless a tiny step for mankind.

THE TALE OF TWO MEETINGS: 2 BELFAST

But the reconciliation didn't stick, and the low point in our relations with DENI came in December when Sean O'Connor and I were suddenly summoned to Belfast, instructed to attend a meeting convened to convey something of the Permanent Secretary's displeasure at the final draft of *Chocolate Cream Soldiers*.

This meeting was in effect a re-run, with rhetorically more powerful backing, of the management committee meeting. The directors of the evaluation elected to attend, whilst reserving their position. Nevertheless, the chairman felt able to open matters firmly; we were all there 'to consider what action needs to be taken to make the Report one that the Department can associate itself with and endorse'.

They were genuinely puzzled that the evaluators appeared indifferent to departmental endorsement. The argument used by DENI officials: ('if people realize how liberal SCSP is, Paisley and the DUP[3] will be down on our heads like a ton of bricks') was similar to that posed by Harry Wolcott at an AERA discussion: 'How should ethnographers feel if their data could be used to *terminate* cultures?'

Again the bifurcation. Where does argument for responsible and prudent behaviour end and illicit pressurizing begin? Can an evaluator play God and construct a morality of consequences? Or is one on surer ground in emphasizing a truth-telling role?

The meeting ended with the conflicting definitions unresolved. DENI supposed itself to have blocked circulation of the report by *dictat*. The evaluators supposed the sensitivities of the situation to require delay, but saw the locus of the decision as resting with them. It was several years before *Chocolate Cream Soldiers* achieved reasonably wide circulation in Northern Ireland, mainly through the taught Master's and Diploma Programme at NUU.

To the irritation of some, it was well regarded by some of the better-known portrayal evaluators in the United States, adding fuel to the argument that the exercise was 'really' aimed at its professional peer groups.

REFLECTIONS: *CHOCOLATE CREAM SOLDIERS* AS EXEMPLUM

Evaluation products may be created in circumstances of benign complicity or creative tension. A recent paper by Sean O'Connor (1980), 'The social role of evaluation products', explored the mismatch between overlapping subcultures, those of the sponsors, the research setting, the perceived audiences and the evaluation team itself. Ploys establishing or negating 'comfortableness' may be constructed around focal issues, the evaluator's alleged subject area competence, milieu-brightness, or ideological/political compatibility, as well as his or her prestige as a researcher and the 'constraints' imposed by contractual negotiation. O'Connor concluded that mismatched programme evaluations are typically conducted alongside problematic subtexts, involving possibilities of co-option, collusion, renegotiation of restricted contracts, deflection towards peripheral 'surrogate tasks', distancing, rejection, labelling as deviant, rhetorical acknowledgement divorced from political action, the management of counter-denunciations, the use of social sensitivities as instruments of social control, and the sponsorship of 'rival products'. Nevertheless, the evaluator had a recognized 'corner' from which to fight.

There is also an epistemological issue. The critics of *Chocolate Cream Soldiers* came armed with lists of passages they wanted deleted from the report. These were so extensive that a full analysis of the 'requests' has not yet been completed, but it went way beyond anything that might be termed 'negotiation for fairness and accuracy'. The wider question is whether any substantial process of negotiation (such as has been envisaged by the SAFARI researchers) is incompatible, ultimately, with the truth-telling role. The defences to the SAFARI[4] line, that social truths are relativistic, or that iterative discourse 'improves' an account, seem to me to be rather weak.

The study leading to *Chocolate Cream Soldiers*, viewed methodologically, owed some of its idiosyncrasies to an unusually composed research team. Also, as I have indicated, other agendas were involved. The evaluation was offered to SCSP in part because I was seeking a 'hands-on' exercise in which the bulk of the fieldwork could be conducted by an MA group at the New University of Ulster who were studying curriculum theory and programme evaluation. Although none of the group had any research experience as such, a certain amount of training was offered.[5] Many were experienced teachers, and were perceived by the trial schools as sympathetic but knowledgeable in a way that precluded them being 'fobbed off'. Perhaps ill-advisedly, we allocated the students in teams to a small number of trial schools in a particular area. In the main, on a limited budget, this was to keep travelling expenses down. So the student–researchers gained extensive experience of SCSP in one or two well-defined geographical settings, but their view of the project was somewhat overfocused. This left a problem. Any confident cross-project generalizations (Crooks, 1982; Stake and Easley, 1978) necessarily depend on some attempt at aggregation and interpretation of the ethnographic and survey data. Overall, the study relied heavily on participant observation, document analysis, observed episodes in classrooms, analysed 'curriculum discourse', and semi-structured interviews concerning emerging pedagogical, curriculum, and community issues. But the unit of analysis (or 'bounded system') in *Chocolate Cream Soldiers* was necessarily the Schools Cultural Studies Project itself. Consequently the evaluation team faced problems equivalent to those faced in the kind of geographically dispersed research that combines 'local' case study with a commitment to produce tentative cross-site generalizations. These problems of research in multi-site settings have been exemplified recently by the 'Executive summary' included by Bob Stake and Jack Easley in their *Case Studies in Science Education* (1978) . . .

The end-in-view of methodological practice is for the researcher to find himself or herself in a position to be able to say something with known levels of confidence or speculation. It is pertinent for us, as authors of *Chocolate Cream Soldiers*, to remind ourselves of the dichotomy between how it felt to be involved in the writing and the available justifying paradigms, positivistic or interpretative, for 'writing it up'. The task of putting the reports together in the centre fell to myself, as principal editor, Sean O'Connor, and the three outside consultants, who had been brought in partly to offset the embarrassment that the evaluation study had the same institutional base as SCSP, partly to 'front' certain aspects – Dr Stephen Kemmis from Deakin, Australia, looking at the SCSP rationale; Chicago's Sister Anne Breslin measuring civil and moral reasoning; Dr Tom Anderson on sabbatical from the University of Illinois focusing on pedagogy. Altogether *Chocolate Cream Soldiers* has seventeen named authors! The conditions under which it was written up, under pressure of deadlines, felt so culpably 'seat of the pants', so hair-raising, so magical, so unlike what any 'justifying' account might look like, that one simply has to say so. All I remember is the weariness, the emotional high, the savagery of the selection, the willingness to begin arguments with only a hazy idea of where they might lead, the hail of crumpled discarded notepaper, and the pure relief when the sacred slog eventually shuddered to a halt. It felt a bit like what I imagine to be the experience of writing a novel. Any judiciousness of comment must have come more out of a sensitivity to language than any explicit weighing of cross-tabulated evidence. At the risk of sounding complacent, I was truly surprised by how much of it sounded about right on my first 'read' of it a couple of days later.

There is no attempt to describe the research process behind *Chocolate Cream Soldiers* as exemplary; indeed, one strong assertion is that we need to learn from our mistakes. But the problems also relate to idiosyncrasies in the setting and it is an open question the extent to which even remotely similar circumstances might be replicated elsewhere. Yet overall it might be possible to identify a trend. Perhaps the climate of the times, stressing accountability, outcome measures, output budgeting, and so on is hostile to expansive non-recommendatory ethnographic reports. Decision-makers are declaring their information needs to lie elsewhere. Social relations in educational settings where ethnographic evaluation research has been conducted have not infrequently deteriorated in spite of protective rules designed to prevent this. Ploys designed to reduce the effectiveness of an evaluation, or deflect it, or manage a counter-denunciation, have become unremarkable and normal. There have been examples of tears, tantrums, ostracization, heavy-handed humour, dismissive silences, threats of litigation. Warmth is possible, but rare.

RESEARCH PROCESSES IN CROSS-SITE SETTINGS

Chocolate Cream Soldiers was faced with a problem of distilling 'understandings' in a cross-site study that involved a largish team of experienced and inexperienced personnel. As Matthew Miles pointed out in his widely circulated Memo to Dave Crandall, the technical problems of data overload and conceptual focus are likely to be severe. Although 'grounded theory' suggests a careful attentiveness ('watchful of serendipity'), the conditions under which the evaluation of the Schools Cultural Studies Project was attempted (short time scales, limited but intensive school visits, a lot of thematic focusing at the centre, relatively inexperienced fieldworkers) meant that the drive towards a clarity of framework was possibly too strong. At worst the fieldwork could be said to have been constructed around a framework of '*known*' issues rather than having the time and space to evolve its own. This problem was worsened by the *partial* view of SCSP available to any particular fieldworker, although weekly team meetings obviated the difficulty to some extent.

Each fieldworker had a research agenda that included observing and reporting classroom 'episodes' and the collection of testimony, wherever possible in the form of a taped interview, with subsequent protocol analysis and edited transcript. There was considerable variation, too, in the style of interviewing employed with the trial-school teachers. The aspiration towards gentle probing proved a difficult one to realize in practice, and a certain passivity and blandness developed, particularly where the interviewers were over-recessive. Some of the paradoxes and ambiguities of SCSP came out rather surprisingly through the survey data. Because these were processed *after* the school visits, opportunities for methodological cross-fertilization were limited. In retrospect it would have been better to have armed the fieldworkers with basic data on the pattern of implementation before placing them in the setting.

As new researchers they weren't always able to 'read' the initial overview in a way that suggested the 'right' follow-up questions. My own view is that recessive interviewing is less a virtue than some educational ethnographers first supposed. But much of the final selection went on the 'newsroom' and was handled (at times brutally) by the subs. One equivocal possible advantage of this type of research is that it bypasses problems of data overload; ethnographic researchers immersed in day-to-day data are not always able to 'extract it out' around an analysis. Also skill at collecting data may not itself confer an ability to write it up, not least in a multi-author set-up where there are problems of an aggregate tone of voice.

METHODOLOGICAL RHETORIC AND RETROSPECTIVE DISTORTION

Finally, as the exercise itself became under siege, the authors of *Chocolate Cream Soldiers* have felt at times under pressure to give a retrospectively distorting account of how the study was actually conducted. What was essentially a modest proposal, a hand-to-mouth low-budget exercise, somehow contrived to end up as a *cause célèbre*. The surprisingly dramatic impact of the exercise carried with it a concomitant temptation – to offer a methodological rhetoric as a professional defence. For example, we were a little bit slow to admit that there is something dishonest in castigating a project for abandoning its initial logic that sectarianism in education can only be combated by engaging in a fine-grain cultural and ideological critique and then conducting an evaluation exercise curiously opaque in its squareness to the same challenge. For all its rich episodic detail, *Chocolate Cream Soldiers* splits on the analysis/portrayal dilemma. The analysis is an issues-based thematic overview of the whole exercise. The 'ethnography' was too often unthematic episodic elaboration for which the summarizing expression is the chapter tellingly called 'Glimpses'. There is something of a gap in the centre. Either as a piece of 'illuminative evaluation', or as a piece of ethnographic research, *Chocolate Cream Soldiers* stands rather awkwardly in relation to the approved animals in the research zoo. Historically it became instead something of a sacred monster, unswallowable like Harry Recher's unpunctured puffer-fish in *Man: A Course of Study*; perhaps what a moralistic pamphleteer might call 'a warning to all'.

NOTES

1. See Jenkins, D., Simons, H. and Walker, R. (1981) for some reflections on the Nuffield International Workshop held at Girton College, Cambridge, 17–20 December 1979.
2. At the workshop on the ethnography of educational settings at Whitelands College, London in March 1982 Paul Atkinson referred to ethnography being in some circumstances a kind of 'surrogate theory'.
3. The Democratic Unionist Party, led by the Rev. Ian Paisley. The DUP is in opposition to the Republican parties but in rivalry with the Official Unionists.
4. SAFARI is an acronym for Success and Failure and Recent Innovation, a research project directed by Barry MacDonald at the Centre for Applied Research in Education, University of East Anglia, to monitor the medium-range effects of curriculum projects. See Jenkins (1978).
5. In the main, the training that was offered was feedback to individual students on their field notes and protocol analysis, together with seminars on interviewing and data analysis.

REFERENCES

Crooks, T. (1982) Generalization in educational research: through a glass darkly, mimeo, University of Otago, New Zealand.
Eisner, E.W. (1972) Emerging models of educational evaluation, *School Review*, No. 70.
Eisner, E.W. (1981) On the differences between scientific and artistic approaches to qualitative research, *Educational Researcher*, No. 10, pp. 5–9.
Hamilton, D., Jenkins, D., King, C., MacDonald, B. and Parlett, M. (eds.) (1977) *Beyond the Numbers Game: A Reader in Educational Evaluation*, Macmillan, London.
Jenkins, D. (1978) An adversary's account of the ethics of case study, in C. Richards (ed.) *Power and the Curriculum*, Nafferton, Driffield.
Jenkins, D. Simons, H. and Walker, R. (1981) Thou nature art my goddess: naturalistic enquiry in educational evaluation, *Cambridge Journal of Education*, Spring.
Jenkins, D., O'Connor, S. *et al.* (1980a) *Chocolate Cream Soldiers: Final Report on the Rowntree Schools Cultural Studies Project*, available from the Education Centre, New University of Ulster, Coleraine.
Jenkins, D., O'Connor, S. *et al.* (1980b) *Chocolate Drops* (A summary of the Rowntree Schools Cultural Studies Project), available from the Education Centre, New University of Ulster, Coleraine.
O'Connor, S. (1980) The social role of evaluation products, mimeo, New University of Ulster.
Shaw, K.E. (1978) Understanding the curriculum: the approach through case studies, *Journal of Curriculum Studies*, No. 10, p. 1.

Stake, R. and Easley, J. (1978) *Case Studies in Science Education: Volume 2 Design Overview and General Findings,* Centre for Instructional Research and Curriculum Evaluation and Committee on Culture and Cognition, University of Illinois School of Education.

4.3
RAISING GENDER ISSUES
IN SUFFOLK TVEI*
Rob Fiddy, Roger Loose and Ian Stronach

The following article comprises two letters. The first (see next page) is from
Rob Fiddy and Ian Stronach to Roger Loose, the Suffolk TVEI Co-
ordinator. The second is his response. The letters followed a weekend
conference where a group of teachers on the MA courses at the Cambridge
Institute of Education and at CARE examined gender issues in TVEI. The
first letter tries to represent what was learned and what the group recom-
mended. Roger Loose's reply completes the account. The exchange reflects
something of an attempt to make the practice of evaluation much more of a
dialogue than an occasional reporting mechanism, and so to avoid being cast
solely in the role of project historians or pathologist.

* Fiddy, R., Loose, R. and Stronach, I. (1986) Raising gender issues in Suffolk TVEI
(correspondence between TVEI co-ordinator), *TVEI Working Papers*, The Centre for
Applied Research in Education.

University of East Anglia

Centre for Applied Research in Education
School of Education
University of East Anglia
Norwich NR4 7TJ

Telephone Norwich (0603) 56161
Telegrams UEANOR NORWICH

29 November 1985

Roger Loose
TVEI Co-ordinator
Northern Area Office
County Hall
Lowestoft
Suffolk

Dear Roger,

Thanks very much for that lucid and helpful introductory talk about TVEI. The teacher–researchers from CARE and CIE subsequently tried to grapple with the gender issues of TVEI for the rest of Saturday and Sunday morning, and this is our version of what ensued. By Sunday lunchtime we were feeling a bit ambivalent about whether we'd got anywhere. It is for you to decide if any of the following will be useful to your TVEI programme.

Our strategy at the residential weekend was to look at gender issues in relation to specific TVEI policy areas, like new technology, learning styles, assessment or vocational education: and then to look more deeply at gender issues, using data available from various TVEI and other sources. But our guess is that we were our own best data, and that what happened between ourselves offers the best guidelines for what you can anticipate in staffrooms if a policy of equal opportunities is to be pursued rather than merely invoked.

At the level of policy and organization, certain guidelines seem useful. The Women's National Commission have made suggestions about the implicit tracking within TVEI that can be attributed to OTFs (Occupational Training Families), 'male-sounding' course labels, setting 'male' and 'female' options against each other in the options, and so on.[1] Moira Kilkenny has just written a report on sex differentiation in Northumberland which is comprehensive and contains over forty specific policy and administrative recommendations at LEA, school, and department levels. It should prove a useful checklist.[2] And of course there's the old Schools Council materials and newsletters on reducing sex differentiation in schools.[3] Most of the data we looked at told us *that* differentiation happened, but not *how* it happened. And it is the latter that has utility for the innovator. There was a thought-provoking recent review in the *Times Educational Supplement* that might be worth following up. Walden and Walkerdine argue that the processes of discrimination are subtly linked to classroom behaviour. Denying that girls need to do worse at maths than boys, they argue that teachers 'watch for and promote those characteristics which they consider to be related to this (real understanding) – confidence, flexibility, risk-taking, rule-breaking'.[4] These attributes, they point out, are all traditionally masculine. Hence differences in achievement. It strikes us that these are also learning styles promoted by TVEI, and that they could therefore *add to* the discrimination against girls in the education process.

We concluded that a strategy for change based solely on policy and organizational recommendations was doomed to failure, because rational models of attitude change always fail. What people know, and how they feel, are not directly related. Committees, advisers, special responsibilities, guidelines, etc. are a necessary framework, but they will not prompt change in themselves, and are often only the trappings of a 'response' to the problem. Indeed, if we are to be honest, we did wonder whether the County would be able to look for an answer, as opposed to a 'response'.

What would a real stab at the problem look like? We thought it would have to start from the self-awareness of the teacher. That could be fostered through school-based initiatives – initially individuals inquiring into their own practices, volunteer teachers observing each other, small groups discussing the issue in terms of their specific classroom practices. Student involvement would be essential, and so too would ways of getting in touch with other groups doing the same kind of thing. Two ground rules emerged from the weekend:

1. 'Create' an awareness of the problem before you address its solution.
2. If policy precedes awareness, then entrenching of attitudes will ensue.

The following table shows roughly what happened when forty teachers approached the issue. Our ground rules emerged from the sometimes painful experience of trying to address gender issues without hurting each others' feelings:

Stage 1 Formal acknowledgement of the problem	*Stage 2* Constraints, dilemmas/ *Evasion, resistance*	*Stage 3* Acceptance of problem/ *Confrontation*	*Stage 4* Change/ *Retrenchment*
● We all support EO ● Options must be open to all ● Sometimes girls are discriminated against	● Other issues are more important ● If girls won't choose, we can't force ● Keep emotions down ● More time needed to think ● Feels uncomfortable ● Fear of hurting other people ● *'Just to regard it as a joke, and defuse the situation'*	● Shifts of position ● Real acknowledge-ment of problem ● 'Hysterical' positions ● 'Personal' attacks ● *'Why are feminists so unattractive to men?'* ● *'Why are men so unattractive to feminists?'* ● *'I shifted my position a lot'*	● Rethink position ● Confirm prejudice ● reject learning ● *It could have destroyed the group if we'd said what we were thinking*

We'd guess that school efforts to come to terms with EO issues might well pass through similar processes, and that's why we suggest a carefully thought-out seed-bed strategy to create awareness and to cope with inevitable tensions at that stage.

Stage 1 produced a few strains for the group. Everyone supports equal opportunities. Stage 2 produced rational objections, and some discomfort. A major rational objection was that freedom of choice was basic. Therefore if girls chose 'wrongly' teachers had no right to pursue the matter. Round and round the mulberry bush of discriminatory practice we went. (That kind of circularity was a bit like the TVEI project that *would* positively discriminate if only the girls would apply.) A major criticism at this stage was that 'token women' in each group were a form of control rather than representation. The real issues would only emerge from a women's group. What implications for TVEI management there? (Actually, this was resisted by most of the women as divisive.) Stage 3 involved a kind of covert confrontation, accompanied by a determination not to let things get too emotive. As a result people tiptoed past words like 'hysterical' and retreated to Stage 2:

'I'm starting to feel very uncomfortable at the sort of reactions that what X (female) has said has brought up . . . I feel it's being taken very lightly here.'

'I'm just saying it's a very emotive area. If it is done in a certain way I think relationships can break up.'

'To him it's not that important, not the kind of thing worth pulling your hair out and destroying the group and all this, but to X and other people in our group it was very important.'

'We pulled back.'

And the positive side of Stage 4? We didn't really get there, and certainly not beyond it. These stages are central to the pursuit of gender awareness. That awareness is the starting point for change. The easy piety of non-discriminatory options, avoiding stereotypes, and equal opportunities actually disguises real confrontation and deeply held beliefs that touch us at the quick of our sexual identities. It's hardly news, of course, but it seems to get forgotten very quickly. And it's a vital factor in planning for change – that's why the small-scale, collaborative strategy is so necessary. 'Awareness' has to be created, and cannot be imposed.

Given the 'awareness' programme and the organizational features Kilkenny recommends, what else? In such a climate, it might then be possible to introduce – as a short-term measure – girls-only classes in science and technology. Or life skills curricula could be devised that stressed 'personhood' rather than gender stereotypes. Texts, language, school practices, and course labels could be scrutinized for discrimination. The absence of females in senior positions (in or out of TVEI) could also be considered, as well as the nature and categories of assessment explicit and implicit within profiling and counselling strategies.

A summary of the policy options:

1. Appoint feminist to LEA/TVEI sub-group on equal opportunities.
2. Balance male and female membership of groups and hierarchies.
3. Encourage male teachers to take 'female' subjects and vice versa.
4. Start dialogue with parents.
5. Start dialogue with employers.
6. Change INSET to gender awareness priority.
7. Change image of technology, course labels, etc.
8. Allocate learners to counter-stereotypical work experience placements.
9. Build 'female' values into technology courses (e.g. technology and handicap).
10. Recruit more positively to ensure balanced course intakes.
11. Appoint senior teacher with EO responsibility.
12. Review existing initiatives in EO via short-term consultancy. Identify further options/practices.

13. Encourage teacher-based research, peer research, collaborative groups, cross-gender discussion in school.
14. Complain to MES/LEA/Government about priorities.
15. Develop gender-based issues in life skill courses: consider idea of 'personhood'.
16. Extend EO teaching further down secondary and primary school: reinvest EO in primary/lower secondary for better returns.
17. Create single-sex groups in science/technology as short-term remedy.
18. Create compulsory core of science/technology for 14–16.
19. Launch whole school self-evaluation of EO issue and practices.
20. Review gender stereotyping in books, resources, etc.

Well, that's a tall order, Roger. It goes without saying that constraints of time and resources, and the political realities of the EO issue in schools, won't allow you to do all of that, even if you so wish. But we hope some of it will be useful and that Suffolk TVEI makes progress on the issue in the next few years.

We would be grateful for any comments you might wish to make – disparaging or otherwise. Thanks once again for helping to set the TVEI scene for us at the weekend conference.

Yours

Ian Stronach
Rob Fiddy

NOTES

1. Cabinet Office (1985) *The other half of our future.* Report of the WNC *ad hoc* working group on training opportunities for women.
2. M. Kilkenny, (1985) *Sex differentiation in the High School Curriculum in Northumberland 1982–85*, University of Newcastle.
3. E.g. Schools Council (1983) *Reducing Sex Differentiation,* Newsletter 4, SC, March.
4. Walden, R. and Walkerdine, V. (1985) *Girls and Mathematics,* Bedford Way Papers 24, London Institute of Education.

Your ref

Our ref RL/LM/SDK

Please ask for Mrs L. Macdonald

Extension 264

19 December 1985

Suffolk
County
Council

DUNCAN G GRAHAM MA

Mr I. Stronach,

Centre for Applied Research in Education,

School of Education,

University of East Anglia,

NORWICH,

Norfolk NR4 7TJ

COUNTY EDUCATION OFFICER

D R WRIGHT

Area Education Officer

Suffolk House

London Road North

Lowestoft

NR32 1BH

Tel (0502) 62262

Dear Ian,

Thank you for your most interesting letter summarizing the outcomes from the gender issues weekend at Newmarket. I found the suggestions made and the analysis of the problem entirely helpful.

We can confirm that we have already found evidence in a Special Needs survey that the learning styles promoted by TVEI that require attributes traditionally classified as masculine, may tend to *add* to the discrimination against girls. This seems to apply, despite the fact that girls opting for TVEI might be expected to identify more readily with these masculine attributes than girls in general. It is the disassociation of these learning styles from the masculine image that is probably the major and most difficult task that faces us.

Our management team recognizes that real progress in the field of equal opportunities depends upon raising the self-awareness of every teacher, student and parent through a variety of non-threatening, in-house initiatives. The first of these must be awareness-raising and attitude change in the senior management team of each establishment. Data collected about sex stereotyping within the institution is seen as vital to this process. Involvement of teaching staff in collecting data and examining materials is a first step to awareness-raising, but it must be accompanied by a simple public declaration of a senior management strategy to show the extent of ownership for the initiative.

The next stage involves individual staff collecting information about their own classroom performance and, where sufficient confidence is gained, that of other staff, in the handling of groups and individuals in a non-stereotyped way. Beyond this, staff may be able to move to a detailed discussion of role models and role model modification in the light of a questionnaire on attitudes and approaches at departmental level.

I found the 'transition model' in your letter very helpful in mapping the likely stages through which a group of staff must go. I suspect that even given the approach I have suggested in the previous paragraph, some staff will get 'stuck' at one of the early stages and be difficult to move thereafter.

The role of feminists in the staff group is one which needs particularly sensitive handling, not least by the feminists themselves. I firmly believe that equal opportunities must always be portrayed as an *'educational'* issue in the widest sense, and therefore sexual politics must not be allowed to cloud it if we are to engage the hearts and minds of *all* staff.

You may know that one of our TVEI schools has been experimenting with girls-only classes in mathematics for several years, with considerable success as far as learning and achievement is concerned. However several of us have deep reservations about this approach, other than as a short-term measure, since it seems to duck the real issues and may serve to heighten sex role stereotyping in the long term.

The absence of females in senior TVEI positions has been discussed on many occasions, since it is obviously a source of concern and embarrassment to me. I must explain that the opportunity for positive discrimination in appointing females did not arise, as the number of applications from women was very low indeed and in every case they had no relevant experiences in the area in which they were showing an interest. It is often claimed that a more careful wording of advertisements can produce a better response from women, but in this case the posts were necessarily so task-specific as to discourage them (even in business technology apparently!).

The balancing of male and female membership of groups and hierarchies is impossible given the low representation of women in high schools and FE, particularly in middle management positions. I do not believe that TVEI can address this issue effectively, given its short time-scale.

Your group of students would clearly like the MSC and its TVEI teams to place equal opportunities much higher in their priorities. As I pointed out at Newmarket, it is *first* in the list of criteria, but it has to be recognized that given the short-term nature of TVEI, higher priority will be given to changing teaching and learning methodologies. This should itself lead towards a clearer recognition of the need for an equal opportunities strategy. In the meantime progress is bound to be slow and painful, for the reasons recognized by your students.

Suffolk County Council has already created an integrated science core programme 14–16 for all students, a form of which has already been implemented in two of the TVEI high schools. We are much further from a compulsory core in technology, but TVEI has set work in hand on this and our schools do have a common programme in technology for all students in the third year.

I am most grateful to you for your summary of the weekend, which will be most helpful in clarifying our management strategy for equal opportunities still further.

Yours sincerely

Roger Loose
Suffolk TVEI Project Co-ordinator

4.4
REPORTING INTERVIEWS:
A CODE OF GOOD PRACTICE*
Janet Powney and Mike Watts

INTRODUCTION

This is an article about good practice in the reporting of interviews. In part it stems from the worrisome problems we have experienced in reading about interviews and in turn reporting some of our own. In part, too, it stems from the general problem that there is no single definition of 'interview' to allow a reader to proceed on the assumption that (s)he understands exactly what is entailed by the term. There are structured, unstructured, focused, semi-focused, clinical, formal, informal, in-depth versions along with a variety of others.

Our worries stem from a disquiet that comes from being provided with (or being able to provide) too little information rather than too much. In trying to derive some useful guidelines for ourselves and others we are keenly aware of the kinds of limitations that are imposed upon researchers, not least of which is the task of tailoring reports to the needs of specific audiences.

INTERVIEWS

Interviewing is a recognized method of gathering information in social research. Survey research in particular has developed sophisticated techniques using trained interviewers (see, for example, Brenner, 1981). Educational researchers have adopted interviewing as an appropriate method for a wide range of investigations, reflecting a similar breadth in theoretical perspectives. Educational research reports, however, usually make

* Powney, J. and Watts, M. (1984) Reporting interviews: a code of good practice, *Research Intelligence*, No. 17, September.

assumptions about a shared view of what constitutes an 'interview'. That this is *not* the case bears some discussion. Massarik (1981), for example, describes a taxonomy of interview types, from a 'limited survey interview' (the typical polling or market research interview) to the 'phenomenal interview' (a commitment to a joint search for shared understanding based upon mutual trust). With the growing trend towards a more humanistic approach to educational research (Pope, Watts and Gilbert, 1983) the more empathetic interview style is becoming increasingly common. With it comes further problems in reporting interviews. Not surprisingly, given the variety of theoretical positions that are to be discerned, there is little attempt at consensus concerning the terms used.

To the question 'What is an interview?', we have opted for a minimum working definition – that is a conversation between two or more people where one or more of the participants takes the responsibility for reporting the substance of what is said.

Before entering into a discussion of the practices of reporting interviews two important points need to be made. The first concerns the interaction of philosophy and methodology. An interview is a particular kind of data-gathering process where verbal interaction, and therefore personal contact, is (presumably) deemed to be important. To be successful as a research tool it is not something to be entered into lightly. As a method, as with all methods (Swift, Watts and Pope, 1983), it needs to be formally consistent with the philosophical assumptions which form the basis for the research being planned.

The second point is that we consider the reporting of interviews to be the construction of a story around the events that have taken place, and of the perceived outcomes of the interaction between interviewer and interviewee. Readers, however, are often provided with so little detail that they can only make assumptions about the content and procedure from the overall context of the research, and from the reputation of the researcher. In reading a research report we want to believe the researcher's story, we want to feel confident that the results obtained are reasonable in the circumstances and that therefore the conclusions and implications that have been drawn can be justified as a basis for debate.

This means that there should be no parts of the interview process where it is uncertain what has been done. Such strictures apply to data collected as part of the process of verification of theory generated by local deductions from prior assumptions. They apply equally forcibly to 'data generated by the research act' which provides the basis for theory. The 'grounded theory' of Glaser and Strauss (1968) should not have to depend on unspecified sources of information. Whatever the style of research, elegance and good experimental design alone cannot compensate for a full description of the researchers' request for meaningful verbal relationships and their consequences for action.

INTERVIEW GUIDELINES

The interview is sensitive to many variables and it is difficult to believe the researchers' story when such sensitive variables have been ignored, or at least not reported. Our dos and don'ts are in part a list and in part a definition of the most sensitive variables involved in the act of interviewing.

The kind and context of the interview

A description of the interview itself is of fundamental importance – as is some rationale for the interview method. It needs to be said whether it takes place with an individual or a group; whether the interviewer/interviewee relationship is formal or informal; if closely structured or very conversational; what the main issues concern; the length, location and occasion of the interview. If these variables seem to be self-evident it has been pointed out that, in a short appraisal of some recent large-scale research reports (Powney, 1982), such information is not often made easily available.

Arguably, the more unstructured is the interview, the more difficult and lengthy a process it is to describe. Unstructured interviews offer the interviewer considerable flexibility and with it more responsibility. The content and direction of the interview may, for instance, be largely determined by the interviewee's responses (for example, see Watts 1983a, 1983b). Successive interviews can thus be very dissimilar and therefore the description of the sessions and the responses becomes increasingly complex. Moreover, alongside the flexibility is the researcher's responsibility to make clear the status of the interview – whether or not, for instance, it is seen to be an exploratory device, preparatory to data collection – possibly in another form; the main instrument of research and data collection; or as a supplement to other methods being used (such as follow-up to a self-completion questionnaire or as confirmation of classroom observations.)

The characteristics of the participants and their relationship

The sensitive variables in this section concern the participants in the interview sessions. It is important to know, for example, the number of participants (whether they are single, small group, or large group interviews); the basis for selection and the method of selection for the interviews. And similarly of the interviewer(s), what experience they have, their status and relationship to the interviewees.

Educational research interviews suggest particular hazards which are likely to occur more frequently than others as various models of teacher-as-researcher proliferate. Most teachers and most academic researchers are inexperienced interviewers. They often use self-taught techniques for preparing, carrying out and reporting interviews. In many cases the people being interviewed are already known to the interviewer either personally or in status terms. Teachers on in-service courses and/or engaged in curriculum development in their own schools may sometimes be interviewing junior and senior colleagues, or well-known or relatively unknown pupils. Simons (1981) has focused on some of the problems associated with adults interviewing pupils. These include, for example, talking too much or listening too little.

In this sense, then, the kind of information suggested here gives the reader some indication of the possible expectations and perceptions of the participants. Mismatches between interviewer and interviewee may well occur, for example, as a result of differences in culture, age, language and sex. Whilst these may be unavoidable, they can and should be reported in detail. It is important for the researcher to note, too, such points as who exercises control over the progress of the interview and who has access to the records of the session afterwards. Anonymity and confidentiality are two normal guarantees of social survey work which may not pertain to small-scale inquiries by teacher–researchers. If informants cannot remain anonymous, however (since any publication of data is likely to make them easily identifiable), they may feel justified in checking or even negotiating the report of the interview.

The purposes of the interview

Research reports using interview data should indicate not just the context and structure of the data from each interview, but also a clear statement of the researcher's purpose(s) in conducting the interview in the first place. It has been common practice in experimental psychology to mislead 'subjects' in order that behavioural observations will not be 'contaminated' by subjects directing their behaviour positively or negatively in relation to the experimenter's purpose. Sharp and Green (1975) and Rosenthal and Jacobson (1968) provide educational examples of this practice.

However, as Pope, Watts and Gilbert (1963) argue, newer directions in educational research benefit from a dissolution of the traditional researcher–subject approach so that genuine two-way interactions between participants can occur.

Whatever the case, it is necessary contextual information to know the purpose of the interview, the expectations of both researcher and researched, and about the outcome(s) (including action) predicted and expected as a result of the interview.

Research methods cannot be neutral – they act as filters through which the environment is selectively experienced. Young (1980) makes this point in his criticisms of the Rutter team (Rutter *et al.*, 1979) who, he says, ignore factors which their implicit model does not regard as important: 'questions of power, conflict, boundary maintenance, categorization, etc'. These might be considered to be the essential contributions of interview material but, as Young points out, no schedules are presented in the report and it might therefore be assumed that the schedules used were precoded and the interviews tightly structured.

The method(s) of data collection

Experienced interviewers (for example those trained in survey research) are aware of the many pitfalls, especially in semi-structured or depth interviews, where the information outcome of the interaction depends not only on the language, content and order of the interview but also on subtle non-verbal cues, silences and practical organization. The use of 'probes', 'prompts', and 'cues' may change the direction of the interview. This presents an immense challenge for 'the softer methodology (which) involves representation of reality for purposes of comparison and analysis of language and meaning' (Cohen and Manion, 1981).

Here, the sensitive variables include not only any use of written notes, tape recordings, full transcripts, recalled information etc., but also what the *interviewees* are told about the session, about the interviewer, the purpose of the discussion and so on. It helps to know the scope the interviewer has to probe responses, his or her maximum tolerance of silence and the legitimate areas for questions by the interviewee.

People are likely to respond differently when their comments are tape recorded (as opposed to noted down on paper) so this aspect of method should be reported. It helps also to know what range (and order) of issues are covered – even if all of these are not subsequently included in the analysis.

Where an interview is only one of several data-collecting strategies some indication ought to be given of the relative importance or weight attached to the interviews.

Analysis and reporting of data

Little has ever been written about the process of analysis either as an 'exact art' (as Hull, 1984, suggests it is) or in practical detail. Some specific tools have been suggested and argued for (see for example Bliss, Monk and Ogborn, 1983), but few writers make explicit the sequence of activities involved in analysis. Aside of this, little is said of who the analysts are, whether or not they were also the original interviewers and what particular perspectives they adopt. If there are several analysts, then how are disagreements resolved, what measure of inter-rater reliability is used? Other questions, such as whether full transcripts are always used, how much is reported, what level of uncodeable or unsortable data is tolerable, what basis is used for filtering the data, are also pertinent and need to be reported.

The scrutiny of results

This final section concerns information that is made available about the other persons involved in the scrutiny of what accrues from the process of analysis. Whoever (if anyone) is deemed to the most suitable judge(s) of the research outcomes requires some description, along with the procedures that are used, the methods of incorporating the fruits of the scrutiny into the analysis process and, again, how any disagreements are resolved. Whether or not one argues that the terms 'validity' and 'reliability' have a meaning within newer paradigms of research, it is still necessary to attempt to be systematic and rigorous about the evaluation of the outcome of interviews. Whatever the processes are that are chosen they need to be outlined and included within a description of research. The academic community needs to pay as much attention to the association between interviewing and data collected as critics usually apply to statistical arguments. Of six critiques of the work of Rutter *et al.* (1979) only Young (1980) makes reference to data generated by interviews.

SUMMARY

This paper has suggested that many research studies underestimate and under-report 'the interview'. Simons (1981, p. 27) suggests that the practice of interviewing 'is not discussed on the grounds that interviewing is an idiosyncratic, interpersonal process that is not susceptible to systematic analysis'. She continues 'we must begin to discuss the problems we experience in practice however self-evident, situation-specific or limited when restricted to the written work they may seem'.

In fact, reports commonly contain the idiosyncratic choices of the researcher rather than what might be required by the research community at large. Whereas it is common practice to include statistical tests, questionnaires and even observation schedules, it is rare to find either interview schedules or *full* accounts of the progress of the interviews. For example, Southgate, Arnold and Johnson (1981) are exceptional in providing a full list of questions asked and a fairly full discussion of the responses. Indeed most of the 'sensitive variables' we have listed were met in that study.

Though we seem to have asked for a lot, much could be broached in the body of a report without necessarily diluting or detracting from the story line. Other pertinent information could well be made clear in an appendix. Along with others (for instance Wragg, 1981) we have hoped to provide a checklist for those about to embark on, or report on, a research project with interviews. Whatever the case, the variables listed above seem to us to provide the very minimum of information for a research report to be properly evaluated.

ELEMENTARY CHECKLIST FOR REPORTING INTERVIEWS IN EDUCATIONAL RESEARCH

1. Kind and context of interview

- What is the rationale for using interviews?
- What kind of interview is it?
- How is the interview structured?
- How much flexibility does the interviewer have?
- What is the length, location and occasion of the interview?

2. Characteristics of the interview participants

   (a) *Interviewees*
   - Who and how many people are involved?
   - What is the basis for their selection and how was the selection made?
   (b) *Interviewers*
   - Who and how many people are involved?
   - What experience of interviewing do they have?
   - What is their relationship to the main research?
   - What is their status and relationship to the interviewees?

3. The purpose of the interview

- What are interviewees told about the purpose of the interview?
- Is this understanding shared with the interviewer?

● Who will have access to the data collected and is it negotiable?

4. The method(s) of data collection

● How strictly controlled is the method of asking questions?
● How are responses recorded?
● What other methods of data collection are being used and what is the relative weighting between the methods?

5. Analysis and reporting of data

● Who analyses what?
● How are the interviewers concerned with the analysis?
● How many analysts are there and how are disagreements resolved?
● Are full transcripts used?
● What basis is used for filtering the data?
● What level of uncodeable or unsortable data is tolerated?

6. Sorting of results

● How are the outcomes of the interviews being evaluated?
● What access may the academic community have to raw data?

REFERENCES

Bliss, J., Monk, M. and Ogborn, J. (1983) *Qualitative Data Analysis for Educational Research,* Croom Helm, London.

Brenner, M. (1981) Survey interviewing, in S. Canter and D. Canter (eds.) *Perspectives on Professional Psychology: Current Developments in the Application of Psychology,* Wiley, Chichester.

Cohen, L. and Manion, L. (1981) *Perspectives on Classrooms and Schools,* Holt, Rinehart & Winston, London.

Glaser, B. and Strauss, A. (1968) *The Discovery of Grounded Theory,* Weidenfeld & Nicholson, London.

Hull, C. (1984) Between the lines: the analysis of interview data as an exact art, *Research Intelligence,* 15 January, pp. 8–11.

Massarik, F. (1981) The interviewing process re-examined, in P. Reason and J. Rowan (eds.) *Human Inquiry. A Sourcebook of New Paradigm Research,* Chichester.

Pope, M., Watts., D.M. and Gilbert, J.K. (1983) Constructive educational research. Paper presented at the 9th Annual Conference of BERA at London University Institute of Education, September.

Powney, J. (1982) The interview – an underestimated technique. Paper presented at the 8th Annual Conference of BERA at University of St Andrews, September.

Rosenthal, R. and Jacobson, L. (1968) Pygmalion in the classroom, *Teacher Expectation and Pupils' Intellectual Development,* Holt, Rinehart & Winston, New York.

Rutter, M., Maughan, B., Mortimore, P. and Ouston, J. (1979) *15,000 Hours, Secondary Schools and their Effects on Children,* Open Books, London.

Sharp, R. and Green, A. (1975) *Education and Social Control – A Study in Progressive Primary Education,* Routledge & Kegan Paul, London.

Simons, H. (1981) Conversation Piece, in C. Adelman, (ed.) *Uttering, Muttering,* Grant McIntyre, London.

Southgate, V., Arnold, H. and Johnson, S. (1981) *Extending Beginning Reading,* Heinemann Educational for Schools Council, London.

Swift, D.J., Watts, D.M. and Pope, M. (1983) Methodological pluralism and personal construct psychology. Paper presented to the 5th International Congress of Personal Construct Psychology, Boston, Massachusetts, July.

Watts, D.M. (1983a) Some alternative views of energy, *Physics Education,* No. 18, pp. 213–17.

Watts, D.M. (1983b) A study of alternative frameworks in school science. Unpublished Ph.D. thesis, University of Surrey, Guildford.

Wragg, E.C. (1981) Conducting and analysing interviews, *Rediguide,* No. 11, Nottingham University.

Young, M. (1980) A case study of the limitation of policy research, in B. Tizard, T. Burgess, H. Francis, H. Goldstein, M. Young and J. Hewion (1980) *15,000 Hours – A Discussion,* University of London, Institute of Education.

INDEX

Index compiled by Peva Keane

UNIVERSITY OF WOLVERHAMPTON
LEARNING RESOURCES